Calcutta. Museum Asiatic Society of Bengal

Asiatic researches; or, Transactions

Calcutta. Museum Asiatic Society of Bengal

Asiatic researches; or, Transactions

ISBN/EAN: 9783741149689

Manufactured in Europe, USA, Canada, Australia, Japa

Cover: Foto ©Andreas Hilbeck / pixelio.de

Manufactured and distributed by brebook publishing software
(www.brebook.com)

Calcutta. Museum Asiatic Society of Bengal

Asiatic researches; or, Transactions

ASIATIC RESEARCHES;

OR,

TRANSACTIONS

OF

THE SOCIETY INSTITUTED IN BENGAL,

FOR INQUIRING INTO

THE HISTORY AND ANTIQUITIES,

THE ARTS, SCIENCES, AND LITERATURE

OF

ASIA.

VOLUME THE SECOND.

Printed verbatim from the Calcutta Edition, in Quarto.

London:

PRINTED FOR VERNOR AND HOOD, IN THE POULTRY.

1799.

ADVERTISEMENT.

IT may greatly conduce to the advancement of useful knowledge, if the learned Societies, established in *Europe*, will transmit to the Secretary of the Society in *Bengal* a Collection of short and precise Queries on every branch of *Asiatic* History, Natural and Civil, on the Philosophy, Mathematics, Antiquities, and Polite Literature of *Asia*, and on Eastern Arts, both liberal and mechanic; since it is hoped that accurate Answers may in due time be procured to any Questions that can be proposed on those subjects; which must in all events be curious and interesting, and may prove, in the highest degree, beneficial to mankind.

I.

THE FOURTH

ANNIVERSARY DISCOURSE,

DELIVERED 15 FEBRUARY, 1787,

BY THE PRÉSIDENT.

Gentlemen,

I HAD the honour last year of opening to you my intention to discourse at our annual meetings on the *five* principal nations who have peopled the continent and islands of *Asia*, so as to trace, by an historical and philological analysis, the number of ancient stems from which those five branches have severally sprung, and the central region from which they appear to have proceeded; you may, therefore, expect that, having submitted to your consideration a few general remarks on the old inhabitants of *India*, I should now offer my sentiments on some other nation, who, from a similarity of *language, religion, arts,* and *manners,* may be supposed to have had an early connection with the *Hindus*; but, since we find some *Asiatic* nations totally dissimilar to them in all or most of those particulars, and since the difference will strike you more forcibly by an immediate and close comparison, I design at present to give a short account of a wonderful people, who seem in every respect so strongly contrasted to the original natives of this country, that they must have been for ages a distinct and separate race

For the purpose of these discourses I discovered *India* on its largest scale, describing it as lying between *Persia* and *China*, *Tartary* and *Java*; and, for the same purpose, I now apply the name of *Arabia*, as the *Arabian* geographers often apply it, to that extensive peninsula which the Red Sea divides from *Africa*, the great *Assyrian* river from *Iran*, and of which the *Erythrean* Sea washes the base; without excluding any part of its western side, which would be completely maritime, if no isthmus intervened between the *Mediterranean* and the Sea of *Kolzom*: that country in short I call *Arabia*, in which the *Arabic* language and letters, or such as have a near affinity to them, have been immemorially current.

Arabia, thus divided from *India* by a vast ocean, or at least by a broad bay, could hardly have been connected in any degree with this country, until navigation and commerce had been considerably improved; yet, as the *Hindus* and the people of *Yemen* were both commercial nations in a very early age, they were probably the first instruments of conveying to the western world the gold, ivory, and perfumes of *India*, as well as the fragrant wood, called *Alluwaea* in *Arabic*, and *Aguru* in *Sanscrit*, which grows in the greatest perfection in *Anam*, or *Cochinchina*. It is possible too that a part of the *Arabian* idolatry might have been derived from the same source with that of the *Hindus*; but such an intercourse may be considered as partial and accidental only; nor am I more convinced than I was fifteen years ago, when I took the liberty to animadvert on a passage in the History of *Prince Kantemir*, that the *Turks* have any just reason for holding the coast of *Yemen* to be a part of *India*, and calling its inhabitants *Yellow Indians*.

The *Arabs* have never been entirely subdued, nor has any impression been made on them, except on their borders; where, indeed, the *Phenicians*, *Persians*, *Ethiopians*, *Egyptians*, and, in modern times, the *Othman Tartars*, have severally acquired settlements; but, with these exceptions, the natives of *Hejaz* and *Yemen* have preserved for ages the sole dominion of their deserts and pastures, their mountains and fertile valleys: thus apart from the rest of mankind, this extraordinary people have retained their primitive manners and language, features and character, as long and as remarkably as the *Hindus* themselves. All the genuine *Arabs* of *Syria* whom I knew in *Europe*, those of *Yemen* whom I saw in the isle of *Hinzuan*, whither many had come from *Muskat* for the purpose of trade, and those of *Hejaz*, whom I have met in *Bengal*, form a striking contrast to the *Hindu* inhabitants of those provinces: their eyes are full of vivacity, their speech voluble and articulate, their deportment manly and dignified, their apprehension quick, their minds always present and attentive, with a spirit of independence appearing in the countenances even of the lowest among them. Men will always differ in their ideas of civilization, each measuring it by the habits and prejudices of his own country; but, if courtesy and urbanity, a love of poetry and eloquence, and the practice of exalted virtues be a juster measure of perfect society, we have certain proof that the people of *Arabia*, both on plains and in cities, in republican and monarchical states, were eminently civilized for many ages before their conquest of *Persia*.

It is deplorable, that the ancient history of this majestic race should be as little known in detail before the time of *Dhu Yezen*, as that of the *Hindus* before *Vicramaditya*; for, although the vast historical work of *Almacairi*, and the *Muryuldhohab* or *Golden Meadows* of *Almasuudi*, contain chapters on the kings of *Himyar*, *Ghasan*, and *Hirah*, with lists of them and sketches of their several reigns; and although genea-

logical tables, from which chronology might be
better ascertained, are prefixed to many compositions
of the old *Arabian* Poets, yet most manuscripts are
so incorrect, and so many contradictions are found in
the best of them, that we can scarce lean upon tradition with security, and must have recourse to the
same media for investigating the history of the *Arabs*
that I before adopted in regard to that of the *Indians*;
namely, their *language*, *letters*, and *religion*, their ancient *monuments*, and the certain remains of their *arts*;
on each of which heads I shall touch very concisely,
having premised that my observations will in general
be confined to the state of *Arabia* before that singular
revolution at the beginning of the *seventh century*,
the effects of which we feel at this day from the *Pyre-
nean* mountains and the *Danube*, to the farthest parts
of the *Indian Empire*, and even to the Eastern Islands.

I. For the knowledge which any *European* who
pleases may attain of the *Arabian* language, we are
principally indebted to the university of *Leyden*; for,
though several *Italians* have assiduously laboured in
the same wide field, yet the fruit of their labours has
been rendered almost useless by more commodious
and more accurate works printed in *Holland*; and,
though *Pocock* certainly accomplished much, and was
able to accomplish any thing, yet the *academical* ease
which he enjoyed, and his theological pursuits, induced him to leave unfinished the valuable work of
Maidani which he had prepared for publication; nor,
even if that mine of *Arabian* philology had seen
the light, would it have borne any comparison with
the fifty dissertations of *Hariri*, which the first *Albert Schultens* translated and explained, though he
sent abroad but few of them, and has left his worthy
grandson, from whom perhaps *Maidani* also may
be expected, the honour of publishing the rest:
but the palm of glory in this branch of litera-

ture is due to *Golius*, whose works are equally profound and elegant; so perspicuous in method, that they may always be consulted without fatigue, and read without languor, yet so abundant in matter, that any man who shall begin with his noble edition of the Grammar compiled by his master *Erpenius*, and proceed with the help of his incomparable dictionary, to study his History of *Taimur* by *Ibni Arabshah*, and shall make himself complete master of that sublime work, will understand the learned *Arabic* better than the deepest scholar at *Constantinople* or at *Mecca*. The *Arabic* language, therefore, is almost wholly in our power; and, as it is unquestionably one of the most ancient in the world, so it yields to none ever spoken by mortals in the number of its words and the precision of its phrases; but it is equally true and wonderful, that it bears not the least resemblance, either in words or the structure of them, to the *Sanscrit*, or great parent of the *Indian* dialects; of which dissimilarity I shall mention two remarkable instances: the *Sanscrit*, like the *Greek*, *Persian*, and *German*, delights in compounds, but in a much higher degree, and indeed to such an excess, that I could produce words of more than twenty syllables, not formed ludicrously, like that by which the buffoon in *Aristophanes* describes a feast, but with perfect seriousness, on the most solemn occasions, and in the most elegant works; while the *Arabic*, on the other hand, and all its sister dialects, abhor the composition of words, and invariably express very complex ideas by circumlocution; so that if a compound word be found in any genuine language of the *Arabian* peninsula *(zemmerdah* for instance, which occurs in the *Hamasah)* it may at once be pronounced an exotic. Again: It is the genius of the *Sanscrit*, and other languages of the same stock, that the roots of verbs be almost universally *biliteral*, so that *five-and-twenty hundred* such roots might be formed by the

B 3

composition of the *fifty Indian* letters; but the *Arabic* roots are as universally *triliteral*, so that the composition of the *twenty-eight Arabian* letters would give near *two-and-twenty thousand elements* of the language: and this will demonstrate the surprising extent of it; for, although great numbers of its roots are confessedly lost, and some, perhaps, were never in use; yet, if we suppose ten thousand of them (without reckoning *quadriliterals*) to exist, and each of them to admit only *five* variations, one with another, in forming *derivative nouns*, even then a perfect *Arabic* dictionary ought to contain *fifty thousand* words, each of which may receive a multitude of changes by the rules of grammar. The derivatives in *Sanscrit* are considerably more numerous: but a farther comparison between the two languages is here unnecessary, since, in whatever light we view them, they seem totally distinct, and must have been invented by two different races of men; nor do I recollect a single word in common between them, except *Suruj*, the plural of *Siraj*, meaning both a *lamp* and the *sun*; the *Sanscrit* name of which is, in *Bengal*, pronounced *Surja*; and even this resemblance may be purely accidental. We may easily believe with the *Hindus*, that *not even Indra himself, and his heavenly bands, much less any mortal, ever comprehended in his mind such an ocean of words as their sacred language contains*; and with the *Arabs*, that no man uninspired was ever a complete master of *Arabic*: in fact, no person, I believe, now living in *Europe* or *Asia*, can read without study an hundred couplets together, in any collection of ancient *Arabian* poems; and we are told, that the great author of the *Kamus* learned by accident from the mouth of a child, in a village of *Arabia*, the meaning of three words, which he had long sought in vain from grammarians, and from books, of the highest reputation. It is by approximation alone that a knowledge of these two venerable languages can be acquired; and, with moderate attention, enough of them may be known to delight and instruct us in an infinite degree. I conclude this head with remarking, that the nature of the *Ethiopic* dialect seems to prove an early establishment of the *Arabs* in part of *Ethiopia*, from which they were afterwards expelled, and attacked even in their own country by the *Abyssinians*, who had been invited over as auxiliaries against the tyrant of *Yemen* about a century before the birth of *Muhammed.*

Of the characters in which the old compositions of *Arabia* were written, we know but little, except that the *Koran* originally appeared in those of *Cufah*, from which the modern *Arabian* letters, with all their elegant variations, were derived, and which unquestionably had a common origin with the *Hebrew* or *Chaldaic*; but, as to the *Himyaric* letters, or those which we see mentioned by the name of *Almusnad*, we are still in total darkness; the traveller *Niebuhr* having been unfortunately prevented from visiting some ancient monuments in *Yemen*, which are said to have inscriptions on them. If those letters bear a strong resemblance to the *Nagari*, and if a story current in *India* be true, that some *Hindu* merchants heard the *Sanscrit* language spoken in *Arabia the Happy*, we might be confirmed in our opinion that an intercourse formerly subsisted between the two nations of opposite coasts,—but should have no reason to believe that they sprang from the same immediate stock. The first syllable of *Hamyar*, as many *Europeans* write it, might perhaps induce an etymologist to derive the *Arabs* of *Yemen* from the great ancestor of the *Indians*; but we must observe, that *Himyar* is the proper appellation of those *Arabs*; and many reasons concur to prove that the word is purely *Arabic.* The similarity of some proper names on the borders of *India* to those of *Arabia*, as the river *Arabius*, a place called *Arabu*, a people named *Aribes* or *Ara-*

B 4

bies, and another called *Sabai*, is indeed remarkable, and may hereafter furnish me with observations of some importance, but not at all inconsistent with my present ideas.

II. It is generally asserted that the old religion of the *Arabs* was entirely *Sabian* ; but I can offer so little accurate information concerning the *Sabian* faith, or even the meaning of the word, that I dare not yet speak on the subject with confidence. This at least is certain, that the people of *Yemen* very soon fell into the common, but fatal, error of adoring the sun and the firmament ; for even the *third* in descent from *Yoktan*, who was consequently as old as *Nahor*, took the surname of *Abdushams*, or *Servant of the Sun* ; and his family, we are assured, paid particular honours to that luminary : other tribes worshipped the planets and fixed stars ; but the religion of the poets at least, seems to have been pure Theism ; and this we know with certainty, because we have *Arabian* verses of unsuspected antiquity, which contain pious and elevated sentiments on the goodness and justice, the power and omnipresence, of *Allah*, or *the God*. If an inscription, said to have been found on marble in *Yemen*, be authentic, the ancient inhabitants of that country preserved the religion of *Eber*, and professed a belief *in miracles and a future state*.

We are also told, that a strong resemblance may be found between the religions of the pagan *Arabs* and the *Hindus* ; but, though this may be true, yet an agreement in worshipping the sun and stars will not prove an affinity between the two nations : the *powers* of God, represented as *female* deities, the adoration of *stones*, and the name of the idol *Wudd*, may lead us indeed to suspect that some of the *Hindu* superstitions had found their way into *Arabia* ; and, though we have no traces in *Arabian*

history of such a conqueror or legislator as the great
Sesac, who is said to have raised pillars in *Yemen* as
well as at the mouth of the *Ganges*, yet, since we
know that *Saoya* is a title of *Buddha*, whom some suppose to be *Woden*, since *Buddha* was not a native of
India, and since the age of *Sesac* perfectly agrees with
that of *Sacya*, we may form a plausible conjecture
that they were in fact the same person who travelled
eastward from *Ethiopia*, either as a warrior or as a lawgiver, about a thousand years before *Christ*, and whose
rites we now see extended as far as the country of
Nison, or, as the *Chinese* call it, *Japuen*, both words
signifying the *Rising Sun*. *Sacya* may be derived from
a word meaning *power*, or from another denoting *vegetable food*; so that this epithet will not determine
whether he was a hero or a philosopher; but the title
Buddha or *wise*, may induce us to believe that he was
rather a benefactor than a destroyer of his species:
if his religion, however, was really introduced into any
part of *Arabia*, it could not have been general in that
country; and we may safely pronounce, that before
the *Mohammedan* revolution, the noble and learned
Arabs were Theists, but that a stupid idolatry prevailed among the lower orders of the people.

I find no trace among them, till their emigration, of
any philosophy but *ethics*; and even their system of
morals, generous and enlarged as it seems to have been
in the minds of a few illustrious chieftains, was on the
whole miserably depraved for a century at least before
Muhammed. The distinguishing virtues which they
boasted of inculcating and practising, were a contempt of riches and even of death; but, in the age
of the *Seven Poets*, their liberality had deviated into
mad profusion, their courage into ferocity, and their
patience into an obstinate spirit of encountering fruitless dangers; but I forbear to expatiate on the manners of the *Arabs* in that age, because the poems, en-

titled *Almoallakat*, which have appeared in our own
language, exhibit an exact picture of their virtues
and their vices, their wisdom and their folly; and
show what may be constantly expected from men of
open hearts and boiling passions, with no law to control, and little religion to restrain them.

III. Few monuments of antiquity are preserved in
Arabia, and of those few the best accounts are very
uncertain; but we are assured that inscriptions on
rocks and mountains are still seen in various parts of
the peninsula; which, if they are in any known language, and if correct copies of them can be procured,
may be decyphered by easy and infallible rules.

The first *Albert Schultens* has preserved in his Ancient Memorials of *Arabia*, the most pleasing of all
his works, two little poems in an elegiac strain, which
are said to have been found, about the middle of the
seventh century, on some fragments of ruined edifices
in *Hadramut*, near *Aden*, and are supposed to be of an
indefinite, but very remote age. It may naturally
be asked,—In what characters were they written?
Who decyphered them? Why were not the original
letters preserved in the book where the verses are cited?
What became of the marbles which *Abdurrahman*,
then governor of *Yemen*, most probably sent to the
Khalifah at *Bagdad?* If they be genuine, they prove
the people of *Yemen* to have been ' herdsmen and
warriors, inhabiting a fertile and well-watered country
' full of game, and near a fine sea abounding with fish,
' under a monarchical government, and dressed in
' green silk, or vests of needlework,' either of their
own manufacture or imported from *India*. The measure of these verses is perfectly regular, and the dialect undistinguishable, at least by me, from that of
Kuraish; so that, if the *Arabian* writers were much
addicted to literary impostures, I should strongly sus-

pect them to be modern compositions on the instability of human greatness, and the consequences of ir-
religion, illustrated by the example of the *Hymyaric*
princes; and the same may be suspected of the first
poem quoted by *Schultens*, which he ascribes to an
Arab in the age of *Solomon.*

The supposed houses of the people called *Thamud*,
are also still to be seen in excavations of rocks; and,
in the time of *Tabrizi* the Grammarian, a castle was
extant in *Yemen* which bore the name of *Aladbut*, an
old bard and warrior, who first, we are told, formed
his army, thence called *alkhamis*, in *five* parts, by which
arrangement he defeated the troops of *Himyar* in an
expedition against *Sanaa.*

Of pillars erected by *Sesac*, after his invasion of
Yemen, we find no mention in *Arabian* histories; and,
perhaps, the story has no more foundation than another told by the *Greeks* and adopted by *Newton*, that
the *Arabs* worshipped *Urania*, and even *Bacchus* by
name, which, they say, means *great* in *Arabic*; but
where they found such a word, we cannot discover:
it is true, that *Beccah* signifies *a great and tumultuous
crowd*, and, in this sense, is one name of the sacred
city commonly called *Meccah.*

The *Cabah*, or *quadrangular* edifice at *Meccah*, is
indisputably so ancient, that its original use and the
name of its builder are lost in a cloud of idle traditions. An *Arab* told me gravely, that it was raised
by *Abraham*, who, as I assured him, was never there:
others ascribe it, with more probability, to *Ismail*, or
one of his immediate descendants; but whether it was
built as a place of divine worship, as a fortress, as a
sepulchre, or as a monument of the treaty between the
old possessors of *Arabia* and the sons of *Kidar*, anti-
quaries may dispute, but no mortal can determine.

It is thought by *Reland* to have been *the mansion of some ancient patriarch, and revered on that account by his posterity*; but the room in which we now are assembled, would contain the whole *Arabian* edifice; and, if it were large enough for the dwelling-house of a patriarchal family, it would seem ill adapted to the pastoral manners of the *Kedarites*. A *Persian* author insists, that the true name of *Meccah* is *Mahcadah*, or the *Temple of the Moon*; but, although we may smile at his etymology, we cannot but think it probable that the *Cabah* was originally designed for religious purposes. Three couplets are cited in an *Arabic* history of this building, which, from their extreme simplicity, have less appearance of imposture than other verses of the same kind : they are ascribed to *Asad*, a *Tobba*, or king *by succession*, who is generally allowed to have reigned in *Yemen* an hundred and twenty-eight years before *Christ's* birth, and they commemorate, without any poetical imagery, the magnificence of the prince *in covering the holy temple with stripped cloth and fine linen, and in making keys for its gate.* This temple, however, the sanctity of which was restored by *Muhammed*, had been strangely profaned at the time of his birth, when it was usual to decorate its walls with poems on all subjects, and often on the triumphs of *Arabian* gallantry and the praises of *Grecian* wine, which the merchants of *Syria* brought for sale into the deserts.

From the want of materials on the subject of *Arabian* antiquity, we find it very difficult to fix the chronology of the *Ismailites* with accuracy beyond the time of *Adnam*, from whom the imposture was descended in the *twenty-first* degree; and, although we have genealogies of *Aikamah* and other *Himyaric* bards as high as the *thirtieth* degree, or for a period of *nine hundred* years at least, yet we can hardly depend on them so far, as to establish a complete chronological system.

By reasoning downwards, however, we may ascertain some points of considerable importance. The universal tradition of *Yemen* is, that *Yoktan*, the son of *Eber*, first settled his family in that country; which settlement, by the computation admitted in *Europe*, must have been above *three thousand six hundred* years ago, and nearly at the time when the *Hindus*, under the conduct of *Rama*, were subduing the first inhabitants of these regions, and extending the *Indian* empire from *Ayodhya*, or *Audh*, as far as the isle of *Sinhal*, or *Silan*. According to this calculation, *Nuuman*, king of *Yemen*, in the *ninth* generation from *Eber*, was contemporary with *Joseph*; and, if a verse composed by that prince, and quoted by *Abulfeda*, was really preserved, as it might easily have been, by oral tradition, it proves the great antiquity of the *Arabian* language and metre. This is a literal version of the couplet:
‘ When thou, who art in power, conductest affairs with
‘ courtesy, thou attainest the high honours of those
‘ who are most exalted, *and* whose mandates are
‘ obeyed.’ We are told that, from an elegant verb in this distich, the royal poet acquired the surname of *Alnnutaser*, or the *Courteous*. Now the reasons for believing this verse genuine are its brevity, which made it easy to be remembered, and the good sense comprized in it, which made it become proverbial; to which we may add, that the dialect is apparently old, and differs in three words from the idiom of *Hejaz*. The reasons for doubting are, that sentences and verses of indefinite antiquity are sometimes ascribed by the *Arabs* to particular persons of eminence; and they even go so far as to cite a pathetic elegy of *Adam* himself on the death of *Abel*, but in very good *Arabic* and correct measure. Such are the doubts which necessarily must arise on such a subject; yet we have no need of ancient monuments or traditions to prove all that our analysis requires, namely that the *Arabs* of *Hejaz* and *Yemen* sprang from a stock entirely differ-

ent from that of the *Hindus*, and that their first establishments in the respective countries where we now
find them, were nearly coeval.

I cannot finish this article without observing, that,
when the King of *Denmark's* ministers instructed the
Danish travellers to collect *historical* books in *Arabic*,
but not to busy themselves with procuring *Arabian
poems*, they certainly were ignorant that the only monuments of old *Arabian* history are collections of poetical pieces and the commentaries on them ; that all
memorable transactions in *Arabia* were recorded in
verse ; and that more certain facts may be known by
reading the *Hamasah*, *the Diwan* of *Hudhail*, and the
valuable work of *Obaidullah*, than by turning over a
hundred volumes in prose, unless indeed those poems
are cited by the historians as their authorities.

IV. The manners of the *Hejazi Arabs*, which have
continued, we know, from the time of *Solomon* to the
present age, were by no means favourable to the cultivation of *arts* ; and, as to *sciences*, we have no reason to believe that they were acquainted with any ;
for the mere amusement of giving names to stars,
which were useful to them in their pastoral or predatory rambles through the deserts, and in their observations on the weather, can hardly be considered as a
material part of astronomy. The only arts in which
they pretended to excellence (I except horsemanship
and military accomplishments) were *poetry* and *rheto-
ric*. That we have none of their compositions in prose
before the *Koran*, may be ascribed, perhaps, to the
little skill which they seem to have had in writing,
to their predilection in favour of poetical measure,
and to the facility with which verses are committed
to memory ; but all their stories prove, that they were
eloquent in a high degree, and possessed wonderful
powers of speaking, without preparation in flowing

and forcible periods. I have never been able to discover what was meant by their books called *Rawa-
sim*; but suppose that they were collections of their
common or customary law. Writing was so little
practised among them, that their old poems, which
are now accessible to us, may almost be considered as
originally unwritten; and I am inclined to think that
Samuel Johnson's reasoning on the extreme imperfec-
tion of unwritten languages, was too general; since a
language that is only spoken, may nevertheless be
highly polished by a people who, like the ancient
Arabs, make the improvement of their idiom a national concern, appoint solemn assemblies for the purpose of displaying their poetical talents, and hold it a
duty to exercise their children in getting by heart
their most approved compositions.

The people of *Yemen* had possibly more *mechanical
arts*, and, perhaps, more *science*; but, although their
ports must have been the emporia of considerable
commerce between *Egypt* and *India*, or part of *Persia*,
yet we have no certain proofs of their proficiency in
navigation or even in manufactures. That the *Arabs*
of the Desert had musical instruments, and names for
the different notes, and that they were greatly delighted
with melody, we know from themselves; but their
lutes and pipes were probably very simple, and their
music, I suspect, was little more than a natural and
tuneful recitation of their elegiac verses and love-
songs. The singular property of their language, in
shunning compound words, may be urged, according
to *Bacon*'s idea, as a proof that they had made no
progress in *arts*, ' which require,' says he, ' a variety
' of combinations to express the complex notions aris-
' ing from them;' but the singularity may perhaps be
imputed wholly to the genius of the language, and the
taste of those who spoke it, since the old *Germans*
who knew no art, appear to have delighted in com-

pound words, which poetry and oratory, one would
conceive, might require as much as any meaner art
whatsoever.

So great, on the whole, was the strength of parts or
capacity, either natural or acquired from habit, for
which the *Arabs* were ever distinguished, that we cannot be surprised when we see that blaze of genius
which they displayed, as far as their arms extended,
when they burst, like their own dyke of *Arim*, through
their ancient limits, and spread, like an inundation,
over the great empire of *Iran*. That a race of *Tazis*,
or *Coursers*, as the *Persians* call them, ‘ who drank
‘ the milk of camels and fed on lizards, should enter-
‘ tain a thought of subduing the kingdom of *Feridun*,’
was considered by the General of *Yczdegird*'s army
as the strongest instance of fortune's levity and muta-
bility ; but *Firdausi*, a complete master of *Asiatic*
manners, and singularly impartial, represents the *Arabs*,
even in the age of *Feridun*, as ‘ disclaiming any kind
‘ of dependence on that monarch, exulting in their
‘ liberty, delighting in eloquence, acts of liberality,
‘ and martial achievements, and thus making the whole
‘ earth,’ says the poet, ‘ red as wine with the blood
‘ of their foes, and the air like a forest of canes with
‘ their tall spears.’ With such a character they were
likely to conquer any country that they could invade ;
and, if *Alexander* had invaded their dominions, they
would unquestionably have made an obstinate, and
probably a successful resistance.

But I have detained you too long, gentlemen, with
a nation who have ever been my favourites, and hope
at our next anniversary meeting to travel with you
over a part of *Asia* which exhibits a race of men distinct both from the *Hindus* and from the *Arabs*. In
the mean time, it shall be my care to superintend the
publication of your transactions; in which if the learned

in *Europe* have not raised their expectations too high, they will not, I believe, be disappointed: my own imperfect essays I always except; but, though my other engagements have prevented my attendance on your society for the greatest part of last year, and I have set an example of that freedom from restraint, without which no society can flourish; yet, as my few hours of leisure will now be devoted to *Sunscrit* literature, I cannot but hope, though my chief object be a knowledge of *Hindu* law, to make some discovery in other sciences, which I shall impart with humility, and which you will, I doubt not, receive with indulgence.

II.

THE FIFTH

ANNIVERSARY DISCOURSE,

DELIVERED 21 FEBRUARY, 1788,

BY THE PRESIDENT.

———————

AT the close of my last address to you, Gentlemen,
I declared my design of introducing to your notice a people of *Asia*, who seemed as different in most
respects from the *Hindus* and *Arabs* as those two nations had been shown to differ from each other; I
mean the people whom we call *Tartars*: but I enter with extreme diffidence on my present subject, because I have little knowledge of the *Tartarean* dialects; and the gross errors of *European* writers on
Asiatic literature, have long convinced me that no satisfactory account can be given of any nation with
whose language we are not perfectly acquainted. Such
evidence, however, as I have procured by attentive
reading and scrupulous enquiries, I will now lay before you; interspersing such remarks as I could not
but make on that evidence, and submitting the whole
to your impartial decision.

Conformably to the method before adopted in describing *Arabia* and *India*, I consider *Tartary* also,
for the purpose of this discourse, on its most extensive
scale; and request your attention whilst I trace the
largest boundaries that are assignable to it. Conceive
a line drawn from the mouth of the *Oby* to that of the

Dneiper, and, bringing it back eastward across the *Euxine*, so as to include the peninsula of *Krim*, extend it along the foot of *Caucasus*, by the rivers *Cur* and *Aras*, to the *Caspian Lake*, from the opposite shore of which follow the course of the *Jaihun*, and the chain of *Caucasean* hills, as far as those of *Imaus*; whence continue the line beyond the *Chinese* wall to the White Mountain and the country of *Yetso*; skirting the borders of *Persia*, *India*, *China*, *Corea*, but including part of *Russia*, with all the districts which lie between the Glacial Sea and that of *Japan*. M. *de Guignes*, whose great work on the *Huns* abounds more in solid learning than in rhetorical ornaments, presents us, however, with a magnificent image of this wide region; describing it as a stupendous edifice, the beams and pillars of which are many ranges of lofty hills, and the dome one prodigious mountain, to which the *Chinese* give the epithet of *Celestial*, with a considerable number of broad rivers flowing down its sides. If the mansion be so amazingly sublime, the land around it is proportionably extended, but more wonderfully diversified; for some parts of it are encrusted with ice, others parched with inflamed air and covered with a kind of lava: here we meet with immense tracts of sandy deserts, and forests almost impenetrable; there, with gardens, groves, and meadows, perfumed with musk, watered by numberless rivulets, and abounding in fruits and flowers; and, from east to west, lie many considerable provinces, which appear as valleys in comparison of the hills towering above them, but in truth are the flat summits of the highest mountains in the world, or at least the highest in *Asia*. Near one fourth in latitude of this extraordinary region is in the same charming climate with *Greece*, *Italy*. and *Provence*; and another fourth in that of *England*, *Germany*, and the northern parts of *France*; but the *Hyperborean* countries can have few beauties to recommend them, at least in the present state of the

earth's temperature. To the south, on the frontiers of
Iran are the beautiful vales of *Soghd*, with the celebrated cities of *Samarkand* and *Bokhara*; on those of
Tibet are the territories of *Cashghar*, *Khoten*, *Chegil*,
and *Khata*, all famed for perfumes, and for the beauty
of their inhabitants; and on those of *China* lies the
country of *Chin*, anciently a powerful kingdom; which
name, like that of *Khata*, has in modern times been
given to the whole *Chinese* empire, where such an appellation would be thought an insult. We must not
omit the fine territory of *Tancut*, which was known to
the *Greeks* by the name of *Serica*, and considered by
them as the farthest eastern extremity of the habitable
globe.

Scythia seems to be the general name which the ancient *Europeans* gave to as much as they knew of the
country thus bounded and described; but whether
that word be derived, as *Pliny* seems to intimate, from
Sacai, a people known by a similar name to the *Greeks*
and *Persians*, or, as *Bryant* imagines, from *Cuthia*, or,
as Colonel *Vallancey* believes, from words denoting
navigation, or, as it might have been supposed, from
a *Greek* root implying *wrath* and ferocity, this at least
is certain, that, as *India*, *China*, *Persia*, *Japan*, are not
appellations of those countries in the languages of the
nations who inhabit them, so neither *Scythia* nor *Tartary* are names by which the inhabitants of the country now under our consideration, have ever distinguished themselves. *Tataristan* is, indeed, a word
used by the *Persians* for the south-western part of
Scythia, where the musk-deer is said to be common;
and the name *Tatar* is by some considered as that of
a particular tribe; by others, as that of a small river
only; while *Turan*, as opposed to *Iran*, seems to
mean the ancient dominion of *Afrasiab* to the north
and east of the *Oxus*. There is nothing more idle
than a debate concerning names, which, after all, are

of little consequence when our ideas are distinct without them. Having given, therefore, a correct notion
of the country which I proposed to examine, I shall
not scruple to call it by the general name of *Tartary*;
though I am conscious of using a term equally impro-
per in the pronunciation and the application of it.

Tartary, then, which contained, according to *Pliny*,
an innumerable multitude of nations, by whom the rest
of *Asia* and all *Europe* has in different ages been over-
run, is denominated, as various images have presented
themselves to various fancies, the *great hive of the
northern swarms*, the *nursery of irresistible legions*, and,
by stronger metaphor, the *foundery of the human race*;
but M. *Bailly*, a wonderfully ingenious man and a
very lively writer, seems first to have considered it as
the *cradle of our species*, and to have supported an
opinion that the whole ancient world was enlightened
by sciences brought from the most northern parts of
Scythia, particularly from the banks of the *Jenisea*, or
from the *Hyperborean* regions. All the fables of old
Greece, Italy, Persia, India, he derives from the north;
and it must be owned, that he maintains his paradox
with acuteness and learning. Great learning and
great acuteness, together with the charms of a most
engaging style, were indeed necessary to render even
tolerable a system which places an earthly paradise,
the gardens of *Hesperus*, the islands of the *Macares*,
the groves of *Elysium*, if not of *Eden*, the heaven
of *Indra*, the *Peristan*, or fairy-land of the *Persian* poets, with its city of diamonds and its
country of *Shadcam*, so named from *Pleasure* and
Love, not in any one climate which the common
sense of mankind considers as the seat of delights, but beyond the mouth of the *Oby*, in the
Frozen Sea, in a region equalled only by that where
the wild imagination of *Dante* led him to fix the
worst of criminals in a state of punishment after

death, and of which *he could not*, he says, *even think without shivering.* A very curious passage in a tract of *Plutarch* on *the figure in the moon's orb,* naturally induced M. *Bailly* to place *Ogygia* in the north; and he concludes that island, as others have concluded rather fallaciously, to be the *Atlantis* of *Plato*; but is at a loss to determine whether it was *Iceland* or *Greenland, Spitzbergen* or *New Zembla.* Among so many charms it was difficult, indeed, to give a preference; but our philosopher, though as much perplexed by an option of beauties as the shepherd of *Ida,* seems on the whole to think *Zembla* the most worthy of the *golden fruit;* because it is indisputably an island, and lies opposite to a gulph near a continent, from which a great number of rivers descend into the ocean. He appears equally distressed among five nations, real and imaginary, to fix upon that which the *Greeks* named *Atlantes;* and his conclusion in both cases must remind us of the showman at *Eton,* who, having pointed out in his box all the crowned heads of the world, and being asked by the school-boys who looked through the glass, which was the Emperor, which was the Pope, which the Sultan, and which the Great Mogul, answered eagerly, ' which you please, young gentlemen, which you please.' His letters, however, to *Voltaire,* in which he unfolds his new system to his friend, whom he had not been able to convince, are by no means to be derided; and his general proposition, that arts and sciences had their source in *Tartary,* deserves a longer examination than can be given to it in this discourse. I shall, nevertheless, with your permission, shortly discuss the question under the several heads, that will present themselves in order.

Although we may naturally suppose that the numberless communities of *Tartars,* some of whom are established in great cities, and some encamped

on plains in ambulatory mansions, which they remove
from pasture to pasture, must be as different in their
features as in their dialects; yet, among those who
have not emigrated into another country, and mixed
with another nation, we may discern a family-likeness,
especially in their eyes and countenance, and in that
configuration of lineaments which we generally call a
Tartar face ; but, without making anxious enquiries,
whether all the inhabitants of the vast region before
described have similar features, we may conclude from
those whom we have seen, and from the original por-
traits of *Taimur* and his descendants, that the *Tartars*
in general differ wholly in complexion and countenance from the *Hindus* and from the *Arabs :* an observation which tends, in some degree, to confirm the
account given by modern *Tartars* themselves of their
descent from a common ancestor. Unhappily, their
lineage cannot be proved by authentic pedigrees, or
historical monuments; for all their writings extant,
even those in the *Mogul* dialect, are long subsequent to
the time of *Muhammed ;* nor is it possible to distinguish
their genuine traditions from those of the *Arabs,* whose
religious opinions they have in general adopted. At
the beginning of the *fourteenth* century, *Khwajah
Rashid,* surnamed *Fadlullah,* a native of *Kazvin,* compiled his account of the *Tartars* and *Mongals* from
the papers of one *Pulad,* whom the great grandson of
Holacu had sent into *Tataristan* for the sole purpose
of collecting historical information ; and the commission itself shows how little the *Tartarian* princes
really knew of their own origin. From this
work of *Rashid,* and from other materials, *Abulghazi,* king of *Khwarezm,* composed in the *Mogul* language his *Genealogical History,* which, having been purchased from a merchant of *Bukhara*
by some *Swedish* officers, prisoners of war in
Siberia, has found its way into several *European*
tongues : it contains much valuable matter, but, like

all *Muhammedan* histories, exhibits tribes or nations as
individual sovereigns; and, if Baron *De Tott* had not
strangely neglected to procure a copy of the *Tartarian*
history, for the original of which he unnecessarily offered a large sum, we should probably have found that it
begins with an account of the deluge, taken from the
Koran, and proceeds to rank *Turc*, *Chin*, *Tatar*, and
Mongal, among the sons of *Yafet*. The genuine traditional history of the *Tartars*, in all the books that I
have inspected, seems to begin with *Oghuz*, as that
of the *Hindus* does with *Rama*: they place their miraculous hero and patriarch *four thousand* years before
Chengiz Khan, who was born in the year 1164, and
with whose reign their historical period commences.
It is rather surprising that Mr. *Bailly*, who makes frequent appeals to etymological arguments, has not derived *Ogyges* from *Oghuz*, and *Atlas* from *Altai*, or
the *Golden Mountain* of *Tartary*: the *Greek* terminations might have been rejected from both words; and
a mere transposition of letters is no difficulty with an
etymologist.

My remarks in this address, Gentlemen, will be
confined to the period preceding *Chengiz*; and, although the learned labours of M. *de Guignes*, and
the Fathers *Visdelou*, *Demailla*, and *Gaubil*, who have
made an incomparable use of their *Chinese* literature,
exhibit probable accounts of the *Tartars* from a
very early age; yet the old historians of *China*
were not only foreign, but generally hostile to them,
and for both those reasons, either through ignorance or malignity, may be suspected of misrepre-
senting their transactions: if they speak truth, the
ancient history of the *Tartars* presents us, like
most other histories, with a series of assassinations,
plots, treasons, massacres, and all the natural fruits
of selfish ambition. I should have no inclination
to give you a sketch of such horrors, even if

the occasion called for it ; and will barely observe,
that the first king of the *Hynznaus*, or *Huns*, began
his reign, according to *Visdelou*, about *three thousand
five hundred and sixty years ago*, not long after the
time fixed in my former discourses for the first regular establishments of the *Hindus* and *Arabs* in their
several countries.

I. Our first enquiry concerning the *languages* and
letters of the *Tartars*, presents us with a deplorable
void, or with a prospect as barren and dreary as that
of their deserts. The *Tartars*, in general, had no
literature (in this point all authorities appear to concur); the *Turcs* had no letters.; the *Huns*, according
to *Procopius*, had not even heard of them ; the magnificent *Chengiz*, whose empire included an area of near
eighty square degrees, could find none of his own
Mongals, as the best authors inform us, able to write
his dispatches ; and *Taimur*, a savage of strong natural parts, and passionately fond of hearing histories
read to him, could himself neither write nor read.
It is true that *Ibnu Arabshah* mentions a set of characters called *Dilberjin*, which were used in *Khata :*
‘ he had seen them,’ he says, ‘ and found them to
‘ consist of *forty-one* letters, a distinct symbol being
‘ appropriated to each long and short vowel, and
‘ to each consonant hard or soft, or otherwise varied
‘ in pronunciation ;’ but *Khata* was in Southern *Tartary*, on the confines of *India* ; and, from his description of the characters there in use, we cannot but
suspect them to have been those of *Tibet*, which are
manifestly *Indian*, bearing a greater resemblance to
those of *Bengal* than to *Devanagari*. The learned
and eloquent *Arab* adds, ‘ that the *Tartars* of *Khata*
‘ write, in the *Dilberjin* letters, all their tales and
‘ histories, their journals, poems, and miscellanies,
‘ their diplomas, records of state and justice, the laws
‘ of *Chengiz*, their public registers, and their composi-

' rions of every species.' If this be true, the people of
Khata must have been a polished, and even a lettered
nation ; and it may be true, without affecting the
general position, that the Tartars were illiterate ; but
Ibnu Arabshah was a professed rhetorician, and it is
impossible to read the original passage without full
conviction that his object in writing it was to display
his power of words in a flowing and modulated period. He says further, that in Jughatai the people of
Oighur, as he calls them, ' have a system of fourteen
' letters only, denominated, from themselves, Oighuri ;'
and those are the characters which the Mongals are
supposed, by most authors, to have borrowed. Abulghazi tells us only, that Chengiz employed the natives
of Eighur as excellent penmen ; but the Chinese assert, that he was forced to employ them, because he
had no writers at all among his natural-born subjects ;
and we are assured by many, that Kublaikhan ordered
letters to be invented for his nation by a Tibetian,
whom he rewarded with the dignity of chief Lama.
The small number of Eighuri letters might induce us
to believe that they were Zend or Pahlawi, which must
have been current in that country when it was governed by the sons of Feridun ; and, if the alphabet
ascribed to the Eighurians by M. Des Hautesrayes be
correct, we may safely decide, that in many of its
letters it resembles both the Zend and the Syriac, with
a remarkable difference in the mode of connecting
them ; but, as we can scarce hope to see a genuine
specimen of them, our doubt must remain in regard to
their form and origin. The page exhibited by Hyde as
Khatayan writing, is evidently a sort of broken Cufick ;
and the fine manuscript at Oxford, from which it was
taken, is more probably a Mendean work on some religious subject, than, as he imagined, a code of Tartarian laws. That very learned man appears to have
made a worse mistake, in giving us for Mongal characters a page of writing which has the appearance of
Japanese, or mutilated Chinese letters.

If the *Tartars* in general, as we have every reason
to believe, had no written memorials, it cannot be
thought wonderful that their *languages*, like those of
America, should have been in perpetual fluctuation,
and that more than fifty dialects, as *Hyde* had been
credibly informed, should be spoken between *Moscow*
and *China*, by the many kindred tribes or their several branches, which are enumerated by *Abulghazi*.
What those dialects are, and whether they really sprang
from a common stock, we shall probably learn from
Mr. *Pallas*, and other indefatigable men employed by
the *Russian* court ; and it is from the *Russians* that we
must expect the most accurate information concerning
their *Asiatic* subjects : I persuade myself that, if their
enquiries be judiciously made, and faithfully reported,
the result of them will prove that all the languages
properly *Tartarian*, arose from one common source ;
excepting always the jargons of such wanderers or
mountaineers as, having long been divided from the
main body of the nation, must, in a course of ages,
have framed separate idioms for themselves.   The
only *Tartarian* language of which I have any knowledge, is the *Turkish* of *Constantinople*, which is however so copious, that whoever shall know it perfectly,
will easily understand, as we are assured by intelligent
authors, the dialects of *Tataristan* ; and we may collect from *Abulghazi*, that he would find little difficulty in the *Calmac* and the *Mogul*. I will not offend
your ears by a dry catalogue of similar words in those
different languages ; but a careful investigation has
convinced me that, as the *Indian* and *Arabian* tongues
are severally descended from a common parent, so
those of *Tartary* might be traced to one ancient
stem essentially differing from the two others.   It
appears, indeed, from a story told by *Abulghazi*, that
the *Virats* and the *Mongals* could not understand each
other ; but no more can the *Danes* and the *English*,
yet their dialects, beyond a doubt, are branches of

the same *Gothic* tree. The dialect of the *Moguls*, in
which some histories of *Taimur* and his descendants
were originally composed, is called in *India*, where a
learned native set me right when I used another word,
Turci; not that it is precisely the same with the *Turkish* of the *Othmanlus*, but the two idioms differ, perhaps, less than *Swedish* and *German*, or *Spanish* and
Portuguese, and certainly less than *Welsh* and *Irish*.
In hope of ascertaining this point, I have long search-
ed in vain for the original works ascribed to *Taimur*
and *Baber*; but all the *Moguls* with whom I have
conversed in this country, resemble the crow in one
of their popular fables, who, having long affected to
walk like a pheasant, was unable, after all, to acquire
the gracefulness of that elegant bird, and in the mean
time forgot his own natural gait. They have not
learned the dialect of *Persia*, bu thave wholly forgotten that of their ancestors. A very considerable part
of the old *Tartarian* language, which in *Asia* would
probably have been lost, is happily preserved in *Europe*; and, if the groundwork of the western *Turkish*,
when separated from the *Persian* and *Arabic*, with
which it is embellished, be a branch of the lost *Oghu-
sian* tongue, I can assert with confidence that it has
not the least resemblance either to *Arabic* or *Sanscrit*,
and must have been invented by a race of men wholly
distinct from the *Arabs* or *Hindus*. This fact alone
oversets the system of M. *Bailly*, who considers the
Sanscrit, of which he gives in several places a most
erroneous account, as ' *A fine monument of his primc-
' aal* Scythians, *the preceptors of mankind, and plant-
' ers of a sublime philosophy even in* India;' for he
holds it an incontestable truth, that *a language which
is dead, supposes a nation which is destroyed*; and he
seems to think such reasoning perfectly decisive of
the question, without having recourse to astronomical
arguments, or the spirit of ancient institutions. For
my part, I desire no better proof than that which the

language of the *Brahmans* affords, of an immemorial and total difference between the *Savages of the Mountains*, as the old *Chinese* justly called the *Tartars*, and the studious, placid, contemplative inhabitants of these *Indian* plains.

II. The *geographical* reasoning of M. *Bailly* may, perhaps, be thought equally shallow, if not inconsistent in some degree with itself. ' An adoration of the ' sun and of fire,' says he, ' must necessarily have ' arisen in a cold region ; therefore it must have been ' foreign to *India*, *Persia*, *Arabia* ; therefore it must ' have been derived from *Tartary*.' No man, I believe, who has travelled in winter through *Bahar*, or has even passed a cold season at *Calcutta* within the tropic, can doubt that the solar warmth is often desirable by all, and might have been considered as adorable by the ignorant in these climates ; or that the return of spring deserves all the salutations which it receives from the *Persian* and *Indian* poets ; not to rely on certain historical evidence, that *Antarah*, a celebrated warrior and bard, actually perished with cold on a mountain of *Arabia*. To meet, however, an objection which might naturally enough be made to the voluntary settlement and amazing population of his primitive race, in the icy regions of the north, he takes refuge in the hypothesis of M. *Buffon*, who imagines that our whole globe was at first of a white heat, and has been gradually cooling from the poles to the equator ; so that the *Hyperborean* countries had once a delightful temperature ; and *Siberia* itself was even *hotter than the climate of our temperate zones* ; that is, was in too hot a climate, by his first proposition, for the primary worship of the sun. That the temperature of countries has not sustained a change in the lapse of ages, I will by no means insist ; but we can hardly reason conclusively from a variation of temperature to the cultivation and diffusion of science. If as many female elephants and tigresses as we now find in

Bengal had formerly littered in the *Siberian* forests, and the young, as the earth cooled, had sought a genial warmth in the climate of the south, it would not follow that other savages, who migrated in the same direction, and on the same account, brought religion and philosophy, language and writing, art and science, into the southern latitudes.

We are told by *Abulghazi* that the primitive religion of human creatures, or the pure adoration of one Creator, prevailed in *Tartary* during the first generations of *Yafet*, but was extinct before the birth of *Oghuz*, who restored it in his dominions; that, some ages after him, the *Mongals* and the *Turcs* relapsed into gross idolatry; but that *Chengiz* was a Theist, and, in a conversation with the *Muhammedan* doctors, admitted their arguments for the being and attributes of the Deity to be unanswerable, while he contested the evidence of their prophet's legation. From old *Grecian* authorities we learn that the *Massagetæ* worshipped the sun; and the narrative of an embassy from *Justin* to the *Rhakan*, or emperor, who then resided in a fine vale near the source of the *Irtish*, mentions the *Tartarian* ceremony of purifying the *Roman* ambassadors by conducting them between two *fires*. The *Tartars* of that age are represented as adorers of the *four elements*, and believers in an invisible spirit, to whom they sacrificed bulls and rams. Modern travellers relate, that, in the festivals of some *Tartarian* tribes, they pour a few drops of a consecrated liquor on the statues of their gods; after which an attendant sprinkles a little of what remains three times toward the south, in honour of fire; toward the west and east, in honour of water and air; and as often toward the north, in honour of the earth, which contained the reliques of their deceased ancestors. Now all this may be very true, without proving a national affinity between the *Tartars*

and *Hindus*; for the *Arabs* adored the planets and
the beauties of Nature; the *Arabs* had carved images, and made libations on a black stone; the *Arabs*
turned in prayer to different quarters of the heavens; yet we know with certainty, that the *Arabs*
are a distinct race from the *Tartars*; and we might
as well infer that they were the same people, because
they had each their *Nomades, or wanderers for pasture*;
and because the *Turcmans*, described by *Ibnuarab-
shah*, and by him called *Tatars*, are, like *most Arabian* tribes, pastoral and warlike, hospitable and
generous, wintering and summering on different
plains, and rich in herds and flocks, horses and camels: but this agreement in manners proceeds from
the similar nature of their several deserts, and their
similar choice of a free rambling life, without evinc-
ing a community of origin, which they could scarce
have had without preserving some remnant at least
of a common language.

Many *Lamas*, we are assured, or priests of *Buddha*,
have been found settled in *Siberia*; but it can hardly
be doubted that the *Lamas* had travelled thither
from *Tibet*; whence it is more than probable, that
the religion of the *Bauddhas* was imported into Southern, or *Chinese Tartary*; since we know that rolls of
Tibetian writing have been brought even from the
borders of the *Caspian*. The complexion of *Buddha*
himself, which, according to the *Hindus*, was *between
white and ruddy*, would perhaps have convinced M.
Bailly, had he known the *Indian* tradition, that the
last great legislator and god of the east was a *Tartar*; but the *Chinese* consider him as a native of
India; the *Brahmans* insist that he was born in a
forest near *Gaya*; and many reasons may lead us to
suspect, that his religion was carried from the west
and the south, to those eastern and northern countries, in which it prevails. On the whole, we meet

with few or no traces in *Scythia* of *Indian* rites and
superstitions, or of that poetical mythology with
which the *Sanscrit* poems are decorated; and we may
allow the *Tartars* to have adored the Sun with more
reason than any southern people, without admitting
them to have been the sole original inventors of that
universal folly. We may even doubt the originality of
their veneration for the *four elements*, which forms a
principal part of the ritual introduced by *Zeratusht*, a
native of *Rai* in *Persia*, born in the reign of *Gushtasp*, whose son *Pashuten* is believed by the *Parsis*
to have resided long in *Tartary*, at a place called *Can-
gidiz*, where a magnificent palace is said to have been
built by the father of *Cyrus*, and where the *Persian*
prince, who was a zealot in the new faith, would naturally have disseminated its tenets among the neighbouring *Tartars*.

Of any philosphy, except natural ethics, which the
rudest society requires and experience teaches, we find
no more vestiges in *Asiatic Scythia* than in ancient *Arabia*; nor would the name of a philosopher and a *Scythian*
have ever been connected, if *Anacharsis* had not visited *Athens* and *Lydia* for that instruction, which his
birth-place could not have afforded him: but *Anacharsis* was the son of a *Grecian* woman, who had
taught him her language; and he soon learned to de-
spise his own. He was unquestionably a man of a
sound understanding and fine parts; and, among the
lively sayings which gained him the reputation of a
wit even in *Greece*, it is related by *Diogenes Laertius*,
that, when an *Athenian* reproached him with being a
Scythian, he answered, ' My country is, indeed, a dis-
' grace to me, but thou art a disgrace to thy country.'
What his country was, in regard to manners and civil
duties, we may learn from his fate in it; for when, on
his return from *Athens*, he attempted to reform it by
introducing the wise laws of his friend *Solon*, he was

killed on a hunting party with an arrow, shot by his
own brother, a *Scythian* chieftain. Such was the
philosophy of M. *Bailly's Atlantes*, the first and most
enlightened of nations! We are assured, however, by
the learned author of the *Dabistan*, that the *Tartars*
under *Chengiz*, and his descendants, were lovers of
truth, and would not even preserve their lives by a
violation of it. *De Guignes* ascribes the same veracity,
the parent of all virtues, to the *Huns*; and *Strabo*,
who might only mean to lash the *Greeks* by praising
Barbarians, as *Horace* extolled the wandering *Scythians*
merely to satirize his luxurious countrymen, informs
us that the nations of *Scythia* deserve the praise due
to wisdom, heroic friendship, and justice; and this
praise we may readily allow them on his authority,
without supposing them to have been the preceptors
of mankind.

As to the laws of *Zamolxis*, concerning whom we
know as little as of the *Scythian Deucalion*, or of
Abaris the *Hyperborean*, and to whose story even *Herodotus* gave no credit, I lament, for many reasons,
that if ever they existed they have not been preserved.
It is certain that a system of laws, called *Yasac*, has been
celebrated in *Tartary* since the time of *Chengiz*, who
is said to have republished them in his empire, as his
institutions were afterwards adopted and enforced by
Taimur; but they seem to have been a common or
traditionary law, and were probably not reduced into
writing till *Chengiz* had conquered a nation who were
able to write.

III. Had the religious opinions and allegorical fables
of the *Hindus* been actually borrowed from *Sythia*,
travellers must have discovered in that country some
ancient monuments of them; such as pieces of gro-
tesque sculpture, images of the Gods and *Avatars*,

and inscriptions on pillars or in caverns, analogous to those which remain in every part of the western peninsula, or to those which many of us have seen in *Baher* and at *Banaras*; but (except a few detached idols) the only great monuments of *Tartarian* antiquity are a line of ramparts on the west and east of the *Caspian*, ascribed indeed by ignorant *Muselmans* to *Yajuj* and *Majuj*, or *Gog* and *Magog*; that is, to the *Scythians*, but manifestly raised by a very different nation, in order to stop their predatory inroads through the passes of *Caucasus*. The *Chinese* wall was built, or finished, on a similar construction and for a similar purpose, by an emperor, who died only two hundred and ten years before the beginning of our æra; and the other mounds were very probably constructed by the old *Persians*, though, like many works of unknown origin, they are given to *Secander*, not the *Macedonian*, but a more ancient hero, supposed by some to have been *Jemshid*. It is related, that pyramids and tombs have been found in *Tataristan*, or *Western Scythia*, and some remnants of edifices in the lake *Saïsan*; that vestiges of a deserted city have been recently discovered by the *Russians* near the *Caspian* Sea, and the *Mountain of Eagles*; and that golden ornaments and utensils, figures of elks and other quadrupeds in metal, weapons of various kinds, and even implements for mining, but made of copper instead of iron, have been dug up in the country of the *Tshudes*; whence M. *Bailly* infers, with great reason, the high antiquity of that people: but the high antiquity of the *Tartars*, and their establishment in that country near four thousand years ago, no man disputes; we are inquiring into their ancient religion and philosophy; which neither ornaments of gold, nor tools of copper, will prove to have had an affinity with the religious rites and the sciences of *India*. The golden utensils might possibly have been fabricated by the *Tartars* themselves; but it is possible too, that they were carried from *Rome* or from *China*, whence occasional embassies were sent to the kings of *Eighur*. Towards the end of the tenth century the *Chinese* emperor dispatched an ambassador to a prince, named *Erslan*, which, in the *Turkish* of *Constantinople*, signifies a *lion*, who resided near the *Golden Mountain*; in the same station, perhaps, where the *Romans* had been received in the middle of the sixth century. The *Chinese* on his return home reported the *Eighuris* to be a grave people, with fair complexions, diligent workmen, and ingenious artificers not only in gold, silver, and iron, but in jasper and fine stones; and the *Romans* had before described their magnificent reception in a rich palace adorned with *Chinese* manufactures: but these times were comparatively modern; and, even if we should admit that the *Eighuris*, who are said to have been governed for a period of two thousand years by an *Idecut*, or sovereign, of their own race, were in some very early age a literary and polished nation, it would prove nothing in favour of the *Huns*, *Turcs*, *Mongals*, and other savages to the north of *Pekin*, who seem in all ages before *Muhammed*, to have been equally ferocious and illiterate.

Without actual inspection of the manuscripts that have been found near the *Caspian*, it would be impossible to give a correct opinion concerning them; but one of them, described as written on blue silky paper in letters of gold and silver, not unlike *Hebrew*, was probably a *Tibetian* composition of the same kind with that which lay near the source of the *Irtish*, and of which *Cassiano*, I believe, made the first accurate version. Another, if we may judge from the description of it, was probably modern *Turkish*; and none of them could have been of great antiquity.

IV. From ancient monuments, therefore, we have

no proof that the *Tartars* were themselves well-in-
structed, much less that they instructed the world;
nor have we any stronger reason to conclude from their
general manners and character, that they had made an
early proficiency in *arts* and *sciences*. Even of poetry,
the most universal and most natural of the fine arts,
we find no genuine specimens ascribed to them, except some horrible war-songs expressed in *Persian* by
Ali of *Yezd*, and possibly invented by him. After
the conquest of *Persia* by the *Mongals*, their princes
indeed encouraged learning, and even made astronomical observations at *Samarkand*; as the *Turc* became
polished by mixing with the *Persians* and *Arabs*,
though *their very nature*, as one of their own writers
confesses, *had before been like an incurable distemper,
and their minds clouded with ignorance :* thus also the
Manchen monarchs of *China* have been patrons of the
learned and ingenious ; and the Emperor *Kien-Long*
is, if he be now living, a fine *Chinese* poet. In all
these instances the *Tartars* have resembled the *Romans*, who, before they had subdued *Greece*, were
little better than tigers in war, and *fauns* or *sylvans*
in science and art.

Before I left *Europe*, I had insisted in conversation,
that the *Tuzuc*, translated by Major *Davy*, was never
written by *Taimur* himself, at least not as *Cæsar* wrote
his commentaries, for one very plain reason, that no
Tartarian king of his age could write at all ; and, in
support of my opinion, I had cited *Ibnu Arabshah*, who,
though justly hostile to the savage, by whom his native city, *Damascus*, had been ruined, yet praises his
genius and the real greatness of his mind; but adds,
"he was wholly illiterate ; he neither read nor wrote
"any thing ; and he knew nothing of *Arabic* ;
"though of *Persian*, *Turkish*, and the *Mogul* dialect,
"he knew as much as was sufficient for his purpose,
"and no more. He used with pleasure to hear histories

" read to him, and so frequently heard the same book,
" that he was able by memory to correct an inaccurate
" reader." This passage had no effect on the translator, whom *great and learned men in* India *had assured,* it seems, *that the work was authentic,* by which
he meant *composed by the conqueror himself :* but the
great in this country might have been *unlearned,* or
the *learned* might not have been *great* enough to answer any leading question in a manner that opposed
the declared inclination of a *British* inquirer; and,
in either case, since no witnesses are named, so general a reference to them will hardly be thought conclu-
sive evidence. On my part, I will name a *Muselman,*
whom we all know, and who has enough both of
greatness and of *learning* to decide the question both
impartially and satisfactorily : The *Nawwab Mozaffer
Jang* informed me of his own accord, that no man
of sense in *Hindustan* believed the work to have been
composed by *Taimur,* but that his favourite, surnamed
Hindu Shah, was known to have written that book and
others, ascribed to his patron, after many confidential
discourses with the *Emir,* and, perhaps, nearly in the
prince's words as well as in his person : a story which
Ali of *Yezd,* who attended the court of *Taimur,* and
has given us a flowery panegyric instead of history,
renders highly probable, by confirming the latter part
of the *Arabian* account, and by total silence as to the
literary productions of his master. It is true, that a
very ingenious but indigent native, whom *Davy* supported, has given me a written memorial on the subject, in which he mentions *Taimur* as the author of
two works in *Turkish ;* but the credit of his information is overset by a strange apocryphal story of a king
of *Yemen,* who invaded, he says, the *Emir's* dominions, and in whose library the manuscript was afterwards found, and translated by order of *Aliskir,* first
minister of *Taimur's* grandson ; and Major *Davy* him-

self, before he departed from *Bengal*, told me, that
he was greatly perplexed by finding in a very accurate and old copy of the *Tuzuc*, which he designed
to republish with considerable additions, a particular
account, written *unquestionably* by *Taimur*, of *his own
death.* No evidence, therefore, has been adduced
to shake my opinion, that the *Moguls* and *Tartars*,
before their conquest of *India* and *Persia*, were wholly
unlettered; although it may be possible, that, even
without art or science, they had, like the *Huns*, both
warriors and lawgivers in their own country some
centuries before the birth of *Christ.*

If learning was ever anciently cultivated in the
region to the north of *India*, the seats of it, I have
reason to suspect must have been *Eighur, Cashghar,
Khata, Chin, Tancut,* and other countries of *Chinese
Tartary,* which lie between the thirty-fifth and forty-
fifth degrees of northern latitude; but I shall, in another discourse, produce my reasons for supposing
that those very countries were peopled by a race allied
to the *Hindus,* or enlightened at least by their vicinity to *India* and *China;* yet in *Tancut,* which by
some is annexed to *Tibet,* and even among its old
inhabitants, the *Seres,* we have no certain accounts of
uncommon talents or great improvements: they were
famed, indeed, for the faithful discharge of moral
duties, for a pacific disposition, and for that longevity which is often the reward of patient virtues and a
calm temper; but they are said to have been wholly
indifferent in former ages to the elegant arts, and even
to commerce; though *Fadhu'llah* had been informed,
that near the close of the *thirteenth* century many
branches of natural philosophy were cultivated in
Cam-chen, then the metropolis of *Serica.*

We may readily believe those, who assure us, that

D 4

some tribes of wandering *Tartars* had real skill in ap-
plying herbs and minerals to the purposes of medicine, and pretended to skill in magic; but the general character of their nation seems to have been this :
They were professed hunters or fishers, dwelling on
that account in forests or near great rivers, under huts
or rude tents, or in waggons drawn by their cattle
from station to station; they were dexterous archers,
excellent horsemen, bold combatants, appearing often
to flee in disorder for the sake of renewing their attack
with advantages; drinking the milk of mares, and
eating the flesh of colts; and thus in many respects
resembling the old *Arabs*, but in nothing more than
in their love of intoxicating liquors, and in nothing
less than in a taste for poetry and the improvement
of their language.

Thus has it been proved, and, in my humble opinion, beyond controversy, that the far greater part of
Asia has been peopled and immemorially possessed by
three considerable nations, whom, for want of better
names, we may call *Hindus, Arabs,* and *Tartars:*
each of them divided and subdivided into an infinite
number of branches, and all of them so different in
form and features, language, manners, and religion,
that, if they sprang originally from a common root,
they must have been separated for ages. Whether more
than three primitive stocks can be found, or, in other
words, whether the *Chinese, Japanese,* and *Persians,*
are entirely distinct from them, or formed by their intermixture, I shall hereafter, if your indulgence to me
continue, diligently inquire. To what conclusions
these inquiries will lead, I cannot yet clearly discern ;
but, if they lead to truth, we shall not regret our
journey through this dark region of ancient history,
in which, while we proceed step by step, and follow
every glimmering of certain light that presents itself,

we must beware of those false rays and luminous vapours which mislead *Asiatic* travellers, by an appearance of water, but are found on a near approach to be deserts of sand.

III.

THE SIXTH

DISCOURSE:

ON THE

PERSIANS.

DELIVERED 19 FEBRUARY, 1789.

Gentlemen,

I TURN with delight from the vast mountains and barren deserts of *Turan*, over which we travelled last year with no perfect knowledge of our course, and request you now to accompany me on a literary journey through one of the most celebrated and most beautiful countries in the world: a country, the history and languages of which, both ancient and modern, I have long attentively studied, and on which I may without arrogance promise you more positive information than I could possibly procure on a nation so disunited and so unlettered as the *Tartars:* I mean that which *Europeans* improperly call *Persia*, the name of a single province being applied to the whole empire of *Iran*, as it is correctly denominated by the present natives of it, and by the learned *Muselmans* who reside in these *British* territories. To give you an account of its largest boundaries, agreeably to my former mode of describing *India*, *Arabia*, and

Tartary, between which it lies, let us begin with the source of the great *Assyrian* stream *Euphrates* (as the *Greeks,* according to their custom, were pleased to miscall the *Forat)* and thence descend to its mouth in the Green Sea, or *Persian* Gulf, including in our line some considerable districts and towns on both sides of the river; then, coasting *Persia,* properly so named, and other *Iranian* provinces, we come to the Delta of the *Sindhu* or *Indus;* whence ascending to the mountains of *Cashghar,* we discover its fountains and those of the *Jaihun,* down which we are conducted to the *Caspian,* which formerly perhaps it entered, though it loses itself now in the sands and lakes of *Khwarezm.* We next are led from the Sea of *Khozar,* by the banks of the *Cur,* or *Cyrus,* and along the *Caucasean* ridges to the shore of the *Euxine,* and thence by the several *Grecian* Seas to the point whence we took our departure, at no considerable distance from the *Mediterranean.* We cannot but include the *Lower Asia* within this outline, because it was unquestionably a part of the *Persian,* if not of the old *Assyrian* empire; for we know that it was under the dominion of *Caikhosrau;* and *Diodorus,* we find, asserts, that the kingdom of *Troas* was dependent on *Assyria,* since *Priam* implored and obtained succours from his emperor *Teutames,* whose name approaches nearer to *Tahmuras* than to that of any other *Assyrian* monarch. Thus may we look on *Iran* as the noblest *island* (for so the *Greeks* and the *Arabs* would have called it) or at least as the noblest *peninsula* on this habitable globe; and if M. *Bailly* had fixed on it as the *Atlantis* of *Plato,* he might have supported his opinion with far stronger arguments than any that he has adduced in favour of *New Zembla.* If the account, indeed, of the *Atlantes* be not purely an *Egyptian,* or an *Utopian* fable, I should be more inclined to place them in *Iran* than in any region with which I am acquainted.

. It may seem strange, that the ancient history of so
distinguished an empire should be yet so imperfectly
known; but very satisfactory reasons may be assigned
for our ignorance of it: the principal of them are
the superficial knowledge of the *Greeks* and *Jews*,
and the loss of *Persian* archives, or historical compositions. That the *Grecian* writers, before *Xenophon*,
had *no* acquaintance with *Persia*, and that *all* their
accounts of it are *wholly* fabulous, is a paradox too
extravagant to be seriously maintained: but their connection with it in war or peace had, indeed, been generally confined to bordering kingdoms under feuda-
tory princes; and the first *Persian* emperor, whose
life and character they seem to have known with tolerable accuracy, was the great *Cyrus*, whom I call,
without fear of contradiction, *Caikhosrau*; for I shall
then only doubt that the *Khosrau* of *Firdausi* was
the *Cyrus* of the first *Greek* historian, and the hero
of the oldest political and moral romance, when I
doubt that *Louis Quatorze* and *Lewis the Fourteenth*
were one and the same *French* King. It is utterly in-
credible that two different princes of *Persia* should
each have been born in a foreign and hostile territory;
should each have been doomed to death in his infancy
by his maternal grandfather in consequence of por-
tentous dreams, real or invented; should each have
been saved by the remorse of his destined murderer;
and should each, after a similar education among
herdsmen, as the son of a herdsman, have found
means to revisit his paternal kingdom; and having
recovered it, after a long and triumphant war, from the
king who had invaded it, should have restored it to
the summit of power and magnificence! Whether so
romantic a story, which is the subject of an epic poem,
majestic and entire as the *Iliad*, be historically true,
we feel perhaps an inclination to doubt; but it
cannot with reason be denied, that the outline of it
related to a single hero, whom the *Asiatics*, convers-

ing with the father of *European* history, described
according to their popular traditions by his true name,
which the *Greek* alphabet could not express : nor will
a difference of names affect the question, since the
Greeks had little regard for truth, which they *sacrificed*
willingly *to the graces* of their language, and the
nicety of their ears ; and, if they could render foreign
words melodious, they were never solicitous to make
them exact ; hence they probably formed *Cambyses*
from *Cumbakhsh*, or *granting desires*, a title rather
than a name ; and *Xerxes* from *Shiruyi*, a prince and
warrior in the *Shahnamah*, or from *Shirshah*, which
might also have been a title ; for the *Asiatic* princes
have constantly assumed new titles or epithets at different periods of their lives, or on different occasions ;
custom which we have seen prevalent in our own
times both in *Iran* and *Hindustan*, and which has
been a source of great confusion even in the scriptural
accounts of *Babylonian* occurrences. Both *Greeks*
and *Jews* have in fact accommodated *Persian* names
to their own articulation ; and both seem to have dis-
regarded the native literature of *Iran*, without which
they could at most attain a general and imperfect
knowledge of the country. As to the *Persians* themselves, who were contemporary with the *Jews* and
Greeks, they must have been acquainted with the history of their own times, and with the traditional accounts of past ages ; but for a reason, which will presently appear, they chose to consider *Cayumers* as the
founder of their empire ; and, in the numerous dis-
tractions which followed the overthrow of *Dara*,
especially in the great revolution on the defeat of
Yezdegird, their civil histories were lost, as those of
India have unhappily been, from the solicitude of
the priests, the only depositaries of their learning, to
preserve their books of law and religion at the expence
of all others. Hence it has happened, that nothing
remains of genuine *Persian* history before the dynasty

of *Sasan*, except a few rustic traditions and fables, which furnished materials for the *Shahnamah*, and which are still supposed to exist in the *Pahlavi* language. All the annals of the *Pishdadi*, or *Assyrian* race, must be considered as dark and fabulous; and those of the *Cayani* family, or the *Medes* and *Persians*, as heroic and poetical; though the lunar eclipses, said to be mentioned by *Ptolemy*, fix the time of *Gushtasp*, the prince by whom *Zeratush* was protected, of the *Parthian* kings descended from *Arshac* or *Arsaces*, we know little more than the names; but the *Sasanis* had so long an intercourse with the emperors of *Rome* and *Byzantium*, that the period of their dominion may be called an historical age. In attempting to ascertain the beginning of the *Assyrian* empire, we are deluded, as in a thousand instances, by names arbitrarily imposed. It had been *settled* by chronologers, that the first monarchy established in *Persia* was the *Assyrian*; and *Newton*, finding some of opinion, that it rose in the first century after the Flood, but unable by his own calculations to extend it farther back than *seven hundred and ninety* years before *Christ*, rejected part of the old system, and adopted the rest of it; concluding, that the *Assyrian* monarchs began to reign about two hundred years after *Solomon*, and that, in all preceding ages, the government of *Iran* had been divided into several petty states and principalities. Of this opinion I confess myself to have been; when, disregarding the wild chronology of the *Muselmans* and *Gabrs*, I had allowed the utmost natural duration to the reigns of eleven *Pishdadi* kings, without being able to add more than a hundred years to *Newton's* computation. It seemed indeed unaccountably strange, that, although *Abraham* had found a regular monarchy in *Egypt*; although the kingdom of *Yemen* had just pretensions to very high antiquity; although the *Chinese*, in the twelfth century before our æra, had made approaches

at least to the present form of their extensive dominion ; and although we can hardly suppose the first
Indian monarchs to have reigned less than three thousand years ago, yet *Persia*, the most delightful, the
most compact, the most desirable country of them
all, should have remained for so many ages unsettled
and disunited. A fortunate discovery, for which I
was first indebted to *Mir Muhammed Husain*, one of
the most intelligent *Muselmans* in *India*, has at once
dissipated the cloud, and cast a gleam of light on the
primeval history of *Iran* and of the human race, of
which I had long despaired, and which could hardly
have dawned from any other quarter.

The rare and interesting tract *on twelve different
religions*, entitled the *Dabistan*, and composed by a
Mohammedan traveller, a native of *Cashmir*, named
Mohsan, but distinguished by the assumed surname of
Fani, or *Perishable*, begins with a wonderfully curious chapter on the religion of *Hushang*, which was
long anterior to that of *Zeratusht*, but had continued to be secretly professed by many learned *Persians* even to the author's time ; and several of the
most eminent of them, dissenting in many points
from the *Gabrs*, and persecuted by the ruling powers
of their country, had retired to *India* ; where they
compiled a number of books, now extremely scarce,
which *Mohsan* had perused, and with the writers of
which, or with many of them, he had contracted an
intimate friendship. From them he learned, that a
powerful monarchy had been established for ages in
Iran before the accession of *Cayumers* ; that it was
called the *Mahabadian* dynasty, for a reason which
will soon be mentioned ; and that many princes, of
whom seven or eight are only named in the *Dabistan*,
and among them *Mahbul*, or *Maha Beli*, had raised
their empire to the zenith of human glory. If we

can rely on this evidence, which to me appears unexceptionable, the *Iranian* monarchy must have been the oldest in the world ; but it will remain dubious to which of the three stocks *Hindu*, *Arabian*, or *Tartar*, the first Kings of *Iran* belonged, or whether they sprang from a *fourth* race distinct from any of the others ; and these are questions which we shall be able, I imagine, to answer precisely, when we have carefully inquired into the *languages* and *letters*, *religion* and *philosophy*, and incidentally into the *arts* and *sciences*, of the ancient *Persians*.

1. In the new and important remarks which I am going to offer on the ancient *languages* and *characters* of *Iran*, I am sensible that you must give me credit for many assertions which, on this occasion, it is impossible to prove; for I should ill deserve your indulgent attention, if I were to abuse it by repeating a dry list of detached words, and presenting you with a vocabulary instead of a dissertation; but, since I have no system to maintain, and have not suffered imagination to delude my judgment ; since I have habituated myself to form opinions of men and things from *evidence*, which is the only solid basis of *civil*, as *experiment* is of *natural* knowledge; and since I have maturely considered the questions which I mean to discuss, you will not, I am persuaded, suspect my testimony, or think that I go too far, when I assure you, that I will assert nothing positively which I am not able satisfactorily to demonstrate. When *Muhammed* was born, and *Anushiravan*, whom he calls *the Just King*, sat on the throne of *Persia*, two languages appear to have been generally prevalent in the great empire of *Iran* ; that of the *Court*, thence named *Deri*, which was only a refined and elegant dialect of the *Parsi*, so called from the province, of which *Shiraz* is now the capital, and that of the learned, in which most books were composed, and which had the

VOL. II. E

name of *Pahlavi*, either from the *heroes*, who spoke
it in former times, or from *Pahlu*, a tract of land,
which included, we are told, some considerable cities
of *Irak*. The ruder dialects of both were, and, I believe, still are spoken by the rustics in several provinces; and in many of them, as *Herat*, *Zabul*, *Sis-
tan*, and others, distinct idioms were vernacular, as it
happens in every kingdom of great extent. Besides
the *Parsi* and *Pahlavi*, a very ancient and abstruse
tongue was known to the priests and philosophers,
called *the language of the Zend*, because a book on
religious and moral duties, which they held sacred,
and which bore that name, had been written in it;
while the *Pazand*, or comment on that work, was
composed in *Pahlavi*, as a more popular idiom; but
a learned follower of *Zeratusht*, named *Bahman*, who
lately died at *Calcutta*, where he had lived with me
as a *Persian* reader about three years, assured me, that
the *letters* of his prophet's book were properly called
Zend, and the *language Avesta*, as the words of the
Vedas are *Sanscrit*, and the characters *Nagari*; or as
the old *Sagas* and poems of *Iseland* were expressed in
Runic letters. Let us however, in compliance with custom, give the name of *Zend* to the sacred language of
Persia, until we can find, as we shall very soon, a fitter
appellation for it. The *Zend* and the old *Pahlavi* are
almost extinct in *Iran*; for among six or seven thousand *Gabrs*, who reside chiefly at *Yezd*, and in *Cir-
man*, there are very few who can read *Pahlavi*, and
scarce any who even boast of knowing the *Zend*;
while the *Parsi*, which remains almost pure in the
Shahnamah, has now become by the intermixture of
numberless *Arabic* words, and many imperceptible
changes, a new language exquisitely polished by a series of fine writers in prose and verse, and analogous
to the different idioms gradually formed in *Europe* after the subversion of the *Roman* empire: but with
modern *Persian* we have no concern in our present in-

quiry, which I confine to the ages that preceded the
Mohammedan conquest. Having twice read the works
of *Firdausi* with great attention since I applied myself to the study of old *Indian* literature, I can assure
you with confidence, that hundreds of *Parsi* nouns
are pure *Sanscrit*, with no other change than such as
may be observed in the numerous *bhashas*, or vernacular dialects of *India*; that very many *Persian* im-
peratives are the roots of *Sanscrit* verbs; and that
even the moods and tenses of the *Persian* verb substantive, which is the model of all the rest, are dedu-
cible from the *Sanscrit* by an easy and clear analogy :
we may hence conclude, that the *Parsi* was derived,
like the various *Indian* dialects, from the language of
the *Brahmans*; and I must add, that in the pure *Persian* I find no trace of any *Arabian* tongue, except what
proceeded from the known intercourse between the
Persians and *Arabs*, especially in the time of *Bahram*,
who was educated in *Arabia*, and whose *Arabic* verses
are still extant, together with his heroic line in *Deri*,
which many suppose to be the first attempt at *Persian*
versification in *Arabian* metre: but, without having recourse to other arguments, *the composition of words*, in
which the genius of the *Persian* delights, and which
that of the *Arabic* abhors, is a decisive proof that the
Parsi sprang from an *Indian*, and not from an *Arabian*
stock. Considering languages as mere instruments of
knowledge, and having strong reasons to doubt the
existence of genuine books in *Zend* or *Pahlavi* (especially since the well-informed author of the *Dabistan*
affirms the work of *Zeratusht* to have been lost, and
its place supplied by a recent compilation) I had no
inducement, though I had an opportunity, to learn
what remains of those ancient languages; but I often
conversed on them with my friend *Bahman*; and both
of us were convinced after full consideration, that the
Zend bore a strong resemblance to *Sanscrit*, and the
Pahlavi to *Arabic*. He had at my request translated

into *Pahlavi* the fine inscription exhibited in the *Gulistan*, on the diadem of *Cyrus*; and I had the patience to read the list of words from the *Pazend* in the appendix to the *Farhangi Jehangiri.* This examination gave me perfect conviction, that the *Pahlavi* was a dialect of the *Chaldaic*; and of this curious fact I will exhibit a short proof. By the nature of the *Chaldean* tongue most words ended in the first long vowel, like *shemia*, heaven ; and that very word, unaltered in a single letter, we find in the *Pazend*, together with *luilia*, night ; *meyd*, water ; *nira*, fire ; *matra*, rain ; and a multitude of others, all *Arabic* or *Hebrew*, with a *Chaldean* termination ; so *zamar*, by a beautiful metaphor, from *pruning' trees*, means in *Hebrew* to *compose verses*, and thence, by an easy transition to *sing* them ; and in *Pahlavi* we see the verb *zamruniten*, to *sing*, with its forms *zamrunemi*, I *sing*, and *zamrunid*, he *sang* ; the verbal terminations of the *Persian* being added to the *Chaldaic* root. Now all those words are integral parts of the language, not adventitious to it like the *Arabic* nouns and verbals engrafted on modern *Persian* ; and this distinction convinces me, that the dialect of the *Gabrs*, which they pretend to be that of *Zeratusht*, and of which *Bahman* gave me a variety of written specimens, is a late invention of their priests, or subsequent at least to the *Muselman* invasion ; for, although it may be possible that a few of their sacred books were preserved, as he used to assert, in sheets of lead or copper, at the bottom of wells near *Yezd*, yet, as the conquerors had not only a spiritual, but a political interest in persecuting a warlike, robust, and indignant race of irreconcileable, conquered subjects, a long time must have elapsed, before the hidden scriptures could have been safely brought to light, and few, who could perfectly understand them, must then have remained ; but, as they continued to profess among themselves the religion of their forefathers, it then became expedient for the *Mubeds*

to supply the lost or mutilated works of their legislator by new compositions, partly from their imperfect recollection, and partly from such moral and religious knowledge as they gleaned, most probably,
among the *Christians*, with whom they had an intercourse. One rule we may fairly establish in deciding
the question, Whether the books of the modern *Gabrs*
were anterior to the invasion of the *Arabs?* When
an *Arabic* noun occurs in them, changed only by the
spirit of the *Chaldean* idiom; as *werta* for *werd*, a
rose; *dahu* for *dhahab*, gold; or *deman* for *zeman*,
time, we may allow it to have been ancient *Pahlavi*;
but when we meet with verbal nouns or infinitives,
evidently formed by the rules of *Arabian* grammar,
we may be sure that the phrases in which they occur
are comparatively modern; and not a single passage,
which *Bahman* produced from the books of his religion would abide this test.

We come now to the language of the *Zend*; and
here I must impart a discovery which I lately made,
and from which we may draw the most interesting
consequences. M. *Anquetil*, who had the merit of
undertaking a voyage to *India*, in his earliest youth,
with no other view than to recover writings of *Zeratusht*, and who would have acquired a brilliant reputation in *France*, if he had not sullied it by his immo-
derate vanity and virulence of temper, which alienated
the good-will even of his own countrymen, has exhibited in his work, entitled *Zendavesta*, two vocabu-
laries in *Zend* and *Pahlavi*, which he had found in
an approved collection of *Rawayat*, or *Traditional
Pieces*, in modern *Persian*. Of his *Pahlavi* no more
need be said than that it strongly confirms my opinion concerning the *Chaldaic* origin of that language;
but, when I perused the *Zend* glossary, I was inexpres-
sibly surprised to find that six or seven words in ten
were pure *Sanscrit*, and even some of their inflexions

formed by the rules of the *Vyacaran*; as *yushmacam*, the genitive plural of *yushmad*. Now M. *Anquetil* most certainly, and the *Persian* compiler most probably, had no knowledge of *Sanscrit*; and could not, therefore, have invented a list of *Sanscrit* words: it is, therefore, an authentic list of *Zend* words which had been preserved in books, or by tradition; and it follows, that the language of the *Zend* was at least a dialect of the *Sanscrit*, approaching perhaps as nearly to it as the *Pracrit*, or other popular idioms, which we know to have been spoken in *India* two thousand years ago. From all these facts it is a necessary consequence, that the oldest discoverable languages of *Persia* were *Chaldaic* and *Sanscrit*; and that, when they had ceased to be vernacular, the *Pahlavi* and *Zend* were deduced from them respectively, and the *Parsi* either from the *Zend*, or immediately from the dialect of the *Brahmans*; but all had perhaps a mixture of *Tartarian*; for the best lexicographers assert, that numberless words in ancient *Persian* are taken from the language of the *Cimmerians*, or the *Tartars* of *Kipchak*; so that the three families, whose lineage we have examined in former discourses, had left visible traces of themselves in *Iran*, long before the *Tartars* and *Arabs* had rushed from their deserts, and returned to that very country from which, in all probability, they originally proceeded, and which the *Hindus* had abandoned in an earlier age, with positive commands from their legislators to revisit it no more. I close this head with observing, that no supposition of a mere political or commercial intercourse between the different nations, will account for the *Sanscrit* and *Chaldaic* words, which we find in the old *Persian* tongues; because they are, in the first place, too numerous to have been introduced by such means; and secondly, are not the names of exotic animals, commodities, or arts, but those of material elements, parts of the body, natural objects and relations, affections of the mind, and other ideas common to the whole race of man.

If a nation of *Hindus*, it may be urged, ever possessed and governed the country of *Iran*, we should find on the very ancient ruins of the temple or palace, now called *the Throne of Jemshid*, some inscriptions in *Devanagari*, or at least in the characters on the stones at *Elephanta*, where the sculpture is unquestionably *Indian*, or in those on the *Staff of Firuz Shah*, which exist in the heart of *India*; and such inscriptions we probably should have found, if that edifice had not been erected after the migration of the *Brahmins* from *Iran*, and the violent schism in the *Persian* religion, of which we shall presently speak; for, although the popular name of the building at *Istakhr*, or *Persepolis*, be no certain proof that it was raised in the time of *Jemshid*, yet such a fact might easily have been preserved by tradition; and we shall soon have abundant evidence, that the temple was posterior to the reign of the *Hindu* monarchs. The *cypresses* indeed, which are represented with the figures in procession, might induce a reader of the *Shahnamah* to believe, that the sculptures related to the new faith introduced by *Zeratusht*; but as a cypress is a beautiful ornament, and as many of the figures appear inconsistent with the reformed adoration of fire, we must have recourse to stronger proofs, that the *Takhti Jemshid* was erected after *Caywmers*. The building has lately been visited, and the characters on it examined, by Mr. *Francklin*; from whom we learn, that *Niebuhr* has delineated them with great accuracy; but without such testimony I should have suspected the correctness of the delineation, because the *Danish* traveller has exhibited two inscriptions in modern *Persian*, and one of them from the same place, which cannot have

E 4

been exactly transcribed: they are very elegant verses of *Nizami* and *Sadi on the instability of human greatness*, but so ill engraved or so ill copied, that if I had not had them nearly by heart, I should not have been able to read them; and M. *Rousseau* of *Isfahan*, who translated them with shameful inaccuracy, must have been deceived by the badness of the copy, or he never would have created a new king *Wakam*, by forming one word of *Jem* and the particle prefixed to it. Assuming, however, that we may reason as conclusively on the characters published by *Niebuhr* as we might on the monuments themselves, were they now before us, we may begin with observing, as *Chardin* had observed on the very spot, that they bear no resemblance whatever to the letters used by the *Gabrs* in their copies of the *Vendidad*. This I once urged, in an amicable debate with *Bahman*, as a proof that the *Zend* letters were a modern invention; but he seemed to hear me without surprize, and insisted that the letters to which I alluded, and which he had often seen, were monumental characters never used in books, and intended either to conceal some religious mysteries from the vulgar, or to display the art of the sculptor, like the embellished *Cufick* and *Nagari* on several *Arabian* and *Indian* monuments. He wondered that any man could seriously doubt the antiquity of the *Pahlavi* letters; and in truth the inscription behind the horse of *Rustam*, which *Niebuhr* has also given us, is apparently *Pahlavi*, and might with some pains be decyphered; that character was extremely rude, and seems to have been written, like the *Roman* and the *Arabic*, in a variety of hands; for I remember to have examined a rare collection of old *Persian* coins in the Museum of the great Anatomist *William Hunter*; and, though I believed the legends to be *Pahlavi*, and had no doubt that they were coins of *Parthian* kings, yet I could not read the inscriptions without wasting more time than I had then at command, in comparing the letters and ascertaining the proportions in which they severally occurred. The gross *Pahlavi* was improved by *Zeratusht* or his disciples into an elegant and perspicuous character, in which the *Zendavesta* was copied; and both were written from the right hand to the left, like other *Chaldaic* alphabets, for they are manifestly both of *Chaldean* origin; but the *Zend* has the singular advantage of expressing all the long and short vowels by distinct marks in the body of each word, and all the words are distinguished by full points between them; so that if modern *Persian* were unmixed with *Arabic*, it might be written in *Zend* with the greatest convenience, as any one may perceive, by copying in that character a few pages of the *Shahnumah*. As to the unknown inscriptions in the palace of *Jemshid*, it may reasonably be doubted whether they contain a system of letters which any nation ever adopted : in *five* of them the letters, which are separated by points, may be reduced to forty, at least I can distinguish no more essentially different; and they all seem to be regular variations and compositions of a straight line and an angular figure like the head of a javelin, or a leaf (to use the language of botanists) *hearted and lanced*. Many of the *Runic* letters appear to have been formed of similar elements; and it has been observed, that the writing at *Persepolis* bears a strong resemblance to that which the *Irish* call *Ogham.* The word *Agam* in *Sanscrit* means *mysterious knowledge*; but I dare not affirm that the two words had a common origin; and only mean to suggest that, if the characters in question be really alphabetical, they were probably secret and sacerdotal, or a mere cypher perhaps, of which the priests only had the key. They might, I imagine, be decyphered if the language were certainly known; but in all other inscriptions of the

same sort, the characters are too complex, and the variations of them too numerous, to admit an opinion
that they could be symbols of articulate sounds ; for
even the *Nagari* system, which has more distinct letters than any known alphabet, consists only of fortyfine simple characters, two of which are mere substitutions, and four of little use in *Sanscrit*, or in any
other language ; while the more complicated figures,
exhibited by *Niebuhr*, must be as numerous at least
as the *Chinese* keys, which are the signs of *ideas* only,
and some of which resemble the old *Persian* letters
at *Istakhr*. The *Danish* traveller was convinced from
his own observation that they were written from the
left hand, like all the characters used by *Hindu* nations; but I must leave this dark subject, which I
cannot illuminate, with a remark formerly made by
myself, that the square *Chaldaic* letters, a few of which
are found on the *Persian* ruins, appear to have been
originally the same with the *Devanagari* before the
latter were enclosed, as we now see them, in angular
frames.

II. The primeval religion of *Iran*, if we rely on the
authorities adduced by *Mohsani Fani*, was that which
Newton calls the oldest (and it may be justly called
the noblest) of all religions : " A firm belief that one
" Supreme God made the world by his power, and
" continually governed it by his providence ; a pious
" fear, love, and adoration of him ; a due reverence
" for parents and aged persons; a fraternal affection
" for the whole human species, and a compassionate
" tenderness even for the brute creation."   A system
of devotion so pure and sublime could hardly, among
mortals, be of long duration ; and we learn from the
Dabistan, that the popular worship of the *Iranians*
under *Hushang*, was purely *Sabian* ; a word of which
I cannot offer any certain etymology, but which has
been deduced by grammarians from *Saba*, an *host*,

and particularly the *host of heaven*, or the *celestial bodies*, in the adoration of which the *Sabian* ritual is believed to have consisted. There is a description in the learned work just mentioned, of the several *Persian* temples dedicated to the Sun and Planets, of the images adored in them, and of the magnificent processions to them on prescribed festivals; one of which is probably represented by sculpture in the ruined city of *Jemshid*. But the planetary worship in *Persia* seems only a part of a far more complicated religion, which we now find in these *Indian* provinces; for *Mohsan* assures us that, in the opinion of the best informed *Persians*, who professed the faith of *Hushang*, distinguished from that of *Zeratusht*, the first monarch of *Iran*, and of the whole earth, was *Mahabad* (a word apparently *Sanscrit*) who divided the people into four orders, the *religious*, the *military*, the *commercial*, and the *servile*, to which he assigned names unquestionably the same in their origin with those now applied to the four primary classes of the *Hindus*. They added, that he received from the Creator, and promulgated among men, *a sacred book in a heavenly language*, to which the *Muselman* author gives the *Arabic* title of *Desatir*, or Regulations, but the original name of which she has not mentioned; and that *fourteen Mahabads* had appeared or would appear in human shapes for the government of this world. Now when we know that the *Hindus* believe in *fourteen Menus*, or celestial personages with similar functions, the *first* of whom left a book of *regulations*, or *divine ordinances*, which they hold equal to the *Veda*, and the language of which they believe to be that of the gods, we can hardly doubt that the first corruption of the purest and oldest religion was the system of *Indian* theology, invented by the *Brahmans*, and prevalent in these territories, where the book of *Mahabad*, or *Menu*, is at this moment the standard of all religious and moral duties. The accession of *Cayu-*

A

mers to the throne of *Persia*, in the eighth or ninth
century before *Christ*, seems to have been accompanied by a considerable revolution both in government
and religion: he was most probably of a different
race from the *Mahabadians* who preceded him, and
began perhaps the new system of national faith
which *Hushang*, whose name it bears, completed;
but the reformation was partial; for, while they rejected the complex polytheism of their predecessors, they
retained the laws of *Mahabad*, with a superstitious veneration for the sun, the planets, and fire; thus resembling the *Hindu* sects, called *Sauras* and *Sagnicas*,
the second of which is very numerous at *Banares*,
where many *agnihotras* are continually blazing, and
where the *Sagnicas*, when they enter on their sacerdotal office, kindle, with two pieces of the hard wood
Semi, a fire which they keep lighted through their
lives for their nuptial ceremony, the performance of
solemn sacrifices, the obsequies of departed ancestors,
and their own funeral pile. This remarkable rite
was continued by *Zeratusht*, who reformed the old religion by the addition of genii, or angels, presiding
over months and days, of new ceremonies in the veneration shown to fire, of a new work which he pretended to have received from heaven, and, above all,
by establishing the actual adoration of one Supreme
Being. He was born, according to *Mohsan*, in the
district of *Rai*; and it was he (not, as *Ammianus* asserts, his protector *Gushtasb*) who travelled into *India*,
that he might receive information from the *Brahmans*
in theology and ethics. It is barely possible that *Py-
thagoras* knew him in the capital of *Irak*; but the
Grecian sage must then have been far advanced in
years; and we have no certain evidence of an intercourse between the two philosophers. The reformed
religion of *Persia* continued in force till that country
was subdued by the *Muselmans*; and, without study-
ing the *Zend*, we have ample information concerning

it in the modern *Persian* writings of several who professed it. *Bahman* always named *Zeratusht* with reverence, but he was in truth a pure Theist, and
strongly disclaimed any adoration of the *fire* or other
elements : he denied that the doctrine of two coeval
principles, supremely good and supremely bad, formed any part of his faith ; and he often repeated with
emphasis the verses of *Firdausi* on the *prostration* of
Cyrus and his paternal grandfather before the blazing
altar : " Think not that they were adorers of fire ;
" for that element was only an exalted object, on the
" lustre of which they fixed their eyes ; they humbled
" themselves a whole week before *God* ; and, if thy
" understanding be ever so little exerted, thou must
" acknowledge thy dependence on the Being supreme-
" ly pure." In a story of *Sadi*, near the close of his
beautiful *Bustan*, concerning the idol of *Somanath*, or
Mahadeva, he confounds the religion of the *Hindus*
with that of the *Gabrs*, calling the *Brahmans* not only
Moghs, (which might be justified by a passage in the
Mesnavi) but even readers of the *Zend* and *Pazend*.
Now, whether this confusion proceeded from real or
pretended ignorance I cannot decide, but am as
firmly convinced that the doctrines of the *Zend* were
distinct from those of the *Veda*, as I am that the religion of the *Brahmans*, with whom we converse every
day, prevailed in *Persia* before the accession of *Cayumers*, whom the *Parsis*, from respect to his memory,
consider as the first of men, although they believe in
an universal deluge before his reign.

With the religion of the old *Persians* their *philosophy* (or as much as we know of it) was inti-
mately connected ; for they were assiduous observ-
ers of the luminaries, which they adored and established, according to *Mohsan*, who confirms in some
degree the fragments of *Berosus*, a number of arti-

ficial cycles with distinct names, which seem to indicate a knowledge of the period in which the equinoxes
appear to revolve. They are said also to have known
the most wonderful powers of nature, and thence to
have acquired the fame of magicians and enchanters;
but I will only detain you with a few remarks on that
metaphysical theology which has been professed immemorially by a numerous sect of *Persians* and *Hindus*, was carried in part into *Greece*, and prevails even
now among the learned *Muselmans*, who sometimes
avow it without reserve. The modern philosophers
of this persuasion are called *Sufis*, either from the
Greek word for a *sage*, or from the *woollen* mantle
which they used to wear in some provinces of *Persia :*
their fundamental tenets are, that nothing exists absolutely but *God*; that the human soul is an emanation
from his essence, and though divided for a time
from its heavenly source, will be finally reunited with
it ; that the highest possible happiness will arise from
its reunion ; and that the chief good of mankind in
this transitory world, consists in as perfect an *union*
with the Eternal Spirit as the incumbrances of a
mortal frame will allow ; that for this purpose they
should break all *connection* (or *taalluk*, as they call it)
with extrinsic objects, and pass through life without
attachments, as a swimmer in the ocean strikes freely
without the impediment of clothes ; that they should
be straight and free as the cypress, whose fruit is hardly
perceptible, and not sink under a load, like fruit-trees
attached to a trellis ; that, if mere earthly charms
have power to influence the soul, the *idea* of celestial
beauty must overwhelm it in extatic delight ; that
for want of apt words to express the divine perfec-
tions and the ardour of devotion, we must borrow
such expressions as approach the nearest to our ideas,
and speak of *Beauty* and *Love* in a transcendent and
mystical sense ; that, like a *reed* torn from its native

bank, like *was* separated from its delicious honey, the soul of man bewails its disunion with *melancholy music*, and sheds burning tears, like the lighted taper waiting passionately for the moment of its extinction, as a disengagement from earthly trammels, and the means of returning to its only beloved. Such in part (for I omit the minuter and more subtil metaphysics of the *Sufis*, which are mentioned in the *Dabistan*) is the wild and enthusiastic religion of the modern *Persian* poets, especially of the sweet *Hafiz* and the great *Mauluvi*. Such is the system of the *Vedanti* philosophers and best lyric poets of *India*; and as it was a system of the highest antiquity in both nations, it may be added to the many other proofs of an immemorial affinity between them.

III. On the ancient *monuments* of *Persian* sculpture and architecture we have already made such observations as were sufficient for our purpose; nor will you be surprized at the diversity between the figures at *Elephanta*, which are manifestly *Hindu*, and those at *Persepolis*, which are merely *Sabian*, if you concur with me in believing that the *Takhti Jemshid* was erected after the time of *Cayumers*, when the *Brahmans* had migrated from *Iran*, and when their intricate mythology had been superseded by the simpler adoration of the planets and of fire.

IV. As to the *sciences* or *arts* of the old *Persians*, I have little to say; and no complete evidence of them seems to exist. *Mohsun* speaks more than once of ancient verses in the *Pahlavi* language; and *Bahman* assured me, that some scanty remains of them had been preserved: their music and painting, which *Nizami* celebrated, have irrecoverably perished; and in regard to *Muni*, the painter and impostor, whose book of drawings, called *Ar-*

tang, which he pretended to be divine, is supposed to have been destroyed by the *Chinese*, in whose dominions he had sought refuge, the whole tale is too modern to throw any light on the questions before us concerning the origin of nations, and the inhabitants of the primitive world.

Thus has it been proved by clear evidence and plain reasoning, that a powerful monarchy was established in *Iran* long before the *Assyrian*, or *Pishdadi* government; that it was in truth a *Hindu* monarchy, though if any chuse to call it *Cusian, Casdean,* or *Scythian*, we shall not enter into a debate on mere names; that it subsisted many centuries, and that its history has been ingrafted on that of the *Hindus*, who founded the monarchies of *Ayodhya* and *Indraprestha*; that the language of the first *Persian* empire was the mother of the *Sanscrit*, and consequently of the *Zend* and *Parsi*, as well as of *Greek, Latin*, and *Gothic*; that the language of the *Assyrians* was the parent of *Chaldaic* and *Pahlavi*, and that the primary *Tartarian* language also had been current in the same empire; although, as the *Tartars* had no books or even letters, we cannot with certainty trace their unpolished and variable idioms.   We discover therefore in *Persia*, at the earliest dawn of history, the *three* distinct races of men, whom we described on former occasions as possessors of *India, Arabia, Tartary*; and, whether they were collected in *Iran* from distant regions, or diverged from it as from a common centre, we shall easily determine by the following considerations.   Let us observe, in the first place, the central position of *Iran*, which is bounded by *Arabia*, by *Tartary*, and by *India*; whilst *Arabia* lies contiguous to *Iran* only, but is remote from *Tartary*, and divided even from the skirts of *India* by a considerable gulf; no country, therefore, but *Persia* seems likely to have sent forth its colonies to all the kingdoms of *Asia*. The *Brahmans* could never have migrated from *India* to *Iran*, because they are expressly forbidden by their oldest existing laws to leave the region which they inhabit at this day; the *Arabs* have not even a tradition of an emigration into *Persia* before *Mohammed*, nor had they indeed any inducement to quit their beautiful and extensive domains; and as to the *Tartars*, we have no trace in history of their departure from their plains and forests till the invasion of the *Medes*, who, according to etymologists, were the sons of *Madai*; and even they were conducted by princes of an *Assyrian* family. The *three* races, therefore, whom we have already mentioned (and more than three we have not yet found) migrated from *Iran* as from their common country; and thus the *Saxon* Chronicle, I presume from good authority, brings the first inhabitants of *Britain* from *Armenia*; while a late very learned writer concludes, after all his laborious researches, that the *Goths* or *Scythians* came from *Persia*; and another contends with great force, that both the *Irish* and old *Britons* proceeded severally from the borders of the *Caspian*; a coincidence of conclusions from different media by persons wholly unconnected, which could scarce have happened if they were not grounded on solid principles. We may therefore hold this proposition firmly established, that *Iran*, or *Persia* in its largest sense, was the true centre of population, of knowledge, of languages, and of arts; which, instead of travelling westward only, as it has been fancifully supposed, or eastward, as might with equal reason have been asserted, were expanded in all directions to all the regions of the world in which the *Hindu* race had settled under various denominations: but whether *Asia* has not produced other races of men, distinct from the *Hindus*, the *Arabs*, or the *Tartars*; or whether any apparent diversity may not have sprung from an intermixture of those three

F

in different proportions, must be the subject of a future inquiry. There is another question of more immediate importance, which you, gentlemen, only can decide; namely, " by what means we can preserve " our Society from dying gradually away? as it has ad- " vanced gradually to its present (shall I say flourish- " ing or languishing?) state." It has subsisted five years without any expence to the members of it, until the first volume of our Transactions was published; and the price of that large volume, if we compare the different values of money in *Bengal* and in *England,* is not more than equal to the *annual* contribution towards the charges of the Royal Society by each of its fellows, who may not have chosen to compound for it on his admission. This I mention not from an idea that any of us could object to the purchase of one copy at least, but from a wish to inculcate the necessity of our common exertions in promoting the sale of the work, both here and in *London.* In vain shall we meet as a literary body, if our meetings shall cease to be supplied with original dissertations and memorials; and in vain shall we collect the most interesting papers, if we cannot publish them occasionally without exposing the superintendents of the Company's press, who undertake to print them at their own hazard, to the danger of a considerable loss. By united efforts the *French* have compiled their stupendous repositories of universal knowledge; and by united efforts only can we hope to rival them, or to diffuse over our own country and the rest of *Europe* the lights attainable by our *Asiatic Researches.*

IV.

A LETTER

FROM

THE LATE HENRY VANSITTART, ESQ.

TO THE PRESIDENT.

Sir,

HAVING some time ago met with a *Persian* abridgment, composed by *Maulavi Khairuddin*, of the *asrarul Afaghinah*, or the secrets of the *Afghans*, a book written in the *Pushto* language by *Husain*, the son of *Sabir*, the son of *Khizr*, the disciple of *Hazrat Shah Kasim Suluimani*, whose tomb is in *Chunargur*, I was induced to translate it. Although it opens with a very wild description of the origin of that tribe, and contains a narrative which can by no means be offered upon the whole as a serious and probable history; yet I conceive that the knowledge of what a nation suppose themselves to be, may be interesting to a Society like this, as well as of what they really are. Indeed the commencement of almost every history is fabulous; and the most enlightened nations, after they have arrived at that degree of civilization and importance which has enabled and induced them to commemorate their actions, have always found a vacancy at their outset which invention, or at best presumption, must supply. Such fictions appear at first in the form of traditions; and having in this shape amused successive generations by a gratification of their national vanity, they are committed to writing, and acquire the authority of history.

F 2

As a kingdom is an assemblage of component parts, condensed by degrees from smaller associations of individuals to their general union, so history is a combination of the transactions not only of the different tribes, but even of the individuals of the nation of which it treats : each particular narrative in such a general collection must be summary and incomplete. Biography, therefore, as well as descriptions of the manners, actions, and even opinions of such tribes as are connected with a great kingdom, are not only entertaining in themselves, but useful, as they explain and throw a light upon the history of the nation.

Under these impressions I venture to lay before the Society the translation of an abridged history of the *Afghans* ; a tribe at different times subject to and always connected with the kingdoms of *Persia* and *Hindustan.* I also submit a specimen of their language, which is called by them *Pukhto* ; but this word is softened in *Persian* into *Pushto.*

I am, *Sir,*

With the greatest respect,

Your most obedient humble servant,

HENRY VANSITTART.

Calcutta, March 3, 1784.

ON

THE DESCENT OF THE AFGHANS FROM THE JEWS

THE *Afghans*, according to their own traditions, are the posterity of *Melic Talut* (king *Saul)* who, in the opinion of some, was a descendant of *Judah,* the son of *Jacob*; and according to others of *Benjamin,* the brother of *Joseph.*

In a war which raged between the children of *Israel* and the *Amalekites*, the latter being victorious, plundered the *Jews*, and obtained possession of the ark of the covenant. Considering this the god of the *Jews*, they threw it into the fire, which did not affect it. They afterwards attempted to cleave it with axes, but without success: every individual who treated it with indignity was punished for his temerity. They then placed it in their temple; but all their idols bowed to it. At length they fastened it upon a cow, which they turned loose in the wilderness.

When the prophet *Samuel* arose, the children of *Israel* said to him, "We have been totally subdued "by the *Amalekites*, and have no king. Raise to us "a king, that we may be enabled to contend for the "glory of God." *Samuel* said, "In case you are led "out to battle, are you determined to fight?" They answered, "What has befallen us that we should not "fight against infidels? That nation has banished "us from our country and children." At this time the angel *Gabriel* descended, and, delivering a wand, said, "It is the command of God that the person "whose stature shall correspond with this wand, shall be king of *Israel*."

F 3

Melic Talut was at that time a man of inferior condition, and performed the humble employment of feeding the goats and cows of others. One day a cow under his charge was accidentally lost. Being disappointed in his searches, he was greatly distressed, and applied to *Samuel*, saying, " I have lost a cow, " and do not possess the means of satisfying the owner. " Pray for me, that I may be extricated from this " difficulty." *Samuel*, perceiving that he was a man of lofty stature, asked his name. He answered, *Talut*. *Samuel* then said, " Measure *Talut* with the wand " which the angel *Gabriel* brought." His stature was equal to it. *Samuel* then said, " *God* has raised *Talut* to be your king." The children of *Israel* answered, " We are greater than our king. We are " men of dignity, and he is of inferior condition. " How shall he be our king." *Samuel* informed them they should know that God had constituted *Talut* their king, by his restoring the ark of the covenant. He accordingly restored it, and they acknowledged him their sovereign.

After *Talut* obtained the kingdom, he seized part of the territories of *Jalut*, or *Goliah*, who assembled a large army, but was killed by *David*. *Talut* afterwards died a martyr in a war against the infidels; and God constituted *David* king of the *Jews*.

Melic Talut had two sons, one called *Berkia*, and the other *Irmia*, who served *David*, and were beloved by him. ' He sent them to fight against the infidels; and, by God's assistance, they were victorious.

The son of *Berkia* was called *Afghan*, and the son of *Irmia* was named *Usbec*. Those youths distinguished themselves in the reign of *David*, and were employed by *Solomon*. *Afghan* was distinguished by his corporal strength, which struck terror into Demons and Genii. *Usbec* was eminent for his learning.

Afghan used frequently to make excursions to the mountains; where his progeny, after his death established themselves, lived in a state of independence, built forts, and exterminated the infidels.

When the select of creatures, *Muhammed*, appeared upon earth, his fame reached the *Afghans*, who sought him in multitudes under their leaders *Khalid* and *Abdul Rashid*, sons of *Walid*. The prophet honoured them with the most gracious reception, saying, " Come, O *Mulue*, or Kings;" whence they assumed the title of *Melic*, which they enjoy to this day. The prophet gave them his ensign, and said that the faith would be strengthened by them.

Many sons were born of *Khalid*, the son of *Walid*, who signalized themselves in the presence of the prophet, by fighting against the infidels. *Muhammed* honoured and prayed for them.

In the reign of Sultan *Mahmud* of *Ghaznah*, eight men arrived, of the posterity, of *Khalid* the son of *Walid*, whose names were *Kalun*, *Alun*, *Daud*, *Yalua*, *Ahmed*, *Awin*, and *Ghazi*. The Sultan was much pleased with them, and appointed each a commander in his army. He also conferred on them the offices of *Vuzir*, and *Vakili Mutlak*, or Regent of the Empire.

Wherever they were stationed they obtained possession of the country, built mosques, and overthrew the temples of idols. They encreased so much, that the army of *Mahmud* was chiefly

F 4

composed of *Afghans*. When *Herhind*, a powerful prince of *Hindustan*, meditated an invasion of *Ghaznah*, Sultan *Mahmud* dispatched against him the descendants of *Khalid* with twenty thousand horse: a battle ensued; the *Afghans* made the attack; and, after a severe engagement, which lasted from daybreak till noon, defeated *Herhind*, killed many of the infidels, and converted some to the *Muhammedan* faith.

The *Afghans* now began to establish themselves in the mountains; and some settled in cities with the permission of Sultan *Mahmud*. They framed regulations, dividing themselves into four classes, agreeably to the following description:—The first is the *pure* class, consiting of those whose fathers and mothers were *Afghans*. The second class consists of those whose fathers were *Afghans*, and mothers of another nation. The third class contains those whose mothers were *Afghans*, and fathers of another nation. The fourth class is composed of the children of women whose mothers were *Afghans*, and fathers and husbands of a different nation. Persons who do not belong to one of these classes, are not called *Afghans*.

After the death of Sultan *Mahmud* they made another settlement in the mountains. *Shihabuddin Gauri*, a subsequent Sultan of *Ghaznah*, was twice repulsed from *Hindustan*. His *Vazir* assembled the people, and asked if any of the posterity of *Khalid* were living. They answered, " Many now live " in a state of independence in the mountains, " where they have a considerable army." The *Vazir* requested them to go to the mountains, and by entreaties prevail on the *Afghans* to come; for they were the descendants of companions of the prophet

The inhabitants of *Ghaznah* undertook this embassy, and, by entreaties and presents, conciliated the minds of the *Afghans*, who promised to engage in the service of the Sultan, provided he would himself come and enter into an agreement with them. The Sultan visited them in their mountains, honoured them, and gave them dresses and other presents. They supplied him with twelve thousand horse, and a considerable army of infantry. Being dispatched by the Sultan before his own army, they took *Dehli*, killed *Roy Pahtoura* the king, his ministers and nobles; laid waste the city, and made the infidels prisoners. They afterwards exhibited nearly the same scene in *Canauj*.

The Sultan, pleased by the reduction of those cities, conferred honours upon the *Afghans*. It is said that he then gave them the titles of *Patan* and *Khan*. The word *Patan* is derived from the *Hindi* verb *Paitna*, *to rush*, in allusion to their alacrity in attacking the enemy. The *Patans* have greatly distinguished themselves in the history of *Hindustan*, and are divided into a variety of sects.

The race of *Afghans* possessed themselves of the Mountain of *Solomon*, which is near *Kandahar*, and the circumjacent country, where they have built forts: this tribe has furnished many kings. The following monarchs of this race have sat upon the throne of *Dehli*:—Sultan *Behlole*, *Afghan Lodi*, Sultan *Secander*, Sultan *Ibrahim*, *Shir Shah*, *Islam Shah*, *Adil Shah Sur*. They also number the following kings of *Gaur*: —*Solaiman Shah Gurzani*, *Bayazid Shah*, and *Kutb Shah*; besides whom their nation has produced many conquerors of provinces. The *Afghans* are called *Solaimani*, either because they were formerly the subjects of *Solomon*, king of the *Jews*, or because they inhabit the Mountain of *Solomon*.

The translation being finished, I shall only add that the country of the *Afghans*, which is a province of *Cabul*, was originally called *Roh*, and from hence is derived the name of the *Rohillahs*. The city, which was established in it by the *Afghans*, was called by them *Paishwer*, or *Paishor*, and is now the name of the whole district. The sects of the *Afghans*, or *Patans*, are very numerous. The principal are these :— *Lodi*, *Lohauni*, *Sur*, *Serwani*, *Yusufzihi*, *Bangish*, *Dilazai*, *Khatti*, *Yusin*, *Khail*, and *Baloje*. The meaning of *Zihi*, is offspring ; and of *Khail*, sect. A very particular account of the *Afghans* has been written by the late *Hafiz Ruhmat Khan*, a chief of the *Rohillahs*, from which the curious reader may derive much information. They are *Muselmans*, partly of the *Sunni*, and partly of the *Shiah* persuasion. They are great boasters of the antiquity of their origin, and reputation of their tribe ; but other *Muselmans* entirely reject their claim, and consider them of modern and even base extraction. However, their character may be collected from history, they have distinguished themselves by their courage, both singly and unitedly, as principals and auxiliaries. They have conquered for their own princes and for foreigners, and have always been considered the main strength of the army in which they have served. As they have been applauded for virtues, they have also been reproached for vices, having sometimes been guilty of treachery, and even acted the base part of assassins.

A Specimen of the PUSHTO LANGUAGE.

لِيتَم ظَالِمَانْ حَاكِمَانْ

اورکور پیشوردری وآره بودی

By the oppression of tyrannical rulers,
Fire, the grave, and *Paishor*, all three have been
rendered equal.

د سنت و پرخصت دی راعلی روا هت

With respect to prayers enjoined by the *Sunnah*,
they are remitted.
It is thus expressed in the reports :

کای اوکاد یره شودی کای نکه هبس پریدنوی

If a *man* perform them, it is very laudable. If
he do not perform them, it is no crime in him.

میرزا خان

ای میرزا که د خوی بهتری نوی
د سید تفاوت سه دی له بامنه

If the disposition be not good, O *Mirza*,
What difference is there between a *Sayyed* and a
Brahman!

(76)

NOTE BY THE PRESIDENT.

THIS account of the *Afghans* may lead to a very interesting discovery. We learn from *Esdras*, that the ten tribes, after a wandering journey, came to a country called *Arsareth*; where, we may suppose, they settled. Now the *Afghans* are said, by the best *Persian* historians, to be descended from the *Jews*; they have traditions among themselves of such a descent; and it is even asserted, that their families are distinguished by the names of *Jewish* tribes, although, since their conversion to the *Islam*, they studiously conceal their origin: the *Pushto* language, of which I have seen a dictionary, has a manifest resemblance to the *Chaldaic*; and a considerable district under their dominion is called *Hazareh*, or *Hazaret*, which might easily have been changed into the word used by *Esdras*. I strongly recommend an inquiry into the literature and history of the *Afghans*.

V.

REMARKS

ON THE

ISLAND OF HINZUAN, OR JOHANNA.

BY THE PRESIDENT.

HINZUAN (a name which has been gradually corrupted into *Anzuanie, Anjuan, Juanny*, and *Johanna*) has been governed about two centuries by a colony of *Arabs*, and exhibits a curious instance of the slow approaches toward civilization, which are made by a small community, with many natural advantages, but with few means of improving them. An account of this *African* island, in which we hear the language and see the manners of *Arabia*, may neither be uninteresting in itself, nor foreign to the objects of inquiry proposed at the institution of our Society.

On *Monday*, the 28th of *July*, 1783, after a voyage, in the *Crocodile*, of ten weeks and two days from the rugged islands of *Cape Verd*, our eyes were delighted with a prospect so beautiful, that neither a painter nor a poet could perfectly represent it, and so cheering to us, that it can justly be conceived by such only as have been in our preceding situation. It was the sun rising in full splendor on the isle of *Mayata* (as the seamen called it) which we had joyfully distinguished the preceding afternoon by the height of its peak, and which now appeared at no great distance from the windows of our cabin; while *Hinzuan*, for which we had so long panted, was plainly discernible a-head, where its high lands presented themselves with remarkable boldness. The weather was fair, the water smooth; and a

gentle breeze drove us easily before dinner-time round
a rock, on which the *Brilliant* struck just a year before,
into a commodious road *, where we dropped our
anchor early in the evening. We had seen *Mohila*,
another sister island, in the course of the day.

The frigate was presently surrounded with canoes,
and the deck soon crowded with natives of all ranks,
from the high born chief, who washed linen, to the
half-naked slave, who only paddled. Most of them
had letters of recommendation from *Englishmen*, which
none of them were able to read, though they spoke
English intelligibly; and some appeared vain of titles,
which our countrymen had given them in play, according to their supposed stations. We had *Lords*,
Dukes, and *Princes* on board, soliciting our custom
and importuning us for presents. In fact, they were
too sensible to be proud of empty sounds, but justly
imagined, that those ridiculous titles would serve as
marks of distinction, and, by attracting notice, procure for them something substantial. The only men
of real consequence in the island, whom we saw before
we landed, were the Governor *Abdulluh*, second cou-
sin to the king, and his brother *Alwi*, with their several sons; all of whom will again be particularly mentioned: they understood *Arabic*, seemed zealots in
the *Mohammedan* faith, and admired my copies of the
Alkoran; some verses of which they read, whilst *Alwi* perused the opening of another *Arabian* manuscript, and explained it in *English* more accurately
than could have been expected.

The next morning showed us the island in all its
beauty; and the scene was so diversified, that a dis-

* Lat. 12° 10' 47" S. Long. 44° 15' 5" E. by the Master.

tinct view of it could hardly have been exhibited by
the best pencil: you must, therefore, be satisfied
with a mere description, written on the very spot,
and compared attentively with the natural landscape.
We were at anchor in a fine bay, and before us was
a vast amphitheatre, of which you may form a general notion by picturing in your minds a multitude of hills infinitely varied in size and figure, and
then supposing them to be thrown together, with a
kind of artless symmetry, in all imaginable positions. The back ground was a series of mountains, one of which is pointed, near half a mile
perpendicularly high from the level of the sea, and
little more than three miles from the shore: all of
them were richly clothed with wood, chiefly fruit-
trees, of an exquisite verdure. I had seen many a
mountain of a stupendous height in *Wales* and
Swisserland, but never saw one before, round the
bosom of which the clouds were almost continually rolling, while its green summit rose flourishing
above them, and received from them an additional
brightness. Next to this distant range of hills was
another tier, part of which appeared charmingly
verdant, and part rather barren; but the contrast
of colours changed even this nakedness into a
beauty. Nearer still were innumerable mountains,
or rather cliffs, which brought down their verdure
and fertility quite to the beach; so that every shade
of green, the sweetest of colours, was displayed at
one view by land and by water. But nothing con-
duced more to the variety of this enchanting prospect, than the many rows of palm-trees, especially the tall and graceful *Arecas* on the shores, in
the valleys, and on the ridges of hills, where one
might almost suppose them to have been planted
regularly by design. A more beautiful appearance
can scarce be conceived, than such a number of elegant palms in such a situation, with luxuriant tops,
like verdant plumes, placed at just intervals, and

showing between them part of the remoter landscape,
while they left the rest to be supplied by the beholder's imagination. The town of *Matsamudo* lay
on our left, remarkable at a distance for the tower
of the principal mosque, which was built by *Halimah*, a queen of the island, from whom the present king is descended: a little on our right was a
small town, called *Buntani*. Neither the territory of
Nice, with its olives, date-trees, and cypresses, nor
the isles of *Hieres*, with their delightful orange-
groves, appeared so charming to me as the view
from the road of *Hinzuan*; which, nevertheless, is
far surpassed, as the Captain of the *Crocodile* assured
us, by many of the islands in the Southern Ocean.
If life were not too short for the complete discharge
of all our respective duties, public and private, and
for the acquisition even of necessary knowledge in
any degree of perfection, with how much pleasure
and improvement might a great part of it be spent
in admiring the beauties of this wonderful orb, and
contemplating the nature of man in all its varieties!

We hastened to tread on firm land, to which we
had been so long disused, and went on shore, after
breakfast, to see the town, and return the Governor's
visit. As we walked, attended by a crowd of natives,
I surprized them by reading aloud an *Arabic* inscription over the gate of a mosque, and still more, when
I entered it, by explaining four sentences, which were
written very distinctly on the wall, signifying, " that
" the world was given us for our own edification,
" not for the purpose of raising sumptuous build-
" ings; life, for the discharge of moral and reli-
" gious duties, not for pleasureable indulgences;
" wealth, to be liberally bestowed, not avariciously
" hoarded; and learning, to produce good actions,
" not empty disputes." We could not but respect
the temple even of a false prophet, in which we

found such excellent morality: we saw nothing better among the *Romish* trumpery in the church at *Madeira*. When we came to *Abdullah*'s house, we were conducted through a small court-yard into an open room, on each side of which was a large and convenient sofa, and above it a high bed-place in a dark recess, over which a chintz counterpoint hung down from the ceiling. This is the general form of the best rooms in the island; and most of the tolerable houses have a similar apartment on the opposite side of the court, that there may be at all hours a place in the shade for dinner or for repose. We were entertained with ripe dates from *Yemen*, and the milk of cocoa-nuts; but the heat of the room, which seemed accessible to all who chose to enter it, and the scent of musk, or civet, with which it was perfumed, soon made us desirous of breathing a purer air; nor could I be detained long by the *Arabic* manuscripts, which the Governor produced, but which appeared of little use, and consequently of no value, except to such as love mere curiosities. One of them, indeed, relating to the penal law of the *Mohammedans*, I would gladly have purchased at a just price; but he knew not what to ask; and I knew that better books on that subject might be procured in *Bengal*. He then offered me a black boy for one of my *Alkorans*, and pressed me to barter an *Indian* dress, which he had seen on board the ship, for a cow and calf. The golden slippers attracted him most, since his wife, he said, would like to wear them; and, for that reason, I made him a present of them; but had destined the book and the robe for his superior. No high opinion could be formed of *Sayyad Abdullah*, who seemed very eager for gain, and very servile where he expected it.

Our next visit was to *Shaikh Salim*, the king's eldest son; and if we had seen him first, the state

of civilization in *Hinzuan* would have appeared
at its lowest ebb. The worst *English* hackney in the
worst stable is better lodged, and looks more princely
than this heir apparent; but though his mien and
apparel were extremely savage, yet allowance should
have been made for his illness; which, as we afterwards learned, was an abscess in the spleen: a disorder not uncommon in that country, and frequently
cured, agreeably to the *Arabian* practice, by the actual
cautery. He was incessantly chewing pieces of the
Areca-nut with shell lime : a custom borrowed, I suppose, from the *Indians*, who greatly improve the
composition with spices and betel-leaves, to which
they formerly added camphor: all the natives of
rank chewed it, but not, I think, to so great an excess. Prince *Salim* from time to time gazed at himself with complacency in a piece of broken looking-
glass, which was glued on a small board : a specimen
of wretchedness, which we observed in no other
house; but many circumstances convinced us that
the apparently low condition of his royal highness,
who was not on bad terms with his father, and seemed not to want authority, proceeded wholly from his
avarice. His brother *Hamdullah*, who generally resides in the town of *Domoni*, has a very different character, being esteemed a man of worth, good sense,
and learning : he had come, the day before, to *Matsamudo*, on hearing that an *English* frigate was in the
road; and I, having gone out for a few minutes to
read an *Arabic* inscription, found him on my return
devouring a manuscript which I had left with some of
the company. He is a *Kadi* or *Mohammedan* judge ;
and as he seemed to have more knowledge than his
countrymen, I was extremely concerned that I had so
little conversation with him. The king, *Shaikh Ahmed*, has a younger son, named *Abdullah*, whose usual
residence is in the town of *Wani*, which he seldom
leaves, as the state of his health is very infirm.
Since the succession to the title and authority of *Sul-*

tan is not unalterably fixed in one line, but requires confirmation by the chiefs of the island, it is not improbable that they may hereafter be conferred on prince *Hamdullah.*

A little beyond the hole in which *Salim* received us, was his *harám*, or the apartment of his women, which he permitted us all to see, not through politeness to strangers, as we believed at first, but as I learned afterwards from his own lips, in expectation of a present. We saw only two or three miserable creatures with their heads covered, while the favourite, as we supposed, stood behind a coarse curtain, and showed her ankles under it, loaded with silver rings; which, if she was capable of reflection, she must have considered as glittering fetters rather than ornaments; but a rational being would have preferred the condition of a wild beast, exposed to perils and hunger in a forest, to the splendid misery of being wife or mistress to *Salim.*

Before we returned, *Alwi* was desirous of showing me his books; but the day was too far advanced, and I promised to visit him some other morning. The governor however prevailed on us to see his place in the country, where he invited us to dine the next day. The walk was extremely pleasant from the town to the side of a rivulet, which formed in one part a small pool very convenient for bathing, and thence through groves and alleys to the foot of a hill; but the dining-room was little better than an open barn, and was recommended only by the coolness of its shade. *Abdullah* would accompany us on our return to the ship, together with two *Muftis* who spoke *Arabic* indifferently, and seemed eager to see all my manuscripts; but they were very moderately learned, and gazed with stupid wonder on a fine copy of the *Hamasah,* and on other collections of ancient poetry.

G 2

Early the next morning a black messenger, with a tawny lad as his interpreter, came from prince *Salim*; who having broken his perspective glass, wished to procure another by purchase or barter. A polite answer was returned, and steps taken to gratify his wishes. As we on our part expressed a desire to visit the king at *Domoni*, the prince's messenger told us that his master would, no doubt, lend us palanquins (for there was not a horse in the island) and order a sufficient number of his vassals to carry us, whom we might pay for their trouble as we thought just. We commissioned him therefore to ask that favour, and begged that all might be ready for our excursion before sun-rise, that we might escape the heat of the noon, which, though it was the middle of winter, we had found excessive. The boy, whose name was *Combo Madi*, staid with us longer than his companion: there was something in his look so ingenuous, and in his broken *English* so simple, that we encouraged him to continue his innocent prattle. He wrote and read *Arabic* tolerably well, and set down at my desire the names of several towns in the island, which he first told me was properly called *Hinzuan*. The fault of begging for whatever he liked, he had in common with the governor and other nobles, but hardly in a greater degree: his first petition for some lavender-water was readily granted; and a small bottle of it was so acceptable to him, that if we had suffered him, he would have kissed our feet: but it was not for himself that he rejoiced so extravagantly: he told us, with tears starting from his eyes, that his mother would be pleased with it, and the idea of her pleasure seemed to fill him with rapture. Never did I see filial affection more warmly felt, or more tenderly and, in my opinion, unaffectedly expressed; yet this boy was not a favourite of the officers, who thought him artful. His mother's name, he said, was *Fatima*; and he importuned us to visit her; conceiving, I suppose, that all mankind must love and admire her. We promised to gratify him; and having made him several presents, permitted him to return. As he reminded me of *Aladdin* in the *Arabian* tale, I designed to give him that name in a recommendatory letter, which he pressed me to write, instead of *St. Domingo*, as some *European* visiter had ridiculously called him; but, since the allusion would not have been generally known, and since the title of *Alau'ldin*, or *eminence in faith*, might have offended his superiors, I thought it advisable for him to keep his *African* name. A very indifferent dinner was prepared for us at the house of the Governor, whom we did not see the whole day, as it was the beginning of *Ramadan*, the *Mohammedan* lent, and he was engaged in his devotions, or made them his excuse; but his eldest son sat by us while we dined, together with *Musa* who was employed, jointly with his brother *Husain*, as purveyor to the Captain of the frigate.

Having observed a very elegant shrub, that grew about six feet high, in the court-yard, but was not then in flower, I learned with pleasure, that it was *hinna*, of which I had read so much in *Arabian* poems, and which *European* botanists have ridiculously named *Lawsonia*. *Musa* bruised some of the leaves, and, having moistened them with water, applied them to our nails and the tips of our fingers, which in a short time became of a dark orange-scarlet. I had before conceived a different idea of this dye, and imagined, that it was used by the *Arabs* to imitate the natural redness of those parts in young and healthy persons, which in all countries must be considered as a beauty:—perhaps a less quantity of *hinna*, or the same differently prepared, might have produced that effect. The old men in *Arabia* used the same dye to conceal their grey hairs, while their daughters were dying their

lips and gums black, to set off the whiteness of their
teeth; so universal in all nations and ages are personal vanity and a love of disguising truth; though
in all cases, the farther our species recede from nature, the farther they depart from true beauty; and
men at least should disdain to use artifice or deceit for
any purpose or on any occasion. If the women of rank
at *Paris*, or those in *London* who wish to imitate
them, be inclined to call the *Arabs* barbarians, let
them view their own head-dresses and cheeks in a
glass, and, if they have left no room for blushes, be
inwardly at least ashamed of their censure.

In the afternoon I walked a long way up the mountains in a winding path amid plants and trees no less new
than beautiful, and regretted exceedingly that very
few of them were in blossom, as I should then have
had leisure to examine them. Curiosity led from
hill to hill; and I came at last to the sources of a rivulet, which we had passed near the shore, and from
which the ship was to be supplied with excellent water. I saw no birds on the mountains but *Gui-
nea-fowl*, which might have been easily caught:
no insects were troublesome to me but mosquitos; and I had no fear of venomous reptiles,
having been assured that the air was too pure for
any to exist in it; but I was often unwillingly a
cause of fear to the gentle and harmless lizard, who
ran among the shrubs. On my return I missed the
path by which I had ascended; but, having met
some blacks laden with yams and plantains, I was
by them directed to another, which led me round,
through a charming grove of cocoa-trees, to the
Governor's country-seat, where our entertainment
was closed by a syllabub, which the *English* had
taught the *Musulmans* to make for them.

We received no answer from *Salim*; nor, indeed, expected one; since we took for granted that he could not but approve our intention of visiting his father; and we went on shore before sun-rise, in full expectation of a pleasant excursion to *Domoni*: but we were happily disappointed. The servants, at the prince's door, told us coolly, that their master was indisposed, and, as they believed, asleep; that he had given them no orders concerning his palanquins, and that they durst not disturb him. *Alewi* soon came to pay us his compliments, and was followed by his eldest son, *Ahmed*, with whom we walked to the gardens of the two princes *Salim* and *Hamdullah*: the situation was naturally good, but wild and desolate; and, in *Salim*'s garden, which we entered through a miserable hovel, we saw a convenient bathing place, well-built with stone, but then in great disorder, and a shed, by way of summer-house, like that under which we dined at the Governor's, but smaller and less neat. On the ground there lay a kind of cradle, about six feet long, and a little more than one foot in breadth, made of cords twisted in a sort of clumsy net-work, with a long thick bambu fixed to each side of it: this, we heard with surprize, was a royal palanquin, and one of the vehicles in which we were intended to have been rocked on mens shoulders over the mountains. I had much conversation with *Ahmed*, whom I found intelligent and communicative: he told me that several of his countrymen composed songs and tunes; that he was himself a passionate lover of poetry and music; and that, if we would dine at his house, he would play and sing to us. We declined his invitation to dinner, as we had made a conditional promise, if ever we passed a day at *Matsanudo*, to eat our curry with *Bana Gibu*, an honest man, of whom we purchased eggs and vegetables, and to whom some *Englishman* had given the title of *Lord*, which made him extremely vain: we could therefore

G 4

make *Sayyad Ahmed* only a morning visit. He sung
a hymn or two in *Arabic*, and accompanied his drawl-
ing, though pathetic, psalmody with a kind of man-
doline, which he touched with an awkward quill : the
instrument was very imperfect, but seemed to give
him delight. The names of the strings were written
on it in *Arabian* or *Indian* figures, simple and compounded ; but I could not think them worth copying.
He gave Captain *Williamson*, who wished to present
some literary curiosities to the library at *Dublin*, a
small roll containing a hymn in *Arabic* letters, but in
the language of *Mombasa*, which was mixed with
Arabic; but it hardly deserved examination, since the
study of languages has little intrinsic value, and is
only useful as the instrument of real knowledge, which
we can scarce expect from the poets of the *Mosam-
bique*. *Ahmed* would, I believe, have heard our *European* airs (I always except *French* melody) with rapture, for his favourite tune was a common *Irish* jig,
with which he seemed wonderfully affected.

On our return to the beach I thought of visiting
old *Alwi*, according to my promise, and prince *Salim*,
whose character I had not then discovered : I resolved
for that purpose to stay on shore alone, our dinner
with *Gibu* having been fixed at an early hour. *Alwi*
showed me his manuscripts, which chiefly related to
the ceremonies and ordinances of his own religion ;
and one of them, which I had formerly seen in *Europe*, was a collection of sublime and elegant hymns
in praise of *Mohammed*, with explanatory notes in the
margin. I requested him to read one of them after
the manner of the *Arabs* ; and he chanted it in a strain
by no means unpleasing ; but I am persuaded that he
understood it very imperfectly. The room, which
was open to the street, was presently crowded with vi-
siters, most of whom were *Muftis*, or *Expounders
of the Law* ; and *Alwi*, desirous perhaps to display

his zeal before them at the expence of good breed-
ing, directed my attention to a passage in a commentary on the *Koran*, which I found levelled at the
Christians. The commentator, having related with
some additions (but on the whole not inaccurately)
the circumstances of the temptation, puts this speech
into the mouth of the tempter: " Though I am un-
" able to delude thee, yet I will mislead, by thy
" means, more human creatures than thou wilt set
" right." ' Nor was this menace vain, (says the
Mohammedan writer) ' for the inhabitants of a region
' many thousand leagues in extent, are still so deluded
' by the Devil, that they impiously call *Isa* the son of
' *God!* Heaven preserve us,' he adds, ' from blas-
' pheming *Christians* as well as blaspheming *Jews.*'
Although a religious dispute with those obstinate zealots would have been unreasonable and fruitless, yet
they deserved, I thought, a slight reprehension, as the
attack seemed to be concerted among them. ' The
' commentator,' said I, ' was much to blame for passing
' so indiscriminate and hasty a censure: the title, which
' gave your legislator and gives you such offence, was
' often applied in *Judea* (by a bold figure agreeable
' to the *Hebrew* idiom, though unusual in *Arabic*)
' to *angels*, to *holy men*, and even to *all mankind*, who
' are commanded to call *God their Father*; and in
' this large sense the apostle, to the *Romans*, calls
' the elect the *children* of *God*, and the *Messiah* the
' *first-born among many brethren*; but the words *only
' begotten* are applied transcendently and incompa-
' rably to him alone *; and, as for me who believes
' the scriptures, which you also profess to believe,
' though you assert without proof that we have al-
' tered them, I cannot refuse him an appellation,
' though far surpassing our reason, by which he is

* Rom. viii. 29. See 1 John iii. 1. IJ. Barrow, 231, 232, 251.

2

' distinguished in the Gospel; and the believers in
' *Muhammed,* who expressly name him *the Messiah,*
' and pronounce him to have been born of a virgin,
' which alone might fully justify the phrase con-
' demned by this author, are themselves condemn-
' able for cavilling at words, when they cannot ob-
' ject to the substance of our faith consistently with
' their own.' The *Muselmans* had nothing to say in
reply; and the conversation was changed.

I was astonished at the questions which *Alwi* put
to me concerning the late peace and the independence
of *America*; the several powers and resources of *Britain* and *France, Spain* and *Holland,* the character
and supposed views of the Emperor, the comparative strength of the *Russian,* Imperial, and *Othman*
armies, and their respective modes of bringing their
forces to action. I answer him without reserve, except on the state of our possessions in *India*; nor
were my answers lost, for I observed, that all the
company were variously affected by them, generally
with amazement, often with concern, especially
when I described to them the great force and admi-
rable discipline of the *Austrian* army, and the stupid
prejudices of the *Turks,* whom nothing can induce to
abandon their old *Tartarian* habits; and exposed the
weakness of their empire in *Africa,* and even in the
more distant provinces of *Asia.* In return, he gave
me clear but general information concerning the government and commerce of his island: " His coun-
" try," he said, " was poor, and produced few articles
" of trade; but if they could get money, *which they
" now preferred to play-things,*" those were his words,
" they might easily," he added, " procure foreign
" commodities and exchange them advantageously
" with their neighbours in the islands and on the
" continent. Thus with a little money," said he,
" we purchase muskets, powder, balls, cutlasses,

" knives, clothes, raw cotton, and other articles
" brought from *Bombay*, and with those we trade to
" *Madagascar* for the natural produce of the country
" or *dollars*, with which the *French* buy cattle,
" honey, butter, and so forth, in that island. With
" *gold*, which we receive from your ships, we can
" procure elephants teeth from the natives of *Mo-*
" *zambique*, who barter them also for ammunition
" and bars of iron; and the *Portugueze* in that
" country give us clothes of various kinds in ex-
" change for our commodities; these cloths we dis-
" pose of lucratively in the three neighbouring islands,
" whence we bring rice, cattle, a kind of bread-fruit,
" which grows in *Comara*, and *slaves*, which we buy
" also at other places to which we trade; and we carry
" on this traffic in our own vessels."

Here I could not help expressing my abhorrence of
their *slave-trade*, and asked him by what law they
claimed a property in rational beings, since our Creator had given our species a dominion, to be moderately exercised, over the beasts of the field and the
fowls of the air, but none *to man over man*. " By no
" law," answered he, " unless necessity be a law.
" There are nations in *Madagascar* and in *Africa*,
" who know neither *God* nor his prophet, nor *Moses*,
" nor *David*, nor the *Messiah* : those nations are in
" perpetual war and take many captives, whom, if
" they could not sell, they would certainly kill. In-
" dividuals among them are in extreme poverty,
" and have numbers of children, who, if they can-
" not be disposed of, must perish through hunger,
" together with their miserable parents. By purchas-
" ing these wretches we preserve their lives, and,
" perhaps, those of many others whom our money
" relieves. The sum of the argument is this: If we
" buy them they will live; if they become valuable
" servants, they will live comfortably; but, if they
" are not sold, they must die miserably." ' There

'may be,' said I, ' such cases; but you fallaciously draw
' a general conclusion from a few particular instances;
' and this is the very fallacy which, on a thousand
' other occasions, deludes mankind.   It is not to be
' doubted, that a constant and gainful traffic in hu-
' man creatures foments war, in which captives are
' always made, and keeps up that perpetual enmity
' which you pretend to be the *cause* of a practice in
' itself reprehensible, while in truth it is its *effect*. The
' same traffic encourages laziness in some parents,
' who might in general support their families by pro-
' per industry, and seduces others to stifle their na-
' tural feelings.   At most, your redemption of those
' unhappy children can amount only to a personal
' contract implied between you, for gratitude and rea-
' sonable service on their part, for kindness and
' humanity on yours; but can you think your part
' performed by disposing of them against their wills,
' with as much indifference as if you were selling
' cattle, especially as they might become readers of the
' *Koran*, and pillars of your faith ?' " The law," said
he, " forbids our selling them, when they are be-
" lievers in the Prophet ; and little children only are
" sold ; nor they often, or by all masters."   ' You,
' who believe in *Muhammed*,' said I, ' are bound
' by the the spirit and letter of his laws to take pains,
' that they also may believe in him ; and if you ne-
' glect so important a duty for sordid gain, I do
' not see how you can hope for prosperity in this world,
' or for happiness in the next.'   My old friend and
the *Muftis* assented, and muttered a few prayers; but
probably forgot my preaching before many minutes
had passed.

So much time had slipped away in this conversation, that I could make but a short visit to Prince
Salim; and my view in visiting him was to fix the
time of our journey to *Domoni* as early as possible on
the next morning.   His appearance was more savage

than ever, and I found him in a disposition to complain bitterly against the *English*. No acknow-
ledgement, he said, had been made for the kind
attentions of himself and the chief men of his
country to the officers and people of the *Brilliant*,
though a whole year had elapsed since the wreck.
I really wondered at the forgetfulness, to which alone
such a neglect could be imputed, and assured him
that I would express my opinion both in *Bengal* and
in letters to *England*. " We have little," said he,
" to hope from letters; for, when we have been paid
" with them instead of money, and have shewn
" them on board your ships, we have commonly
" been treated with disdain, and often with impreca-
" tions." I assured him, that either those letters
must have been written coldly and by very obscure
persons, or shown to very ill-bred men, of whom
there were too many in all nations; but that a few
instances of rudeness ought not to give him a general
prejudice against our national character. " But you,"
said he, " are a wealthy nation, and we are indigent,,
" yet, though all our groves of cocoa-trees, our
" fruits, and our cattle, are ever at your service, you
" always try to make hard bargains with us for what
" you chuse to dispose of; and frequently will neither
" sell nor give those things which we principally
" want." ' To form,' said I, ' a just opinion of
' *Englishmen*, you must visit us in our own island,
' or at least *India*; here we are strangers and travel-
' lers: many of us have no design to trade in any
' country, and none of us think of trading in
' *Hinzuan*, where we stop only for refreshment.
' The clothes, arms, or instruments, which you
' may want, are commonly necessary or convenient
' to us; but, if *Sayyad Alwi* or his sons were to be
' strangers in our country, you would have no rea-
' son to boast of superior hospitality.' He then
showed me, a second time, a part of an old silk vest,
with the star of the Order of the Thistle, and beg-

ged me to explain the motto ; expressing a wish, that the order might be conferred on him by the King of *England*, in return for his good offices to the *English*. I represented to him the impossibility of his being gratified, and took occasion to say, that there was more true dignity in their own native titles, than in those of *prince*, *duke*, and *lord*, which had been idly given them, but had no conformity to their manners or the constitution of their government.

This conversation being agreeable to neither of us, I changed it, by desiring that the palanquins and bearers might be ready next morning as early as possible. He answered, that his palanquins were at our service for nothing, but that we must pay him ten dollars for each set of bearers; that it was the stated price, and that Mr. *Hastings* had paid it when he went to visit the king. This, as I learned afterwards, was false; but, at all events, I knew that he would keep the dollars himself, and give nothing to the bearers, who deserved them better, and whom he would compel to leave their cottages, and toil for his profit. " Can you imagine," I replied, " that we would employ four-and-twenty men " to bear us so far on their shoulders without reward- " ing them amply ? But since they are freemen (so he had assured me)." and not your slaves, we will pay " them in proportion to their diligence and good beha- " viour ; and it becomes neither your dignity nor ours " to make a previous bargain." I showed him an ele- gant copy of the *Koran*, which I destined for his father, and described the rest of my present; but he coldly asked, " if that was all?" Had he been king, a purse of dry dollars would have given him more pleasure than the finest or holiest manuscript. Finding him, in conversing on a variety of subjects, utterly void of in- telligence or principle, I took my leave, and saw him no more; but promised to let him know for certain whe- ther we should make our intended excursion.

We dined in tolerable comfort, and had occasion, in the course of the day, to observe the manners of the natives in the middle rank, who are called *Banas*, all of whom have slaves constantly at work for them. We visited the mother of *Combomadi*, who seemed in a station but little raised above indigence; and her husband, who was a mariner, bartered an *Arabic treatise* on astronomy and navigation, which he had read, for a sea-compass, of which he well knew the use.

In the morning I had conversed with two very old *Arabs* of *Yemen*, who had brought some articles of trade to *Hinzuan*; and in the afternoon I met another, who had come from *Muskat* (where at that time there was a civil war) to purchase, if he could, an hundred stand of arms. I told them all that I loved their nation; and they returned my compliment with great warmth, especially the two old men, who were near fourscore, and reminded me of *Zohair* and *Hareth*.

So bad an account had been given me of the road over the mountains, that I dissuaded my companions from thinking of the journey, to which the captain became rather disinclined; but as I wished to be fully ac-quainted with a country which I might never see again, I wrote the next day to *Salim*, requesting him to lend me one palanquin and to order a sufficient number of men. He sent me no written answer, which I ascribe rather to his incapacity than to rudeness; but the Governor, with *Akvi* and two of his sons, came on board in the evening, and said, that they had seen my letter; that all should be ready; but that I could not pay less for the men than ten dollars. I said I would pay more, but it should be to the men them-selves, according to their behaviour. They return-ed somewhat dissatisfied, after I had played at chess with *Alwi's* younger son, in whose manner and address there was something remarkably pleasing.

Before sun-rise, on the 2d of *August*, I went alone on shore, with a small basket of such provisions as I might want in the course of the day, and with some cushions to make the prince's palanquin at least a tolerable vehicle; but the prince was resolved to receive the dollars to which his men were entitled; and he knew that, as I was eager for the journey, he could prescribe his own terms. Old *Alwi* met me on the beach, and brought excuses from *Salim*, who he said was indisposed. He conducted me to his house, and seemed rather desirous of persuading me to abandon my design of visiting the king; but I assured him, that, if the prince would not supply me with proper attendants, I would walk to *Domoni* with my own servants and a guide. *Shaikh Salim*, he said, was miserably avaricious, and that he was ashamed of a kinsman with such a disposition; but that he was no less obstinate than covetous; and that, without ten dollars paid in hand, it would be impossible to procure bearers. I then gave him three guineas, which he carried, or pretended to carry to *Salim*; but returned without the change, alleging that he had no silver, and promising to give me on my return the few dollars that remained. In about an hour the ridiculous vehicle was brought by nine sturdy blacks, who could not speak a word of *Arabic*, so that I expected no information concerning the country through which I was to travel; but *Alwi* assisted me in a point of the utmost consequence. ' You cannot go,' said he, ' without an interpreter, for the king speaks only
' the language of this island; but I have a servant,
' whose name is *Tumuni*, a sensible and worthy man,
' who understands *English*, and is much esteemed
' by the king; he is known and valued all over

'*Hinzuan.* This man shall attend you; and you
' will soon be sensible of his worth.'

Tumuni desired to carry my basket; and we set out
with a prospect of fine weather, but some hours later
than I had intended. I walked, by the gardens of
the two princes, to the skirts of the town, and came
to a little village consisting of several very neat huts
made chiefly with the leaves of the cocoa-tree; but
the road a little farther was so stony, that I sat in the
palanquin, and was borne with perfect safety over some
rocks. I then desired my guide to assure the men
that I would pay them liberally; but the poor peasants, who had been brought from their farms on the
hills, were not perfectly acquainted with the use of
money, and treated my promise with indifference.

About five miles from *Matsamudo* lies the town of
Wani, where *Shaikh Abdullah,* who has already been
mentioned, usually resides: I saw it at a distance,
and it seemed to be agreeably situated. When I had
passed the rocky part of the road, I came to a stony
beach where the sea appeared to have lost some
ground, since there was a fine sand to the left, and
beyond it a beautiful bay, which resembled that of
Weymouth, and seemed equally convenient for bathing; but it did not appear to me that the stones over
which I was carried had been recently covered with
water. Here I saw the frigate, and, taking leave
of it for two days, turned from the coast into a fine
country very neatly cultivated, and consisting partly
of hillocks exquisitely green, partly of plains, which
were then in a gaudy dress of rich yellow blossoms.
My guide informed me they were plantations of a
kind of vetch, which was eaten by the natives. Cottages and farms were interspersed all over this gay
champaign, and the whole scene was delightful; but
it was soon changed for beauties of a different kind.

We descended into a cool valley, through which
ran a rivulet of perfectly clear water; and there, finding my vehicle uneasy, though from the laughter and
merriment of my bearers I concluded them to be
quite at their ease, I bade them set me down, and
walked before them all the rest of the way. Mountains, clothed with fine trees and flowering shrubs,
presented themselves on our ascent from the vale; and
we proceeded for half an hour through pleasant wood-
walks, where I regretted the impossibility of loi-
tering a while to examine the variety of new blossoms,
which succeeded one another at every step, and the
virtues, as well as names, of which seemed familiar
to *Tumuni*. At length we descended into a valley
of greater extent than the former: a river or large
wintery torrent ran through it, and fell down a steep
declivity at the end of it, where it seemed to be lost
among rocks. Cattle were grazing on the banks of
the river, and the huts of their owners appeared on
the hills: a more agreeable spot I had not before
seen even in *Swisserland* or *Merionethshire*; but it was
followed by an assemblage of natural beauties, which I
hardly expected to find in a little island twelve degrees to the south of the Line. I was not sufficiently
pleased with my solitary journey to discover charms
which had no actual existence, and the first effect of
the contrast between *St. Jago* and *Hinzuan* had
ceased; but, without any disposition to give the
landscape a high colouring, I may truly say, what I
thought at the time, that the whole country which
next presented itself, as far surpassed *Ermenonville*, or
Blenheim, or any other imitations of nature, which I
had seen in *France* or *England*, as the finest bay surpasses an artificial piece of water. Two very high
mountains, covered to the summit with the richest
verdure, were at some distance on my right hand,
and separated from me by, meadows diversified with
cottages and herds, or by vallies resounding with tor-

rents and waterfalls; on my left was the sea, to which there were beautiful openings from the hills and woods; and the road was a smooth path naturally winding through a forest of spicy shrubs, fruit-trees, and palms. Some high trees were spangled with white blossoms, equal in fragrance to orange-flowers : my guide called them *Monongos*; but the day was declining so fast that it was impossible to examine them: the variety of fruits, flowers, and birds, of which I had a transient view in this magnificent garden, would have supplied a naturalist with amusement for a month; but I saw no remarkable insect, and no reptile of any kind. The woodland was diversified by a few pleasant glades, and new prospects were continually opened : at length a noble view of the sea burst upon me unexpectedly; and, having passed a hill or two, we came to the beach, beyond which were several hills and cottages. We turned from the shore; and, on the next eminence, I saw the town of *Domoni* at a little distance below us. I was met by a number of natives, a few of whom spoke *Arabic*, and thinking it a convenient place for repose, I sent my guide to apprize the king of my intended visit. He returned in half an hour with a polite message; and I walked into the town, which seemed large and populous. A great crowd accompanied me; and I was conducted to a house built on the same plan with the best houses at *Matsamudo*. In the middle of the court-yard stood a large *Monongo-tree*, which perfumed the air; the apartment on the left was empty; and in that on the right sat the king on a sofa or bench, covered with an ordinary carpet. He rose when I entered, and grasping my hands, placed me near him on the right; but as he could speak only the language of *Hinzuan*, I had recourse to my friend *Tumuni*, than whom a readier or more accurate interpreter could not have been found. I presented the king with a very handsome *Indian* dress of blue silk with golden flowers,

which had been worn only once at a masquerade, and
with a beautiful copy of the *Koran*, from which I
read a few verses to him. He took them with great
complacency, and said, he wished I had come by
sea, that he might have loaded one of my boats
with fruit, and with some of his finest cattle. He
had seen me, he said, on board the frigate, where
he had been, according to his custom, in disguise,
and had heard of me from his son *Shaikh Hamdullah*. I gave him an account of my journey, and
extolled the beauties of his country: he put many
questions concerning mine, and professed great regard
for our nation. " But I hear," said he, " that you are
" a magistrate, and consequently profess peace: why
" are you armed with a broad sword?" ' I was a
' man,' I said, ' before I was a magistrate; and, if it
' should ever happen that law could not protect
' me, I must protect myself.' He seemed about
sixty years old, had a very cheerful countenance, and
great appearance of good-nature mixed with a certain
dignity, which distinguished him from the crowd of
ministers and officers who attended him. Our conversation was interrupted by notice, that it was the
time for evening prayers; and, when he rose, he said
" this house is yours, and I will visit you in it, after
" you have taken some refreshment." Soon after,
his servants brought a roast fowl, a rice pudding, and
some other dishes, with papayas and very good pomegranates; my own basket supplied the rest of my
supper. The room was hung with old red cloth, and
decorated with pieces of porcelain and festoons of
English bottles; the lamps were placed on the ground
in large sea-shells; and the bed-place was a recess,
concealed by a chintz hanging, opposite to the sofa,
on which we had been sitting. Though it was not a
place that invited repose, and the gnats were inex-
pressibly troublesome, yet the fatigue of the day procured me very comfortable slumber. I was waked

by the return of the king and his train ; some of whom
were *Arabs*, for I heard one of them say *hūwa rukīd*,
or, *he is sleeping*. There was immediate silence, and I
passed the night with little disturbance, except from
the unwelcome songs of the mosquitos.   In the
morning all was equally silent and solitary ; the house
appeared to be deserted ; and I began to wonder what
had become of *Tumuni* : he came at length with concern on his countenance, and told me that the bearers
had run away in the night ; but that the king, who
wished to see me in another of his houses, would
supply me with bearers, if he could not prevail on me
to stay till a boat could be sent for.   I went immediately to the king, whom I found sitting on a raised
sofa in a large room, the walls of which were adorned
with sentences from the *Koran* in very legible characters : about fifty of his subjects were seated on the
ground in a semicircle before him ; and my interpreter to his place in the midst of them.   The good
old king laughed heartily, when he heard the adven-
ture of the night, and said, " you will now be my
" guest for a week, I hope ; but, seriously, if you
" must return soon, I will send into the country for
" some peasants to carry you."   He then apologized
for the behaviour of *Shaikh Salim*, which he had
heard from *Tumuni*, who told me afterwards that he
was much displeased with it, and would not fail to
express his displeasure.   He concluded with a long
harangue on the advantage which the *English* might
derive from sending a ship every year from *Bombay* to
trade with his subjects, and on the wonderful cheap-
ness of their commodities, especially of their cowries.
Ridiculous as this idea might seem, it showed an en-
largement of mind, a desire of promoting the interest
of his people, and a sense of the benefits arising
from trade, which could hardly have been expected
from a petty *African* chief, and which, if he had

H 3

been sovereign of *Yemen*, might have been expanded
into rational projects proportioned to the extent of
his dominion? I answered, that I was imperfectly
acquainted with the commerce of *India*; but that I
would report the substance of his conversation, and
would ever bear testimony of his noble zeal for
the good of his country, and to the mildness with
which he governed it. As I had no inclination to
pass a second night in the island, I requested leave
to return without waiting for bearers: he seemed very
sincere in pressing me to lengthen my visit, but
had too much *Arabian* politeness to be impor-
tunate. We therefore parted; and at the request
of *Tumuni*, who assured me that little time would
be lost in showing attention to one of the wor-
thiest men in *Hinzuan*, I made a visit to the Governor of the town, whose name was *Mulekka*: his
manners were very pleasing, and he showed me
some letters from the officers of the *Brilliant*,
which appeared to flow warm from the heart, and
contained the strongest *eloge* of his courtesy and
liberality. He insisted on filling my basket with
some of the finest pomegranates I had ever seen;
and I left the town, impressed with a very favourable
opinion of the king and his governor. When I
reascended the hill, attended by many of the natives, one of them told me in *Arabic* that I was
going to receive the highest mark of distinction
that it was in the king's power to show me;
and he had scarce ended, when I heard the report
of a single gun: *Shaikh Ahmed* had saluted me
with the whole of his ordnance. I waved my hat,
and said *Allah Acbar*: the people shouted, and I
continued my journey, not without fear of inconvenience from excessive heat, and the fatigue of climb-
ing rocks. The walk, however, was not on the
whole unpleasant: I sometimes rested in the valleys,
and forded all the rivulets, which refreshed me with

their coolness, and supplied me with exquisite water to
mix with the juice of my pomegranates, and occasionally with brandy. We were overtaken by some peasants, who came from the hills by a nearer way, and
brought the king's present of a cow with her calf, and
a she-goat with two kids: they had apparently been
selected for their beauty, and were brought safe to
Bengal. The prospects, which had so greatly delighted me the preceding day, had not lost their
charms, though they wanted the recommendation of
novelty; but I must confess, that the most delightful
object in that day's walk, of near ten miles, was the
Black Frigate, which I discerned at sunset from a '
rock near the prince's gardens. Close to the town I
was met by a native, who, perceiving me to be weary,
opened a very fine cocoa-nut, which afforded a delicious draught: he informed me, that one of his countrymen had been punished that afternoon for a theft
on board the *Crocodile*, and added, that, in his opinion, the punishment was no less just than the offence
was disgraceful to his country. The offender, as I
afterwards learned, was a youth of good family, who
had married a daughter of old *Alwi*, but, being left
alone for a moment in the cabin, and seeing a pair of
blue Morocco slippers, could not resist the temptation, concealed them so ill under his gown, that he
was detected with the mainer. This proves, that no
principle of honour is instilled by education into
the gentry of this island: even *Alwi*, when he had
observed that, " in the month of *Ramadan*, it was
" not lawful to paint with *huma*, or to tell *lies*," and
when I asked, whether both were lawful all the rest of
the year, answered, that " lies were innocent, if no
" man was injured by them." *Tumuni* took his leave,
as well satisfied as myself with our excursion. I told
him, before his master, that I transferred also to him
the dollars, which were due to me out of the three
guineas; and that, if ever they should part, I should

H 4

be very glad to receive him into my service in *India*.
Mr. *Roberts*, the master of the ship, had passed the
day with *Sayyad Ahmed*, and had learned from him
a few curious circumstances concerning the government of *Hinzuan*; which he found to be a monarchy
limited by aristocracy. The king, he was told, had
no power of making war by his own authority; but,
if the assembly of nobles, who were from time to
time convened by him, resolved on a war with any of
the neighbouring islands, they defrayed the charges
of it by voluntary contributions, in return for which
they claimed as their own all the booty and captives
that might be taken. The hope of gain or the want
of slaves is usually the real motives for such enter-
prizes, and ostensible pretexts are ea ly found. At that
very time he understood they meditated a war, because they wanted hands for the following harvest.
Their fleet consisted of sixteen or seventeen small vessels, which they manned with about two thousand five
hundred islanders armed with muskets and cutlasses,
or with bows and arrows. Near two years had elapsed before they had possessed themselves of two towns
in *Mayata*, which they still kept and garrisoned. The
ordinary expences of the government were defrayed
by a tax from two hundred villages: but the three
principal towns were exempt from all taxes, except
that they paid annually to the chief *Mufti* a fortieth
part of the value of all their moveable property; and
from that payment neither the king nor the nobles
claimed an exemption. The kingly authority, by the
principles of their consitution, was considered elective,
though the line of succession had not been altered since
the first election of a sultan. He was informed that a
wandering *Arab*, who had settled in the island,
had, by his intrepidity in several wars, acquired the
rank of a chieftain, and afterwards of a king with
limited powers; and that he was the *grandfather*
of *Shaikh Ahmed*. I had been assured that Queen

Halimah was his *grandmother*; and, that he was the *sixth* king; but it must be remarked, that the words *jedd* and *jeddah* in *Arabic* are used for a male and female *ancestor* indefinitely; and, without a correct pedigree of *Ahmed*'s family, which I expected to procure but was disappointed, it would scarce be possible to ascertain the time when his forefather obtained the highest rank in the government. In the year 1600 Captain *John Davis*, who has written an account of his voyage, found *Mayata* governed by a king, and *Antuame*, or *Hinzuan*, by a queen, who showed him great marks of friendship. He anchored before the town of *Demos* (does he mean *Domoni?*) which was as large, he says, as *Plymouth*; and he concludes, from the ruins around it, that it had once been a place of strength and grandeur. I can only say, that I observed no such ruins. Fifteen years after, Captain *Peyton* and Sir *Thomas Roe* touched at the *Comara* islands; and, from their several accounts, it appears that an old sultaness at that time resided in *Hinzuan*, but had a dominion paramount over all the isles, three of her sons governing *Mohila* in her name. If this be true, *Sohaili* and the successors of *Halimah* must have lost their influence over the other islands; and, by renewing their dormant claim as it suits their convenience, they may always be furnished with a pretence for hostilities. Five generations of eldest sons would account for an hundred and seventy of the years which have elapsed since *Davis* and *Peyton* found *Hinzuan* ruled by a sultaness; and *Ahmed* was of such an age, that his reign may be reckoned equal to a generation. It is probable, on the whole, that *Halimah* was the widow of the first *Arabian* king, and that her mosque has been continued in repair by his descendants; so that we may reasonably suppose two centuries to have passed since a single *Arab* had the courage and address to establish in that beautiful island a form of government, which,

though bad enough in itself, appears to have been administered with advantage to the original inhabitants.
We have lately heard of civil commotions in *Hinzuan*, which, we may venture to pronounce, were not
excited by any cruelty or violence of *Ahmed*, but
were probably occasioned by the insolence of an oli-
garchy naturally hostile to king and people. That
the mountains in the *Comara* islands contain diamonds, and the precious metals, which are studiously
concealed by the policy of the several governments,
may be true, though I have no reason to believe it,
and have only heard it asserted without evidence;
but I hope, that neither an expectation of such treasures, nor of any other advantage, will ever induce
an *European* power to violate the first principles of
justice by assuming the sovereignty of *Hinzuan*,
which cannot answer a better purpose than that of
supplying our fleets with seasonable refreshment;
and, although the natives have an interest in receiving us with apparent cordiality, yet, if we wish their
attachment to be unfeigned and their dealings just,
we must set them an example of strict honesty in the
performance of our engagements. In truth, our nation
is not cordially loved by the inhabitants of *Hinzuan*,
who, as it commonly happens, form a general
opinion from a few instances of violence or breach
of faith. Not many years ago an *European*, who
had been hospitably received and liberally supported
at *Mutsamudo*, behaved rudely to, a young married
woman, who, being of low degree, was walking
veiled through a street in the evening. Her husband
ran to protect her, and resented the rudeness, probably with menaces, possibly with actual force; and
the *European* is said to have given him a mortal
wound with a knife or bayonet, which he brought,
after the scuffle, from his lodging. This foul mur-
der, which the law of nature would have justified
the magistrate in punishing with death, was reported

to the king, who told the governor (and I use the
very words of *Alwi*) that " it would be wiser to hush
it up." *Alwi* mentioned a civil case of his own,
which ought not to be concealed. When he was on
the coast of *Africa*, in the dominions of a very savage
prince, a small *European* vessel was wrecked; and
the prince not only seized all that could be saved from
the wreck, but claimed the captain and the crew as
his slaves, and treated them with ferocious insolence.
Alwi assured me, that, when he heard of the accident, he hastened to the prince, fell prostrate before
him, and by tears and importunity prevailed on him
to give the *Europeans* their liberty; that he supported
them at his own expence, enabled them to build another vessel, in which they sailed to *Hinzuan*, and departed thence for *Europe* or *India*. He showed me
the Captain's promissory notes for sums, which to an
African trader must be a considerable object, but
which are no price for liberty, safety, and, perhaps,
life, which his good though disinterested offices had
procured. I lamented that, in my situation, it was
wholly out of my power to assist *Alwi* in obtaining
justice; but he urged me to deliver an *Arabic* letter
from him, inclosing the notes, to the Governor General, who, as he said, knew him well: and I com-
plied with his request. Since it is possible that a
substantial defence may be made by the person thus
accused of injustice, I will not name either him or
the vessel which he had commanded; but, if he be
living, and if this paper should fall into his hands,
he may be induced to reflect how highly it imports
our national honour, that a people whom we call
savage, but who administer to our convenience, may
have no just cause to reproach us with a violation of
our contracts.

(

VI.

ON THE BAYA, OR INDIAN GROSS-BEAK.

BY AT'HAR ALI KHAN OF DEHLI.

THE little bird, called *Baya* in *Hindi*, *Berbera* in *Sanscrit*, *Babui* in the dialect of *Bengal*, *Cibu* in *Persian*, and *Tenawwit* in *Arabic*, from his remarkably *pendent* nest, is rather larger than a sparrow, with yellow-brown plumage, a yellowish head and feet, a light coloured breast, and a conic beak, very thick in proportion to his body. This bird is exceedingly common in *Hindustan*: he is astonishingly sensible, faithful, and docile, never voluntarily deserting the place where his young were hatched, nowise averse, like most other birds, to the society of mankind, and easily taught to perch on the hand of his master. In a state of nature he generally builds his nest on the highest tree that he can find, especially on the Palmyra, or on the *Indian* fig-tree; and he prefers that which happens to overhang a well or a rivulet: he makes it of grass, which he weaves like cloth, and shapes like a large bottle, suspending it firmly on the branches, but so as to rock with the wind; and placing it with its entrance downwards, to secure it from birds of prey. His nest usually consists of two or three chambers; and it is the popular belief that he lights them with fire-flies, which he catches alive at night and confines with moist clay, or with cowdung: that such flies are often found in his nest, where pieces of cow-dung are also stuck, is indubitable; but, as their light could be of little use to him, it seems probable that he only feeds on them. He may be taught with ease to fetch a piece of paper, or any small thing that his master points out to him. It is an attested fact, that, if a ring be dropped into a deep well, and a signal given to him, he will fly down with amazing celerity, catch the ring before it touches the water, and bring it up to his master with apparent exultation; and it is confidently asserted, that, if a house or any other place be shown to him once or twice, he will carry a note thither immediately on a proper signal being made. One instance of his docility I can myself mention with confidence, having often been an eye-witness of it: the young *Hindu* women at *Banares* and in other places wear very thin plates of gold, called *ticas*, slightly fixed, by way of ornament, between their eye-brows; and, when they pass through the streets, it is not uncommon for the youthful libertines, who amuse themselves with training *Bayas*, to give them a sign which they understand, and send them to pluck the pieces of gold from the foreheads of their mistresses, which they bring in triumph to the lovers. The *Baya* feeds naturally on grasshoppers and other insects, but will subsist, when tame, on pulse macerated in water. His flesh is warm and drying, of easy digestion, and recommended, in medical books, as a solvent of stone in the bladder or kidneys; but of that virtue there is no sufficient proof. The female lays many beautiful eggs, resembling large pearls: the white of them, when they are boiled, is transparent, and the flavour of them is exquisitely delicate. When many *Bayas* are assembled on a high tree, they make a lively din, but it is rather chirping than singing; their want of musical talents is, however, amply supplied by their wonderful sagacity, in which they are not excelled by any feathered inhabitants of the forest.

VII.

ON THE CHRONOLOGY OF THE HINDUS.

WRITTEN IN JANUARY 1788,

BY THE PRESIDENT.

THE great antiquity of the *Hindus* is believed so firmly by themselves, and has been the subject of so much conversation among *Europeans*, that a short view of their Chronological System, which has not yet been exhibited from certain authorities, may be acceptable to those who seek truth without partiality to received opinions, and without regarding any consequences that may result from their inquiries. The consequences, indeed, of truth cannot but be desireable, and no reasonable man will apprehend any danger to society from a general diffusion of its light; but we must not suffer ourselves to be dazzled by a false glare, nor mistake enigmas and allegories for historical verity. Attached to no system, and as much disposed to reject the *Mosaic* history, if it be proved erroneous, as to believe it, if it be confirmed by sound reasoning from indubitable evidence, I propose to lay before you a concise account of *Indian* Chronology, extracted from *Sanscrit* books, or collected from conversations with *Pundits*, and to subjoin a few remarks on their system, without attempting to decide a question, which I shall venture to start, " Whether it is not in fact the same with our " own, but embellished and obscured by the fancy " of their poets and the riddles of their astronomers ?"

One of the most curious books in *Sanscrit*, and one of the oldest after the *Vedas*, is a tract on *religious and civil duties*, taken, as it is believed, from the oral instructions of *Menu*, son of *Brahma*, to the first inhabitants of the earth. An exceeding well-collated copy of this most interesting law-tract is now before me; and I begin my dissertation with a few couplets from the first chapter of it: " The sun " causes the division of day and night, which are " of two sorts, those of men and those of the " Gods ; the day, for the labour of *all* creatures in " their several employments; the night for their " slumber. A month is a day and night of the " patriarchs; and it is divided into two parts; the " bright half is *their* day for laborious exertions ; the " dark half, *their* night for sleep. A year is a day " and night of the Gods; and that is also divided " into two halves ; the day is, when the sun moves " toward the north ; the night, when it moves to- " ward the south. Learn now the duration of a " night and day of *Brahma* with that of the ages " respectively and in order. Four thousand years " *of the Gods* they call the *Crita* (or *Satya*) age ; " and its limits at the beginning and at the end *are*, " in like manner, as many hundreds. In the three " successive ages, together with their limits at the " beginning and end of them, are thousands and " hundreds diminished by one. This aggregate of " four ages, amounting to twelve thousand divine " years, is called an age of the Gods ; and a thou- " sand such divine ages added together must be con- " sidered as a day of *Brahma* : his night has also the " same duration. The before mentioned age of the " Gods, or twelve thousand of their years, multi- " plied by seventy-one, form what is named here " below a *Manwantara*. There are *alternate* crea- " tions and destructions *of worlds* through innumer- " able *Manwantaras* : the Being supremely desir- " able performs all this again and again."

Such is the arrangement of infinite time, which the *Hindus* believe to have been revealed from Heaven, and which they generally understand in a literal sense: it seems to have intrinsic marks of being purely astronomical; but I will not appropriate the observations of others, nor anticipate those in particular, which have been made by two or three of our members, and which they will, I hope, communicate to the Society. A conjecture, however, of Mr. *Paterson* has so much ingenuity in it, that I cannot forbear mentioning it here, especially as it seems to be confirmed by one of the couplets just cited: he supposes, that, as a *month* of mortals is a day and night of the patriarchs, from the analogy of its bright and dark halves, so, by the same analogy, a day and night of mortals might have been considered by the ancient *Hindus* as a month of the lower world; and then a year of such months will consist only of twelve days and nights, and thirty such years will compose a lunar year of mortals; whence he surmises that the *four million three hundred and twenty thousand* years, of which the four *Indian* ages are supposed to consist, mean only years of twelve days; and, in fact, that sum divided by *thirty*, is reduced to *an hundred and forty-four thousand*: now *a thousand four hundred and forty* years are one *pada*, a period in the *Hindu* astronomy; and that sum multiplied by *eighteen*, amounts precisely to *twenty-five thousand nine hundred and twenty*, the number of years in which the fixed stars appear to perform their long revolution eastward. The last mentioned sum is the product also of *an hundred and forty-four*, which, according to M. *Bailly*, was an old *Indian* cycle, into *an hundred and eighty*, or the *Tartarian* period, called *Van*, and of *two thousand eight hundred and eighty* into *nine*, which is not one only of the lunar cycles, but considered by the *Hindus* as a mysterious number and an emblem of Divinity, because, if it be multiplied by any other

I

whole number, the sum of the figures in the different products remain always nine, as the Deity, who appears in many forms, continues One immutable essence. The important period of *twenty-five thousand nine hundred and twenty* years is well known to arise from the multiplication of *three hundred and sixty* into *seventy-two*, the number of years in which a fixed star seems to move through a degree of a great circle; and, although M. *Le Gentil* assures us, that the modern *Hindus* believe a complete revolution of the stars to be made in *seventy-four thousand* years, or *fifty-four* seconds of a degree to be passed in one year, yet we may have reason to think that the old *Indian* astronomers had made a more accurate calculation, but concealed their knowledge from the people under the veil of *fourteen Manwantaras, seventy-one* divine ages, compound cycles, and years of different sorts, from those of *Brahma* to those of *Patala*, or the *infernal regions*. If we follow the analogy suggested by *Menu*, and suppose only a day and night to be called a *year*, we may divide the number of years in a divine age by *three hundred and sixty*, and the quotient will be *twelve thousand*, or the number of his *divine years* in one age: but, conjecture apart, we need only compare the two periods 4320000 and 25920, and we shall find, that among their common divisors, are 6, 9, 12 &c. 18, 36, 72, 144, &c.; which numbers with their several multiples, especially in a decuple progression, constitute some of the most celebrated periods of the *Chaldeans, Greeks, Tartars*, and even of the *Indians*. We cannot fail to observe, that the number 432, which appears to be the basis of the *Indian* system, is a 60th part of 25920, and, by continuing the comparison we might probably solve the whole enigma. In the preface to a *Varanes* Almanac I find the following wild stanza : " A *thousand* Great Ages are a day of " *Brahma*; a *thousand* such days are an *Indian* hour

" of *Vishnu; six hundred thousand* such hours make
" a period of *Rudra*; and a million of *Rudras*
" (or *two quadrillions five hundred and ninety-two*
" *thousand trillions of lunar years)* are but a second
" to the Supreme Being." The *Hindu* theologians
deny the conclusion of the stanza to be orthodox:
" *Time*," they say, " *exists not at all with God*;" and
they advise astronomers to mind their own business,
without meddling with theology. The astronomical
verse, however, will answer our present purpose; for
it shows, in the first place, that cyphers are added
at pleasure to swell the periods; and, if we take ten
cyphers from a *Rudra*, or divide by ten thousand
millions, we shall have a period of 259200000 years,
which, divided by 60 (the usual divisor of *time*
among the *Hindus*) will give 4320000, or a Great
Age, which we find subdivided in the proportion of
4, 3, 2, 1, from the notion of *virtue* decreasing
arithmetically in the *golden, silver, copper,* and *earthen* ages. But, should it be thought improbable
that the *Indian* astronomers in very early times had
made more accurate observations than those of *Alex-
andria, Bagdad,* or *Maraghah,* and still more improbable that they should have relapsed with apparent cause into error, we may suppose that they
formed their divine age by an arbitrary multiplication
of 24000 by 180, according to *Le Gentil,* or of 21600
by 200, according to the comment on the *Surya Siddhanta.* Now, as it is *hardly* possible that such
coincidences should be accidental, we may hold it
nearly demonstrated, that the period of a *divine age*
was at first merely astronomical, and may consequently reject it from our present inquiry into the
historical or civil chronology of *India.* Let us, however, proceed to the avowed opinions of the *Hindus,*
and see, when we have ascertained their system, whether we can reconcile it to the course of nature and '
the common sense of mankind.

The aggregate of their four ages they call a divine age, and believe that, in every thousand such ages, or in every *day* of *Brahma*, *fourteen Menus* are successively invested by him with the sovereignty of the earth: each *Menu*, they suppose, transmits his empire to his sons and grandsons during a period of seventy-one divine ages; and such a period they name a *Manwantara*; but, since *fourteen* multiplied by *seventy-one* are not quite a *thousand*, we must conclude that *six divine ages* are allowed for intervals between the *Manwantaras*, or for the twilight of *Brahma's* day. Thirty such days, or *Calpas*, constitute, in their opinion, *a month* of *Brahma*; twelve such months, one of his years; and an hundred such years, his *age*; of which age they assert, that fifty years have elapsed. We are now then, according to the *Hindus* in the first day or *Calpa* of the first month of the fifty-first year of *Brahma's* age, and in the twenty-eighth divine age of the seventh *Manwantara*, of which divine age the *three first* human ages have passed, and *four thousand eight hundred and eighty-eight* of the *fourth*.

In the present day of *Brahma* the first *Menu* was surnamed *Swayambhuva*, or *son of the self-existent*; and it is he by whom the *institutes of religious and civil duties* are supposed to have been delivered. In his time the Deity descended at a *sacrifice*, and, by his wife *Satarupa*, he had two distinguished sons, and three daughters. This pair were created for the multiplication of the human species, after that new creation of the world which the *Brahmans* call *Padmacalpiya*, or the *Lotos*-creation.

If it were worth while to calculate the age of *Menu's* institutes, according to the *Brahmans*, we must multiply four million three hundred and twenty thousand by six times seventy-one, and add to the product the number of years already past in the seventh *Manwantara*. Of the five *Menus* who succeeded him, I have seen little more than the names; but the *Hindu* writings are very diffuse on the life and posterity of the *seventh Menu*, surnamed *Vaivaswata*, or *Child of the Sun*: he is supposed to have had ten sons, of whom the eldest was *Ieshwacu*; and to have been accompanied by seven *Rishis*, or holy persons, whose names were, *Casyapa*, *Atri*, *Vasishtha*, *Viswamitra*, *Gautama*, *Jamadagni*, and *Bharadwaja*; an account which explains the opening of the fourth chapter of the *Gita:* " This immutable system of devotion," says *Crishna*, " I revealed to *Vivaswat*, or *the Sun*; *Vivaswat* declared it to *his son Menu*; *Menu* explained it to *Ieshwacu*: thus the chief *Rishis* know this sublime *doctrine* delivered from one to another."

In the reign of this *sun born* monarch, the *Hindus* believe the whole earth to have been drowned, and the whole human race destroyed by a flood, except the pious prince himself, the seven *Rishis*, and their several wives; for they suppose his children to have been born after the deluge. This general *praylaya*, or destruction, is the subject of the first *Purana*, or *sacred poem*, which consists of fourteen thousand stanzas; and the story is concisely, but clearly and elegantly, told in the eighth book of the *Bhagawata*, from which I have abstracted the whole, and translated it with great care, but will only present you here with an abridgment of it. " The demon *Hayagriva* having purloined the " *Vedas* from the custody of *Brahma*, while he was " reposing at the close of the sixth *Manwantara*, " the whole race of men became corrupt, except " the seven *Rishis* and *Satyavrata*, who then reigned

" in *Dravira*, a maritime region to the south of
" *Carnata*: this prince was performing his ablutions
" in the river *Critamala*, when *Vishnu* appeared to
" him in the shape of a small fish, and, after seve-
" ral augmentations of bulk in different waters,
" was placed by *Satyavrata* in the ocean, where
" he thus addressed his amazed votary: " In *seven*
" days all creatures, who have offended me, shall be
" destroyed by a deluge, but thou shalt be secured
" in a capacious vessel miraculously formed: take
" therefore all kinds of medicinal herbs and esculent
" grain for food, and, together with the seven holy
" men, your respective wives, and pairs of all ani-
" mals, enter the ark without fear; then shalt thou
" know God face to face, and all thy questions shall
" be answered." Saying this, he disappeared; and
after seven days, the ocean ' began to overflow the
' coasts, and the earth to be flooded by constant
' showers, when *Satyavrata*, meditating on the
' Deity, saw a large vessel moving on the waters:
' he entered it, having in all respects conformed to
' the instructions of *Vishnu*; who, in the form of a
' vast fish, suffered the vessel to be tied with a great
' sea-serpent, as with a cable, to his measureless
' horn. When the deluge had ceased, *Vishnu* slew
' the demon, and recovered the *Vedas*, instructed
' *Satyavrata* in divine knowledge, and appointed
' him the seventh *Menu* by the name of *Vaivas-*
' *wata*.' Let us compare the two *Indian* accounts
of the *Creation* and the *Deluge* with those delivered
by *Moses*. It is not made a question in this tract,
whether the first chapters of *Genesis* are to be understood in a literal, or merely in an allegorical sense;
the only points before us are, whether the creation
described by the *first Menu*, which the *Brahmans*
call that of the *Lotos*, be not the same with that recorded in our Scripture; and whether the story of

the *seventh Menu* be not one and the same with that of *Noah*. I propose the questions, but affirm nothing; leaving others to settle their opinions, whether *Adam* be derived from *adim*, which in *Sanscrit* means the *first*; or *Menu* from *Nuh*, the true name of the patriarch; whether the *sacrifice*, at which *God* is believed to have descended, alludes to the offering of *Abel*; and, on the whole, whether the two *Menus* can mean any other persons than the great progenitor, and the restorer of our species.

On a supposition that *Vaivaswata*, or *sun-born*, was the *Noah* of Scripture, let us proceed to the *Indian* account of his posterity, which I extract from the *Puranart'haprecasa*, or *The Puranas Explained*: a work lately composed in *Sanscrit* by *Radhacanta Sarman*, a *Pandit* of extensive learning and great fame among the *Hindus* of this province. Before we examine the genealogies of kings, which he has collected from the *Puranas*, it will be necessary to give a general idea of the *avataras*, or *descents*, of the Deity. The *Hindus* believe innumerable such descents or special interpositions of Providence in the affairs of mankind, but they reckon *ten* principal *avataras* in the current period of four ages; and all of them are described, in order as they are supposed to occur, in the following Ode of *Jayadeva*, the great lyric poet of *India*.

1. " Thou recoverest the *Veda* in the water of the ocean of destruction, *placing it* joyfully in the bosom of an ark fabricated *by thee*, O *Cesava*, assuming the body of a *fish*. Be victorious, O *Heri*, lord of the universe!

2. " The earth stands firm on thy immensely broad back, which grows larger from the callus.

I 4

occasioned by bearing that vast burden, O *Cesava*, assuming the body of a *tortoise*. Be victorious, O *Heri*, lord of the universe!

3. " The earth, placed on the point of thy tusk, remains fixed like the figure of a black antelope on the moon, O *Cesava*, assuming the form of a *boar*. Be victorious, O *Heri*, lord of the universe!

4. " The claw with a stupendous point, on the exquisite lotos of thy lion's paw, is the black bee that stung the body of the embowelled *Hiranyacasipu*, O *Cesava*, assuming the form of a *man-lion*. Be victorious, O *Heri*, lord of the universe.

5. " By thy power thou beguilest *Bali*, O thou miraculous dwarf, thou purifier of men with the water (of *Ganga*) springing from thy feet, O *Cesava*, assuming the form of a *dwarf*. Be victorious, O *Heri*, lord of the universe!

6. " Thou bathest in pure water, consisting of the blood of *Cshatriyas*, the world, whose offences are removed, and who are relieved from the pain of other births, O *Cesava*, assuming the form of *Parasu-Rama*. Be victorious, O *Heri*, lord of the universe!

7. " With ease to thyself, with delight to the Genii of the eight regions, thou scatterest on all sides in the plain of combat the demon with ten heads, O *Cesava*, assuming the form of *Rama Chandra*. Be victorious, O *Heri*, lord of the universe!

8. " Thou wearest on thy bright body a mantle

shining like a blue cloud, or like the water of *Yamuna* tripping towards thee through fear of thy sorrowing *ploughshare*, O *Cesava*, assuming the form of *Halla-Rama*. Be victorious, O *Heri*, lord of the universe!

9. "Thou blamest,(Oh, wonderful!) the whole *Veda*, when thou seest, O kind-hearted, the slaughter of cattle prescribed for sacrifice, O *Cesava*, assuming the body of *Buddha*. Be victorious, O *Heri*, lord of the universe!

10. "For the destruction of all the impure thou drawest thy cimeter like a blazing comet (how tremendous!) O *Cesava*, assuming the body of *Calci*. Be victorious, O *Heri*, lord of the universe!"

These ten *Avataras* are by some arranged according to the thousands of divine years in each of the four ages, or in an arithmetical proportion from four to one; and, if such an arrangement were universally received, we should be able to ascertain a very material point in the *Hindu* chronology; I mean the birth of *Buddha*, concerning which the different *Pandits*, whom I have consulted, and the same *Pandits* at different times, have expressed a strange diversity of opinion. They all agree that *Calci* is yet to come, and that *Buddha* was the last considerable incarnation of the Deity; but the astronomers at *Varanes* place him in the *third* age, and *Radhacant* insists that he appeared after the *thousandth* year of the *fourth*. The learned and accurate author of the *Dabistan*, whose information concerning the *Hindus* is wonderfully correct, mentions an opinion of the *Pandits*, with whom he had conversed, that *Buddha* began his career *ten* years before the close of the third age; and *Goverdhana* of *Cashmir*, who had once informed me that *Crishna* descended *two centuries* before *Buddha*, assured me lately that the *Cashmirians* admitted an interval of *twenty-four* years (others allow only *twelve*) between these two divine persons.   The best authority, after all, is the *Bhagawat* itself, in the first chapter of which it is expressly declared, that " *Bud-* " *dha,* the son of *Jina,* would appear at *Cicata* for " the purpose of confounding the demons, *just at* " *the beginning* of the *Caliyug.*"   I have long been convinced, that, on these subjects, we can only reason satisfactorily from *written* evidence, and that our forensick rule must be invariably applied *to take the de-* *clarations of the* Brahmans *most strongly against them-* *selves;* that is, *against their pretensions to antiquity;* so that, on the whole, we may safely place *Buddha* *just at the beginning* of the *present* age : but what is the *beginning* of it ?   When this question was proposed to *Radhacant,* he answered, " Of a period com- " prising more than four hundred thousand years, " the first two or three thousand may reasonably be " called *the beginning.*"   On my demanding *written* evidence, he produced a book of some authority, composed by a learned *Goswami,* and entitled *Bhagawa-* *tamurita,* or the *Nectar* of the *Bhagawat,* on which it is a metrical comment ; and the couplet which he read from it deserves to be cited.   After the just mentioned account of *Buddha* in the text, the commentator says,

Asau vyactah calerabdasahasradwitaye gate,
Murtih patalaverna'sya dwibhuja chicurojj'hita.

' He *became* visible, the-thousand-and-second-year-of- the-Cali-*age being* past ; his body of-a-colour-be- ' tween-white and-ruddy, with-two-arms, without- ' hair *on his head.*'

Cicata, named in the text as the birth-place of

Buddha, the *Goswami* supposes to have been *Dher-maranya*, a wood near *Gaya*, where a colossal image of that ancient deity still remains. It seemed to me of black stone: but, as I saw it by torch-light, I cannot be positive as to its colour, which may indeed have been changed by time.

The *Brahmans* universally speak of the *Bauddhas* with all the malignity of an intolerant spirit; yet the most orthodox among them consider *Buddha* himself as an incarnation of *Vishnu*. This is a contradiction hard to be reconciled, unless we cut the knot, instead of untying it, by supposing with *Giorgi*, that there were *two Buddhas*, the younger of whom established the new religion, which gave so great offence in *India*, and was introduced into *China* in the first century of our æra. The *Cashmirian* before mentioned asserted this fact, without being led to it by any question that implied it; and we may have reason to suppose that *Buddha* is in truth only a general word for a *Philosopher*. The author of a celebrated *Sanscrit* Dictionary, entitled from his name *Amara-cosha*, who was himself a *Bauddha*, and flourished in the first century before *Christ*, begins his vocabulary with nine words that signify *heaven*, and proceeds to those which mean *a deity in general*; after which come different *classes* of *Gods*, *Demigods*, and *Demons*, all by *generic* names; and they are followed by two very remarkable heads; first (not the *general names* of *Buddha*, but) the names of a *Buddha-in-general* of which he gives us eighteen, such as *Muni*, *Sastri*, *Muninidra*, *Vinayaca*, *Samantabhadra*, *Dhermaraja*, *Sugata*, and the like; most of them significative of *excellence*, *wisdom*, *virtue*, and *sanctity*; secondly, the names of *a particular-Buddha-Muni*-who-descended-in-the-family-of-*Sacya* (these are the very words of the original) and his titles are, *Sacyamuni*, *Sacyasinha*,

Servart'hasiddha, *Saudhodani*, *Gautama*, *Arcabandhu*,
or *Kinsman of the Sun*, and *Mayadevisuta*, or *Child
of Maya*. Thence the author passes to the different
epithets of particular *Hindu* deities When I pointed out this curious passage to *Radhacant*, he contend-
ed that the first eighteen names were *general* epithets,
and the following seven *proper names*, or *patronymics*,
of one and the same person; but *Ramalochan*, my
own teacher, who though not a *Brahman* is an excellent scholar and a very sensible unprejudiced man,
assured me that *Buddha* was a *generic* word, like
Deva, and that the learned author, having exhibited
the names of a *Devata* in genearl, proceeded to those
of a *Buddha* in general, before he came to particulars:
he added, that *Buddha* might mean a *Sage* or *Philosopher*, though *Budha* was the word commonly used
for a mere *wise man* without supernatural powers.
It seems highly probable, on the whole, that the
Buddha, whom *Jayadeva* celebrates in his Hymn, was
the *Sacyasinha*, or *Lion of Sacya*, who, though he forbade the sacrifices of cattle, which the *Vedas* enjoin,
was believed to be *Vishnu* himself in a human form,
and that another *Buddha*, one perhaps of his followers
in a later age, assuming his name and character, attempted to overset the whole system of the *Brahmans*,
and was the cause of that persecution, from which
the *Bauddhas* are known to have fled into very distant
regions. May we not reconcile the singular difference
of opinion among the *Hindus* as to the time of *Buddha's* appearance, by supposing that they have confounded the *two Buddhas*, the first of whom was born
a few years before the close of the last age, and the
second, when above a thousand years of the present
age had elapsed ? We know from better authorities,
and with as much certainty as can justly be expected
on so doubtful a subject, the real time, compared
with our own æra, when the ancient *Buddha* began to

distinguish himself; and it is for this reason principally that I have dwelt with minute anxiety on the subject of the last *Avatar*.

The *Brahmans*, who assisted *Abulfazl* in his curious but superficial account of his master's empire, informed him, if the figures in the *Ayini Acbari* be correctly written, that a period of 2962 years had elapsed from the birth of *Buddha* to the 40th year of *Acbar's* reign; which computation will place his birth in the 1366th year before that of our Saviour; but, when the *Chinese* government admitted a new religion from *India* in the first century of our æra, they made particular inquiries concerning the age of the old *Indian Buddha*, whose birth, according to *Couplet*, they place in the 41st year of their 28th cycle, or 1036 years before *Christ*; and they call him, says he, *Foe*, the son of *Moye* or *Maya*; but M. *De Guignes*, on the authority of four *Chinese* historians asserts, that *Fo* was born about the year before *Christ* 1027, in the kingdom of *Cashmir*. *Giorgi*, or rather *Cassiano*, from whose papers his work was compiled, assures us, that, by the calculation of the *Tibetians*, he appeared only 959 years before the *Christian* epoch; and M. *Bailly*, with some hesitation, places him 1031 before it, but inclines to think him far more ancient, confounding him, as I have done in a former tract, with the *first Buddha*, or *Mercury*, whom the *Goths* called *Woden*, and of whom I shall presently take particular notice. Now, whether we assume the medium of the four last-mentioned dates, or implicitly rely on the authorities quoted by *De Guignes*, we may conclude, that *Buddha* was first distinguished in this country *about a thousand* years before the beginning of our æra; and whoever, in so early an age, expects a certain epoch unqualified with *about* or *nearly*, will be greatly disappointed. Hence it is clear, that, whe-

ther the fourth age of the *Hindus* began about *one*
thousand years before *Christ*, according to *Gover-
dhan's* account of *Buddha's* birth, or *two* thousand,
according to that of *Radhacant*, the common opinion
that 4888 years of it are now elapsed, is erroneous;
and here for the present we leave *Buddha*, with an
intention of returning to him in due time; observing
only, that if the learned *Indians* differ so widely in
their accounts of the age, when their ninth *Avatar*
appeared in their country, we may be assured that they
have no certain chronology before him, and may
suspect the certainty of all the relations concerning
even *his* appearance.

The received chronology of the *Hindus* begins
with an absurdity so monstrous, as to overthrow the
whole system; for, having established their period of
seventy one divine ages as the reign of each *Menu*, yet
thinking it incongruous to place a holy personage in
times of *impurity*, they insist that the *Menu* reigns
only in every *golden* age, and disappears in the *three
human ages* that follow it, continuing to dive and
emerge like a water-fowl, till the close of his *Manwantara*. The learned author of the *Puranart'hapra-
casa*, which I will now follow step by step, mentioned this ridiculous opinion with a serious face; but,
as he has not inserted it in his work, we may take his
account of the seventh *Menu* according to its obvious
and rational meaning, and suppose that *Vaivaswata*,
the son of *Surya*, the son of *Casyapa*, or *Uranus*, the
son of *Marichi*, or *Light*; the son of *Brahma*, which
is clearly an allegorical pedigree, reigned in the last
golden age, or, according to the *Hindus*, three million eight hundred and ninety-two thousand eight
hundred and eighty eight years ago. But they contend that he actually reigned on earth *one million seven
hundred and twenty-eight thousand* years of mortals, or

four thousand eight hundred years of the Gods; and this opinion is another monster so repugnant to the course of nature and to human reason, that it must be rejected as wholly fabulous, and taken as a proof, that the *Indians* know nothing of their *sun-born Menu* but his name and the principal event of his life; I mean the *universal deluge*, of which the *three* first *Avatars* are merely allegorical representations, with a mixture, especially in the *second*, of astronomical mythology.

From this *Menu* the whole race of men is believed to have descended; for the seven *Rishis*, who were preserved with him in the ark, are not mentioned as fathers of human families; but, since his daughter *Ila* was married, as the *Indians* tell us, to the first *Buddha*, or *Mercury*, the son of *Chandra*, or the *Moon*, a male deity, whose father was *Atri*, son of *Brahma*, (where again we meet with an allegory purely astronomical or poetical) his posterity are divided into two great branches, called the *Children of the Sun*, from his own supposed father, and the *Children of the Moon*, from the parent of his daughter's husband. The lineal male descendants in both these families are supposed to have reigned in the cities of *Ayodhya*, or *Audh*, and *Pratisht'hana*, or *Vitora*, respectively till the *thousandth year of the present age*, and the names of all the princes in both lines having been diligently collected by *Radhacant* from several *Puranas*, I exhibit them in two columns, arranged by myself with great attention.

SECOND AGE.

CHILDREN OF THE

SUN.	MOON.	
Icshwacu,	Budha,	
Vicucshi	Pururavas,	
Cucutst'ha,	Ayush,	
Aneas,	Nabusha,	
5. Prit'hu	Jayati,	5.
Viswagandhi,	Puru,	
Chandra,	Janamejaya	
Yuvanaswa,	Prachinwat,	
Srava,	Pravira,	
10. Vribadaswa,	Menasyu,	10.
Dhundhumara	Charupada,	
Drid'haswa,	Sudyu,	
Heryaswa,	Bahugava,	
Nicumbha,	Sanyati,	
15. Crisaswa,	Ahanyati,	15.
Senajit,	Raudraswa,	
Yuvanaswa,	Riteyush,	
Mandhatri,	Rantinava,	
Purucutsa	Sumati,	
20. Trasadasyu,	Aiti	20.
Anaranya,	Dushmanta,	
Heryaswa,	Bharata, *	
Praruna,	(Vitat'ha,	

CHILDREN OF THE

SUN.	MOON.	
Trivindhana,	Manyu,	
25. Satyavrata,	Vrihatcshetra,	25.
Trisancu,	Hastin,	
Harischandra,	Ajamid'ha,	
Rohita,	Ricsha,	
Harita,	Samwarana,	
30. Champa,	*Curu*,	30.
Sudeva,	*Juhnu*,	
Vijaya,	Surat'ha,	
Bharuca,	Vidurat'ha,	
Vrica,	Sarvabhauma,	
35. Babuca,	Jayatsena,	35.
Sagara,	Radhica,	
Asamanjas,	Ayutayush,	
Ansumat,	Acrodhana,	
Bhagirat'ha,	Devatit'hi,	
40. Sruta,	Ricsha,	40.
Nabha,	*Dilipa*,	
Sindhudwipa,	Pratipa,	
Ayutayush,	Santanu,	
Ritaperna,	*Vichitravirya*,	
45. Saudasa,	Pandu,	45.
Asmaca	*Yudhisht'hir*)	
Mulaca,		
Dasarat'ha,		

CHILDREN OF THE

SUN.   MOON.

Aidabidi,
50. Viswasaha,
C'hatwanga,
Dirghabahu,.
Raghu,
Aja,
55. *Dasarat'ha,*
Rama.

It is agreed among all the *Pandits,* that *Rama,*
their *seventh* incarnate Divinity, appeared as king
of *Ayodhya* in the *interval* between the *silver* and
the *brazen* ages; and, if we suppose him to have
began his reign at the very beginning of that interval,
still *three thousand three hundred* years of the Gods,
or *a million one hundred and eighty-eight thousand*
lunar years of mortals will remain in the *silver* age,
during which the *fifty-five* princes between *Vaivaswata* and *Rama* must have governed the world; but,
reckoning *thirty* years for a generation, which is rather too much for a long succession of *eldest* sons,
as they are said to have been, we cannot, by the
course of nature, extend the *second* age of the *Hindus* beyond *sixteen hundred and fifty* solar years. If we
suppose them not to have been eldest sons, and even
to have lived longer than modern princes in a dissolu-
lute age, we shall find only a period of *two thousand*
years; and, if we remove the difficulty by admitting
miracles, we must cease to reason, and may as well
believe at once whatever the *Brahmans* chuse to tell
us.

In the *lunar* pedigree we meet with another absurdity equally fatal to the credit of the *Hindu* system. As far as the twenty-second degree of descent from *Vaivaswata*, the synchronism of the two families appears tolerably regular, except that the Children of the Moon were not all *eldest* sons; for king *Yayati* appointed the youngest of his five sons to succeed him in *India*, and allotted inferior kingdoms to the other four, who had offended him; part of the *dacshin*, or the *south*, to *Yadu*, the ancestor of *Crishna*; the north to *Anu*, the east to *Druhya*, and the west to *Turvasu*, from whom the *Pandits* believe, or pretend to believe, in compliment to our nation, that we are descended. But of the subsequent degrees in the lunar line they know so little, that, unable to supply a considerable interval between *Bharat* and *Vitat'ha*, whom they call son and successor, they are under a necessity of asserting, that the great ancestor of *Yudhisht'hir* actually reigned *seven-and-twenty thousand years*; a fable of the same class with that of his wonderful birth, which is the subject of a beautiful *Indian* drama. Now, if we suppose his life to have lasted no longer than that of other mortals, and admit *Vitat'ha* and the rest to have been his regular successors, we shall fall into another absurdity; for then, if the generations in both lines were nearly equal, as they would naturally have been, we shall find *Yudhisht'hir*, who reigned confessedly at the close of the *brazen* age, nine generations older than *Rama*, before whose birth the *silver* age is allowed to have ended. After the name of *Bharat*, therefore, I have set an asterisk, to denote a considerable chasm in the *Indian* history, and have inserted between brackets, as out of their places, his *twenty-four* successors, who reigned, if at all, in the following age, immediately before the war of the *Mahabharat*. The fourth *Avatar*, which is placed in the interval between the *first* and *second* ages, and the

K 2

fifth which soon followed it, appear to be moral fables grounded on historical facts. The *fourth* was the punishment of an impious monarch, by the Deity himself *bursting from a marble column* in the shape of a *lion*; and the *fifth* was the humiliation of an arrogant prince, by so contemptible an agent as a mendicant *dwarf.* After these, and immediately before *Buddha,* come three great warriors, all named *Rama*; but it may justly be made a question, whether they are not three representations of one person, or three different ways of relating the same history. The first and second *Ramas* are said to have been contemporary; but whether all or any of them mean *Rama,* the son of *Cush,* I leave others to determine. The mother of the second *Rama* was named *Caushalya,* which is a derivative of *Cushala,* and, though his father be distinguished by the title or epithet of *Dasarat'ha,* signifying that *his war-chariot bore him to all quarters of the world*; yet the name of *Cush,* as the *Cashmirians* pronounce it, is preserved entire in that of his son and successor, and shadowed in that of his ancestor *Ticurshi*; nor can a just objection be made to this opinion from the nasal *Arabian* vowel in the word *Rumah,* mentioned by *Moses,* since the very word *Arab* begins with the same letter, which the *Greeks* and *Indians* could not pronounce; and they were obliged, therefore, to express it by the vowel which most resembled it. On this question, however, I assert nothing; nor on another, which might be proposed: " Whether the " *fourth* and *fifth Avatars* be not allegorical stories " of the two presumptuous monarchs, *Nimrod* and " *Belus ?*" The hypothesis, that *government* was first established, *laws* enacted, and *agriculture* encouraged in *India* by *Rama* about *three thousand eight hundred* years ago, agrees with the received account of *Noah's* death, and the previous settlement of his immediate descendants.

THIRD AGE.

CHILDREN OF THE

SUN.	MOON.
Cusha,	
Atit'hi,	
Nishadha,	
Nabhas,	
5. Pundarica,	
Cshemadhanwas,	Vitat'ha,
Devanica,	Manyu,
Ahinagu,	Vrihatcshetra,
Paripatra,	Hastin,
10. Ranach'hala.	Ajamid'ha, 5.
Vajranabha,	Ricsha,
Arca,	Samwarana,
Sugana,	Curu,
Vidhriti,	Juhnu,
15. Hiranyanabha,	Surat'ha,
Pushya,	Vidurat'ha,
Dhruvasandhi,	Sarvabhauma,
Sudersana,	Jayatsena,
Agniverna,	Radhica,
20 Sighra,	Ayutayush, 15.
Maru, supposed to	Acrodhana,
be still alive,	
Prasusruta,	Devatit'hi,
Sandhi,	Ricsha,

K 3

CHILDREN OF THE

S U N.	M O O N.	
Amersana,	Dilipa,	
25. Mahaswat,	Pratipa,	20.
Viswabhalu,	Santanu,	
Prasenajit,	Vichitravirya,	
Tacshaca,	Pandu,	
Vrihadbala,	*Yudhisht'hira*,	
30. Vrihadrana, Y. B. C.	Paricshit,	25.
. 3100.		

Here we have only *nine*-and-*twenty* princes of the
solar line between *Rama* and *Vrihadrana* exclusively ;
and their reigns, during the whole *brazen* age, are
supposed to have lasted near *eight hundred* and *sixty-
four thousand* years : a supposition evidently against
nature, the uniform course of which allows only a
period of *eight hundred* and *seventy*, or, at the very
utmost, of *a thousand*, years for *twenty-nine* generations. *Paricshit*, the great nephew and successor
of *Yudhisht'hir*, who had recovered the throne from
Duryodhan, is allowed without controversy to have
reigned in the interval between the *brazen* and *earthen*
ages, and to have died at the setting in of the
Caliyug ; so that, if the *Pandits* of *Cashmir* and *Varanes* have made a right calculation of *Buddha's* appearance, the present, or *fourth*, age must have begun about *a thousand* years before the birth of *Christ*,
and consequently the reign of *Icshwacu*, could not
have been earlier than *four thousand* years before that
great epoch ; and even that date will, perhaps, appear, when it shall be strictly examined, to be near
two thousand years earlier than the truth. I cannot
leave the third *Indian* age, in which the virtues and
vices of mankind are said to have been equal, with-

ont observing, that even the close of it is manifestly fabulous and poetical, with hardly more *appearance* of historical truth than the tale of *Troy*, or of the *Argonauts*; for. *Yudhisht'hir*, it seems, was the son of *Dherma*, the *Genius of Justice*; *Bhima* of *Pavan*, or the *God of Wind*; *Arjun* of *Indra*, or the *Firmament*; *Nacul* and *Sahadeva*, of the two *Cranars*, the *Castor* and *Pollus* of *India*; and *Bhishmu*, their reputed great uncle, was the child of *Gangu*, or the *Ganges*, by *Santanu*, whose brother *Devapi* is supposed to be still alive in the city of *Calapa*; all which fictions may be charming embellishments of an heroic poem, but are just as absurd in civil history as the descent of two royal families from the Sun and the Moon.

FOURTH AGE.

CHILDREN OF THE

SUN.	MOON.	
Urucriya,	*Janamejaya*,	
Vatsavriddha,	*Satanica*,	
Prativyoma,	Sahasranica,	
Bhanu,	Aswamedhaja,	
5. Devaca,	Asimacrishna,	5.
Sahadeva,	Nemichacra,	
Vira,	Upta,	
Vrihadaswa,	Chitrarat'ha,	
Bhanumat,	Suchirat'ba,	
10. Praticaswa,	Dhritimat,	10.
Supratica,	Sushena,	

K 4

CHILDREN OF THE

SUN.	MOON.	
Marudeva,	Sunit'ha,	
Sunacshatra.	Nrichacshuh,	
Pushcara,	Suc'hinala,	
15. Antaricsha,	Pariplava,	15.
Sutapas,	Sunaya,	
Amitrajit,	Medhavin,	
Vrihadraja,	Nripanjaya,	
Barhi,	Derva,	
20. Critanjaya,	Timi,	20.
Rananjaya,	Vrihadrat'ha,	
Sanjaya,	Sudasa,	
Slocya,	Satanica,	
Suddhoda,	Durmadana,	
25. Langalada,	Rahinara,	25.
Prasenajit,	Dandapani,	
Cshudraca,	Nimi,	
Sumitra, Y. B. C.	Cshemaca.	
2100.		

In both families, we see, *thirty* generations are reckoned from *Yudhisht'hir*, and from *Vrihadbala* his contemporary (who was killed in the war of *Bharat* by *Abhimanyu*, son of *Arjun* and father of *Paricshit*), to the time when the *solar* and *lunar* dynasties are believed to have become extinct in the present divine age; and for these generations the *Hindus* allot a period of *one thousand* years only, or a *hundred* years for *three* generations; which calculation, though pro-

bably too large, is yet moderate enough, compared
with their absurd accounts of the preceding ages;
but they reckon exactly the same number of years for
twenty generations only in the family of *Jarasandha*,
whose son was contemporary with *Yudhisht'hir*, and
founded a new dynasty of princes in *Magadha*, or
Bahar; and this exact coincidence of the times, in
which the three races are supposed to have been extinct, has the appearance of an artificial chronology,
formed rather from imagination than from historical
evidence, especially as twenty kings, in an age comparatively modern, could not have reigned a thousand years. I, nevertheless, exhibit the list of them
as a curiosity, but am far from being convinced that
all of them ever existed; that, if they did exist, they
could not have reigned more than *seven hundred years*,
I am fully persuaded by the course of nature and the
concurrent opinion of mankind.

KINGS of MAGADHA.

Sahadeva,	Suchi,
Marjari,	Cshema,
Srutasravas,	Suvrata,
Ayutayush,	Dhermasutra,
5. Niramitra,	Srama, 15.
Sunacshatra,	Drid'hasena,
Vrihetsena,	Sumati,
Carmajit,	Subala,
Srutanjaya,	Sunita,
10. Vipra,	Satyajit. 20.

Puranjaya, son of the twentieth king, was put to
death by his minister, *Sunaca*, who placed his own
son *Pradyota* on the throne of his master; and this

revolution constitutes an epoch of the highest importance in our present enquiry; first, because it happened according to the *Bhagawatamrita*, two years exactly before *Buddha*'s appearance in the same kingdom; next, because it is believed by the *Hindus* to have taken place *three thousand eight hundred and eighty-eight* years ago, or *two thousand one hundred* years before *Christ*; and lastly, because a regular chronology, according to the number of years in each dynasty, has been established from the accession of *Pradyota* to the subversion of the genuine *Hindu* government; and that chronology I will now lay before you, after observing only, that *Radhacant* himself says nothing of *Buddha* in this part of his work, though he particularly mentions the two preceding *Avataras* in their proper places.

KINGS of MAGADHA.

	Y. B. C.
Pradyota,	2100
Palaca,	
Visac'hayupa,	
Rajaca,	
Nandiverdhana, 5 reigns = 138 years.	

Sisunaga,	
Cacaverna,	1962
Cshemadherman,	
Cshetrajnya.	
Vidhisara 5.	
Ajatasatru,	
Darbhaca.	

KINGS of MAGADHA.

Y. B. C.

Ajaya
Nandiverdhana
Mahanandi,   10 r. = 360 y.

Nanda,   1602

This prince, of whom frequent mention is made in the *Sanscrit* books, is said to have been murdered, after a reign of *a hundred years*, by a very learned and ingenious, but passionate and vindictive, *Brahman*, whose name was *Chanacya*, and who raised to the throne a man of the *Maurya* race, named *Chandragupta*. By the death of *Nanda*, and his sons, the *Cshatrya* family of *Pradyota* became extinct.

MAURYA KINGS.

Y. B. C.

Chandragupta,   1502
Varisara,
Asocaverdhana
Suyasas,
Desarat'ha,   5.
Sangata,
Salisuca,
Somasarman,
Satadhanwas,
Vrihadrat'ha,   10 r. = 137 y.

On the death of the tenth *Maurya* king, his place was assumed by his commander in chief, *Pushpami-tra*, of the *Sunga* nation or family.

SUNGA KINGS.

		Y. B. C.
Pushpamitra,		1365
Agnimitra,		
Sujyesht'ha,		
Vasumitra,		
Abhadraca,	5.	
Pulinda,		
Ghosha,		
Vajramitra,		
Bhagavata,		
Devabhuti,	10 *r.* = 112 *y.*	

The last prince was killed by his minister *Vasu-deva*, of the *Canna* race, who usurped the throne of *Magadha*.

CANNA KINGS.

		Y. B. C.
Vasudeva,		1253.
Bhumitra,		
Narayana,		
Susarman,	4 *r.* = 345 *y.*	

A *Sudra*, of the *Andhra* family, having murdered his master *Susarman*, and seized the government, founded a new dynasty of

ANDHRA KINGS.

		Y. B. C.
Balin,		908
Crishna,		
Srisantacarna,		
Paurnamasa,		
Lambodara,	5.	
Vivilaca,		
Meghaswata,		
Vatamana,		
Talaca,		
Sivaswati,	10.	
Purisbabheru,		
Sunandana,		
Chacoraca,		
Bataca,		
Gomatin	15.	
Purimat,		
Medasiras,		
Sirascand'ha,		
Yajnyasri,		
Vijaya,	20.	
Chandrabija,	21 r = 456 y.	

After the death of *Chandrabija*, which happened, according to the *Hindus*, 396 years before *Vicramáditya*, or 452 B. C. we hear no more of *Magadha* as an independent kingdom ; but . *Radhacant* has exhibited the names of *seven* dynasties, in which *seventy-six* princes are said to have reigned *one thousand three hundred and ninety-nine years* in *Avabhriti*, a town of the *Dacshin*, or *South*, which we commonly call *Decan*. The names of the seven dynasties, or of the families who established them, are *Abhira, Gardabhin, Canca, Yavana, Turushcara, Bhurunda, Maula*; of which the *Yavanas* are by some, not generally, supposed to have been *Ionians* or *Greeks*, but the *Turushcaras* and *Maulas* are universally believed to have been *Turcs* and *Moguls*; yet *Radhacant* adds, " when " the *Maula* race was extinct, five princes, named *Bhu-* " *nanda Bangira, Sisunandi, Yasonandi*, and *Pravi-* " *raca* reigned *an hundred and six years* (or till the year " 1053) in the city of *Cilacila*," which he tells me, he understands to be in the country of the *Maharash-tras*, or *Mahrattas*; and here ends his *Indian* chronology ; for " after *Praviraca*," says he, " this empire " was divided among *Mlech'has*, or Infidels." This account of the *seven modern dynasties* appears very doubtful in itself, and has no relation to our present inquiry ; for their dominion seems confined to the *Decan*, without extending to *Magadha* ; nor have we any reason to believe that a race of *Grecian* princes ever established a kingdom in either of those countries. As to the *Moguls*, their dynasty still subsists at least nominally, unless that of *Chengiz* be meant ; and his successors could not have reigned in any part of *India* for the period of *three hundred* years, which is assigned to the *Maulas* ; nor is it probable that the word *Turc*, which an *Indian* could have easily pronounced and clearly expressed in the *Nagari* letters, should have been corrupted into *Turushcara*. On the whole, we may safely close the most authentic

system of *Hindu* Chronology that I have yet been
able to procure, with the death of *Chandrabija*. Should
any farther information be attainable, we shall, perhaps, in due time attain it either from books or inscriptions in the *Sanscrit* language ; but from the materials
with which we are at present supplied, we may establish as indubitable the two following propositions :
That the *three first* ages of the *Hindus* are chiefly *mythological*, whether their mythology was founded on
the dark enigmas of their astronomers, or on the heroic
fictions of their poets ; and that the *fourth*, or *historical* age, cannot be carried farther back than about two
thousand years before *Christ*. Even in the history of
the present age, the generations of men and the reigns
of kings, are extended beyond the course of nature,
and beyond the average resulting from the accounts of
the *Brahmans* themselves ; for they assign to *an hundred and forty-two* modern reigns a period of *three
thousand one hundred and fifty-three* years, or about
twenty-two years to a reign one with another; yet they
represent only four *Cunna* princes on the throne of
Magadha for a period of *three hundred* and *forty-five*
years ; now it is even more improbable that four successive kings should have reigned *eighty-six years and
three months* each, than that *Nanda* should have been
king a *hundred* years, and murdered at last. Neither
account can be credited ; but, that we may allow the
highest probable antiquity to the *Hindu* government,
let us grant that *three generations* of men were equal
on an average to *an hundred* years, and that *Indian*
princes have reigned, one with another, *two-and-
twenty*: then reckoning thirty generations from *Arjun*,
the brother of *Yudhist'hira*, to the extinction of his
race, and taking the *Chinese* account of *Buddha*'s birth
from M. *De Guignes*. as the most authentic medium
between *Abulfazl* and the *Tibetians*, we may arrange
the corrected *Hindu* Chronology according to the fol-

lowing table, supplying the word *about* or *nearly* (since
perfect accuracy cannot be obtained, and ought not to
be required) before every date.

	Y. B. C.
Abhimanyu, *son of Arjun*,	2029
Pradyota,	1029
Buddha,	1027
Nanda,	699
Balin,	149
Vicramaditya,	56
Devapala, king of Gaur,	23

If we take the date of *Buddha*'s appearance from
Abu'lfazl, we must place *Abhimanyu* 2368 years before *Christ*, unless we calculate from the twenty kings
of *Magadha*, and allow *seven hundred* years, instead
of *a thousand*, between *Arjun* and *Pradyota*, which
will bring us again very nearly to the date exhibited
in the table; and, perhaps, we can hardly approach
nearer to the truth. As to *Raja Nanda*, if he
really sat on the throne a whole century, we must
bring down the *Andhra* dynasty to the age of *Vicramaditya*, who with his feudatories had probably obtained so much power during the reign of those princes,
that they had little more than a nominal sovereignty,
which ended with *Chandrabija* in the *third* or *fourth*
century of the *Christian* æra; having, no doubt,
been long reduced to insignificance by the kings of
Gaur, descended from *Gopala*. But, if the author of
the *Dabistan* be warranted in fixing the birth of
Buddha ten years before the *Caliyug*, we must thus
correct the Chronological Table:

Y. B. C.

Buddha,	—	1027
Paricshit,	—	1017
Pradyota (reckoning 20 *or* 30 generations)	}	317 *or* 17

Y. A. C.

Nanda,	—	13 *or* 313

This correction would oblige us to place *Vicramaditya* before *Nanda*, to whom, as all the *Pundits* agree, he was long posterior; and, if this be an historical fact, it seems to confirm the *Bhagawatamrita*, which fixes the beginning of the *Caliyug* about *a thousand years before Buddha*; besides that *Balin* would then be brought down at least to the sixth and *Chundrabija* to the tenth century after *Christ*, without leaving room for the subsequent dynasties, if they reigned successively.

Thus have we given a sketch of *Indian* history through the longest period fairly assignable to it, and have traced the foundation of the *Indian* empire above *three thousand eight hundred years* from the present time; but, on a subject in itself so obscure, and so much clouded by the fictions of the *Brahmans*, who, to aggrandize themselves, have designedly raised their antiquity beyond the truth, we must be satisfied with probable conjecture and just reasoning from the best attainable data; nor can we hope for a system of *Indian* Chronology, to which no objection can be made, unless the astronomical books in *Sanscrit* shall clearly ascertain the places of the colures in some precise years of the historical age, not by loose traditions, like that of a coarse observation by

Chiron, who possibly never existed (for " he lived," says *Newton,* " in the *golden* age," which must long have preceded the *Argonautic* expedition) but by such evidence as our own astronomers and scholars shall allow to be unexceptionable.

A CHRONOLOGICAL TABLE,

according to one of the Hypotheses intimated in the preceding Tract.

CHRISTIAN AND MUSELMAN.	HINDU.	Years from 1788 of our æra.
Adam,	*Menu* I. Age I.	5794
Noah,	*Menu* II:	4737
Deluge,	— —	4138
Nimrod,	*Hiranyacaśipu.* Age II.	4006
Bel,	*Bali,*	3892
Rama,	*Rama.* Age III.	3817
Noah's death,	— —	3787
	Pradyota,	2817
	Buddha. Age IV.	2815
	Nanda,	2487
	Balin,	1937
	Vicramaditya,	1844
	Devapala,	1811
Christ,	— —	1787
	Narayanpala,	1721
	Saca,	1709
Walid,	— —	1080
Mahmud,	— —	786
Chengiz,	— —	548
Taimur,	— —	391
Babur,	— —	276
Nadirshah,	— —	49

L 2

VIII.

ON THE CURE OF THE ELEPHANTIASIS.

BY AT'HAR ALI KHAN OF DEHLI.

INTRODUCTORY NOTE.

AMONG the afflicting maladies which punish the vices and try the virtues of mankind, there are few disorders of which the consequences are more dreadful or the remedy in general more desperate than the *judham* of the *Arabs*, or *khorah* of the *Indians*. It is also called in *Arabia daul'asad:* a name corresponding with the *Leontiasis* of the *Greeks*, and supposed to have been given in allusion to the grim distracted and *lion-like* countenances of the miserable persons who are affected with it. The more common name of the distemper is *Elephantiasis*, or, as *Lucretius* calls it, *Elephas*, because it renders the skin, like that of an *Elephant*, uneven and wrinkled, with many tubercles and furrows ; but this complaint must not be confounded with the *daul'fil*, or *swelled legs*, described by the *Arabian* physicians, and very common in this country. It has no fixed name in *English*, though *Hillary*, in his *Observations on the Diseases of Barbadoes*, calls it the *Leprosy of the joints*, because it principally affects the extremities, which in the last stage of the malady are distorted, and at length drop off; but, since it is in truth a distemper corrupting the whole mass of blood, and therefore considered by *Paul* of *Ægina* as an *universal ulcer*, it requires a more general appellation, and may properly be named the *Black Leprosy :* which term is in fact adopted by M. *Boissieu de Sauvages* and *Gorræus*, in contradistinction to the *White*

L 3

Leprosy, or the *Beres* of the *Arabs* and *Leuce* of the *Greeks*.

This disease, by whatever name we distinguish it, is peculiar to hot climates, and has rarely appeared in *Europe*. The philosophical poet of *Rome* supposes it confined to *the Banks of the Nile*; and it has certainly been imported from *Africa* into the *West India* islands by the black slaves, who carried with them their resentment and their revenge; but it has been long known in *Hindustan:* and the writer of the following Dissertation, whose father was physician to *Nadirshah* and accompanied him from *Persia* to *Dehli*, assures me that it rages with virulence among the native inhabitants of *Calcutta* His observation, that it is frequently a consequence of the *venereal infection*, would lead us to believe that it might be radically cured by *mercury*; which has, nevertheless, been found ineffectual, and even hurtful, as *Hillary* reports, in the *West Indies*. The juice of *hemlock*, suggested by the learned *Michaelis*, and approved by his medical friend *Roederer*, might be very efficacious at the beginning of the disorder, or in the milder sorts of it; but, in the case of a malignant and inveterate *judham*, we must either administer a remedy of the highest power, or, agreeably to the desponding opinion of *Celsus*, *leave the patient to his fate*, *instead of teasing him with fruitless medicines*, and suffer him, in the forcible words of *Aretæus*, *to sink from inextricable slumber into death*. The life of a man is, however, so dear to him by nature, and in general so valuable to society, that we should never despond while a spark of it remains; and, whatever apprehensions may be formed of future danger from the distant effects of *arsenic*, even though it should eradicate a present malady, yet, as no such inconvenience has arisen from the use of it in *India*, and as experience

must ever prevail over theory, I cannot help wishing
that this ancient *Hindu* medicine may be fully tried
under the inspection of our *European* surgeons,
whose minute accuracy and steady attention must
always give them a claim to superiority over the
most learned natives ; but many of our countrymen
have assured me, that they by no means entertain a
contemptuous opinion of the native medicines, especially in diseases of the skin. Should it be thought
that the mixture of sulphur must render the poison
less active, it may be adviseable at first to administer
orpiment, instead of the *crystalline arsenic.*

ON THE CURE OF THE ELEPHANTIASIS,
AND OTHER DISORDERS OF THE BLOOD.

GOD IS THE ALL-POWERFUL HEALER.

IN the year of the *Messiah* 1783, when the worthy and respectable *Maulavi Mir Muhammed Husain*, who excels in every branch of useful knowledge, accompanied Mr. *Richard Johnson* from *Luc'hnau* to *Calcutta*, he visited the humble writer of this tract, who had long been attached to him with sincere affection; and, in the course of their conversation, ‘ One of the fruits of my late excursion,’ said he, ‘ is a present for you, which suits your profession, ‘ and will be generally useful to our species. Conceiv- ‘ ing you to be worthy of it, by reason of your assi- ‘ duity in medical inquiries, I have brought you a pre- ‘ scription, the ingredients of which are easily found, ‘ but not easily equalled as a powerful remedy against ‘ all corruptions of the blood, the *judham*, and the ‘ *Persian* fire, the remains of which are a source of ‘ infinite maladies. It is an old secret of the *Hindu* ‘ physicians, who applied it also to the cure of cold ‘ and moist distempers; as the palsy, distortions of the ‘ face, relaxation of the nerves, and similar diseases. ‘ Its efficacy too has been proved by long experience; ‘ and this is the method of preparing it :—

‘ Take of white *arsenic*, fine and fresh, one *tola*; ‘ of picked black pepper six times as much : let both ‘ be well beaten at intervals for four days successively ‘ in an iron mortar, and then reduced to an impalpa-

' ble powder in one of stone with a stone pestle, and
' thus co.npletely levigated, a little water being mixed
' with them. Make pills of them as large as tares
' or small pulse, and keep them dry in a shady
' place *.

' One of those pills must be swallowed morning
' and evening with some betel-leaf, or, in countries
' where betel is not at hand, with cold water. If the
' body be cleansed from foulness and obstructions by
' gentle cathartics and bleeding before the medicine
' is administered, the remedy will be speedier.'

The principal ingredient of this medicine is the
arsenic, which the *Arabs* call *Shuce*; the *Persians*
mergi mush, or mouse-bane; and the *Indians*, sanc'hya:
a mineral substance ponderous and *crystalline*. The
orpiment, or *yellow* arsenic, is the weaker sort. It is
deadly poison, and so subtil, that, when mice are
killed by it, the very smell of the dead will destroy
the living of that species. After it has been kept about

---

* The lowest weight in general use among the *Hindus* is the
reti, called in *Sanscrit* either *rettica* or *ractica*, indicating redness;
and *crishnala*, from *crishna*, black; it is the *red* and *black* seed
of the *ganja* plant, which is a creeper of the same class and
order at least with *glycyrrhiza*: but I take this from report,
having never examined its blossoms. One *rattica* is said to
be of equal weight with three barley-corns, or four grains
of rice in the husk; and eight *reti*-weights, used by jewellers,
are equal to seven carats. I have weighed a number of
the seeds in diamond-scales, and find the average Apothecary's
weight of one seed to be a grain and *five-sixteenths*. Now, in the
Hindu medical books, ten of the *rattica* seeds are one *mashaca*; and
eight *mashacas* make a *tolaca*, or *tola*; but in the law-books of
Bengal a *mashaca* consists of *sixteen racticas*, and a *tolaca* of *five*
mashas; and, according to some authorities, *five retis* only go
to one *masha*, *sixteen* of which make a *tolaca*. We may observe,
that the silver *reti*-weights, used by the goldsmiths at *Banares* are
twice as heavy as the *seeds*; and thence it is that *eight retis* are
commonly said to constitute one *masha*; that is, *eight silver weights*,
or *sixteen seeds*; *eighty* of which seeds, or 105 grains, constitute
the quantity of arsenic in the *Hindu* prescription.

seven years, it loses much of its force; its colour becomes turbid, and its weight is diminished. This mineral is hot and dry in the fourth degree: it causes suppuration, dissolves or unites, according to the quantity given, and is very useful in closing the lips of wounds when the pain is too intense to be borne. An unguent made of it with oils of any sort, is an effectual remedy for some cutaneous disorders; and, mixed with rose water, it is good for cold tumours, and for the dropsy; but it must never be administered without the greatest caution; for such is its power, that the smallest quantity of it in powder, drawn, like *alcohol*, between the eye-lashes, would in a single day entirely corrode the coats and humours of the eye; and fourteen *retis* of it would in the same time destroy life. The best antidote against its effects are the scrapings of leather reduced to ashes. If the quantity of arsenic taken be accurately known, four times as much of those ashes, mixed with water and drank by the patient, will sheath and counteract the poison.

The writer, conformably to the directions of his learned friend, prepared the medicine; and, in the same year, gave it to numbers, who were reduced by he diseases above mentioned to the point of death. *God* is his witness that they grew better from day to day, were at last completely cured, and are now living (except one or two, who died of other disorders) to attest the truth of this assertion. One of his first patients was a *Parsi*, named *Menuchehr*, who had come from *Surat* to this city, and had fixed his abode near the writer's house: he was so cruelly afflicted with a confirmed lues, here called *the Persian Fire*, that his hands and feet were entirely ulcerated and almost corroded, so that he became an object of disgust and abhorrence. This man consulted the writer on his case, the state of which he disclosed without re-

serve. Some blood was taken from him on the same
day, and a cathartic administered on the next. On
the third day he began to take the *arsenic-pills*, and,
by the blessing of *God*, the virulence of his disorder
abated by degrees, until signs of returning health appeared. In a fortnight his recovery was complete,
and he was bathed, according to the practice of our
physicians. He seemed to have no virus left in his
blood, and none has been since perceived by him.

But the power of this medicine has chiefly been
tried in the cure of the *Juzam*, as the word is pronounced in *India*; a disorder infecting the whole
mass of blood, and thence called by some *fisadi khun*.
The former name is derived from an *Arabic* root
signifying, in general, *amputation, maiming, excision*,
and, particularly, the *truncation* or *erosion of the fingers*, which happens in the last stage of the disease.
It is extremely contagious; and, for that reason, the
prophet, said, *Ferru mina'lmejdhumi cama teferru
mina'l asad*, or, ' Flee from a person afflicted with the
' *judham*, as you would flee from a lion.' The author
of the *Bahhru'ljawahir*, or *Sea of Pearls*, ranks it
as an infectious malady with the *measles*, the *small pox*,
and the *plague*. It is also *hereditary*, and, in that respect, classed by medical writers with the *gout*, the
consumption, and the *white leprosy*.

A common cause of this distemper is the unwholesome diet of the natives, many of whom are accus-
tomed, after eating a quantity of *fish*, to swallow
copious draughts of milk, which fail not to cause an
accumulation of yellow and black bile, which min-
gles itself with the blood and corrupts it: but it has
other causes; for a *Brahmen*, who had never tasted
fish in his life, applied lately to the composer of this
essay, and appeared in the highest degree affected by

a corruption of blood ; which he might have inherited, or acquired by other means. Those, whose religion permits them to eat *beef*, are often exposed to the danger of heating their blood intensely through the knavery of the butchers in the *Bazar*, who fatten their calves with *Balawer* ; and those who are so ill-advised as to take *provocatives* (a folly extremely common in *India*) at first are insensible of the mischief, but, as soon as the increased moisture is dispersed, find their whole mass of blood inflamed and, as it were, adust; whence arises the disorder of which we now are treating. The *Persian*, or venereal fire, generally ends in this malady ; as one *Devi Prasad*, lately in the service of Mr. *Vansittart*, and some others, have convinced me by an unreserved account of their several cases.

It may be here worth while to report a remarkable case, which was related to me by a man who had been afflicted with the *juzam* near four years ; before which time he had been disordered with the *Persian* fire, and, having closed an ulcer by the means of a strong healing plaister, was attacked by a violent pain in his joints. On this he applied to a *Cabiraju*, or *Hindu* physician, who gave him some pills, with a positive assurance, that the use of them would remove his pain in a few days ; and in a few days it was, in fact, wholly removed ; but, a very short time after, the symptoms of the *juzam* appeared, which continually encreased to such a degree, that his fingers and toes were on the point of dropping off. It was afterwards discovered, that the pills which he had taken were made of cinnabar, a common preparation of the *Hindus* ; the heat of which had first stirred the humours ; which, on stopping the external discharge, had fallen on the joints, and then had occasioned a quantity of adust bile to mix itself with the blood and infect the whole mass.

Of this dreadful complaint, however caused, the first symptoms are a numbness and redness of the whole body, and principally of the face, an impeded hoarse voice, thin hair and even baldness, offensive perspiration and breath, and whitlows on the nails. The cure is best begun with copious bleeding, and cooling drink, such as a decoction of the *nilufer*, or *Nymphea*, and of violets, with some doses of manna : after which stronger cathartics must be administered. But no remedy has proved so efficacious as the pills composed of arsenic and pepper : one instance of their effect may here be mentioned, and many more may be added, if required.

In the month of *February* in the year just mentioned, one *Shaikh Ramazani*, who then was an upper-servant to the Board of Revenue, had so corrupt a mass of blood, that a black leprosy of his joints was approaching ; and most of his limbs began to be ulcerated. In this condition he applied to the writer, and requested immediate assistance. Though the disordered state of his blood was evident on inspection, and required no particular declaration of it, yet many questions were put to him ; and it was clear, from his answers, that he had a confirmed *juzam* : he then lost a great deal of blood, and, after due preparation, took the arsenic-pills. After the first week his malady seemed alleviated ; in the second it was considerably diminished ; and, in the third, so entirely removed, that the patient went into the bath of health, as a token that he no longer needed a physician.

IX

ON THE INDIAN GAME OF CHESS.

BY THE PRESIDENT.

IF evidence be required to prove that chess was invented by the *Hindus*, we may be satisfied with the testimony of the *Persians*; who, though as much inclined as other nations to appropriate the ingenious inventions of a foreign people, unanimously agree, that the game was imported from the west of *India*, together with the charming fables of *Vishnusarman*, in the sixth century of our æra. It seems to have been immemorially known in *Hindustan* by the name of *Chaturanga*, that is, the four *angas*, or *members* of an army, which are said in the *Amaracosha* to be *hastyaswarat'hapadatam*, or *elephants, horses, chariots, and foot soldiers*; and in this sense the word is frequently used by epic poets in their descriptions of real armies. By a natural corruption of the pure *Sanscrit* word, it was changed by the old *Persians* into *Chatrang*; but the *Arabs*, who soon after took possession of their country, had neither the initial nor final letter of that word in their alphabet, and consequently altered it further into *Shatranj*, which found its way presently into the modern *Persian*, and at length into the dialects of *India*, where the true derivation of the name is known only to the learned. Thus has a very significant word in the sacred language of the *Brahmans* been transformed by successive changes into *axedrez, scacchi, echecs, chess*, and, by a whimsical concurrence of circumstances, given birth to the *English* word *check*; and even a name to the *Exchequer* of *Great Britain*. The beautiful simplicity and extreme perfection of the game, as it is

commonly played in *Europe* and *Asia*, convince me
that it was invented by one effort of some great genius; not completed by gradual improvements, but
formed, to use the phrase of *Italian* critics, *by the
first intention*; yet of this simple game, so exquisitely
contrived, and so certainly invented in *India*, I cannot
find any account in the classical writings of the *Brahmans*. It is, indeed, confidently asserted, that *Sanscrit* books on Chess exist in this country; and, if they
can be procured at *Banares*, they will assuredly be
sent to us. At present I can only exhibit a description of a very ancient *Indian* game of the same kind;
but more complex, and, in my opinion, more modern
than the simple Chess of the *Persians*. This game
is also called *Chaturanga*, but more frequently *Chaturaji*, or the *Four Kings*, since it is played by four
persons representing as many princes, two allied armies combating on each side. The description is taken
from the *Bhawishya Puran*, in which *Yudhisht'hir* is
represented conversing with *Vyasa*, who explains at
the king's request the form of the fictitious warfare
and the principal rules of it. " Having marked *eight*
" squares on all sides," says the sage, " place the *red*
" army to the east, the *green* to the south, the *yellow*
" to the west, and the *black* to the north : let the
" *elephant* stand on the left of the *king*; next to him,
" the *horse*; then the *boat*; and, before them all,
" four *foot-soldiers*; but the *boat* must be placed in
" the *angle* of the board." From this passage it
clearly appears, that an army, with its four *angas*,
must be placed on each side of the board, since an
elephant could not stand in any other position on the
left hand of each *king*; and *Radhacant* informed me,
that the board consisted, like ours, of *sixty-four*
squares, half of them occupied by the forces, and
half vacant. He added, that this game is mentioned
in the oldest law-books, and that it was invented by the
wife of *Ravan*, king of *Lanca*, in order to amuse him

with an image of war, while his metropolis was closely besieged by *Rama*, in the second age of the world. He had not heard the story told by *Firdausi*, near the close of the *Shahnamah*; and it was probably carried into *Persia* from *Canyacuvja*, by *Borzu* the favourite physician, thence called *Vaidyaprya*, of the, great *Anushiravan*; but he said that the *Brahmans* of *Gaur*, or *Bengal*, were once celebrated for superior skill in the game, and that his father, together with his spiritual preceptor *Jaganuat'h*, now living at *Tribeni*, had instructed two young *Brahmans* in all the rules of it, and had sent them to *Jayanagar* at the request of the late *Raja*, who had liberally rewarded them. A *ship* or *boat* is substituted, we see, in this complex game for the *rat'h*, or armed *chariot*, which the *Bengalese* pronounce *rot'h*, and which the *Persians* changed into *rokh*, whence came the *rook* of some *European* nations; as the *vierge* and *fol* of the *French* are supposed to be corruptions of *ferz* and *fil*, the *prime minister* and *elephant* of the *Persian* and *Arabs*. It were in vain to seek an etymology of the word *rook* in the modern *Persian* language; for, in all the passages extracted from *Firdausi* and *Jami*, where *rokh* is conceived to mean a *hero* or a *fabulous bird*, it signifies, I believe, no more than a *cheek* or a *face*; as in the following description of a procession in *Egypt*:—
" When a thousand youths, like cypresses, box-trees,
" and firs, with locks as fragrant, cheeks as fair, and
" bosoms as delicate as lilies of the valley, were
" marching gracefully along, thou wouldst have said
" that the new spring was *turning his face* (not, as
Hyde translates the words, *carried on rokhs*) from
" station to station." And as to the battle of the *du-wazdeh rakh*, which *D'Herbelot* supposes to mean *douze preux chevaliers*, I am strongly inclined to think that the phrase only signifies a combat of *twelve persons face to face*, or six on a side. I cannot agree with my friend *Radhacant*, that a *ship* is properly introduced

in this imaginary warfare instead of a *chariot*, in which
the old *Indian* warriors constantly fought ; for, though
the *king* might be supposed to sit in a car, so that
the four *angas* would be complete, and though it may
often be necessary in a real campaign to pass rivers or
lakes, yet no river is marked on the *Indian*, as it is
on the *Chinese* chess-board ; and the intermixture of
ships with horses, elephants, and infantry embattled on
a plain, is an absurdity not to be defended.   The use
of *dice* may, perhaps, be justified in a representation of war, in which *fortune* has unquestionably a
great share ; but it seems to exclude chess from the rank
which has been assigned to it among the sciences, and
to give the game before us the appearance of *whist*,
except that pieces are used openly, instead of cards
which are held concealed : nevertheless, we find that
the moves in the game described by *Vyasa* were to a
certain degree regulated by *chance*; for he proceeds to
tell his royal pupil, that, " if *cinque* be thrown, the
" *king* or a *pawn* must be moved; if *quatre*, the
" *elephant* ; if *trois*, the *horse* ; and if *deux*, the *boat*."

He then proceeds to the moves : " The *king* passes
" freely on all sides, but over *one* square only ; and
" with the same limitation, the *pawn* moves, but he
" advances straight forward, and kills his enemy
" through an angle; the *elephant* marches in all direc-
" tions, as far as his driver pleases; the *horse* runs
" obliquely, traversing three squares; and the *ship*
" goes over two squares diagonally."   The elephant,
we find, has the powers of our *queen*, as we are pleased
to call the *minister*, or *general*, of the *Persians*; and the
ship has the motion of the piece to which we give the
unaccountable appellation of *bishop*; but with a restric-
tion which must greatly lessen his value.

The bard next exhibits a few general rules and superficial directions for the conduct of the game: " the *pawns* and the *ship* both kill and may be volun-" tarily killed; while the *king*, the *elephant*, and the " *horse* may slay the foe, but cannot expose them-" selves to be slain. Let each player preserve his own " forces with extreme care, securing his *king* above all, " and not sacrificing a superior to keep an inferior " piece." Here the commentator on the *Puran* ob-serves, that the *horse*, who has the choice of *eight* moves from any central position, must be preferred to the *ship*, who has only the choice of *four*; but this argument would not have equal weight in the com-mon game, where the *bishop* and *tower* command a whole line, and where a knight is always of less value than a tower in action, or a bishop of that side on which the attack is begun. " It is by the overbearing " power of the *elephant* that the king fights boldly; " let the whole army, therefore, be abandoned, in or-" der to secure the *elephant*: the king must never place " one elephant before another, according to the rule " of *Gotama*, unless he be compelled by want of room, " for he would thus commit a dangerous fault; and, if " he can slay one of two hostile elephants, he must " destroy that on his left hand." The last rule is ex-tremely obscure; but, as *Gotama* was an illustrious lawyer and philosopher, he would not have conde-scended to leave directions for the game of *Chatu-ranga*, if it had not been held in great estimation by the ancient sages of *India*.

All that remains of the passage, which was copied for me by *Radhacant* and explained by him, relates to the several modes in which a partial success or com-plete victory may be obtained by any one of the four players; for we shall see that, as if a dispute had arisen between two allies, one of the kings may assume the command of all the forces, and aim at separate con-

quest. First, " When any one king has placed himself
" on the square of another king, which advantage is
" called *Sinhasana*, or *the throne*, he wins a stake;
" which is doubled, if he kills the adverse monarch
" when he seizes his place; and, if he can seat himself
" on the throne of his ally, he takes the command of
" the whole army." Secondly, "If he can occupy suc-
" cessively the thrones of all the three princes, he ob-
" tains the victory, which is named *Chaturaji*; and the
" stake is doubled if he kill the last of the three just
" before he takes possession of his throne; but if he
" kill him on his throne, the stake is quadrupled."
Thus, as the commentator remarks, in a real warfare, a
king may be considered as victorious when he seizes
the metropolis of his adversary; but if he can destroy
his foe, he displays greater heroism, and relieves his
people from any further solicitude. " Both in gaining
" the *Sinhasana* and the *Chaturaji*," says *Vyasa*, " the
" king must be supported by the *elephants*, or all the
" forces united." Thirdly, " When one player has
" his own king on the board, but the king of his
" partner has been taken, he may replace his captive
" ally, if he can seize both the adverse kings; or, if
" he cannot effect their capture, he may exchange his
" king for one of them, against the general rule,
" and thus redeem the allied prince, who will supply
" his place." This advantage has the name of *Nri-
pacrishta*, or *recovered by the king*; and the *Nauca-
crishta* seems to be analogous to it, but confined to
the case of *ships*. Fourthly, " If a pawn can march
" to any square on the opposite extremity of the board,
" except that of the king or that of the ship, he as-
" sumes whatever power belonged to that square; and
" this promotion is called *Shatpada*, or the *six strides*."
Here we find the rule, with a singular exception, concerning the advancement of the *pawns*, which often
occasions a most interesting struggle at our common
chess, and which has furnished the poets and moralists

of *Arabia* and *Persia* with many lively reflections on human life. It appears that this privilege of *Shatpada* was not allowable, in the opinion of *Gotama*, when a player had three pawns on the board; but, when only one pawn and one ship remained, the pawn might advance even to the square of a king or a ship, and assume the power of either. Fifthly, " According " to the *Racshasas*, or *giants* (that is, the people of *Lanca*, where the game was invented) there could " be neither victory nor defeat if a king were left on the " plain without force: a situation which they named " *Cacacasht'ha*." Sixthly, " If three ships happen to " meet, and the fourth can be brought up to them in " the remaining angle, this has the name of *Vrihan-* " *nauca*, and the player of the fourth seizes all the " others." Two or three of the remaining couplets are so dark, either from an error in the manuscript or from the antiquity of the language, that I could not understand the *Pandit's* explanation of them, and suspect that they gave even him very indistinct ideas; but it would be easy, if it were worth while, to play at the game by the preceding rules; and a little practice would, perhaps, make the whole intelligible. One circumstance, in this extract from the *Puran*, seems very surprizing; all games of hazard are positively forbidden by *Menu*, yet the game of *Chaturanga*, in which dice are used, is taught by the great *Vyasa* himself, whose law tract appears with that of *Gotama* among the eighteen books which form the *Dhermasastra*; but, as *Radhacant* and his preceptor *Jagannat'h*, are both employed by government in compiling a digest of *Indian* laws, and as both of them, especially the venerable sage of *Tribeni*, understand the game, they are able I presume to assign reasons why it should have been excepted from the general prohibition, and even openly taught by ancient and modern *Brahmans*.

M 3

X.

TWO INSCRIPTIONS

FROM THE VINDYA MOUNTAINS.

Translated from the Sanscrit by Charles Wilkins, Esq.

FIRST INSCRIPTION,

In a Cavern, called the Grot of the Seven Rishis, near Gaya.

1. ANANTA VARMA, master of the hearts of
the people, who was the good son of *Sree
Sardoola,* by his own birth and great virtues classed
amongst the principal rulers of the earth, gladly
caused this statue of *Kreeshna,* of unsullied renown,
confirmed in the world like his own reputation, and
the image of *Kanteematée* * to be deposited in this
great mountain-cave.

2. *Sree Sardoola,* of established fame, jewel of the
diadems of kings, emblem of time to the martial
possessors of the earth, to the submissive the tree of
the fruit of desire, a light to the Military Order,
whose glory was not founded upon the feats of a
single battle, the ravisher of female hearts, and the
image of *Smara* †, became the ruler of the land.

---

* *Radha,* the favourite mistress of *Kreeshna.*
† *Kama Deva,* the Cupid of the *Hindus.*

3. Wherever *Sree Sardoola* is wont to cast his own discordant sight towards a foe, and the fortunate star, his broad eye, is enflamed with anger between its expanded lids; *there* falleth a shower of arrows from the ear-drawn string of the bow of his son, the renowned *Ananta Varma*, the bestower of infinite happiness.

SECOND INSCRIPTION,

In a Cave behind Nagarjeni.

1. THE auspicious *Sree Yunjo Varma*, whose movement was as the sportive elephant's in the season of lust, was like *Manoo* *, the appointer of the military station of all the chiefs of the earth.—By whose divine offerings, the God with a thousand eyes † being constantly invited, the emaciated *Pow- lgmee* ‡; for a long time, sullied the beauty of her cheeks with falling tears.

2. *Ananta Varma* by name, the friend of strangers, renowned in the world in the character of valour, by nature immaculate as the lunar beams, and who is the offspring of *Sree Sardoola*:—By him this wonderful statue of *Bhootspatee* and of *Devee* ‖, the maker of all things visible and invisible and the granter of boons, which hath taken sanctuary in this cave, was caused to be made. May it protect the universe !

---

* The first legislator of the *Hindus*.

† *Eudra* a deification of the Heavens.

‡ The wife of *Eudra*.

‖ *Seevo*, or *Mahadeva* and his consort in one image, as a type of the deities, *Graitor* and *Geojiris*.

3. The string of his expanded bow, charged with arrows and drawn to the extremity of the shoulder, bursteth the circle's centre. Of spacious brow, propitious distinction, and surpassing beauty, he is the image of the moon with an undiminished countenance. *Ananta Varma* to the end! Of form like *Smura* * in existence, he is seen with the constant and affectionate standing with their tender and fascinated eyes constantly fixed upon him.

4. From the machine his bow, reproacher of the crying *Koorara* †, bent to the extreme, he is endued with force; from his expanded virtue he is a provoker; by his good conduct his renown reacheth to afar; he is a hero by whose coursing steeds the elephant is disturbed, and a youth who is the seat of sorrow to the women of his foes. He is the director, and his name is *Ananta* ‡.

---

* The Hindoo *Cupid*.

† A bird that is constantly making a noise before rain.

‡ This word signifies eternal or infinite.

XI

A DESCRIPTION OF ASAM,

BY MOHAMMED CAZIM.

Translated from the Persian, by Henry Vansittart, Esq. *

ASAM, which lies to the north-east of *Bengal*, is divided into two parts by the river *Brahmaputra*, that flows from *Khuta*. The northern portion is called *Uttarcul*, and the southern *Dacshincul*. *Uttarcul* begins at *Gowahutty*, which is the boundary of his Majesty's territorial possessions, and terminates in mountains inhabited by a tribe called *Meeri Mechmi*. *Dacshincul* extends from the village *Sidea* to the hills of *Srinagar*. The most famous mountains to the northward of *Uttarcul*, are those of *Duleh* and *Landah* ; and to the southward of *Dacshincul* are those of *Namrup, (Camrup?)* situated four days journey above *Ghergong*, to which the *Raja* retreated. There is another chain of hills, which is inhabited by a tribe called *Nanqc*, who pay no revenue to the *Raja*, but profess allegiance to him, and obey a few of his orders. But the † *Zemleh* tribe are entirely independent of him ; and, whenever they find an opportunity, plunder the country contiguous to their mountains. *Asam* is of an oblong figure ; its length about 200 standard coss, and its breadth, from the northern to the southern mountains, about eight days journey. From

---

* This account of *Asam* was translated for the Society, but afterwards printed by the learned translator as an appendix to his *Aelrujirnamab*. It is reprinted here, because our government has an interest in being as well acquainted as possible with all the nations *bordering* on the *British* territories.

† In another copy this tribe are called *Daftcb.*

Gnrahutty to *Ghergong* are seventy-five standard coss :
and from thence it is fifteen days journey to *Khoten*,
which was the residence of *Peeran Wiseh* *, but is
now called *Ava* †, and is the capital of the *Raja* of
Pegu, who considers himself of the posterity of that
famous General. The first five days journey from the
mountains of *Camrup*, is performed through forests,
and over hills, which are arduous and difficult to pass.
You then travel eastward to *Ava* through a level
and smooth country. To the northward is the plain
of *Khata*, that has been before mentioned as the
place from whence the *Brahmaputra* issues, which is
afterwards fed by several rivers that flow from the
southern mountains of *Asam*. The principal of these
is the *Dhonee*, which has before occurred in this history : it joins that broad river at the village *Lucki-
gerah.*

Between these rivers is an island well inhabited,
and in an excellent state of tillage. It contains a spacious, clear, and pleasant country, extending to the
distance of about fifty coss. The cultivated tract is
bounded by a thick forest, which harbours elephants,
and where those animals may be caught, as well as
in four or five other forests of *Asam*. If there be occasion for them, five or six hundred elephants may be
procured in a year. Across the *Dhonee*, which is the
side of *Ghergong*, is a wide, agreeable, and level
country, which delights the heart of the beholder.
The whole face of it is marked with population and
tillage ; and it presents on every side charming pros-

* According to *Khondemir*, *Peeran Wiseh* was one of the nobles
of *Afrasiab*, King of *Turan*, contemporary with *Kaicaus*, second
Prince of the *Kianian* Dynasty. In the *Ferhang Jehangyrry* and
Borhaun Katca (two Persian Dictionaries) *Peeran* is described as
one of the *Pehlevan* or heroes of *Turan*, and General under *Afrasiab*, the name of whose father was *Wiseh*.

† This is a palpable mistake. *Khoten* lies to the north of *Him-
alaya* ; and *Piran Visab* could never have seen *Ava*.

pects of ploughed fields, harvests, gardens, and groves. All the island before described lies in *Dac-shincul*. From the village *Salagerch* to the city of *Ghergong* is a space of about fifty ross, filled with such an uninterrupted range of gardens, plentifully stocked with fruit-trees, that it appears as one garden. Within them are the houses of the peasants, and a beautiful assemblage of coloured and fragrant herbs, and of garden and wild flowers blowing together. As the country is overflowed in the rainy season, a high and broad causeway has been raised for the convenience of travellers from *Salagereh* to *Ghergong*, which is the only uncultivated ground that is to be seen. Each side of this road is planted with shady bamboos, the tops of which meet, and are intertwined. Amongst the fruits which this country produces, are mangoes, plantains, jacks, oranges, citrons, limes, pine-apples, and *punialeh*, a species of *amlch*, which has such an excellent flavour, that every person who tastes it prefers it to the plum. There are also cocoa-nut trees, pepper vines, *Areca* trees, and the *Sudij* *, in great plenty. The sugar-cane excels in softness and sweetness, and is of three colours, red, black, and white. There is ginger free from fibres, and betel vines. The strength of vegetation and fertility of the soil are such, that whatever seed is sown, or slips planted, they always thrive. The environs of *Ghergong* furnish small apricots, yams, and pomegranates; but as these articles are wild, and not assisted by cultivation and engraftment, they are very indifferent. The principal crop of this country consists in rice and † mash. *Ades* is very scarce; and wheat and barley are never sown. The silks are excellent, and resemble

---

* The *Sadij* is a long aromatic leaf, which has a pungent taste, and is called in Sanscrit, *Tejapatra*. In our botanical books it bears the name of *Malabathrum*, or the *Indian* Leaf.

† *Mash* is a species of grain, and *Ades* a kind of pea.

those of *China* ; but they manufacture very few more
than are required for use. They are successful in
embroidering with flowers, and in weaving velvet
and *tauthund*, which is a species of filk of which they
make tents and * *kenauts*. Salt is a very precious
and scarce commodity ; it is found at the bottom of
some of the hills, but of a bitter and pungent quality.
A better sort is in common, which is extracted from
the plantain-tree. The mountains inhabited by the
tribe called *Nanac*, produce plenty of excellent *Lig-
num Aloes*, which a society of the natives import
every year into *Asam*, and barter for salt and grain.
This evil disposed race of mountaineers are many degrees removed from the line of humanity, and destitute
of the characteristical properties of a man. They go
naked from head to foot, and eat dogs, cats, snakes,
mice, rats, ants, locusts, and every thing of this sort
which they can find. The hills of *Cumrup*, *Sidea*,
and *Luckigereh*, supply a fine species of *Ligmam Aloes*,
which sinks in water. Several of the mountains contain musk-deer.

The country of *Uttarcul*, which is on the northern
side of the *Brahmaputra*, is in the highest state of
cultivation, and produces plenty of pepper and *Areca*-nuts. It even surpasses *Dacshincul* in population
and tillage ; but, as the latter contains a greater
tract of wild forests, and places difficult of access,
the rulers of *Asam* have chosen to reside in it for the
convenience of control, and have erected in it the
capital of the kingdom. The breadth of *Uttarcul*,
from the bank of the river to the foot of the mountains, which is a cold climate, and contains snow, is
various ; but is nowhere less than fifteen coss, nor
more than forty-five coss. The inhabitants of those

---

* *Knauts* are walls made to surround tents.

mountains are strong, have a robust and respectable
appearance, and are of the middling size. Their complexions, like those of the natives of all cold climates,
are red and white; and they have also trees and fruits
peculiar to frigid regions. Near the fort of *Jum
Dereh*, which is on the side of *Gowahutty*, is a chain
of mountains, called the country of *Dereng*; all the
inhabitants of which resemble each other in appearance, manners, and speech, but they are distinguished by the names of their tribes, and places of residence. Several of these hills produce musk, *katnus*[*],
bhoot [+], *peree*, and two species of horses, called *goont*
and *tanyans*. Gold and silver are procured here, as in
the whole country of *Asam*, by washing the sand of the
rivers. This, indeed, is one of the sources of revenue.
It is supposed that 12,000 inhabitants, and some say
20,000, are employed in this occupation; and it is a
regulation, that each of these persons shall pay a fixed
revenue of a *tola* [‡] of gold to the *Raja*. The people of *Asam* are a base and unprincipled nation, and
have no fixed religion. They follow no rule but that
of their own inclinations, and make the approbation
of their own vicious minds the test of the propriety
of their actions. They do not adopt any mode of
worship practised either by *Heathens* or *Mohammedans*;
nor do they concur with any of the known sects which
prevail amongst mankind. Unlike the Pagans of
Hindustan, they do not reject victuals which have been
dressed by *Muselmans*; and they abstain from no flesh

---

[*] Katnus is thus described in the *Borbura Kotea*: " This word,
in the language of *Rum*, is a sea-cow; the tail of which is hung
upon the necks of horses, and on the summits of standards.
Some say that it is a cow which lives in the mountains of
Chen." It here means the mountain-cow, which supplies the
tail that is made into *chowries*; and in *Sanscrit* is called *chamara*.

[+] *Bhoot* and *peree* are two kinds of blanket.

[‡] Eighty *rui-weights*. See page 154, *note*.

except human. They even eat animals that have died
a natural death; but, in consequence of not being
used to the taste of ghee, they have such an antipa-
thy to this article, that if they discover the least
smell of it in their victuals, they have no relish for
them. It is not their custom to veil their women;
for even the wives of the *Raja* do not conceal their
faces from any person. The females perform work
in the open air, with their countenances exposed and
heads uncovered. The men have often four or five
wives each, and publicly buy, sell, and change them.
They shave their heads, beards, and whiskers, and
reproach and admonish every person who neglects this
ceremony. Their language has not the least affinity
with that of *Bengal* *. Their strength and courage
are apparent in their looks; but their ferocious manners and brutal tempers are also betrayed by their
physiognomy. They are superior to most nations in
corporal force and hardy exertions. They are enter-
prizing, savage, fond of war, vindictive, treacherous,
and deceitful. The virtues of compassion, kindness,
friendship, sincerity, truth, honour, good faith,
shame, and purity of morals, have been left out of
their composition. The seeds of tenderness and humanity have not been sown in the field of their frames.
As they are destitute of the mental garb of manly qualities, they are also deficient in the dress of their bodies.
They tie a cloth round their heads, and another round
their loins, and throw a sheet upon their shoulder;
but it is not customary in that country to wear turbans,
robes, drawers, or shoes. There are no buildings of
brick or stone, or with walls of earth, except the gates
of the city of *Ghergong*, and some of their idolatrous
temples. The rich and poor construct their habita-

* This is an error: young *Brahmins* often come from *Asam* to
Nadiya for instruction; and their vulgar dialect is understood by
the *Bengal* teachers.

tions of wood, bamboos, and straw. The *Raja* and his courtiers travel in stately litters; but the opulent and respectable persons amongst his subjects are carried in lower vehicles called doolies. *Asam* produces neither horses*, camels, nor asses; but those cattle are sometimes brought thither from other countries. The brutal inhabitants, from a congenial impulse, are fond of seeing and keeping asses, and buy and sell them at a high price; but they discover the greatest surprize at seeing a camel; and are so afraid of a horse, that if one trooper should attack a hundred armed *Asamians*, they would all throw down their arms and flee; or should they not be able to escape, they would surrender themselves prisoners. Yet, should one of that detestable race encounter two men of another nation on foot, he would defeat them.

- The ancient inhabitants of this country are divided into two tribes, the *Asamians* and the *Cultanians*. The latter excel the former in all occupations except war and the conduct of hardy enterprises, in which the former are superior. A body-guard of six or seven thousand *Asamians*, fierce as demons, of unshaken courage, and well provided with warlike arms and accoutrements, always keep watch near the *Raja*'s sitting and sleeping apartments; these are his loyal and confidential troops and patrol. The martial weapons of this country are the musquet, sword, spear, and arrow and bow of bamboo. In their forts and boats they have also plenty of cannon, *serbans*†, and *ramchangee*, in the management of which they are very expert.

Whenever any of the *Rajahs*, magistrates, or principal men die, they dig a large cave for the deceased, in which they inter his women, attendants, and servants, and some of the magnificent equipage and useful furniture which he possessed in his life-time ; such as elephants, gold and silver, *badcash* (large fans), carpets, clothes, victuals, lamps, with a great deal of oil, and a torch-bearer; for they consider these articles as stores for a future state.   They afterwards construct a strong roof over the cave upon thick timbers. The people of the army entered some of the old caves, and took out of them the value of 90,000 rupees, in gold and silver.   But an extraordinary circumstance is said to have happened, to which the mind of man can scarcely give credit, and the probability of which is contradicted by daily experience.   It is this : All the nobles came to the imperial general and declared, with universal agreement, that a golden betel-stand was found in one of the caves that was dug eighty years before, which contained betel-leaf quite green and fresh ; but the authenticity of this story rests upon report.

Ghergong has four gates, constructed of stone and earth ; from each of which the *Raja*'s palace is distant three coss.   The city is encompassed with a fence of bamboos ; and within it high and broad causeways have been raised for the convenience of passengers during the rainy season.   In the front of every man's house is a garden, or some cultivated ground.   This is a fortified city, which encloses villages and tilled fields.   The *Raja*'s palace stands upon the bank of the *Degoo*, which flows throughout the city.   This river is lined on each side with houses ; and there is a small market, which contains no shopkeepers except sellers of betel.   The reason is, that it is not customary for the inhabitants to buy provisions for daily use, because they lay up a stock for themselves, which lasts them a year. The *Raja's* palace is surrounded by a causeway, planted on each side with a close hedge of bamboos, which serves instead of a wall. On the outside there is a ditch, which is always full of water. The circumference of the enclosure is one coss and fourteen jereebs. Within it have been built lofty halls and spacious apartments for the *Raja*, most of them of wood, and a few of straw, which are called *thuppers*. Amongst these is a *diwan khanah*, or public saloon, one hundred and fifty cubits long, and forty broad, which is supported by sixty-six wooden pillars, placed at an interval of about four cubits from each other. The *Raja's* seat is adorned with lattice-work and carving. Within and without have been placed plates of brass, so well polished, that when the rays of the sun strike upon them, they shine like mirrors. It is an ascertained fact, that 3000 carpenters and 1200 labourers were constantly employed on this work, during two years before it was finished. When the *Raja* sits in this chamber, or travels, instead of drums and trumpets, they beat the *dhol* and *dand*. The latter is a round thick instrument made of copper, and is certainly the same as the drum †, which it was customary, in the time of the ancient kings, to beat in battles and marches.

The *Rajas* of this country have always raised the crest of pride and vainglory, and displayed an ostentatious appearance of grandeur, and a numerous train of attendants and servants. They have not bowed the head of submission and obedience, nor have they paid tribute or revenue to the most powerful monarch; but they have curbed the ambition, and

* The *dhol* is a kind of drum, which is beaten at each end.
† This is a kind of kettle-drum, and is made of a composition of several metals.

N 2

checked the conquests, of the most victorious princes of *Hindustan*. The solution of the difficulties
attending a war against them, has baffled the pene-
tration of heroes who have been stiled Conquerors
of the World. Whenever an invading army has entered their territories, the *Asamians* have covered
themselves in strong posts, and have distressed the
enemy by stratagems, surprises, and alarms, and by
cutting off their provisions. If these means have
failed, they have declined a battle in the field, but
have carried the peasants into the mountains, burnt
the grain, and left the country empty. But when
the rainy season has set in upon the advancing enemy,
they have watched their opportunity to make excursions, and vent their rage; the famished invaders
have either become their prisoners, or been put to
death. In this manner powerful and numerous armies
have been sunk in that whirlpool of destruction, and
not a soul has escaped.

Formerly *Husain Shah*, a king of *Bengal*, undertook an expedition against *Asam*, and carried with
him a formidable force in cavalry, infantry, and boats.
The beginning of this invasion was crowned with
victory. He entered the country, and erected the
standard of superiority and conquest. The *Raja*
being unable to encounter him in the field, evacuated
the plains, and retreated to the mountains. *Husain*
left his son, with a large army, to keep possession of
the country, and returned to *Bengal*. The rainy
season commenced, and the roads were shut up by
the inundation. The *Raja* descended from the mountains, surrounded the *Bengal* army, skirmished with
them, and cut off their provisions, till they were reduced to such straits, that they were all, in a short
time, either killed or made prisoners.

In the same manner *Mohammed Shah*, the son of *Toghuc Shah*, who was king of several of the provinces of *Hindustan*, sent a well-appointed army of an hundred thousand cavalry to conquer *Asam*; but they were all devoted to oblivion in that country of enchantment; and no intelligence or vestige of them remained. Another army was dispatched to revenge this disaster; but when they arrived in *Bengal*, they were panic-struck, and shrunk from the enterprize; because if any person passes the frontier into that district, he has not leave to return. In the same manner, none of the inhabitants of that country are able to come out of it, which is the reason that no accurate information has hitherto been obtained relative to that nation. The natives of *Hindustan* consider them as wizzards and magicians, and pronounce the name of that country in all their incantations and counter-charms. They say that every person who sets his foot there, is under the influence of witchcraft, and cannot find the road to return.

Jeidej Sing [*], the *Raja of Ascan*, bears the title of *Swergi*, or *Celestial. Swerg*, in the *Hindustani* language, means heaven. That frantic and vainglorious prince is so excessively foolish and mistaken, as to believe that his vicious ancestors were sovereigns of the heavenly host; and that one of them, being inclined to visit the earth, descended by a golden ladder. After he had been employed some time in regulating and governing his new kingdom, he became so attached to it, that he fixed his abode in it and never returned.

In short, when we consider the peculiar circumstances of *Asam*; that the country is spacious, popu-

---

[*] Properly *Jeyedswe, a Sinha, or the Lion with Banners of Com-*

lous, and hard to be penetrated; that it abounds in perils and dangers; that the paths and roads are beset with difficulties; that the obstacles to the conquest of it are more than can be described; that the inhabitants are a savage race, ferocious in their manners, and brutal in their behaviour; that they are of a gigantic appearance, enterprising, intrepid, treacherous, well armed, and more numerous than can be conceived; that they resist and attack the enemy from secure posts, and are always prepared for battle; that they possess forts as high as heaven, garrisoned by brave soldiers, and plentifully supplied with warlike stores, the reduction of each of which would require a long space of time; that the way was obstructed by thick and dangerous bushes, and broad and boisterous rivers: when we consider these circumstances, we shall wonder that this country, by the aid of *God*, and the auspices of his Majesty, was conquered by the imperial army, and became a place for erecting the standard of the faith. The haughty and insolent heads of several of the detestable *Asamians*, who stretch the neck of pride, and who are devoid of religion and remote from *God*, were bruised by the hoofs of the horses of the victorious warriors. The *Musselman* heroes experienced the comfort of fighting for their religion; and the blessings of it reverted to the sovereignty of his just and pious Majesty.

The *Raja*, whose soul had been enslaved by pride, who had been bred up in the habit of presuming the stability of his own government, never dreamed of this reverse of fortune; but being now overtaken by the punishment due to his crimes, fled, as has been before mentioned, with some of his nobles, attendants, and family; and a few of his effects, to the mountains of *Commup*. That spot, by its bad air and water, and confined space, is rendered the worst place in the world, or rather it is in one of the pits of hell,

The *Raja's* officers and soldiers, by his orders, crossed the *Dhonec*, and settled in the spacious island between that and the *Brahmaputra*, which contains numerous forests and thickets. A few took refuge in other mountains, and watched an opportunity of committing hostilities.

Camrup is a country on the side of *Dacshincul*, situated between three high mountains, at the distance of four days journey from *Ghergong*. It is remarkable for bad water, noxious air, and confined prospects. Whenever the *Raja* used to be angry with any of his subjects, he sent them thither. The roads are difficult to pass, insomuch that a foot-traveller proceeds with the greatest inconvenience. There is one road wide enough for a horse; but the beginning of it contains thick forests for about half a coss. Afterwards there is a defile, which is stony and full of water. On each side is a mountain towering to the sky.

The Imperial General remained some days in *Ghergong*, where he was employed in regulating the affairs of the country, encouraging the peasants, and collecting the effects of the *Raja*. He repeatedly read the *Khotbeh*, or prayer, containing the name and titles of the Prince of the Age, King of Kings, *Alamgeer*, Conqueror of the World; and adorned the faces of the coins with the imperial impression. At this time there were heavy showers, accompanied with violent wind, for two or three days; and all the signs appeared of the rainy season, which in that country sets in before it does in *Hindustan*. The General exerted himself in establishing posts, and fixing guards, for keeping open the roads and supplying the army with provisions. He thought now of securing himself during the rains, and determined, after the sky should be cleared from the clouds, the

lightning cease to illuminate the air, and the swelling
of the water should subside, that the army should
again be set in motion against the *Raja* and his attendants, and be employed in delivering the country from
the evils of their existence.

The author then mentions several skirmishes,
which happened between the *Raja*'s forces and the
Imperial troops; in which the latter were always victorious. He concludes thus:

" At length all the villages of *Dacshincul* fell into the
possession of the Imperial army. Several of the inhabitants and peasants, from the diffusion of the fame
of his Majesty's kindness, tenderness, and justice,
submitted to his government, and were protected in
their habitations and property. The inhabitants of
Uttarcul also became obedient to his commands.
His Majesty rejoiced when he heard the news of this
conquest, and rewarded the General with a costly
dress, and other distinguishing marks of his favour."

The narrative, to which this is a supplement, gives
a concise history of the military expedition into *Asam*.
In this description the author has stopt at a period
when the Imperial troops had possessed themselves of
the capital, and were masters of any part of the plain
country which they chose to occupy or over-run.
The sequel diminishes the credit of the conquest, by
showing that it was temporary, and that the *Raja* did
not forget his usual policy of harassing the invading
army during the rainy season: but this conduct produced only the effect of distressing and disgusting it
with the service, instead of absolutely destroying it,
as his predecessors had destroyed former adventurers.
Yet the conclusion of this war is far from weaken-
ing the panegyric which the author has passed upon
the Imperial General, to whom a difference of situa-

tion afforded an opportunity of displaying additional
virtues, and of closing that life with heroic fortitude
which he had always hazarded in the field with martial spirit.   His name and titles were, *Mir Jumlah,
Maazzim Khan, Khani Khanan, Sipahi Salar.*

REMARK.

The preceding account of the *Asamians,* who are
probably superior in all respects to the *Moguls,* exhibits a specimen of the black malignity and frantic in-
tolerance with which it was usual, in the reign of
Aurangzib, to treat all those whom the crafty, cruel,
and avaricious emperor was pleased to condemn as
infidels and barbarians.

XII.

ON THE MANNERS, RELIGION, AND LAWS
OF THE CUCIS, OR MOUNTAINEERS
OF TIPRA.

Communicated, in Persian, by John Rawlins, Esq.

THE inhabitants of the mountainous districts to the east of *Bengal* give the name of *Patiyan* to the Being who created the universe; but they believe that a deity exists in every tree, that the sun and moon are Gods, and that whenever they worship those subordinate divinities, *Patiyan* is pleased.

If any one among them put another to death, the chief of the tribe, or other persons who bear no relation to the deceased, have no concern in punishing the murderer; but, if the murdered person has a brother, or other heir, he may take blood; nor has any man whatever a right to prevent or oppose such retaliation.

When a man is detected in the commission of theft or other atrocious offence, the chieftain causes a recompense to be given to the complainant, and reconciles both parties; but the chief himself receives a customary fine: and each party gives a feast of pork, or other meat, to the people of his respective tribe.

In ancient times it was not a custom among them to cut off the heads of the women whom they found in the habitations of their enemies; but it happened

once that a woman asked another why she came so
late to her business of sowing grain: she answered,
that her husband was gone to battle, and that the
necessity of preparing food and other things for him
had occasioned her delay. This answer was overheard
by a man at enmity with her husband; and he was
filled with resentment against her, considering, that,
as she had prepared food for her husband for the purpose of sending him to battle against his tribe, so, in
general, if women were not to remain at home, their
husbands could not be supplied with provision, and
consequently could not make war with advantage.
From that time it became a constant practice to cut off
the heads of the enemy's women; especially, if they
happen to be pregnant, and therefore confined to their
houses. And this barbarity is carried so far, that if a
Cuci assail the house of an enemy, and kill a woman
with child, so that he may bring two heads, he acquires honour and celebrity in his tribe, as the destroyer of two foes at once.

As to the marriages of this wild nation; when a
rich man has made a contract of marriage, he gives four
or five head of *gayals* (the cattle of the mountains)
to the father and mother of the bride, whom he carries to his own house: her parents then kill the *gayals*,
and, having prepared fermented liquors and boiled
rice, with other eatables, invite the father, mother,
brethren, and kindred of the bridegroom to a nuptial
entertainment. When a man of small property is inclined to marry, and a mutual agreement is made, a
similar method is followed in a lower degree: and a
man may marry any woman, except his own mother.
If a married couple live cordially together, and have a
son, the wife is fixed and irremoveable; but, if they
have no son, and especially if they live together on bad
terms, the husband may divorce his wife, and marry
another woman.

- They have no idea of heaven or hell, the reward of good, or the punishment of bad actions; but they profess a belief, that when a person dies, a certain spirit comes and seizes his soul, which he carries away; and that whatever the spirit promises to give at the instant when the body dies, will be found and enjoyed by the dead; but that, if any one should take up the corse and carry it off, he would not find the treasure.

The food of this people consists of elephants, hogs, deer, and other animals; of which, if they find the carcasses or limbs in the forests, they dry and eat them occasionally.

When they have resolved on war, they send spies before hostilities are begun, to learn the stations and strength of the enemy, and the condition of the roads; after which they march in the night; and two or three hours before daylight, make a sudden assault with swords, lances, and arrows. If their enemies are compelled to abandon their station, the assailants instantly put to death all the males and females who are left behind, and strip the houses of all their furniture; but, should their adversaries, having gained intelligence of the intended assault, be resolute enough to meet them in battle, and should they find themselves overmatched, they speedily retreat and quietly return to their own habitations. If at any time they see a star very near the moon, they say, ' to-night we shall undoubtedly be attacked by some enemy;" and they pass that night under arms with extreme vigilance. They often lie in ambush in a forest near the path where their foes are used to pass and repass, waiting for the enemy with different sorts of weapons, and killing every man or woman who happens to pass by. In this situation, if a leech, or a worm, or a snake should bite one of them, he bears the pain in perfect silence;

and whoever can bring home the head of an enemy
which he has cut off, is sure to be distinguished and
exalted in his nation.   When two hostile tribes appear to have equal force in battle, and neither has hopes
of putting the other to flight, they make a signal of
pacific intentions, and, sending agents reciprocally,
soon conclude a treaty; after which they kill several
head of *gayals* and feast on their flesh, calling on
the sun and moon to bear witness of the pacifica-
tion : but if one side, unable to resist the enemy, be
thrown into disorder, the vanquished tribe is considered
as tributary to the victors, who every year receive
from them a certain number of *gayals*, wooden dishes,
weapons, and other acknowledgments of vassalage.
Before they go to battle they put a quantity of roasted
alus (esculent roots like *potatoes*) and paste of rice-
flour into the hollow of bamboos, and add to them
a provision of dry rice, with some leathern bags full of
liquor : then they assemble and march with such celerity, that in one day they perform a journey ordi-
narily made by letter-carriers in three or four days,
since they have not the trouble and delay of dressing
victuals.   When they reach the place to be attacked,
they surround it in the night, and, at early dawn, enter
it, putting to death both young and old, women
and children, except such as they chuse to bring
away captive.   They put the heads which they cut off
into leathern bags ; and if the blood of their enemies
be on their hands they take care not to wash it off.
When, after this slaughter, they take their own food,
they thrust a part of what they eat into the mouths of
the heads which they have brought away, saying to
each of them, ' Eat, quench thy thirst, and satisfy thy
' appetite.   As thou hast been slain by my hand, so
' may thy kinsmen be slain by my kinsmen!' During
their journey, they have usually two such meals ; and
every watch, or two watches, they send intelligence

of their proceedings to their families. When any of them sends word that he has cut off the head of an enemy, the people of his family, whatever be their age or sex, express great delight, making caps and ornaments of red and black ropes; then filling some large vessels with fermented liquors, and decking themselves with all the trinkets they possess, they go forth to meet the conqueror, blowing large shells and striking plates of metal, with other rude instruments of music. When both parties are met they show extravagant joy, men and women dancing and singing together; and if a married man has brought an enemy's head, his wife wears a head-dress with gay ornaments, the husband and wife alternately pour fermented liquor into each other's mouths, and she washes his bloody hands with the same liquor which they are drinking; thus they go revelling, with excessive merriment to their place of abode; and, having piled up the heads of their enemies in the court-yard of their chieftain's house, they sing and dance round the pile; after which they kill some *gayals* and hogs with their spears, and, having boiled the flesh, make a feast of it, and drink the fermented liquor. The richer men of this race fasten the heads of their foes on a bamboo, and fix it on the graves of their parents, by which act they acquire great reputation. He who brings back the head of a slaughtered enemy, receives presents from the wealthy of cattle and spirituous liquors; and if any captives are brought alive, it is the prerogative of those chieftains who were not in the campaign, to strike off the heads of the captives. Their weapons are made by particular tribes; for some of them are unable to fabricate instruments of war.

In regard to their civil institutions, the whole management of their household affairs belongs to the women; while the men are employed in clearing fo-

rests, building huts, cultivating land, making war,
or hunting game and wild beasts. Five days (they
never reckon by months or years) after the birth of a
male child, and three days after that of a female, they
entertain their family and kinsmen with boiled rice and
fermented liquor; and the parents of the child partake
of the feast. They begin the ceremony with fixing a
pole in the court-yard; and then, killing a *gayal* or a
hog with a lance, they consecrate it to their deity; after
which all the party eat the flesh and drink liquor,
closing the day with dancing and with songs. If any
one among them be so deformed, by nature or by accident, as to be unfit for the propagation of his species,
he gives up all thought of keeping house, and begs
for his subsistence, like a religious mendicant, from
door to door, continually dancing and singing. When
such a person goes to the house of a rich and liberal
man, the owner of the house usually strings together a
number of white and red stones, and fixes one end of
the string on a long cane, so that the other end may
hang down to the ground; then, paying a kind of
superstitious homage to the pebbles, he gives alms to
the beggar; after which he kills a *gayal* and a hog,
and some other quadrupeds, and invites his tribe to
a feast. The giver of such an entertainment acquires
extraordinary fame in the nation: and all unite in
applauding him with every token of honour and reverence.

When a *Cuci* dies, all his kinsmen join in killing
a hog and a *gayal*; and, having boiled the meat,
pour some liquor into the mouth of the deceased, round
whose body they twist a piece of cloth by way of shroud.
All of them taste the same liquor as an offering to his
soul; and this ceremony they repeat at intervals for
several days. Then they lay the body on a stage, and,
kindling a fire under it, pierce it with a spit, and

dry it : when it is perfectly dried, they cover it with two or three folds of cloth; and, enclosing it in a little cafe within a chest, bury it under ground. All the fruits and flowers that they gather within a year after the burial, they scatter on the grave of the deceased; but fome bury their dead in a different manner, covering them first with a shroud, then with a mat of woven reeds, and hanging them on a high tree. Some, when the flesh is decayed, wash the bones, and keep them dry in a bowl, which they open on every sudden emergence; and fancying themselves at a consultation with the bones, purfue whatever measures they think proper, alledging, that they act by the command of their departed parents and kinsmen. A widow is obliged to remain a whole year near the grave of her husband, where her family bring her food: if she die within the year, they mourn for her; if she live, they carry her back to her house, where all her relations are entertained with the usual feast of the *Cuci*.

If the deceased leave three sons, the eldest and the youngest share all his property, but the middle son takes nothing: if he have no sons, his estate goes to his brothers; and if he have no brothers, it escheats to the chief of the tribe.

NOTE.

A party of *Cuci* visited the late CHARLES CROFTES, Esq. at *Jafarabad* in the spring of 1776, and entertained him with a dance: they promised to return after their harvest, and seemed much pleased with their reception.

XIII.

SECOND CLASSICAL BOOK

OF THE

CHINESE.

BY THE PRESIDENT.

THE vicinity of *China* to our *Indian* territories, from the capital of which there are not more than *six hundred miles* to the province of *Yunan*, must necessarily draw our attention to that most ancient and wonderful empire, even if we had no commercial intercourse with its more distant and maritime provinces; and the benefits that might be derived from a more intimate connection with a nation long famed for their useful arts and for the valuable productions of their country, are too apparent to require any proof or illustration. My own inclinations and the course of my studies lead me rather to consider at present their *laws, politics,* and *morals,* with which their general literature is closely blended, than their manufactures and trade : nor will I spare either pains or expense to procure translations of their most approved *law-tracts,* that I may return to *Europe* with distinct ideas, drawn from the fountain-head, of the wisest *Asiatic* legislation. It will probably be a long time before accurate returns can be made to my inquiries concerning the *Chinese Laws;* and, in the interval, the Society will not, perhaps, be displeased to know that a translation of a most venerable and excellent work may be expected from *Canton* through the kind assistance of an inestimable correspondent.

According to a *Chinese* writer, named *Li Yang Ping,* " the ancient characters used in his country ' were the outlines of visible objects, earthly and

O 2

'celestial : but as things merely intellectual could
' not be expressed by those figures, the grammarians
' of *China* contrived to represent the various opera-
' tions of the mind by metaphors drawn from the
' productions of nature : thus the idea of roughness
' and of rotundity, of motion and rest, were con-
' veyed to the eye by signs representing a mountain,
' the sky, a river and the earth ; the figures of the
' sun, the moon, and the stars, differently combined,
' stood for smoothness and splendour, for any thing
' artfully wrought, or woven with delicate workman-
' ship ; extension, growth, increase, and many other
' qualities, were painted in characters taken from
' clouds, from the firmament, and from the vege-
' table part of the creation ; the different ways of
' moving, agility and slowness, idleness and dili-
' gence, were expressed by various insects, birds,
' fish, and quadrupeds. In this manner passions
' and sentiments were traced by the pencil, and ideas
' not subject to any sense were exhibited to the sight,
' until by degrees new combinations were invented,
' new expressions added ; the characters deviated
' imperceptibly from their primitive shape, and the
' *Chinese* language became not only clear and forcible, but rich and elegant in the highest degree.'

In this language, so ancient and so wonderfully
composed, are a multitude of books abounding in
useful, as well as agreeable, knowledge; but the
highest class consists of *Five* works ; one of which,
at least, every *Chinese* who aspires to literary honours,
must read again and again, until he possess it perfectly.

The *first* is purely *Historical*, containing annals of
the empire from the *two-thousand three-hundred thirty-
seventh* year before CHRIST : it is entitled *Shuking*,
and a version of it has been published in *France* ; to

which country we are indebted for the moft authentic
and moft valuable fpecimens of *Chinefe* hiftory and
literature, from the compofitions which preceded
thofe of *Homer* to the poetical works of the prefent
Emperor, who feems to be a man of the brighteft
genius and the moft amiable affections. We may
fmile, if we pleafe, at the levity of the *French*, as
they laugh without fcruple at our ferioufnefs: but let
us not fo far undervalue our rivals in arts and in arms,
as to deny them their juft commendation, or to relax
our efforts in that noble ftruggle, by which alone we
can preferve our own eminence.

The fecond claffical work of the *Chinefe* contains
three hundred odes, or fhort poems, in praife of ancient fovereigns and legiflators, or defcriptive of ancient manners, and recommending an imitation of
them in the difcharge of all public and domeftic
duties: they abound in wife maxims and excellent
precepts, ' their whole doctrine,' according to *Cun-
fu-tsu*, in the *Lunyu* or *Moral Difcourfes*, ' being re-
' ducible to this grand rule, that we fhould not even
' entertain a thought of any thing bafe or culpable;'
but the copies of the *Shi King*, for that is the title of
the book, are fuppofed to have been much disfigured,
fince the time of that great philofopher, by fpurious
paffages and exceptionable interpolations; and the
ftyle of the poems is in fome parts too metaphorical,
while the brevity of other parts renders them ob-
fcure; though many think even this obfcurity
fublime and venerable, like that of ancient cloyfters
and temples, ' *Shedding*,' as *Milton* expreffes it, ' *a
' dim religious light*.' There is another paffage in the
Lunyu, which deferves to be fet down at length:
' Why, my fons, do you not ftudy the book of Odes?
' If we creep on the ground, if we lie ufelefs and
' inglorious, thofe poems will raife us to true glory:

O 3

‘ in them we fee, as in a mirror, what may beft be-
‘ come us, and what will be unbecoming ; by their
‘ influence we fhall be made focial, affable, benevo-
‘ lent ; for as mufic combines founds in juft melody,
‘ fo the ancient poetry tempers and compofes our
‘ passions: the Odes teach us our duty to our parents
‘ at home, and abroad to our prince ; they instruct
‘ us also delightfully in the various productions of
‘ nature.’   ‘ Haft thou studied,’ said the philosopher
to his son *Peyu*, ‘ the first of the three hundred Odes
‘ on the nuptials of Prince *Venvam* and the virtuous
‘ *Tai Jin ?*   He who studies them not resembles a
‘ man with his face against a wall, unable to advance
‘ a step in virtue and wisdom.’   Most of those Odes
are near *three thoufand* years old, and some, if we give
credit to the *Chinefe* annals, considerably older ; but
others are somewhat more recent, having been composed under the later emperors of the *third* family,
called *Sheu*.   The work is printed in *four* volumes ;
and towards the end of the *first*, we find the Ode,
which *Couplet* has accurately translated at the beginning of the *Tabio*, or *Great Science*, where it is finely
amplified by the philosopher : I produce the original
from the *Shi King* itself, and from the book in which
it is cited, together with a double version, one verbal
and another metrical ; the only method of doing
justice to the poetical compositions of the *Asiatics*.
It is a panegyric on *Vucun*, Prince of *Guey* in the
province of *Honang*, who died, near a century old,
in the *thirteenth* year of the emperor *Pingvang*, seven
hundred and fifty-six years before the birth of *Christ*,
or *one hundred and forty-eight*, according to *Sir Isaac
Newton*, after the taking of *Troy* ; so that the *Chinese*
Poet might have been contemporary with *Hesiod* and
Homer, or, at least, must have written the Ode before the *Iliad* and *Odyssey* were carried into *Greece* by
Lycurgus.

The verbal translation of the thirty-two original characters is this:

'   Behold yon reach of *the river* Ki;
'   Its green reeds how luxuriant! how luxuriant!
'   Thus is our prince adorned with virtues;
'   As a carver, as a filer, of ivory,
'   As a cutter, as a polisher, of gems.
'   O how elate and sagacious! O how dauntless and composed!
'   How worthy of fame! How worthy of reverence!
'   We have a prince adorned with virtues,
'   Whom to the end *of time* we cannot forget.'

THE PARAPHRASE.

Behold, where yon blue riv'let glides
    Along the laughing dale;
Light reeds bedeck its verdant sides,
    And frolic in the gale:

So shines our Prince! In bright array
    The Virtues round him wait;
And sweetly smil'd th' auspicious day,
    That rais'd him o'er our state.

As pliant hands in shapes refin'd
    Rich iv'ry carve and smoothe,
His *Laws* thus mould each ductile mind,
    And every passion soothe.

O 4

As gems are taught by patient art
In sparkling ranks to beam,
With *manners* thus he forms the heart,
And spreads a gen'ral gleam.

What soft, yet awful, dignity!
What meek, yet manly, grace!
What sweetness dances in his eye,
And blossoms in his face!

So shines our Prince! A sky-born crowd
Of Virtues round him blaze:
Ne'er shall Oblivion's murky cloud
Obscure his deathless praise.

The prediction of the poet has hitherto been accomplished; but he little imagined that his composition would be admired, and his prince celebrated in a language not then formed, and by the natives of regions so remote from his own.

In the *tenth* leaf of the *Ta Hio*, a beautiful comparison is quoted from another ode in the *Shi King*, which deserves to be exhibited in the same form with the preceding:

' The peach-tree, how fair! how graceful!
' Its leaves, how blooming! how pleasant!
' Such is a bride, when she enters her bridegroom's
　house,
' And pays due attention to her whole family.'

The simile may thus be rendered:

> Gay child of Spring, the garden's queen,
>   Yon peach-tree charms the roving sight:
> Its fragrant leaves how richly green !
>   Its blossoms how divinely bright!
>
> So softly smiles the blooming bride,
>   By Love and conscious Virtue led
> O'er her new mansion to preside,
>   And placid joys around her spread.

The next leaf exhibits a comparison of a different nature, rather sublime than agreeable, and conveying rather censure than praise:

O how horridly impends yon southern mountain !

Its rocks in how vast, how rude a heap !

Thus loftily thou sittest, O minister of YN !

All the people look up to thee with dread.

Which may be thus paraphrased:

> See, where yon crag's imperious height
>   The sunny highland crowns,
> And hideous as the brow of night,
>   Above the torrent frowns !
>
> So scowls the Chief, whose will is law,
>   Regardless of our state;
> While millions gaze with painful awe,
>   With fear allied to hate.

It was a very ancient practice in *China* to paint or
engrave moral sentences and approved verses on
vessels in constant use; as the words *Renew thyself
daily* were inscribed on the bason of the emperor
Tang, and the poem of *Kien Long*, who is now on
the throne, in praise of tea, has been published on a
set of porcelain cups; and if the description just
cited of a selfish and insolent statesman were, in the
same manner, constantly presented to the eyes and
attention of rulers, it might produce some benefit to
their subjects and to themselves; especially if the
comment of *Tsem Tsu*, who may be called the
Xenoplon, as *Cun Fu Tsu* was the *Socrates*, and *Mem
Tsu* the *Plato*, of *China*, were added to illustrate and
enforce it.

If the rest of the *three hundred* Odes be similar to
the specimens adduced by those great moralists in
their works, which the *French* have made public, I
should be very solicitous to procure our nation the
honour of bringing to light the *second* classical book
of the *Chinese*. The *third*, called *Yeking*, or the
book of changes, believed to have been written by
Fo, the *Hermes* of the East, and consisting of right
lines variously disposed, is hardly intelligible to the
most learned *Mandarins*; and *Cun Fu Tsu* himself,
who was prevented by death from accomplishing his
design of elucidating it, was dissatisfied with all the
interpretations of the earliest commentators.   As to
the *fifth*, or *Liki*, which that excellent man compiled
from old monuments, it consists chiefly of the *Chinese*
ritual, and of tracts on moral duties; but the *fourth* .
entitled *Chung Cieu*, or *Spring* and *Autumn*, by which
the same incomparable writer meaned the *flourishing*
state of an empire under a virtuous monarch, and the
fall of kingdoms under bad governors, must be an
interesting work in every nation.   The powers, how-

ever, of an individual are so limited, and the field of knowledge is so vast, that I dare not promise more than to procure, if any exertions of mine will avail, a complete translation of the *Shi King*, together with an authentic abridgement of the *Chinese* laws, civil and criminal. A native of *Canton*, whom I knew some years ago in *England*, and who passed his first examinations with credit in his way to literary distinctions, but was afterwards allured from the pursuit of learning by a prospect of success in trade, has favoured me with the *Three Hundred Odes* in the original, together with the *Lun Yu*, a faithful version of which was published at *Paris* near a century ago; but he seems to think, that it would require three or four years to complete a translation of them; and Mr. Cox informs me that none of the *Chinese* to whom he has access, *possess leisure and perseverance enough for such a task*; yet he hopes, with the assistance of *Whang Atong*, to send me next season some of the poems translated into *English*. A little encouragement would induce this young *Chinese* to visit *India*, and some of his countrymen would, perhaps, accompany him; but though considerable advantage to the public, as well as to letters, might be reaped from the knowledge and ingenuity of such emigrants, yet we must wait for a time of greater national wealth and prosperity, before such a measure can be formally recommended by us to our patrons at the helm of government.

A Letter to the PRESIDENT *from a young*
CHINESE.

SIR,

I RECEIVED the favour of your letter dated 28th
March, 1784, by Mr. *Cox*. I remember the
pleasure of dining with you in company with Captain
Blake and Sir *Joshua Reynolds*; and I shall always
remember the kindness of my friends in *England*.

The *Chinese* book, *Shi King*, that contains three
hundred poems, with remarks thereon, and the work
of *Con-fu-tsu*, and his grandson, the *Tai Ho*, I beg
you will accept: but to translate the work into
English will require a great deal of time, perhaps
three or four years; and I am so much engaged in
business, that I hope you will excuse my not undertaking it.

If you wish for any books or other things from
Canton, be so good as to let me know, and I will
take particular care to obey your orders.

Wishing you health,

I am, S I R,

Your most obedient humble Servant,

WHANG ATONG.

To Sir WILLIAM JONES,
Dec. 10, 1784.

تَوَاضُع submission,	وضع		
مُتَوَاتِر succeeding another,	وتر		
مُتَوَاصِل united,	وصل		
تَجَاوُز excess,	جوز	اِنْقِيَاد sumiss	انقياد
مُتَجَاوِز exceeding,	جوز	مُنْقَاد ob'ing	
مُتَعَاوِر received in loan,	عور		
تَلَافِي prosecution,	لفو	اِنْجِلَا brihtn	
مُتَعَالِي raising on high,	علو	مُنْعَدِي coragi	
تَبَاجُر the act of revolting,	يجر		
مُتَبَاجِر revolting,	يجر		
مُتَبَاجِر revolted,	يجر		
تَمَايُل inflection,	ميل	اِنْقِيَاد submis	
مُتَغَايِر altering,	غبر	مُنْقَاد obeying	
تَعَالِي exaltation,	علي	اِنْقَضَا expirati	
مُتَنَاهِي complicating,	نهي	مُنْقَضِي coming	

10*b.*

From

ا

مُسْتَانِي waiting with patience, اني

متَرَائِي looking at one another, راي

تَوَالِي a series of succession, ولي
مُتَوَالِي following in succession, ولى

تَقَاوِي the act of empowering, قوي
مُتَقَاوِي empowering, قوي

ADVERTISEMENT.

EXAMPLES of derivatives from Arabic quadriliterals rarely occur in the Persian language;
and from the 9th, 11th, 12th, and 13th, conjugations of triliteras there are none to be met with. I
have, therefore, confined my observations to the nine
conjugations included in the table. And al·hough
particular senses and uses are assigned to each of these
by grammarians, (which may be seen in Mr. *Richardson*'s Gram. p. 65) it is at the same time to be observed, that they are nevertheless frequently used in
other senses; many of them retaining the simple
signification of their primitives: and that every root
does not extend through every conjugation, but that
some are used in one form, many in several, none
in all.

These observations are applicable to the present
subject; and the derivatives of such conjugations as
are more frequently used in the Arabic, seem also to
be more frequently than any other introduced into
the Persian.

Where no example of any particular form is to be
found in Golius and Meninski, I have left a blank
in the table, which may be filled up whenever any
can be met with.

With regard to the examples which I have brought
to illustrate the following rules, they are such as
came first to hand; and *one* example of an infinitive
or participle is intended as a representation of the
infinitives and participles of every species and conjugation. To have attempted a complete system of

examples would have carried me far beyond the
limits of my present undertaking.

OF ARABIC INFINITIVES.

I. Their Masculine Singulars are used in the Persian as Substantives; and in every respect serve the
same purposes, and are subject to the same rules of
construction as substantives originally Persian.

Ex.

1. governing a fub. fol.	اظهار یکانگی	demonstrations of unanimity
2. agreeing with an ad. fol.	استعجال تمام	great haste
3. agreeing with a part. pas. fol.	تحریر مسطور	the said writing
4. nominatives to verbs,	نظر براین بود	my view was this
5. governed by verbs,	احتظا ظو افر یافت	he received great delight
6. governed by a prep.	بعد از تقدیم مراسم	after perform- ing the duties
7. united by a conjunction	اقبال و اجلال	prosperity and splendour
8. rendered definite by affixing ی	اتحادی که درمیان بود	the union that was between

II. Their Masculine Plurals are used in the Persian as substantives; and in every respect serve the
same purposes, and are subject to the same rules of
construction as substantives originally Persian.

Ex.   .

1. governing a sub. fol.	اخلاق مردم	the dispositions of men

Ex.

2. agreeing with an ad. fol.   افعال نیک   good actions

3. agreeing with a part. pas. fol.   اطوار مسطور   the qualifica-
tions described

III. Their Feminine Singulars are used in the
Persian as substantives; and in every respect serve
the same purposes, and are subject to the same rules
of construction as substantives originally Persian.

Ex.

1. nominatives to verbs,   اجازت است   there is permission

2. governing a sub. fol.   معا ملت ملک   the business of
the empire

3. agreeing with an ad. fol.   مقا تله عظیمه   a bloody battle

4. agreeing with a part.   مکاتبه مرقومه بدوستی   a letter written
pas. fol.   in friendship

IV. Their Feminine Plurals are used in the Persian
as substantives; and in every respect serve the same
purposes, and are subject to the same rules of construction as substantives originally Persian.

Ex.

1. governing a sub. fol.   توجهات دوستان   the civilities of
friends

2. agreeing with an ad. fol.   معاملات کلی   public affairs

3. agreeing with a part. pas. fol.   تکلیفات مزبور   the said burthens

V. The Infinitives of the first conjugation of transitive verbs are regularly of the form exhibited in the
table. But those of Intransitives are reducible to no

proper rule without innumerable exceptions. Grammarians make of them in all thirty-two different
forms, which may be seen in Mr. Richardson's Grammar, p. 92. but for these irregularities, he justly
observes, that a dictionary is the only proper guide.
These Infinitives, both Singulars and Plurals, are
introduced freely into the Persian as Substantives.

Ex. governing another sub. fol. وصول مکتوب the arrival of the
letter & ca & ca

OF ARABIC PARTICIPLES ACTIVE.

I. Their Masculine Singulars are used in the
Persian as participles, as substantives, and as adjectives.

Ex.

1. as participles with a verb fol. منتظر ماند he remained ex-
pecting

طالع و لامع باد be shining and
blazing

2. as sub. governing another sub. fol. حاکم شهر governor of the
city

موجب خوشنودی causing gladness
—the cause of
gladness

مصنف این کتاب composing this
book—the author
of this book

مطابق شرع شریف following the noble law—follower
of the noble law

3: as an ad. qualifying a sub. مردم قابل an able man

4. following another sub. signify- حضرت خالق God the creator
ing the same thing

Ex.

5. agreeing with an ad. fol.   عامِل نِیک   a good agent.

6. agreeing with a part. pas. fol.   حاکِم مستقل   absolute judge

7. governed by a verb,   قاتلرا کُشت   he put the mur-
der to death

8. nominatives to verbs,   اگر عاشِق صادق است   if the lover be sincere

9. with a prep. fol. an un-
common construction,   مشتمل بر مصادقت   containing friendship

II. Their masculine perfect plurals are used in the Persian as substantives in the form of the oblique case which terminates in ین . But they do not seem to be used in the form of the nominative which terminates in ون .

Ex. 1. governed by a sub.
going before,   علم اولین وآخرین   the knowledge of the moderns and ancients

قوم مسلمین   the sect of the faithful

III. Their masculine imperfect plurals are used in the Persian as substantives.

Ex.

1. governing a sub. fol.   حکام حال واستقبال   officers of the present and future

2. agreeing with an ad. fol.   عمال جدید وقدیم   the new and old agents

IV. Their feminine singulars are used in the Persian as participles, as substantives, and as adjectives.

Ex.

1. as a part. act. with a verb. fol.   حامله است   she is pregnant

2. as a sub. governing another fol.   مالکه ملک   queen of the empire

P

Ex.

3. as an ad. qualifying a sub. going before, زني حامله a pregnant wo- man

4. as a sub. qualified by an ad. following, مشفقه مهربان kind friend

5. as a sub. qualified by a part. pas. following, صاحبه موصوفه accomplished lady

V. Their feminine perfect p'urals are used in the Persian as substantives expressing things without life.

Ex.

1. governing a sub. following, واقعات زمان the incidents of time

2. agreeing with an ad. fol. واردات ناگهانی unforeseen events

OF ARABIC PARTICIPLES PASSIVE.

I. Their masculine singulars are used in the Persian as participles passive, as substantives, and as adjectives.

Ex.

1. as a part. pas. جملكي همت مصروف بران است the sum of my desire is be- stowed on that

ظلِ شفقت ممد و دباد be the shade of clemency ex- tended

2. as a sub. go- verning another following it مشهود ضمير منير ميكر دانند I make it the perception (i.e. the thing per- ceived) of your enlightened soul; i.e. I re- present it, &c.

مرغوب طبایع — the desire, (i. e. the thing desired) of the soul

3. as an ad. qualifying a sub. going before, — بند ه مظلوم — the injured slave

4. joined with another sub. by a con. — مقصودومرام — intention and design

5. governed by verbs, — خلایق رامحظوظ کردانند — make the people glad

6. nominatives to verbs, — مقصود اوشان برایی بود — their intention was this

II. Their masculine perfect plural does not seem to be used in the Persian, either in the form of the nominative or the oblique case.

III. Their feminine singulars are used in the Persian as substantives, and as adjectives.

Ex.

1. as a sub. governing another fol. it, — معشوقه من — my beloved, i. e. the beloved of me

2. as a sub. agreeing with a part. pas. fol. — معشوقه مذکوره — the said beloved woman

3. as an ad. agreeing with a sub. going before, — والده محترومه — respected mother

IV. Their feminine perfect plurals are used in the Persian as substantives, to express things without life.

Ex.

1. governing a sub. fol. — مطلوبات آن مهربان — the demands of that friend

2. agreeing with an ad. fol. — مقدمات شرعی — law affairs

P 2

V. The active and passive participles of transitive verbs form, with a following substantive having the article ال prefixed to it, compounds corresponding to that of خوب‌روی , which are used in the Persian as substantives and as adjectives.

Ex.

1. as a sub. a nominative to the verb, متعذّر آلفصل است he evades a decision

2. as an ad. qualifying a sub. شخص واجب التعظیم a person deserving respect

قلم مقطوع اللسان a pen cut short in the point

OF ARABIC ADJECTIVES *resembling* PARTICIPLES.

I. The forms حسن صعب صریر represent three species of Arabic words which are derived from intransitive verbs ; and called by Arabic grammarians, adjectives resembling participles. The singulars of these forms are used in the Persian both as adjectives and substantives.

Ex.

1. as a sub. qualified by the pronoun dem. آن عزیز that respectable person

2. with a verb, شریر است he is wicked

3. as an ad. qualifying a sub. دوست قدیم an old friend

II. Their plurals are used in the Persian as substantives.

Ex.

1. governing a sub. fol. حکمای یونان the learned men of Greece

2. agreeing with an ad. fol, شرفای پاک‌نهاد noblemen of integrity

III. These three forms of adjectives, resembling participles, form, with a following substantive having the article ال prefixed to it, compounds corresponding to that of خوب روئ, which are used in the Persian both as substantives and adjectives.

Ex.

1. as a sub. qualified by the   أرى حسن الوجه   that beauty
pro. demon.

     أرى قديم الخدمت   that old servant

2. as a sub. qualified   قديم الخدمت مذكور   the said old ser-
by an ad. fol.   vant

3. as an ad. qualifying a   مردم قديم الخدمت   a man of long ser-
sub. going before,   vice

OF PARTICIPLES *expressing the Sense of their PRIMITIVES in a stronger Degree.*

I. The forms نصير نصار نصور نصر منصار are participles which express the sense of their primitives in a stronger degree; and are sometimes used in the Persian as adjectives.

Ex.

1. agreeing with a sub. going before,   ادويه قتاله   a poisonous medicine

2. agreeing with a verb. fol.   صبور است   he is full of patience

صريب is the form of a participle expressing the sense of the primitive in a less degree; but it does not seem to be used in the Persian.

OF ARABIC SUBSTANTIVES.

I. The Arabic noun of time and place are frequently employed in the Persian; and the following list exhibits the forms of such as are derived from the first conjugations of the different species of tri-literals.

CONJUGATION FIRST.

		FROM		Roots

NOUNS of TIME and PLACE from TRILITERALS.

I.   مكتب the time and place of writing,   كتب

II.   مقر a place of rest—residence,   قر

III.   مامن a place of safety,   امن

V.   مبدأ the place and time of beginning,   بدا

VI.   موضع place—opportunity,   وضع

VII.   مقام the place and time of standing,   قوم

VIII.   مدعا the place or object of desire,   دعو

X.   مبيع the place and time of selling,   بيع

XI.   مرمى the place and time of throwing,   رمي

XII.   مآب the place of return—the center,   اوب

XV.   مجيء the time of coming—arrival,   جي

XVII.   ماتى the place, the way of approaching,   اتى

XVIII.   مرءا the place of looking, beholding,   راى

XIX.   مولا و مولى the place of power—and thus lord, master, &c.   ولي

XXI.   مهوا a place of division—the interval,   هوى

XXII.   محيا the time and place of living,   حي

XXIII.   مأوا و ماوى a place of habitation—refuge,   اوى

————To express the *place* more particularly, ت is sometimes added to the common form, as مقبرة a burning place.

II. The noun of time and place from the derivative conjugations is exactly the same with the participle passive; and is also used in the Persian.

Ex. 1. a part. pas. from the 10th con. مستودع deposited—also a place of deposit

III. The Persian language has terms proper to
itself for expressing the instrument of action; it does
not however reject the use of the Arabic instru-
mental noun, which is represented by the forms,
منصرت or منصر منصار

Ex. 1. governing another بميزان عقل سنجيد he weighed in scale of reason

مفتاح مقصود the key of his intention

IV. All Arabic proper names, and the names of
things, are introduced into the Persian at pleasure.

Ex. مريم Mary, مكة Mecca, عين the eye, لحم
flesh, جد an ancestor, &c. &c.

OF ARABIC ADJECTIVES.

I. Besides the Arabic participles which we have
already observed are used as adjectives, there is also
a plentiful source of real adjectives formed by affixing
ی to substantives of almost every denomination,
which are freely introduced into the Persian.

Ex. انسانی humane, اراضی earthly, مصری Egyptian, &c. &c.

II. The masculine singulars of Arabic superlatives are used in the Persian both as substantives and adjectives.

Ex.

1. as a sub. governing another fol. it اسعدزمان the most fortunate of times

2. as an ad. qualifying a sub. going before, دروقت احسن at a most lucky time

III. The masculine plurals of Arabic superlatives are used in the Persian both as substantives and adjectives.

Ex.

1. as a sub. governing another fol. it, اکابروقت the great men of the age

2. as an ad. qualifying a sub. going before, اشخاص اکابر most illustrious personages

IV. The feminine singulars of Arabic superlatives are used in the Persian as adjectives.

Ex. 1. qualifying a sub. going before, دولت عظمی prosperity most great

V. Arabic ordinal numbers are used in the Persian as adjectives.

Ex. 1. qualifying a sub. before, باب اول the first chapter

Of the FORM of ARABIC WORDS when used in the PERSIAN.

I. All Arabic infinitives, participles, substantives, and adjectives, are introduced into the Persian in the form of the nominative, which throws away from the last letter every species of nunnation (ـٌ), or short vowel (ـُ), which they may posses as Arabic words, and remain without motion; but when their construction in the Persian requires them to assume the termination of another case, they receive it in the same manner as if they were originally Persian words; with the following exceptions.

1st. When an Arabic word terminating in ى, that must be pronounced as ١*, becomes the first substantive in construction with another substantive following it, ى is actually changed into ١, to which short g (ـ) is afterwards affixed to shew the construction.

Ex. تمنى in construction becomes تمناى, as تمناى شفاعت the petition of intercession, and so also مولى دعوى معنى &c.

2d. Feminine Arabic *substantives* terminating in ة, when introduced into the Persian, change ة, sometimes into ه, and sometimes into ت.

Ex. محبت friendship, being found written by the same author محبه and محبت.

3d. Feminine Arabic *adjectives* and *participles* terminating in ت, when introduced into the Persian, always change ت into ه.

* See Richardson's Arabic Gram. p. 109. Canon. III.

Ex. خالصت pure, is always written خالصه, as معبت خالصه pure friendship.

4*tb.* Arabic participles plural terminating in ین, although introduced into the Persian as nominatives, are originally the oblique case.

Ex. دانایان، متقد مبی چنبی فر مودند the learned ancients thus said.

5*tb.* When an Arabic infinitive is used in the Persian language as an adverb, it is introduced in the form of the Arabic accusative without any change.

Ex. اتفاقا accidentally, &c. &c.

OF ARABIC ADVERBS, PREPOSITIONS, AND CONJUNCTIONS.

I. Arabic adverbs, prepositions, and conjunctions, seem to be introduced into the Persian language at pleasure. Of these Mr. Richardson has made a very useful collection in his chapter of separate particles, to which I beg leave to refer; observing, at the same time, that a knowledge of such as are most frequently employed, will easily be acquired from experience without any particular instructions.

OF ARABIC COMPOUNDS.

I. The manner in which different Arabic parts of speech are employed to form a variety of compounded words made use of in the Persian, is well explained by Sir William Jones in his Persian Grammar; and

with respect to phrases purely Arabic, and whole
sentences, which are often met with in Persian au‐
thors, they require a perfect knowledge of the Arabic
language, and do not belong to this place.

OF THE CONSTRUCTION OF ARABIC
INFINITIVES, PARTICIPLES, SUB-
STANTIVES, AND ADJECTIVES.

I. In the Persian language, when Arabic adjectives
or participles are made use of to qualify Arabic or
Persian substantives singular, they agree with them
in gender and number.

Ex.

1. an Arabic sub. mas. qualified   عاشق مذکور   the said lover
   by an Arabic part. mas.

2. an Arabic sub. fem. qualified   والده مکرمه   respected mother
   by an Arabic part. pas. fem.

3. a Pers. sub. mas. qualified by   دوست قدیم   an old friend
   an Arabic ad. mas.

4. a Pers. sub. fem. qualified by   همشیره عزیزه   dear sister
   an Arabic ad. fem.

II. When Arabic adjectives and participles are
made use of to qualify Arabic and Persian substan‐
tives masculine and plural, they remain in the mas‐
culine singular.

Ex.

1. an Arabic sub. mas. plu. with   حکام مذکور   the said officers
   an Arabic part. mas. sing.

2. a Pers. sub. mas. plu. with   برادران مذکور   the said brethren
   an Arab. part. mas. sing.

III. When Arabic adjectives and participles are
made use of to qualify Arabic or Persian substantives
feminine and plural, they are put in the feminine singular; and often, though not so properly, in the
masculine singular.

Ex.
1. an Arabic sub.
fem. plur. with
Arabic part. sin.

both fem. masc. تكليفات مذكوره مذكور the said burthens

2. a Persian sub. fem.
plur. with Arabic
part. sing. both fem.

and mas. زنان موصوفه موصوف accomplished women

IV. An Arabic substantive, in the Persian, is often
rendered definite by a following Arabic adjective or
participle having the article ال prefixed.

Ex. a sub. with a part. pas. نبي المختار the prophet elect

For an account of the genders of Arabic words,
and of their perfect and imperfect plurals, I must
again refer to Mr. *Richardson*'s Arabic Grammar;
and to that of *Erpenius*, where the latter subject is
treated at still greater length.

Of the INTRODUCTION of the ARABIC
into the LANGUAGE of HINDOSTAN.

I. All the different species of infinitives, participles, substantives, and adjectives, which we have
enumerated; and all compounds formed by *Arabic*

and *Persian* words, are introduced into the language
of *Hindostan*, in the same form, for the same purposes, and with the same freedom as in the *Persian*:
submitting themselves to the different rules of regi-
men and concord that are peculiar to *that* language;
in the same manner as if they were words originally
belonging to it. *Arabic* adverbs, prepositions, and
conjunctions, are also used in the language of *Hindostan*; but I think less frequently than in the Persian.

XV.

ON THE

ASTRONOMICAL COMPUTATIONS

OF THE

HINDUS.

BY SAMUEL DAVIS, Esq.

Bhagalpur, 15th Feb. 1789.

IT is, I believe, generally admitted, that inquiries
into the astronomy of the *Hindus* may lead to much
curious information, besides what relates merely to
the science itself; and that attempts to ascertain the
chronology of this ancient nation will, as they have
hitherto done, prove unsatisfactory unless assistance
be derived from such researches.

The following communication is not expected to
contribute towards so desirable a purpose; but, with
all its imperfections, it may have the useful effect of
awakening the attention of others in this country who
are better qualified for such investigations, and of in-
citing them to pursue the same object more success-
fully, by showing that numerous treatises in *Sanscrit*
on astronomy are procurable, and that the *Brahmens*
are extremely willing to explain them. As an encouragement to those who may be inclined to amuse
themselves in this way, I can farther venture to de-
clare, from the experience I have had, that *Sanscrit*
books in this science are more easily translated than
almost any others, when once the technical terms are
understood: the subject of them admitting neither
of metaphysical reasoning nor of metaphor, but being delivered in plain terms and generally illustrated
with examples in practice, the meaning may be well
enough made out, by the help of a *Pandit,* through
the medium of the *Persian* or the *Hindi* language,

Moreover, it does not appear that skill in the abstruse parts of modern mathematics is indispensably necessary; but that, with as much knowledge of geometry and the circles of the sphere as, it may be supposed, most of the members of this society possess, a considerable progress might be made in revealing many interesting particulars, which at present lie hid to *Europeans* in the *Jyotish*, or astronomical, *Sastra*.

The prediction of eclipses and other phenomena, published in the *Hindu Patra*, or almanac, excited my curiosity long ago to know by what means it was effected; but it was not until lately that I had any means of gratification. I had before this been inclined to think, with many others, that the *Brahmens* possess no more knowledge in astronomy than they have derived from their ancestors in tables ready calculated to their hands, and that few traces of the principles of the science could be found among them; but by consulting some *Sanscrit* books, I was induced to alter my opinion. To satisfy myself on this subject, I begin with calculating, by a modern *Hindu* formula, an eclipse which will happen in next *November*; the particulars of which process, although in some measure interesting, were not sufficient for my purpose, as it yet remained to be learnt on what grounds some tables used in it were constructed; and for this information I was referred to the *Surya Siddhanta*, an original treatise, and reputed a divine revelation. For a copy of the *Surya Siddhanta* I am indebted to Sir *Robert Chambers*, who procured it among other books at *Benares*; but the obscurity of many technical terms made it some times difficult to be understood even by the *Pandit* I employed, who was by no means deeply versed in the science he professed. By his diligence, however, and through the obliging assistance of Mr. *Duncan* at *Benares*, who procured for me the *Tica*, or Commentary, this

difficulty was at length surmounted ; and a computation of the above-mentioned eclipse, not merely on
the principles, but strictly by the rules, of the *Surya
Siddhanta*, is what I propose now to present you with,
after such preliminary observations as may be necessary to make it intelligible.

I suppose it sufficiently well known, that the *Hindu*
division of the ecliptic into signs, degrees, &c. is the
same as ours ; that their astronomical year is sydereal,
or containing that space of time in which the sun, departing from a star, returns to the same ; that it commences on the instant of his entering the sign *Aries*, or
rather the *Hindu* constellation *Mesha* [a] ; that each astronomical month contains as many even days and
fractional parts as he stays in each sign ; and that the
civil differs from the astronomical account of time
only in rejecting those fractions, and beginning the
year and month at sunrise, instead of the intermediate
instant of the artificial day or night. Hence arises the
unequal portion of time assigned to each month dependent on the situation of the sun's apsis, and the
distance of the vernal equinoctial colure from the
beginning of *Mesha* in the *Hindu* sphere; and by
these means they avoid those errors which *Europeans*,
from a different method of adjusting their calendar by
intercalary days, have been subject to. An explanation of these matters would lead me beyond my present intention, which is to give a general account only
of the method by which the *Hindus* compute eclipses,
and thereby to show, that a late *French* author was too
hasty in asserting generally that they determine them

---

[a] Or, to be more particular, on his entering the *Nacshatra*, or
lunar mansion (*Aswini*). There were formerly only twenty-seven
Nacshatras: a 28th (*Abhijit*) has been since added, taken out of the
21st and 22d, named *Uttarashara* and *Sravana*. These three in
their order comprehend 10°, 5°, and 11° 40' of the Zodiac : the
rest comprehend 13° 20' each.

" by set forms, couched in enigmatical verses,[*]" &c,
So far are they from deserving the reproach of ignorance which Mons. *Sonnerat* has implied, that on inquiry, I believe, the *Hindu* science of astronomy will
be found as well known now as it ever was among
them, although, perhaps, not so generally, by reason
of the little encouragement men of science at present
meet with, compared with what they formerly did under their native princes.

It has been common with astronomers to fix on some
epoch, from which, as from a radix, to compute the
planetary motions; and the ancient *Hindus* chose that
point of time counted back when, according to their
motions as they had determined them, they must have
been in conjunction in the beginning of *Mesha*, or
Aries; and coeval with which circumstance they supposed the creation.   This, as it concerned the planets
only, would have produced a moderate term of years
compared with the enormous antiquity, that will be
hereafter stated; but, having discovered a slow motion of the nodes and apsides also, and taking it into
the computation, they found it would require a length
of time corresponding with 1955884890 years now
expired, when they were so situated, and 2364115110
years more, before they would return to the same situation again, forming together the grand anomalistic
period denominated a *Calpa*, and fancifully assigned as
the day of *Brahma*.   The *Calpa* they divided into
Manwantaras, and greater and less *Yugas*.   The use
of the *Manwantara* is not stated in the *Surya Siddhanta*; but that of the *Maha*, or greater *Yug*, is sufficiently
evident, as being an anomalistic period of the sun and
moon, at the end of which the latter, with her apogee
and ascending node, is found, together with the sun,

---

[*] See the translation of Mons. *Sonnerat's* Voyage.

In the first of *Aries*; the planets also deviating from that point only as much as is their latitude and the difference between their mean and true anomaly.

These cycles being so constructed as to contain a certain number of mean solar days, and the *Hindu* system assuming that at the creation, when the planets began their motions, a right line, drawn from the equinoctial point *Lanca* through the centre of the earth, would, if continued, have passed through the centre of the sun and planets to the first star in *Aries*: their mean longitude for any proposed time afterwards may be computed by proportion. As the revolutions a planet makes in any cycle are to the number of days composing it, so are the days given to its motion in that time; and the even revolutions being rejected, the fraction, if any, shows its mean longitude at midnight under their first meridian of *Lanca*: for places east or west of that meridian a proportional allowance is made for the difference of longitude on the earth's surface, called in *Sanscrit* the *Desantara*. The positions of the apsides and nodes are computed in the same manner; and the equation of the mean to the true place, determined on principles which will be hereafter mentioned.

The division of the *Maha Yug* into the *Satya*, *Treta*, *Dwapar*, and *Cali* ages, does not appear from the *Surya Siddhanta* to answer any practical astronomical purpose, but to have been formed on ideas similar to the *golden*, *silver*, *brazen*, and *iron* ages of the *Greeks*. Their origin has however been ascribed to the precession of the equinoxes by those who will of course refer the *Manwantera* and *Calpa* to the same foundation: either way the latter will be found anomalistic, as has been described, if I rightly understand the following passage in the first section of the *Surya Siddhanta*; the translation of which is, I believe, here correctly given. Q 2

—— "Time, of the denomination *Murta* *, is
" estimated by respirations; six respirations make a
" *Vicala*, sixty *Vicalas* a *Danda*, sixty *Dandas* a *Nac-*
" *shatra* day, and thirty *Nacshatra* days a *Nacshatra*
" month· The *Savan* month is that contained be-
" tween thirty successive risings of *Surya*, and varies in
" its length according to the *Lagna Bhuja*. Thirty
" *Tit'his* compose the *Chandra* month. The *Saura*
" month is that in which the sun describes one sign
" of the Zodiac, and his passage through the twelve
" signs is one year, and one of those years is a *Deva*
" day, or day of the Gods. When it is day at *Asura* †
" it is night with the *Gods*, and when it is day with the
" *Gods* it is night at *Asura*. Sixty of the *Deva* days
" multiplied by six give the *Deva* year, and twelve
" hundred of the *Deva* years form the aggregate of
" the four *Yugas*. To determine the *Saura* years
" contained in this aggregate, write down the following
" numbers, 4, 3, 2, which multiply by 10,000; the
" product 4,320,000 is the aggregate of *Maha Yuga*,
" including the *Sandhi* and *Sundhyansa* ‡. This is
" divided into four *Yugas*, by reason of the diffe-
" rent proportions of *Virtue* prevailing on earth, in
" the following manner:—— Divide the aggregate
" 4,320,000 by 10, and multiply the quotient by four
" for the *Satya Yug*, by three for the *Treta*, by two

* This is mean sydereal time:—A *Nacshatra*, or sydereal day, is
the time in which the earth makes a turn upon its axis, or, according to the *Hindus*, in which the stars make one complete revolution.
This is shorter than the *Savan*, or solar day, which varies in its
length according to the *Lagna Bhuja*, or right ascension, and also
from the sun's unequal motion in the ecliptic; for both which
circumstances the *Hindus* have their *equation of time*, as will appear in the calculation of the eclipse.

† *Asura*, the south pole, the habitation of the *Asura Loca*, or
demons, with whom the *Devas*, who reside at *Sumeru*, the north
pole, wage eternal war.

‡ *Sandhi* and *Sandhyansa*, the morning and evening twilight.
The proper words, I believe, are *Sandhya* and *Sandhyansa*.

" for the *Dwapar*, and by one for the *Cali Yug*. Di-
" vide either of the *Yugs* by six for its *Sandhi* and
" *Sandhyansa*. Seventy one *Yugs* make a *Manwan-*
" *tera*; and at the close of each *Manwantera* there is
" a *Sandhi* equal to the *Satya Yug*, during which
" there is an universal deluge. Fourteen *Manwan-*
" *teras*, including the *Sandhi*, compose a *Calpa*, and
" at the commencement of each *Calpa* there is a
" *Sandhi* equal to the *Satya Yug*, or 1,728,000 *Saura*
" years.) A *Calpa* is therefore equal to 1000 *Maha*
" *Yugs*. One *Calpa* is a day with *Brahma*, and his
" night is of the same length; and the period of his
" life is 100 of his years. One half of the term of
" *Brahma's* life, or fifty years, is expired, and of the
" remainder the first *Calpa* is begun; and six *Man-*
" *wanteras*, including the *Sandhi*, are expired. The
" seventh *Manwantera*, into which we are now ad-
" vanced, is named *Vaivaswata*. Of this *Manwantera*
" twenty-seven *Maha Yugs* are elapsed, and we are
" now in the *Satya Yug* of the twenty-eighth, which
" *Satya Yug* consists of 1,728,000 *Saura* years. The
" whole amount of years, expired from the begin-
" ning of the *Calpa* * to the present time, may hence

---

* Construction of the *Calpa*.

		Years.
Cali,	$\frac{4320000}{10} =$	432000
Dwapar,	$\frac{4320000}{10} \times 2 =$	864000
Trita,	$\frac{4320000}{10} \times 3 =$	1296000
Satya,	$\frac{4320000}{10} \times 4 =$	1728000
Aggregate or *Maha Yug*,		4320000
		71
Manwantera,	- -	306720000
With a *Sandhi* equal to the *Satya Yug*,	- - -	1728000
		308448000
		14
Calpa, - - - -		4318272000
With a *Sandhi* equal to the *Satya Yug*	- - -	1728000
Whole duration of *Calpa*,		4320000000

Computation of the period elapsed of the *Calpa* at the end of the last *Satya* age, when the *Surya Siddhanta* is supposed to have been written.

	Years.
Sandhi at the beginning of the *Calpa*, - - -	1728000
6 *Manwanteras*, or 1848480000 × 6 =	1850880000
27 *Maha Yugs* of the 7th *Manwantera*, or 4320000 × 27 =	116640000
Satya Age of the 28th *Maha Yug*, - - =	1728000
	1970784000

Q 3

" be computed ; but from the number of years so
" found, must be made a deduction of one hundred
" times four hundred and seventy-four divine years,.
" or of that product multiplied by three hundred and
" sixty for human years, that being the term of *Brah-*
" *ma*'s employment in the creation ; after which the
" planetary motions commenced.

" Sixty *Vicalas* make one *Cala*, sixty *Calas* one
" *Bhoga*, thirty *Bhagas* one *Rasi*, and there are
" twelve *Rasis* in the *Bhogana* *.

" † In one *Yug*, *Surya*, *Budha*, and *Sucra* perform
" 4320000 *Madhyama* revolutions through the Zodiac.
" *Mangala*, *Vrihaspati*, and *Sani* make the same num-
" ber of *Sighra* revolutions through it ; *Chandra* makes
" 57753336 ‡ *Madhyama* revolutions ; *Mangala*
" 2296632 *Madhyama* revolutions ; *Budha*'s *Sighras*
" are 17937060 ; *Vrihaspati*'s *Madhyamas* 364220 ;
" *Sucru*'s *Sighras* 7022376 ; *Sani*'s *Madhyamas* are
" 146568. The *Chandrochcha* revolutions are 488203 ;
" the retrograde revolutions of the *Chandrapata* are
" 232238.

" The time contained between sunrise and sunrise
" is the *Bhumi Savan* day : the number of those days

---

* The division of the *Bhagana*, or Zodiac, into signs, degrees, &c.

† *Surya* the Sun ; *Budha*, Mercury ; *Sucra*, Venus ; *Mangala*,
Mars ; *Vrihaspati*, Jupiter ; *Sani*, Saturn ; *Chandra*, the Moon ;
the *Chandra Uchcha*, or *Chandrochcha*, the Moon's apogee ; *Chandra Pata*, the Moon's ascending node. The *Madhyama* revolutions of Mars, Jupiter, and Saturn, and the *Sighra* revolutions of
Venus and Mercury, answer to their revolutions about the Sun.

‡ 57753336—4320000=53433336 lunar months, or lunations
in a *Yug* ;   *D. D. P.*
                    and $\frac{147791781.8}{53433336}$=29 31 50, 6, &c.
                                                 D. H. M. S.
in each mean lunation, or in English time 29 . 12 . 44 . 2 47'''36''''.
53433336—51840000= 1593336 *Adhi* or intercalary lunar months
in 4320000 solar sydereal years.

" contained in a *Yug* is 1577917828 ". The number
" of *Nacshatra* days 1582237828 + ; of *Chandra* days
" 1603000080 ; of *Adhi* months 1593336 ; of *Cshaya*
" *Ti'his* 25082252 ; of *Saura* months 51840000.
" From either of the planets *Nacshatra* days deduct

* $\frac{1577917828}{4320000}$ = 365. 15. 31. 31. 24. diurnal revolutions of the Sun, the length of the *Hindu* year.

+ $\frac{1582117828}{4320000}$ = 365. 15. 31. 31. 24. diurnal revolutions of the stars in one year.

$\frac{1577917828}{57753336}$ = 27. 19. 18. 1. 37. &c. the Moon's periodical month. The 1603000080 *Chandra*, or lunar days, called also *Ti'bis*, are each one-thirtieth part of the moon's synodical month or relative period, and vary in length according to the inequality of her motion from the sun. The *Cshaya Ti'bi* and *Adbi*, or intercalary lunar months, are sufficiently evident.

The sun and planets preside alternately over the days of the week, which are named accordingly. The first day after the creation was *Revivar*, or *Sunday* : it began at midnight, under the meridian of *Lanca* ; and the *Revivar* of the *Hindus* corresponds with our Sunday. The sun and planets in the same manner govern the years ; hence they may be said to have *weeks* of years. *David's* prophecy is supposed to mean *weeks* of years.

The *Hindu* cycle of 60, supposed by some to be the Chaldean *Sosos*, is referred to the planet Jupiter : " one of these years is
" equal to the time in which by the mean motion, he (*Vrihaspati*)
" advances one degree in his orbit." (Commentary on the *Surya*
Siddhanta.) This cycle is, I believe, wholly applied to astrology.
Neither this cycle of 60 nor the *Pitri's* day are mentioned in this
part of the *Surya Siddhanta*, where they might be expected to occur. Perhaps on inquiry there may be found some reason for supposing them both of a later invention. " The *Pitris* inhabit be-
" hind *Chandra*, and their mid-day happens when *Chandra* is in
" conjunction with *Surya*; and their midnight, when *Chandra* is in
" opposition to *Surya* ; their morning, or sunrise, is at the end
" of half the *Crishna Pacsha* ; and their sunset at the end of half
" the *Sucla Pacsha* ; this is declared in the *Sacrlys Sanhita*. Their
" names are *Agni*, *Swati*, &c. their day and night are therefore
together equal to one *Chandra* month." (Commentary). Hence,
it appears, the *Hindus* have observed that the moon revolves once
on her axis in a lunar month, and consequently has the same side
always opposed to the earth. They have also noticed the difference of her apparent magnitude in the horizon and on the meridian, and endeavour to explain the cause of a phenomenon, which
Europeans as well as themselves are at a loss to account for.

" the number of its revolutions, the remainder will
" be the number of its *Savan* days contained in a *Yug*.
" The difference between the number of the revolu-
" tions of *Surya* and *Chandra* gives the number of
" *Chandra* months ; and the difference between the
" *Saura* months and *Chandra* months gives their num-
" ber of *Adhi* months. Deduct the *Savan* days from
" the *Chandra* days, the remainder will be the num-
" ber of *Tit'hi Cshayas*. The number of *Adhi* months,
" *Tit'hi Cshayas*, *Nacshatra*, *Chandra*, and *Savan*
" days, multiplied severally by 1000, gives the num-
" ber of each contained in a *Calpa*.

" The number of *Mandochcha* revolutions, which
" revolutions are direct, or according to the order of
" the signs contained in a *Calpa*, is of *Surya* 387 ;
" of *Mangala* 204 ; of *Buddha* 368 ; of *Frihaspati*
" 900 ; of *Sucra* 535 ; of *Sani* 39.

" The number of revolutions of the *Patas*, which
" revolutions are retrograde, or contrary to the order
" of the signs, contained in a *Calpa*, is of *Mangala*
" 214 ; of *Buddha* 488 ; of *Frihaspati* 174 ; of *Su-*
" *cra* 903 ; of *Sani* 662. The *Pata* and *Uchcha* of
" *Chandra* are already mentioned."

It must be observed, that, although the planetary
motions as above determined might have served for
computations in the time of *Meya*, the author of the
Surya Siddhanta, yet for many years past they have not
been found to agree with the observed places in the
heavens in every instance ; and that corrections have
accordingly been introduced, by increasing or reducing
those numbers. Thus the motions of the moon's apo-
geo and node are now increased in computations of
their places by the addition of four revolutions each in
a *Yug* to their respective numbers above given. The
nature of these corrections, denominated in *Sanscrit*

I

Bija, is explained in a passage of the *Tica*, or Commentary, on the *Surya Siddhanta*, wherein is maintained the priority of that *Sastra* in point of time to all others. The translation of that passage, together with the text it illustrates, is as follows :

(Surya Siddhanta). " *Arca* (the Sun) addressing " *Meya*, who attended with reverence, said, Let your " attention, abstracted from human concerns, be wholly " applied to what I shall relate. *Surya* in every for- " mer *Yug* revealed to the *Munis* the invariable science " of astronomy. The planetary motions may alter ; " but the principles of that science are always the " same."

The Commentary. — " Hence it appears, that the " *Surya Siddhanta* was prior to the *Brahma Siddhanta* " and every other *Sastra* ; because this *Sastra* must be " the same that was revealed *in every former Yug*, al- " though the motions of the planets might have been " different. This variation in the planetary motions " is mentioned in the *Vishnu Dhermotter*, which di- " rects that the planets be observed with an instru- " ment, whereby their agreement or disagreement " may be determined in regard to their computed " places ; and in case of the latter, an allowance of " *Bija* accordingly made. *Vasisht'ha* in his *Siddhanta* " also recommends this occasional correction of *Bija*, " saying to the *Muni Mandavya*, " I have shown you " how to determine some matters in astronomy ; but " the mean motion of *Surya* and the other planets " will be found to differ in each *Yug*." Accordingly " *Aryabhatta, Brahmagupta*, and others, having ob- " served the heavens, formed rules on the principles " of former *Sastras*, but which differed from each " other in proportion to the disagreements which " they severally observed of the planets, with re- " spect to their computed places.

" Why the *Munis*, who certainly knew, did not
" give the particulars of those deviations, may seem
" unaccountable, when the men *Aryabhatta, Brah-*
" *magupta*, and others have determined them. The
" reason was, that those deviations are not in them-
" selves uniform ; and to state their variations would
" have been endless. It was therefore thought better,
" that examinations at different times should be made,
" and due corrections of the *Bija* introduced. A
" *Ganita Sastra*, whose rules are demonstrable, is
" true ; and when conjunctions, oppositions, and
" other planetary phenomena, calculated by such
" *Sastras*, are found not to agree with observation,
" a proportionable *Bija* may be introduced without
" any derogation from their credit. It was therefore
" necessary, that this *Sastra* (the *Surya Siddhanta*)
" should be revealed in each *Yug*, and that other
" *Sastra* should be composed by the *Munis*.

" The original *Sastra* then appears to be the *Surya*
" *Siddhanta* ; the second, the *Brahma Siddhanta* ; the
" third, the *Paulastya Siddhanta* ; the fourth, the *Soma*
" *Siddhanta*."

In the following table are given the periodical revolutions of the planets, their nodes and apsides, according to the *Surya Siddhanta*. The corrections of *Bija*
at present used, are contained in one column *, and
the inclination of their orbits to the ecliptic in another. The obliquity of the ecliptic is inserted ac-

---

* This I must, however, at present om.it, not having as yet discovered the corrections of this kind that will bring even the Sun's
place, computed by the *Surya Siddhanta*, exactly to an agreement
with the astronomical books in present use. Of these books, the
principal are the *Grahalaghava*, composed about 268 years ago, the
tables of *Macaranda* used at *Benares* and *Tirhut*, and the *Sidd-*
hanta Rahasya, used at *Nadya* ; the last written in 1513 *Saca*, or
198 years ago.

cording to the same *Sastra*. Its diminution does not
appear to have been noticed in any subsequent
treatise. In the tables of *Macaranda* and also in the
Grahalaghava, the latter written only 268 years ago,
it is expressly stated at twenty-four degrees.

The motion of the equinoxes, termed in *Sanscrit*
the *Cranti*, and spoken of in the *Tica*, or commentary, on the *Surya Siddhanta* as the Sun's *pata* or
node, is not noticed in the foregoing passage of that
book; and, as the *Hindu* astronomers seem to entertain an idea of the subject different from that of
its revolution through the *Platonic* year I shall farther on give a translation of what is mentioned, both
in the original and commentary, concerning it.

The next requisite for the computation of the eclipse
is the portion of the *Calpa* expired to the present
time, which is determined in the following manner :

The *Surya Siddhanta* is supposed to have been received, through divine revelation, towards the close of
the *Satya* age, at the end of which, 50 of the years
of *Brahma* were expired, and of the next *Calpa*, or
day, 6 *Manwanteras*, 27 greater Jugs, and the *Satya*
age of the the 28th *Jug*, together with the *Sandhya*
or twilight at the beginning of the *Calpa* ; the aggregate of which several periods is 1970781000 years
elapsed of the *Calpa* to the beginning of the last
Treta age ; to which add the *Treta* and *Dwapar* ages,
together with the years elapsed of the present *Cali*
age, for the whole amount of sydereal years from the
beginning of the *Calpa* to the present *Bengal* year.
But in the foregoing quotation it is observed, from
that amount of years must be made a deduction of
47400 divine, or 17064000 human or sydereal years,
the term of *Brahma's* employment in the work of

The TABLE. See page 236.

The Planets in their order.	Sydereal Period.	Period of the Apsides.	Period of the Nodes.	Mean motion per day '" per danda '"	Inclination of the Orbit.	Cacsha, or circumference of the Orbit.
	Days. D. P. V.	Days. D.	Days. D.	' ''		Yojan.
The Moon,	27 19 18 1 &c.	3232 50 —	6794 23	790 35	4 30	324000
Mercury,	87 58 10	1189820164 46 —	3331724558 11	186 24	2 —	1043208
Venus,	88 39 38	2949379117 45 &c.	17471173 06 45	37	2	2664 0637
The Sun,	365 15 13 31 24	4977307949 5 —	Precession of the equinoxes 54" per year.	59 8	Obliquity of the Ecliptic 24°	4331500
Mars,	686 59 50 38	775587192 9 &c.	7371447794 23 &c.	31 26	1 30	8146929
Jupiter,	4332 19 14 20 &c.	1751242091 6 &c.	9608403264 20 &c.	5 —	1 —	51375764
Saturn,	10785 46 2 18 &c.	14976711701 52 &c.	2183361673 42 &c.	2 —	2 —	127668255

The longitude of the Sun's apogee in the *Hindu* sphere is 2', 17°, 17', 15", to which add the *Ayanansa* 19°, 21', 27", the sum 3°, 6°, 38', 42", is its place according to *European* expression. In this the *Hindu* account differs about 1° 22' from the observations of *European* astronomers, who determine the place of the earth's aphelion in the present age to be in 9°, 8°, 1'. There is much greater disagreement with respect to the aphelia and nodes of the other planets.

On supposition that the obliquity of the ecliptic was accurately observed by the ancient *Hindus*, as 24°, and that its decrease has been from that time half a second a year, the date of the *Surya Siddhanta* will be about 3840 years. It is remarkable that the *Hindus* do not appear to have noticed its decrease.

The *Cacshas* are explained farther on.

creation; for, as the universe was not completed, the planetary motions did not commence until that portion of the *Calpa* was elapsed.

This deduction appears to have been intended as a correction, which, without altering the date of the *Calpa* as settled, probably, by yet more ancient astronomers, might (joined perhaps with other regulations) bring the computed places of the planets to an agreement with their observed places, when the *Surya Siddhanta* was written; and, as the arguments of its commentator in support of the propriety of it, without prejudice to other authors, contain some curious particulars, I hope I may be excused for departing from my immediate object to insert a translation of them.

" In the *Surya Siddhanta, Soma Siddhanta, Praja-
" peti, Vasisht'ha,* and other *Sastras,* this deduction
" is required to be made from the *Calpa,* because at
" the end of that term the planetary motions com-
" menced. The son of *Jishnu,* who understood four
" *Vedas,* and *Bhascaracharya,* considered these mo-
" tions as commencing with the *Calpa.* It may seem
" strange that there should be such a disagreement.
" Some men say, As it is written that the *Calpa* is
" the day of *Brahma,* and as a day is dependent on
" the rising and setting of the sun, the motion of the
" sun and planets must have begun with the *Calpa*;
" and therefore *Brahmagupta* should be followed;
" but I think otherwise. The *Calpa* or *Brahma's* day
" is not to be understood as analogous to the solar day
" otherwise than as containing a determined portion
" of time; neither is it at all dependent on the com-
" mencement of the *Calpa*; but, being composed of the
" same periods as the latter, it will not end until the
" term of years here deducted shall be expired of the
" next *Calpa.* The motions of the *Grahas* must

" therefore be computed from the point of time there
" stated, as the beginning of *Brahma*'s day, and not
" as *Brahmagupta* and others direct, from the begin-
" ning of the *Culpa* ; which will not be found to an-
" swer.

" Other men say, that rules derived from the *Ganita*
" *Sastra* and agreeing with observation, are right ;.
" that any period deduced from such a mode of com-
" putation, and the planets determined to have been
" then in the first of *Mesha*, may be assumed ; that
" it will therefore answer either way, to consider these
" motions as beginning with the *Calpa*, or after the
" above-mentioned period of it was expired. This
" however is not true; for in the instance of *Mangala*
" there will be found a great difference, as is here
" shown. The revolutions of *Mangala* in a *Culpa*,
" according to *Brahmagupta*, are 2296823522, and,
" by the rule of proportion, the revolutions of *Man-*
" *gala* in 17064000 years are 9072472 7' 28° 0' 16" *.
" For any other planet, on trial, a similar disagree-,
" ment will be found, and the proposition of comput-
" ing from either period must be erroneous. More-
" over, of what use is it to make computations for a
" space of time, when the planets and their motions
" were not in being ?

" It might, however, from the foregoing circum-
" stances, be imputed to *Brahmagupta* and the
" rest, that they have given precepts through igno-

---

* Because $\frac{2296823522 \times 17064000}{4320000000}$ = $\underset{\text{Revolutions.}}{9072472}$ 7, 28° 0' 16"

" rance, or with intent to deceive—That, having
" stated the revolutions of the planets different from
" the account revealed by *Surya*, they must certainly
" have been in error—That *Brahmagupta* could not
" have counted the revolutions from the beginning of
" the *Calpa*: neither could he from the mean mo-
" tion of the planets have so determined them.—He
" was a mortal, and therefore could not count the re-
" volutions.—Although the rule of proportion should
" be granted to have served his purpose for the revo-
" lutions of the planets, yet it certainly could not for
" those of their *Mandochcha*, because it was not within
" the term of a man's life to determine the mean mo-
" tion of the *Mandochcha*; and this assertion is justi-
" fied by the opinion of *Bhascaracharya*. But the rule
" of proportion could not have answered even for the
" planets; for, although their mean motion be ob-
" served one day, and again the next, how can a man
" be certain of the exact time elapsed between the two
" observations? And if there be the smallest error in
" the elapsed time, the rule of proportion cannot
" answer for such great periods. An error of the
" 10-millionth part of a second *(Vicala)* in one day,
" amounts to forty degrees * in the computation of a
" *Calpa*; and the mistake of 1-tenth of a respiration in
" one *Saura* year, makes a difference in the same pe-
" riod of 20000 days. That it is therefore evident,
" *Brahmagupta*'s motive for directing the planetary
" motions to be computed as commencing with the
" *Calpa*, was to deceive mankind, and that he had
" not the authority of the *Munis*, because he differs
" from the *Surya Siddhanta*, *Brahma Siddhanta*, *Soma*
" *Siddhanta*; from *Vasishtha*, and other *Munis*.

---

* The error would be more than 43°

" Such opinions would have no foundation, as I
" shall proceed to show. *Brahmagupta's* rules are
" consistent with the practice of the *Pandits* his pre-
" decessors; and he formed them from the *Purana*
" *Vishnu Dhermottara*, wherein is contained the
" *Brahma Siddhanta* ; and the periods given by *Ary-*
" *abhatta* are derived from the *Parasera Siddhanta* :
" the precepts of the *Munis* are therefore the autho-
" rities of *Brahmagupta, Aryabhatta*, and *Bhasca-*
" *racharya*, whose rules cannot be deceitful. The
" *Munis* themselves differed with regard to the num-
" ber of *Savan* days in a *Yug*, which is known from
" the *Pancha Siddhanta*, composed by *Vara Acharya* ;
" wherein are proposed two methods of computing
" the sun's place, the one according to the *Surya*
" *Siddhanta*, the other according to the *Romaca Sidd-*
" *hanta* ; whence it appears that there were diffe-
" rent rules of computation even among the *Munis*.
" It is also mentioned in the *Tica* on the *Varaha*
" *Sanhita*, that, according to the *Paulastya Siddhanta*,
" there was formerly a different number of *Savan*
" days estimated in a *Yug*. The maxims therefore of
" *Brahmagupta* and the other two, agreeing with those
" of the *Munis*, are right ; but, should it even be
" supposed that the *Munis* themselves could be
" mistaken, yet *Brahmagupta* and the other two had
" the sanction of the *Vedas*, which in their numerous
" *Sac'has* (branches) have disagreements of the same
" kind ; and, according to the *Sacalya Sanhita*,
" *Brahma*, in the revelation he made to *Nared*, told
" him, although a circumstance or thing were not
" perceptible to the senses, or reconcileable to rea-
" son, if authority for believing it should be found
" in the *Vedas*, it must be received as true.

" If a planet's place, computed both by the *Surya*
" *Siddhanta* and *Parasera Siddhanta*, should be found

" to differ, which rule must be received as right?
" I answer, that which agrees with his place
" by observation: and the *Munis* gave the same di-
" rection. If computations from the beginning of
" the *Calpa*, and from the period stated in the *Surya*
" *Siddhanta* give a difference, as appears in the in-
" stance of *Mangala*, which of the two periods to be
" computed from is founded in truth? I say it is
" of no consequence to us which, since our ob-
" ject is only to know which period answers for com-
" putation of the planetary places in our time, not
" at the beginning of the *Calpa*. The difference
" found in computing according to *Brahmagupta* and
" the *Munis*, must be corrected by an allowance of
" *bija*, or by taking that difference as the *eshepa*;
" but the books of the *Munis* must not be altered,
" and the rules given by *Brahmagupta*, *Varacharya*,
" and *Aryabhatta* may be used with such precautions.
" Any person may compose a set of rules for the com-
" mon purposes of astronomy; but, with regard to
" the duties necessary in eclipses, the computation
" must be made by the books of the *Munis*, and the
" *bija* applied; and in this manner it was that *Vara-
" ha*, *Aryabhatta*, *Brahmagupta*, and *Cesava Samvat-
" sara*, having observed the planets and made due al-
" lowance'of *bija*, composed their books.

" *Ganesa* mentions, that the *Grahas* were right in
" their computed places in the time of *Brahma*,
" *Acharya*, *Vasisht'ha*, *Casyapa*, and others, by the
" rules they gave, but in length of time they differed;
" after which, at the close of the *Satya* age, *Surya* re-
" vealed to *Meya* a computation of their true places.
" The rules then received answered during the *Treta*
" and *Dwapar* ages, as also did other rules formed
" by the *Munis* during those periods. In the begin-
" ning of the *Cali Yug*, *Parasera*'s book answered;
" but *Aryabhatta*, many years after, having examined

" the heavens, found some deviation, and introduced
" a correction of *bija*. After him, when further de-
" viations were observed, *Durga Sinha*, *Mihira*, and
" others, made corrections. After them came the
" son of *Jistnu* and *Brahmagupta*, and made correc-
" tions. After them *Cesava* settled the places of
" the planets ; and, sixty years after *Cesava*, his son
" *Ganesa* made corrections."

We have now, according to the *Hindu* system, the
mean motion of the planets, their nodes and apsides,
and the elapsed time since they were in conjunction
in the first of *Mesha*, with which, by the rule of proportion, to determine their mean longitude for any
proposed time of the present year. It is, however,
observed in the *Surya Siddhanta*, that to assume a
period so great is unnecessary; for use, the computation may be made from the beginning of the *Treta*
age, at which instant all the *Grahas*, or moveable
points in the heavens, were again in conjunction in
Mesha, except the apogees and ascending nodes,
which must therefore be computed from the creation.
The same is true of the beginning of the present *Cali*
age; for the greatest common divisor of the number
of days composing the *Maha Yug* and the planetary
revolutions in that period, is four, which quotes
394479457 days, or 1080000 years ; and the *Treta*
and *Dwapar* ages contain together just that number
of years. The present *Hindu* astronomers therefore
find it unnecessary to go farther back than the beginning of the *Cali Yug* * in determining the mean lon-

* Neither do they, in computing by the formulas in common
use, go farther back than to some assigned date of the æra *Sara* ;
but, having the planets places determined for that point of time,
they compute their mean places and other requisites for any proposed date afterwards by tables, or by combinations of figures contrived to facilitate the work : as in *Grahalaghava*, *Siddhanta Ra-
haya*, and many other books. An inquirer into *Hindu* astronomy
having access to such books only, might easily be led to suppose

girdle of the planets themselves; but for the position of their apsides and nodes, the elapsed time since
the creation must be used; or at least in instances, as
of the sun, when the numbers 387 and 432,000000
are incommensurable but by unity. I have however
in the accompanying computation, taken the latter
period in both cases.

For the equation of the mean to the true anomaly,
in which the solution of triangles is concerned, and
which is next to be considered, the *Hindus* make use
of a canon of sines, constructed according to the
Surya Siddhanta, in the following manner:—" Divide
" the number of minutes contained in one sine 1800
" by eight, the quotient 225 is the first *Jyapinda*, or
" the first of the twenty-fourth portions of half the
" string of the bow. Divide the first *Jyapinda* by
" 225, the quotient 1 deduct from the dividend,
" and the remainder 224 add to the first for the se-
" cond *Jyapinda* 449. Divide the second *Jyapinda*
" by 225, the quotient being 1, and the fraction
" more than half a minute, deduct 2 from the fore-
" going remainder 224, and add the remainder
" so found to the second for the third *Jyapinda* 671.
" Divide this by 225, the quotient 3 deduct from
" the last remainder 222; the remainder so found
" 219, add to the third for the fourth *Jyapinda* 890.
" Divide this by 225, and the quotient deduct from
" the last remainder; the remainder so found add
" to the fourth for the fifth *Jyapinda* 1105, and
" proceed in this manner until the twenty-four *Cra-*

that the *Brahmans* compute eclipses *by set forms, couched in enigmatical verses*, out of which it would be difficult to develop their system of astronomy; and this I apprehend was the case with Mons.
Sonnerat. The *Jyotish Pandits* in general, it is true, know little
more of astronomy than they learn from such books, and they
are consequently very ignorant of the principles of the science;
but there are some to be met with who are better informed.

" *majyas* ‡ are completed, which will be as follows :

" ¹225, ²449, ³671, ⁴890, ⁵1105, ⁶1315, ⁷1520, ⁸1719,

" ⁹1910, ¹⁰2093, ¹¹2267, ¹²2431, ¹³2585, ¹⁴2728, ¹⁵2859, ¹⁶2978,

" ¹⁷3084, ¹⁸3177, ¹⁹3256, ²⁰3321, ²¹3372, ²²3409, ²³3431, ²⁴3438.

" For the *utcramajya* *, the twenty-third *cramajya*
" deducted from the *trijya* or twenty-fourth *cramajya*,
" leaves the first *utcramajya* ; the twenty-second de-
" ducted from the twenty-third, leaves the second
" *utcramajya* ; the twenty-first from the twenty-second,
" leaves the third ; the twentieth from the twenty-
" first, leaves the fourth. In the same manner pro-
" ceed until the *utcramajyas* are completed ; which

" will be as follows : ¹7, ²29, ³66, ⁴117, ⁵182, ⁶261, ⁷354,

" ⁸460, ⁹579, ¹⁰710, ¹¹853, ¹²1007, ¹³1171, ¹⁴1345, ¹⁵1528, ¹⁶1719,

" ¹⁷1928, ¹⁸2125, ¹⁹2233, ²⁰2548, ²¹2767, ²²2989, ²³3213, ²⁴3438."

So far the *Surya Siddhanta* on the subject of the
sines. The commentator shows how they are geo-
metrically constructed : " With a radius describe a
" circle, the periphery of which divide into 21600
" equal parts, or minutes. Draw north and south,
" and east and west, lines through the centre : set
" off contrarywise from the east point, 225 on the
" periphery, and draw a string from those extremi-
" ties across the *trijya* †. The string is the *jya*, and
" its half the *ardhajya*, called *jiva*. The *Pandits* say,
" a planet's place will correspond with the *ardhajya* ;
" by which, therefore, computations of their places
" are always made ; and by the term *jya* is always
" understood the *ardhajya*. The first *jya* will be
" found to contain 449 minutes, and the operation,
" repeated to twenty-four divisions, will complete the
" *cramajya*. In each operation, the distance con-

---

‡ *Cramajyas*, right sines.   * *Utcramajyas*, versed sines.
† *Trijya*, the radius.

"tained between the *jya* and its arc, or that line
"which represents the arrow of a bow, must be exa-
"mined, and the number of minutes therein con-
"tained and taken for the *utcramajya*. The circle
"may represent any space of land; the *bhujajya* * is
"the *bhuja*; the *cotijya* the *coi*, and the *trijya* the
"*carna*. The square of the *bhujajya* deducted from
"the square of the *trijya*, leaves the square of the
"*cotijya*; the root of which is the *cotijya*; and, in
"the same manner, from the *cotijya* is determined the
"*bhujajya*. The *cotyutcramajya* deducted from the
"*trijya*, leaves the *bhujacramajya*. The *bhujot-cramu-*
"*jya* deducted from the *trijya*, leaves the *coticramajya*.
"When the *bhujajya* is the first division of the *trijya*,
"the *cotijya* is the twenty-three remaining divisions;
"which *cotijya* deducted from the *trijya*, leaves the
"*bhujotcramajya*. On this principle are the *jyas* gi-
"ven in the text : +they may be determined by calcu-
"lation also, as follows :

"The *trijya* take as equal to 3438 minutes, and con-
"taining twenty-four *jyapindas*; its half is the *jya* of
"one sine or 1719'; which is the eighth *jyapindu*, or
"the sixteenth *cotijyapinda*. The square of the
"*trijya* multiply by 3, and divide the product by
"4, the square root of the quotient is the *jya* of
"two sines, or 2977'. The square root of half the
"square of the *trijya* is the *jya* of one sine and an half
"(45°) or 2431; which deducted from the *trijya*
"leaves the *utcramajya* 1007'. By this *utcramajya*
"multiply the *trijya*; the square root of half the pro-
"duct is the *jya* of 22°, 30', or 1315". The square
"of this deduct from the square of the *trijya*, the

* *Bhujajya*, the sine complement.

† A diagram might here be added for illustration, but it must
be unnecessary to any one who has the smallest knowledge of
Geometry.

" square root of the difference is the *jya*, of 67', 30',
" or 3177', which is the *cotijya* of 22°, 30' equal
" to 1315'. The *bhujajya* and *cotijya* deducted
" severally from the *trijya*, leaves the *utcramajya* of
" each 2123", and 261'."—&c.

This is sufficient to show, that the *Hindus* have the
right construction of the sines, although they do not
appear, from any thing I can learn, ever to have carried it farther than to twenty-four divisions of the quadrant, as in the following table. Instances of the like
inaccuracy will occur in the course of this paper. The
table of sines may perhaps be more clearly represented
in the following manner:

Right Sines, the Radius containing 3438 *Minutes.*

Arc	Sine	Arc.	Sine	Arc.	Sine.
1st = 11 = 3°,45	225	9th = 1225 = 33",45	1910	17th = 3825 = 0,°,45	3084
2d = 450 = 7,30	449	10th = 2250 = 37,30	2093	18th = 4050 = 67,30	3177
3d = 675 = 11,15	671	11th = 1475 = 41,15	2267	19th = 4275 = 71,15	3256
4th = 900 = 15,—	890	12th = 1700 = 45,—	2431	20th = 4500 = 75,—	3321
5th = 1125 = 18,45	1105	13th = 1925 = 48,45	2585	21st = 4725 = 78,45	3376
6th = 1350 = 22,30	1315	14th = 2150 = 52,30	2728	22d = 4950 = 82,30	1409
7th = 1575 = 26,15	1520	15th = 2375 = 56,15	2859	23d = 5175 = 86,15	3431
8th = 1800 = 30,—	1719	16th = 1800 = 60,—	2978	24th = 5400 = 90,—	3438

Versed Sines.

Arc	Sine	Arc.	Sine.	Arc.	Sine.
1st = 225 = 3°,45	7	9th = 2025 = 33°,45	579	17th = 3825 = 63°,45	1923
2d = 450 = 7,30	29	10th = 2250 = 37,30	710	18th = 4050 = 67,30	2103
3d = 675 = 11,15	66	11th = 2475 = 41,15	853	19th = 4275 = 71,15	2283
4th = 900 = 15,—	117	12th = 2700 = 45,—	1107	20th = 4500 = 75,—	2548
5th = 1125 = 18,45	182	13th = 2925 = 48,45	1171	21st = 4725 = 78,45	2767
6th = 1350 = 22,30	261	14th = 3150 = 52,30	1145	22d = 4950 = 82,30	2989
7th = 1575 = 26,15	354	15th = 3375 = 56,15	1229	23d = 5175 = 86,15	3211
8th = 1800 = 30,—	460	16th = 3600 = 60,—	1319	24th = 5400 = 90,—	3438

For the sines of the intermediate arcs, take a mean
proportion of the tabular difference, as for the sine of
14°, which is between the third and fourth tabular arcs,
or 16, minutes exceeding the third; therefore 225'

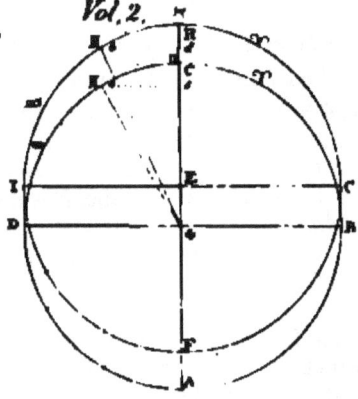

Fig. 1.   *Vol. 2.*   *P. 249.*

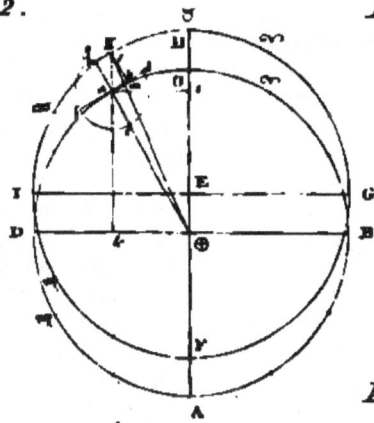

Fig. 2.   *P. 250.*

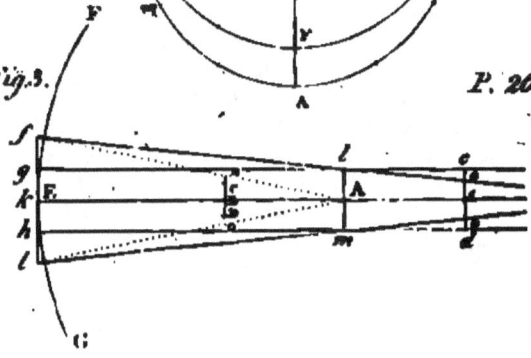

Fig. 3.   *P. 263.*

being the difference of those arcs, and 219 the difference of their sines, $\frac{165' \times 219'}{225'} = 160', 36''$, or a mean proportional number, to be added to the sine of the third tabular arc, for the sine required of 14° or 831' 36''. In the sexagesimal arithmetic, which appears to be universally used in the *Hindu* astronomy, when the fraction exceeds half unity, it is usually taken as a whole number: Thus, 831', 35'', 35''', would be written 831', 36.

To account for the apparent unequal motions of the planets, which they suppose to move in their respective orbits through equal distances in equal times, the *Hindus* have recourse to excentric circles, and determine the excentricity of the orbits of the sun and moon with respect to that circle, in which they place the earth as the centre of the universe, to be equal to the sines of their greatest anomalistic equations, and accordingly that the delineation of the path of either may be made in the following manner:

Describe a circle, which divide as the ecliptic into signs, degrees, and minutes; note the place of the *Mandochcha*, or higher apsis, which suppose in ४°. Draw a diameter to that point, and set off from the centre ⊕ towards the place of the apogee, the excentricity equal to the sine of the greatest equation, which of the sun is 130' 32''. Here the excentricity is represented much greater, that the figure may be better understood. Round the point E, as the centre, describe the excentric circle FGHI, which is the sun's orbit, and in the point H, where it is cut by the line ⊕ ४ prolonged, is the place of the *Mandochcha*, or higher apsis; and in the opposite point F is the lower. From the place of the apogee H, set off its longitude in reverse, or contrary to the order of the signs, for the beginning of *Aries*, and divide this

circle, as the former, into signs and degrees. Note
the sun's mean longitude in each circle, as suppose
in *Gemini*, and from both points draw right lines to
the earth at ⊖. According to the *Hindu* system, which
appears to be the same as the *Ptolemaic*, the angle
$a \oplus C$ will be the mean anomaly, the angle $b \oplus C$
the true anomaly, and the angle $a \oplus b$ their difference, or the equation of the mean to the true place ;
to be subtracted in the first six signs of anomaly, and
added in the last six. The *Europeans*, in the old
astronomy, found the angle $b \oplus C$ by the following
proportion, and which subtracted from $a \oplus C$, left
the equation, which as the *Hindus*, they inserted in
tables calculated for the several degrees of the quadrant ;—as the co-sine of the mean anomaly $\oplus e = Ed$
added to the excentricity $E \oplus$, is to the sine of the
mean anomaly $ae = bd$; so is the radius to the tangent
of the true anomaly : or, in the right angled triangle
$d \oplus b$, in which are given $d \oplus$ and bd, if $d \oplus$ be made
radius, bd will be the tangent of the angle $b \oplus d$, required. The *Hindus*, who have not the invention of
tangents, take a different method, on principles equally true. They imagine the small circle or epicycle,
cdef, drawn round the planet's mean place a with a
radius equal to the excentricity, which in this case,
of the sun, is 130′ 30″, and whose circumference in
degrees, or equal divisions of the deferent A B C D,
will be in proportion as their semi-diameters ; or, as
$\oplus C = 3438'$, to A B C D $= 360°$, so $ag = 130'$ 32″, to
$efgd = 13°$ 40′, which is called the *paridhi-ansa*, or *paridhi* degrees. In the same proportion also will be
the correspondent sines hc and ai, and their co-sines
cb and lk, which are therefore known by computation, in minutes or equal parts of the radius $a \ominus$,
which contains, as before mentioned, 3438′. In the
right angled triangle $h \oplus c$, right angled at h, there
are given the sides $h \oplus$ ($= a \oplus + c b$, because $cb = ha$)

and hc; to find the hypotenuse $c\oplus$, by means of which the angle $a\ominus m$ may be determined; for its sine is lm, and, in the similar triangles $hc\oplus$ and $lm\oplus$, as $c\oplus$ is to $m\oplus$, so is hc to lm, the sine of the angle of equation. From the third to the ninth sine of anomaly, the co-sine cb must be subtracted from the radius 3438′ for the side $h\oplus$.

It is, however, only in computing the retrogradations and other particulars respecting the planets *Mercury, Venus, Mars, Jupiter,* and *Saturn,* where circles greatly excentric are to be considered, that the *Hindus* find the length of the *carna,* or hypotenuse $c\oplus$; in other cases, as for the anomalistic equations of the sun and moon, they are satisfied to take hc as equal to the sine lm, their difference, as the commentator on the *Siddhanta* observes, being inconsiderable.

Upon this hypothesis are the *Hindu* tables of anomaly computed with the aid of an adjustment, which, as far as I know, may be peculiar to themselves. Finding that, in the first degree of anomaly, both from the higher and lower apsis, the difference between the mean and observed places of the planets was greater than became thus accounted for, they enlarged the epicycle in the apogee and perigee, proportionably to that observed difference for each planet respectively, conceiving it to diminish in inverse proportion to the sine of the mean anomaly, until at the distance of three sines, or half-way between those points, the radius of the epicycle should be equal to the excentricity or sine of the greatest equation. This assumed difference in the magnitude of the epicycle, they called the difference of the *paridhi ansa,* between *vishama* and *sama*; the literal meaning of which is *odd* and *even*. From the first to the third sign of anomaly, or rather in the third, a planet is in *vishama*; from the third to the sixth, or in the perigee, in *sama*; in the ninth sign, in *vishama*; and in the twelfth, or the apogee, in *sama*. The *paridhi* degrees, or circumference of the epicycle in *sama* arc, of the sun $14°$; in *vishama* $13°$ $40'$; of the moon in *sama* $32°$; in *vishama*, $31°40'$; the difference assigned to each between *sama* and *vish-ama*, $20'$.

To illustrate these matters by examples, let it be required to find the equation of the sun's mean to his true place in the first degree of anomaly. The sine of $1°$ is considered as equal to its arc, or 60.— The circumference of the epicycle in *sama*, or the apogee, is $14°$, but diminishing in this case towards *vish-ama*, in inverse proportion to the sine of anomaly.— Therefore, as radius 3438 is to the difference between *sama* and *vishama* $20'$, so is the sine of anomaly $60'$ to the diminution of the epicycle in the point of anomaly proposed, $20''$ ($= \frac{60 \times 10'}{1411^\circ}$) which, subtracted from $14°$, leaves $13°59'40''$. Then, as the circumference of the great circle $360°$ is to the circumference of the epicycle $13°59'40''$, so is the sine of anomaly $60'$ to its correspondent sine in the epicycle hc; which, as was observed, is considered as equal to lm, or true sine of the angle of equation $2'19''56''$ ($= \frac{13°59'40'' \times 60'}{360°}$), which, in the *Hindu* canon of sines, is the same as its arc, and is therefore the equation of the mean to the true place in $1°$ of anomaly, to be added in the first six sines and subtracted in the last six.

For the equation of the mean to the true place in $5°14'$ of anomaly. The sine of $5°14'$ is $313'36$ $8'''$ and $\frac{311'36''8''+10'=6271'2'40''}{1411^\circ} = 1'49''$, to be deducted from the *paridhi* degrees in *sama*.—$14°1'49''=13°58.11''$, and $\frac{211',16'',5''+13°58,11''=4779.10.17''}{363°} = 12'9''59''$ the sine of the angle of equation, which is equal to its arc.

For the same in 14° of anomaly. The sine of 14°, is 831.36. — $\frac{831'16''\times 20'}{3418}$ = 4' 50'', and, $\frac{14'-4'50''\times 831'36''}{360°}$ = 32' 9'' the sine of the angle of equation.

For the same in two sines of anomaly. The sine of 60° is 2978'' $\frac{29:8'\times 10'}{3418}$ = 17', 19''; and $\frac{14°-17'. 19''\times 2978''}{360°}$ = 113' 25'' 20''', the sine of equation equal to its arc.

For the equation of the mean to the true place of the moon in 1° of anomaly. The *paridhi* degrees of the moon in *sama* are 32°, in *vishama* 31°, 40', the difference 20'. The sine of 1° is 60' and $\frac{60'\times 20''}{3418}$ = 21'' to be deducted from the *paridhi* degrees in *sama*, 32° — 21'' = 31° 59' 39''. $\frac{31°. 59'. 39'+6.7}{360°}$ = 5', 20'', the equation required.

For the same in ten degrees of anomaly. The sine of 10° is 597' $\frac{597\times 20'}{3418}$ = 3' 28'', and $\frac{31°-1'. 18''\times 597'}{360°}$ = 52' 28'', the equation required.

For the same in three sines of anomaly. The sine of 90° is the radius or 3438', and $\frac{3418'\times 20'}{3418}$ = 20', $\frac{31°-27'\times 3418'}{360°}$ = 302', 25'', the sine of the greatest angle of equation, equal to the radius of the epicycle in this point of anomaly, the arc corresponding with which is 302' 45'', the equation required.

For the equation of the mean to the true motion in these several points of anomaly, say, as radius 3438 is to the mean motion, so is the co-sine *c b* of the anomalistic angle *g a c* in the epicycle, to the difference between the mean and apparent motion, or the equation required, to be subtracted from the

mean motion from the first three sines of anomaly;
added in the next six, and subtracted in the last
three.

Example, for the sun, in $5°\ 14'$ of anomaly. The
co-sine of $5°\ 14'$ in the *Hindu* canon is $3422'\ 17''\ 52'''$.
The *paridhi* circle in this point, found before, is $13°$
$58'\ 11''$; and $\frac{3422'\ 17'\ 52''+13°\ 58'\ 11''}{360°} = 132'\ 48''$ the
co-sine $c\ b$ in the epicycle; then, as radius 3438
is to the sun's mean motion $59'\ 8''$ per day, or
$59''\ 8'''$ per *danda*, so is the co-sine $c\ b = 132'\ 48''$,
to the equation required, $2'\ 17''$ per day, or $2''\ 17'''$
per *danda*. The motion of the sun's apsis is so slow
as to be neglected in these calculations; but that of
the moon is considered, in order to know her mean
motion from her apogee, which is $783'\ 54''$.

In this manner may be determined the equation of
the mean to the true anomaly and motion for each
degree of the quadrant; and which will be found to
agree with the tables of *Macaranda*. The following
tables are translated from that book:

| Solar Equations, *Ravi p'hala* |

Anomaly	Eq. of the mean to the true place.		Eq. of the mean to the true motion.	Anomaly	Eq. of the mean to the true place.		Eq. of the mean to the true motion.	Anomaly	Eq. of the mean to the true place.			Eq. of the mean to the true motion.
	°	′ ″	′ ″	°	° ′	″	′ ″		°	′	″	′ ″
1		2 20	2 18	31	1 8	—	1 55	61	1	54	30	1 4
2		4 40	2 18	32	1 9	57	1 54	62	1	55	34	1
3		7 —	2 18	33	1 11	57	1 53	63	1	56	35	58
4		9 19	2 17	34	1 13	47	1 51	64	1	57	34	57
5		11 37	2 17	35	1 15	40	1 51	65	1	58	34	55
6		13 56	2 17	36	1 17	32	1 49	66	1	59	30	55
7		16 15	2 16	37	1 19	23	1 47	67	2	—	23	52
8		18 33	2 16	38	1 21	11	1 45	68	2	1	14	49
9		20 51	2 15	39	1 23	57	1 43	69	2	2	4	46
10		23 7	2 14	40	1 24	42	1 42	70	2	2	51	43
11		25 23	2 14	41	1 26	26	1 40	71	2	3	35	41
12		27 39	2 13	42	1 28	7	1 38	72	2	4	17	39
13		29 55	2 13	43	1 29	46	1 36	73	2	4	57	37
14		32 10	2 12	44	1 31	23	1 34	74	2	5	35	35
15		34 24	2 11	45	1 32	58	1 32	75	2	6	12	32
16		36 37	2 11	46	2 34	32	1 30	76	2	6	45	31
17		38 39	2 10	47	1 36	4	1 29	77	2	7	17	28
18		41 1	2 9	48	1 37	35	1 28	78	2	7	45	25
19		43 12	2 8	49	1 39	6	1 28	79	2	8	12	23
20		45 23	2 7	50	1 40	36	1 26	80	2	8	36	22
21		47 31	2 6	51	1 42	3	1 23	81	2	8	58	20
22		49 39	2 6	52	1 43	26	1 19	82	2	9	18	18
23		51 47	2 5	53	1 44	43	1 16	83	2	9	36	15
24		53 53	2 3	54	1 46	2	1 14	84	2	9	51	12
25		55 57	2 2	55	1 47	17	1 13	85	2	10	3	10
26		58 1	2 1	56	1 48	33	1 13	86	2	10	13	8
27	1	— 2	2 —	57	1 49	47	1 12	87	2	10	20	6
28	1	2 53	1 58	58	1 51	—	1 11	88	2	10	27	4
29	1	4 3	1 57	59	1 52	12	1 11	89	2	10	31	1
30	1	6 2	1 56	60	1 53	25	1 8	90	2	10	33	

Lunar Equations, *Chandra p'hala.*

Anomaly	Eq. of the mean to the true place.	Eq. of the mean to the true medium.	Anomaly	Eq. of the mean to the true place.	Eq. of the mean to the true medium.	Anomaly	Eq. of the mean to the true place.	Eq. of the mean to the true medium.
°	° ′ ″	′ ″	°	° ′ ″	′ ″	°	° ′ ″	′ ″
1	5 20	66 39	31	2 36 37	59 20	61	4 25 26	33 41
2	10 40	69 38	32	2 41 11	58 41	62	4 27 36	32 39
3	16 —	69 31	33	2 45 36	58 —	63	4 29 59	31 35
4	21 19	69 28	34	2 49 58	57 19	64	4 32 19	30 29
5	26 36	69 21	35	2 54 20	56 37	65	4 34 37	29 22
6	31 54	69 13	36	2 58 39	55 56	66	4 36 47	28 13
7	37 12	69 4	37	3 2 54	55 14	67	4 38 54	27 7
8	42 29	68 54	38	3 7 5	54 30	68	4 40 54	26 1
9	47 44	68 43	39	3 11 12	53 44	69	4 42 50	24 55
10	52 58	68 28	40	3 15 16	52 58	70	4 44 40	23 49
11	58 11	68 11	41	3 19 18	51 26	71	4 46 24	22 42
12	1 3 23	67 52	42	3 23 24	50 57	72	4 48 5	21 34
13	1 8 40	67 35	43	3 27 26	50 48	73	4 49 38	20 24
14	1 13 45	67 17	44	3 30 54	49 46	74	4 51 9	19 14
15	1 18 53	66 55	45	3 34 39	48 54	75	4 52 53	18 3
16	1 24 —	66 38	46	3 38 21	48 —	76	4 53 54	16 51
17	1 29 5	66 18	47	3 41 58	47 5	77	4 55 6	15 38
18	1 34 9	65 57	48	3 45 32	46 9	78	4 56 15	14 25
19	1 39 10	65 36	49	3 49 59	45 13	79	4 57 17	13 14
20	1 44 9	65 14	50	3 52 24	44 19	80	4 58 13	12 3
21	1 49 17	64 50	51	3 55 16	43 27	81	4 59 6	10 53
22	1 54 3	64 24	52	3 59 2	42 32	82	4 59 53	0 41
23	1 58 3	63 56	53	4 2 13	41 37	83	5 — 27	8 34
24	2 3 47	63 24	54	4 5 16	40 41	84	5 1 8	7 14
25	2 8 35	63 53	55	4 8 18	39 44	85	5 1 40	6 2
26	2 13 22	63 22	56	4 11 16	38 47	86	5 2 3	4 51
27	2 18 6	61 48	57	4 14 11	37 50	87	5 2 10	3 40
28	2 22 47	61 13	58	4 17 —	36 51	88	5 2 36	2 37
29	2 27 35	60 35	59	4 19 46	35 48	89	5 2 44	1 44
30	2 32 2	59 56	60	4 22 29	34 48	90	5 2 49	— —

Having the true longitude of the sun and moon, and the place of the node determined by the methods explained, it is easy to judge, from the position of the latter, whether at the next conjunction or opposition there will be a solar or a lunar eclipse; in which case the *tit'hi*, or date of the moon's synodical month, must be computed from thence, to determine the time counted from midnight of her full or change. Her distance in longitude from the sun, divided by 720, the minutes contained in a *tit'hi*, or the thirtieth part of 360°, the quotient shows the *tit'hi* she has passed, and the fraction, if any, the part performed of the next; which, if it be the fifteenth, the difference between that fraction and 720' is the distance she has to go to her opposition, which will be in time proportioned to her actual motion; and that being determined, her longitude, the longitude of the sun, and place of the node may be known for the instant of full moon, or middle of the lunar eclipse. The *Hindu* method of computing these particulars is so obvious in the accompanying instance, as to require no further description here; and the same may be said with respect to the declination of the sun and the latitude of the moon.

It is evident from what has been explained, that the *Pandits*, learned in the *Jyotish Sastra*, have truer notions of the form of the earth and the economy of the universe than are ascribed to the *Hindus* in general: and that they must reject the ridiculous belief of the common *Brahmens*, that eclipses are occasioned by the intervention of the monster *Rahu*, with many other particulars equally unscientific and absurd. But, as this belief is founded on explicit and positive declarations contained in the *Vedas* and *Puranas*, the divine authority of which writings no devout *Hindu* can dispute, the astronomers have some of them cautiously explained such passages in those writings as disagree with the

principles of their own science; and, where reconcilia-
tion was impossible, have apologized, as well as they
could, for propositions necessarily established in the
practice of it, by observing, that certain things, as
stated in other *Sastras*, " might have been so formerly,
" and may be so still; but for astronomical purposes,
" astronomical rules must be followed." Others have,
with a bolder spirit, attacked and refuted unphilosophical
opinions. *Bhascara* argues, that it is more reasonable
to suppose the earth to be self-balanced in infinite space,
than that it should be supported by a series of animals,
with nothing assignable for the last of them to rest upon;
And *Nerasinha*, in his commentary, shows that by *Rahu*
and *Cetu*, the head and tail of the monster, in the sense
they generally bear, could only be meant the position
of the moon's nodes and the quantity of her latitude,
on which eclipses do certainly depend; but he does
not therefore deny the reality of *Rahu* and *Cetu*: on
the contrary, he says, that their actual existence and
presence in eclipses ought to be believed, and may be
maintained as an article of faith, without any prejudice
to astronomy. The following *Sloca*, to which a literal translation is annexed, was evidently written by a
Jyotish, and is well known to the *Pandits* in general:

Vip'halanyanyasastrani, vivadasteshu cevalum:

Sap'halam jyotisham sastram, chandrarcau yatra sac-
        shinau.

" Fruitless *are all* other *Sastras*; in them *is* conten-
tion only. Fruitful *is* the *Jyotish Sastra*, where the sun
and moon *are* two witnesses."

    The argument of *Varahacharya* concerning the
monster *Rahu*, might here be annexed, but, as this

c

paper will without it be sufficiently prolix, I shall
next proceed to show how the astronomical *Pandits*
determine the moon's distance and diameter, and other
requisites for the prediction of a lunar eclipse.

The earth they consider as spherical, and imagine
its diameter divided into 1600 equal parts, or *Yojanes*.
An ancient method of finding a circle's circumference
was to multiply the diameter by three; but this being
not quite enough, the *Munis* directed that it should be
multiplied by the square root of ten. This gives for
the equatorial circumference of the earth in round
numbers 5059 *Yojanas*, as it is determined in the *Surya Siddhanta*. In the table of sines, however, found
in the same book, the radius being made to consist of
3438 equal parts or minutes, of which equal parts
the quadrant contains 5400, implies the knowledge
of a much more accurate ratio of the diameter to the
circumference; for by the first it is as 1. to 3. 1627.&c.
by the last, as 1. to 3. 14136; and it is determined
by the most approved labours of the *Europeans*, as
1. to 3. 14159, &c. In the *Puranas* the circumference of the earth is declared to be 500,000,000
Yojuns; and, to account for this amazing difference
the commentator before quoted thought, " the *Yojan*
" stated in the *Surya Siddhanta* contained each
" 100,000 of those meant in the *Puranas*; or per-
" haps, as some suppose, the earth was really of that
" size in some former *Calpa*. Moreover, others say,
" that from the equator south ward, the earth increa-
" ses in bulk: however, for astronomical purposes,
" the dimensions given by *Surya* must be assumed."
The equatorial circumference being assigned, the
circumference of a circle of longitude in any latitude
is determined. As radius 3438 is to the *Lambajya*
or sine of the polar distance, equal to the complete-
ment of the latitude to ninety degrees, so is the equa-

torial dimension 5059, to the dimension in *Yojana* required.

Of a variety of methods for finding the latitude of a place, one is by an observation of the *palabha*, or shadow, projected from a perpendicular *Gnomon* when the sun is in the equator. The *Sancu*, or *Gnomon*, is twelve *angulas*, or digits, in length divided, each into sixty *vingulas*; and the shadow observed at *Benares* is $\overset{\wedge}{5}$, $\overset{\vee}{45}$. Then, by the proportion of a right angled triangle $\sqrt{\overline{12.^2 + 5,45}} = 13 \ 18$ the *acsha carna* (hypotenuse) or distance from the top of the *Gnomon* to the extremity of the shadow; which take as radius, and the projected shadow will be the sine of the zenith distance, in this case, equal to the latitude of the place $\frac{2418 \times 545}{13 \ 18} = 1487$, the arc corresponding with which, in the canon of sines, is $25°\ 26'$ the latitude of *Benares*. The sine complement of the latitude is $3101'\ 57''$, and again by trigonometry $\frac{3101'\ 4'' + 5059\ 18}{3418} = 4565$, 4 *Yogans* the circumference of a circle of longitude in the latitude of *Benares*.

The longitude is directed to be found by observation of lunar eclipses calculated for the first meridian, which the *Surya Siddhanta* describes as passing over *Lanca*, *Rohitaca*, *Avanti*, and *Sannihita-saras*. *Avanti* is said by the commentator to be " now called *Ujjayíni*," or *Ougein*, a place well known to the *English* in the *Mahratta* dominions. The distance of *Benares* from this meridian is said to be sixty-four *Yojan* eastward; and as 4565 *Yojan*, a circle of longitude at *Benares*, is to sixty *dandas*, the natural day, so is sixty-four *Yojan* to 0, 50, the difference of longitude in time, which marks the time after midnight, when, strictly speaking, the astronomical day begins at *Benares* *. A total lunar eclipse was observed to happen at *Benares* fifty-one *palas* later than a calculation gave it for *Lanca*, and $\frac{51+45^{5}5.4}{60}$ = sixty-four *Yojana*, the difference of longitude on the earth's surface.

According to *Rennel's* map, in which may be found *Ongein*, and agreeably to the longitude assigned to *Benares*, the equinoctial point *Lanca* falls in the Eastern Ocean, southward from *Ceylon* and the *Maldiva* Islands. *Lanca* is fabulously represented as one of four cities built by *Devatas*, at equal distances from each other, and also from *Sumeru* and *Badawanal*, the north and south poles, whose walls are of gold, &c. and with respect to *Meya's* performing his famous devotions, in reward of which he received the astronomical revelations from the sun, recorded in the *Surya Siddhanta*, the commentator observes, " he performed " those devotions in *Salmala*, a country a little to the " eastward of *Lanca :* the dimensions of *Lanca* are " equal to one twelfth part of the equatorial circumfe- " rence of the earth," &c. Hence, perhaps on inquiry, may be found whether by *Salmala* is not meant *Ceylon.* In the history of the war of *Rama* with *Rawan*, the tyrant of *Lanca*, the latter is said to have married the daughter of an *Asura*, named *Meya :* but these disquisitions are foreign to my purpose.

For the dimensions of the moon's *caesha* (orbit) the rule in the *Sanscrit* text is more particular than is necessary to be explained to any person, who has informed

* " This day (*astronomical day*) is accounted to begin at mid-
" night under the *rec'ha* (meridian) of *Lanca ;* and at all places
" east or west of that meridian, as much sooner or latter as is their
" *disantera* (longitude) reduced to time, according to the *Surya*
" *Siddhanta*, *Brahma Siddhanta*, *Vasishtha Siddhanta*, *Soma Sidd-*
" *hanta*, *Parasara Siddhanta*, and *Aryabhatta.* According to *Brah-*
" *magupta* and others, it begins at sunrise ; according to the *Ro-*
" *maca* and others, it begins at noon ; and according to the *Arabs*
" *Siddhanta*, at sunset." (*Tica* on the *Surya Siddhanta*).

S 2

himself of the methods used by *European* astronomers to determine the moon's horizontal parallax.' In general terms, it is to observe the moon's altitude, and thence, with other requisites, to compute the time of her ascension from the sensible *cshitija*, or horizon, and her distance front the sun when upon the rational horizon, by which to find the time of her passage from the one point to the other; or, in other words, ' to 'find the difference in time between the meridian to 'which the eye referred her at rising, and the meridian 'she was actually upon;' in which difference of time she will have passed through a space equal to the earth's semidiameter or 800 *Yojan*: and, by proportion, as that time is to her periodical month, so is 800 *Yojan* to the circumference of her *cacsha*, 324000 *Yojan*. The errors arising from refraction, and their taking the moon's motion as along the sine instead of its arc, may here be remarked; but it does not seem that they had any idea of the first [*], and the latter they perhaps thought too inconsiderable to be noticed. Hence it appears that they made the horizontal parallax 53′ 20″ and her distance from the earth's centre 51570 *Yojan*; for $\frac{180°\times 1600}{324000} = 53′\ 20″$; and as 90° or 5406′ is to the radius 3438′, so is one-fourth of her orbit 81000 *Yojan* to 51570, and $\frac{51570\times 21600}{5059} = 220184$, the same distance in geographical miles. *European* astronomers compute the mean distance of the moon about 240000, which is something above a fifteenth part more than the *Hindus* found it so long ago as the time of *Maya*, the author of the *Surya Siddhanta*.

By the *Hindu* system the planets are supposed to move in their respective orbits at the same rate; the dimensions therefore of the moon's orbit being

---

[*] But they are not wholly ignorant of optics: they know the angles of *incidence* and *reflection* to be equal, and compute the place of a star or planet, as it would be seen reflected from water or a mirror.

known, those of the other planets are determined, according to their periodical revolutions, by proportion. As the sun's revolutions in a *Maha Yug* 4320000 are to the moon's revolutions in the same cycle 57533336, so is her orbit 324000 *Yojan* to the sun's orbit 4331500 *Yojan*; and in the same manner for the *cacshas*, or orbits of the other planets. All true distance and magnitude derivable from parallax, is here out of the question; but the *Hindu* hypothesis will be found to answer their purpose in determining the duration of eclipses, &c.

For the diameters of the sun and moon, it is directed to observe the time between the appearance of the limb upon the horizon and the instant of the whole disk being risen, when their apparent motion is at a mean rate, or when in three signs of anomaly; then, by proportion, as that time is to a natural day, so are their orbits to their diameters respectively; which of the sun is 6500 *Yojan*; of the moon, 480 *Yojan*. These dimensions are increased or diminished as they approach the lower or higher apsis, in proportion as their apparent motion exceeds or falls short of the mean, for the purpose of computing the diameter of the earth's shadow at the moon, on principles which may perhaps be made more intelligible by a figure.

Let the earth's diameter be $lm=gh=cd$; the distance of the moon from the earth A B, and her diameter C D. By this system, which supposes all the planets moving at the same rate, the dimensions of the sun's orbit will exceed the moon's, in proportion as his period in time exceeds hers; let his distance be A E, and E F G part of his orbit. According to the foregoing computation also, the sun's apparent diameter $f\,i$, at this distance from the earth, is 6500 *Yojan*; or rather, the angle his diameter subtends when viewed in three signs of anomaly, would be 6500 parts of the circumference of a circle consisting of 4331500, and described round the earth as a centre with a radius equal to his mean distance, which is properly all that is meant by the *vishcambha*, and which, therefore, is increased or diminished according to his equated motion. This in three signs of anomaly is equivalent to 32′ 24″; for, as 4331500 to 360°, so 6500 to 32′ 24″. The *Europeans* determine the same to be 32′ 22″. In the same manner, the sun's *vishcambha* in the mean *cacsha* of the moon, or the portion of her orbit in *Yojans*, included in this angle, is found, as 4331500 is to 324000, so is 6500 to 486 *Yojan* or *n*, *o*, of use in solar eclipses; but this I am endeavouring to explain is a lunar one. It is evident that the diameter of the earth's shadow at the moon will be *c*, *d*,—*c*, *a + b*, *d*, or *a b* when her distance is *A e*; and that *c a* and *b d* will be found by the following proportion: as *A k* is to *f i—g h=f g+h i*, so is *A e* to *c a +b d*. But it has been observed that *A k* and *f i* are proportioned by the *Hindus* according to the moon's distance *A e*, the apparent motion of the sun and moon, and the angles subtended by their diameters. The *Hindu* rule therefore states, As the sun's *vishcambha* or diameter is to the moon's, so is the difference of the diameters of the sun and earth, in *Yojans*, to a fourth number, equal to *c a + b d* to be subtracted from the *suchi*, or *lm=cd* to find *a b*; also, that the number of *Yojans*, thus determined as the diameters of the moon and shadow, may be reduced to minutes of a great circle by a divisor of fifteen. For, as the minutes contained in 360°=21600, are to the moon's orbit in *Yojan* 324000, so is one minute to fifteen *Yojan*.

The diameter of the moon's disk, of the earth's shadow, and the place of the node being found, for the instant of opposition or full moon, the remaining

I

part of the operation differs in no respect that I know
of from the method of *European* astronomers to
compute a lunar eclipse. The translation of the Formula for this purpose, in the *Surya Siddhanta*, is as
follows: " The earth's shadow is always six signs
" distant from *Surya*; and *Chandra* is eclipsed when-
" ever at the *purnima* the *pata* is found there; as is
" also *Surya*, whenever at the end of the *amavasya* the
" *pata* is found in the place of *Surya*; or, in either
" case, when the *pata* is nearly so situated. At the
" end of the *amavasya tit'hi* the signs, degrees,
" and minutes of *Surya* and *Chandra* are equal; and
" at the end of the *purnima tit'hi* the difference is ex-
" actly six signs; take therefore the time unexpired
" of either of those *tit'his*, and the motion for that
" time add to the *madhyama*, and the degrees and mi-
" nutes of *Surya* and *Chandra* will be equal. For
" the same instants of time compute the place of the
" *pata* in its retrograde motion, and, if it should be in
" conjunction with *Surya* and *Chandra*, then, as from
" the intervention of a cloud, there will be an obscu-
" rity of *Surya* or of *Chandra*. *Chandra*, from the
" west, approaches from the earth's shadow, which on
" entering, he is obscured. For the instant of the *puri-*
" *nima*, from the half sum of the *chandramana* and the
" *tamoliptamana* subtract the *vicshepa*, the remainder is
" the *ch'channa*. If the *ch'channa* is greater * than the
" *grahyamana*, the eclipse will be total; and if less, the
" eclipse will be proportionably less. The *grahya* and
" *grahaca* deduct and also add; square the difference
" and the sum severally; subtract the square of the
" *vicshepa* from each of those squares, and the square
" root of each remainder multiply by sixty; divide
" each product by the difference of the *gati* of *Surya*

___
* Or, when the *ch'channa* and *grahyamana* are equal, the eclipse
is *total*.

S 4

" and *Chandra* ; the first quotient will be half the
" duration of the eclipse in *dandas* and *palas* ; and the
" second quotient will be half the *vimardardha* dura-
" tion in *dandas* and *palas*," &c. The *ch'chayma*, or
portion of the disk eclipsed, is here found in degrees and minutes of a great circle : it may also be
estimated in *digits*; but the *angulas* or digits of the
Hindu are of various dimensions in different books.

The beginning, middle, and end of the eclipse
may now be supposed found for the time in *Hindu*
hours, when it will happen after midnight ; but, for
the corresponding hour of the civil day, which begins
at sunrise, it is further necessary to compute the length
of the artificial day and night ; and, for this purpose,
must be known the *ayanansa* or distance of the vernal
equinox from the first of *mesha*, the sun's right ascension and declination ; which several requisites shall be
mentioned in their order.

Respecting the precession of the equinoxes and
place of the colure, the following is a translation of all
I can find on the subject in the *Surya Siddhanta* and
its commentary :—

Text. " The *ayanansa* moves eastward thirty times
" twenty in each *Maha Yug* ; by that number (600)
" multiply the *ahargana* (number of mean solar days
" for which the calculation is made) and divide the
" product by the *savan* days in a *Yug*, and of the quo-
" tient take the *bhuja*, which multiply by three, and
" divide the product by ten; the quotient is the *ayan-*
" *a sa*. With the *ayanansa* correct the *graha*, *cranti*,
" the *ch'hava*, *charadala*, and other requisites to find
" the *pus'hti* and the two *vishuvas*. When the *carna*
" is less than the *surya ch'haya*, the *pracchacra* moves

2

" eastward, and the *ayanansa* must be added ; and
" when more, it moves westward, and the *ayanansa*
" must be subtracted.

Commentary. " By the text, the *ayana bhagana* is
" understood to consist of 600 *bhaganas* (periods) in
" a *Maha Yug* ; but some persons say, the meaning is
" thirty *bhaganas* only, and accordingly that there
" are 30,000 *bhaganas*. Also that *Bhascar Acharya*
" observes, that, agreeably to what has been delivered
" by *Surya*, there are 30,000 *bhaganas* of the *ayanansa*
" in a *Calpa*. This is erroneous ; for it disagrees
" with the *Sastras* of the *Rishis*. The *Sacalya San-*
" *hita* states that the *bhagunas* of the *Cranti pata* in
" a *Maha Yug* are 600 eastward. The same is ob-
" served in the *Vasisht'ha Siddhanta* ; and the rule
" for determining the *ayanansa* is as follows :—The
" expired years divide by 600, of the quotient make
" the *bhuja*, which multiply by three, and divide the
" product by ten. The meaning of *Bhascar, Acha-*
" *rya* was not, that *Surya* gave 30,000 as the *bhaganas*
" of the *ayanansa* in a *Calpa*, the name he used being
" *Saura* not *Surya*, and applied to some other book.
" From the *natansa* is known the *crantyansa*, and
" from the *crantijya* the *bhujajya*, the arc of which
" is the *bhujansa* of *Surya*, including the *ayanansa* :
" this for the first three months; after which, for
" the next three months, the place of *Surya*, found by
" this mode of calculation, must be deducted from
" six signs. For the next three months the place of
" *Surya* must be added to six signs, and for the last
" three months the place of *Surya* must be deducted
" from twelve signs. Thus, from the shadow may
" be computed the true place of *Surya*. For the
" same instant of time compute his place by the
" *ahargana*, from which will appear whether the
" *ayanansa* is to be added or subtracted. If the place
" found by the *ahargana* be less than the place

" found by the shadow, the *ayanansa* must be added.
" In the present time the *ayanansa* is added. Ac-
" cording to the author of the *Varasanhita*, it was
" said to have been formerly deducted ∗; and the
" southern *ayana* of *Surya* to have been in the first
" half of the *nacshatra Aslesha* +; and the northern
" *ayana* in the beginning of *Dhanishta:* that in his
" time the southern *ayana* was in the beginning of
" *Cacara*, or Cancer; and the northern in the be-
" ginning of *Macara*, or Capricorn.

" The *bhaganas* of the *ayanansa* in a *Maha Yug* are
" 600, the *saura* years in the same period 4,320,000;
" one *bhagana* of the *ayanansa* therefore contains
" 7,200 years. Of a *bhagana* there are four *padas.*
" *First pada*, when there was no *ayanansa*; but the
" *ayanansa* beginning from that time and increasing,
" it was added. It continued increasing 1800 years;
" when it became at its utmost, or twenty-seven de-
" grees. *Second pada:*—After this it diminished;

∗ " It was said to have been formerly *rina*." In the *Hindu*
specious arithmetic, or algebra, *dhana* signifies affirmation or addition, and *rina* negation or subtraction: the sign of the latter is
a point placed over the figure, or the quantity noted down; thus,
four added to seven, is equal to three. See the *bija ganita*, where
the mode of computation is explained thus: " When a man has
four pieces of money, and owes seven of the same value, his circumstances reduced to the form of an equation, or his books
balanced, show a deficiency of three pieces."

† This describes the place of the solstitial colure; and, according to this account of the *ayanansa*, the equinoctial colure must
then have passed through the tenth degree of the *nacshatra Bharani* and the 3° 20′ of *Visac'ha*. The circumstance, as it is mentioned in the *Vara Sanhita*, is curious and deserving of notice. I
shall only observe here, that, although it does not disagree with
the present system of the *Hindus* in regard to the motion of the
equinoctial points, yet the commentator on the *Varasanhita* supposes that it must have been owing to some preternatural cause.
The place here described of the colure, is on comparison of the
Hindu and *European* spheres about 3° 40′ eastward of the position,
which it is supposed by Sir *Isaac Newton*, on the authority of
Eudoxus, to have had in the *primitive* sphere at the time of the
Argonautic expedition.

" but the amount was still added, until, at the end
" of 1800 years more, it was diminished to nothing.
" *Third pada*: The *ayanansa* for the next 1800 years
" was deducted; and the amount deducted at the
" end of that term was twenty-seven degrees. *Fourth*
" *pada*: The amount deduction diminished; and at
" the end of the next term of 1800 years, there was
" nothing either added or subtracted. The *Munis*,
" having observed these circumstances, gave rules ac-
" cordingly: if in the *savan* days of a *Maha Yug*
" there are 600 *bhaganas*, what will be found in the
" *ahargana* proposed? which statement will produce
" *bhaganas*, sines, &c.; reject the *bhaganas*, and
" take the *bhuja* of the remainder, which multiply
" by three and divide by ten, because there are four
" *padas* in the *bhagana*; for if in 90° there is a cer-
" tain number found as the *bhuja*, when the *bhuja*
" degrees are twenty-seven, what will be found?
" and the numbers twenty-seven and ninety used in
" the computation being in the ratio of three to ten,
" the latter are used to save trouble.

" There is another method of computing the *aya-*
" *nansa*: The *cranti-pata-gati* is taken at one minute
" per year; and according to this rule the *ayanansa*
" increases to twenty-four degrees; the time neces-
" sary for which, as *one pada* is 1440 years. This is
" the *gati* of the *nacshatras* of the *cranti mandala*.

" The *nacshatra Revati* rises where the *nari man-*
" *dala* and the *cshitija* intersect *; but it has been

* This can happen only when there is no *ayanansa*. The *nari
mandala* is the equator. The *yoga* star of *Revati* is in the last of
Mina (Pisces) or, which is the same, in the *first* of *Mesha* (Aries)
and has no latitude in the *Hindu* tables. Hence, from the *ayanansa* and time of the beginning of the *Hindu* year, may be known
their zodiacal stars. *Revati* is the name of the twenty-seventh
lunar mansion, which comprehends the last 13° 20' of *Mina*.
When the *ayanansa* was 0, as at the creation, the beginning of the

" observed to vary twenty-seven degrees north and
" south. The same variation is observed in the other
" nacshatras: it is therefore rightly said, that the
" chacra moves eastward. The chacra means all the
" nacshatras. The planets are always found in the
" nacshatras, and the cranti-pata-gati is owing to
" them, not to the planets ; and hence it is observed
" in the text, that the pata draws chandra to a dis-
" tance equal to the cranti degrees."

Here, to my apprehension, instead of a revolution
of the equinoxes through all the signs in the course of
the Platonic year, which would carry the first of Vaisac'h through all the seasons, is clearly implied a libra-
tion of those points from the third degree of Pisces
to the twenty-seventh of Aries, and from the third of
Virgo to the twenty-seventh of Libra, and back again
in 7200 years; but, as this must seem to Europeans
an extraordinary circumstance to be stated in so ancient a treatise as the Surya Siddhanta, and believed
by Hindu astronomers ever since, I hope the above
quotations may attract the attention of those who are
qualified for a critical examination of them, and be
compared with whatever is to be found in other Sastras,
on the same subject. Whatever may be the result of
such an investigation, there is no mistaking the rule for
determining the ayanansa, which was at the beginning
of the present year 19° 21', and consequently the
vernal equinox in Pisces 10° 39' of the Hindu sphere ;
or, in other words, the sun entered Mesha or Aries,
and the Hindu year began when he was advanced 19°
21' into the northern signs, according to European expression.

Cali Yug, &c. the colure passed through the yoga star of Revati.
It is plain, that in this passage Revati applies either to the particular yoga star of that name or to the last, or twenty-seventh
lunar mansion, in which it is situated. (See a former note.) In
each nacshatra, or planetary mansion, there is one star called the
yoga, whose latitude, longitude, and right ascension the Hindus
have determined and inserted in their astronomical tables.

The *ayanansa* added to the sun's longitude in the *Hindu* sphere, gives his distance from the vernal equinox : of the sum take the *bhuja* ; that is, if it exceeds three sines, subtract it from six sines ; if it exceeds six sines, subtract six from it ; and if it exceeds nine sines, subtract it from twelve. The quantity so found will be the sun's distance from the nearest equinoctial point from which is found his declination—as radius is to the *paramapacramajya*, or sine of the greatest declination 24°, so is the sun's distance from the nearest equinoctial point to the declination sought ; which will agree with the table of declination in present use, to be found in the tables of *Macaranda*, and calculated for the several degrees of the quadrant. The declination thus determined for one sign, two signs, and three signs, is 11° 43', 20° 38', and the greatest declination, or the angle of inclination of the ecliptic and equator 24°. The co-sines of the same in the *Hindu* canon are 3366', 3217' and 3141'; and, as the co-sine of the declination for one sine, is to the co-sine of the greatest declination, so is the sine of 30° to the sine of the right ascension for a point of the ecliptic at that distance from either of the two *vishuvas*, or equinoctial points. In this manner is found the right ascension for the twelve signs of the ecliptic, reckoned from the vernal equinox ; and also, by the same management of triangles, the ascensional difference and oblique ascension for any latitude : which several particulars are inserted in the *Hindu* books, as in the following table, which is calculated for *Bhagalpur*, on supposition that the *palabha* or equinoctial shadow is 5 30.

By the *Lagna* of *Lanca*, *Madhyama*, or mean *Lagna*, the *Hindus* mean those points of the equator which rise respectively with each thirtieth degree of the ecliptic counted from *Aries* in a right sphere, answering to the right ascension in any latitude ; by the *Lagna* of a particular place, the oblique ascension, or the divisions of the equator which rise in succession with each sign in an oblique sphere, and by the *chara* the ascensional difference.

Signs.	Hindu Names.	Lagna of Lanca.		Chara of Bhagalpur.		Ullagna.	
		In respirations answering to minutes of the equator.	In palas, or minutes of time, 3600 to a Nacshatra day.	In respirations answering to minutes of the equator.	In palas, or minutes of time, 3600 to a Nac-shatra day.	In respirations answering to minutes of the equator.	In palas, or minutes of time, 3600 to a Nacshatra day.
	Mesha,	1670	278	327	55	1343	224
	Vrisha,	1795	299	268	45	1527	255
	Mit'huna,	1935	323	110	18	1825	304
	Carcata,	1935	323	110	18	2045	341
	Sinha,	1795	299	268	45	2063	343
	Canya,	1670	278	327	55	1997	333
	Tula,	1670	278	327	55	1997	333
	Vrischica,	1795	299	268	45	2063	343
	Dhanus,	1935	323	110	18	2045	341
	Macara,	1935	323	110	18	1825	304
	Cumbha,	1735	299	268	45	1527	255
	Mina.	1670	278	327	55	1343	224
		21600	3600			21600	3600

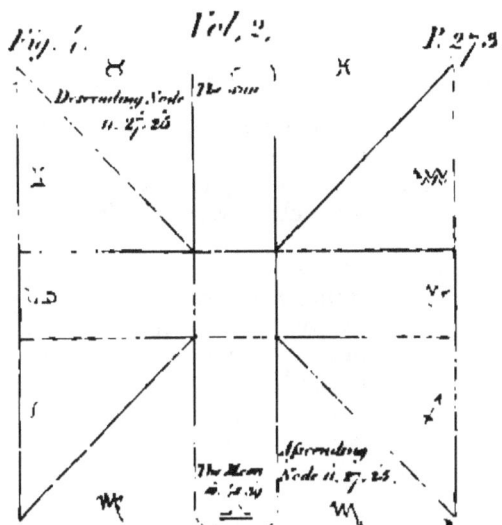

A Chinese Ode. P.199.

COMPUTATION OF THE ECLIPSE.

Let it be premised that the position of the sun, moon, and nodes, by calculation, will on the first of next *Vaisac'h* be as here represented in the *Hindu* manner, excepting the characters of the signs.

By inspection of the figure, and by considering the motion of the sun, moon, and nodes, it appears that, when the sun comes to the sign *Tula, Libra,* corresponding with the month of *Cartic,* the descending node will have gone back to *Aries* ; and that consequently a *lunar* eclipse may be expected to happen at the end of the *purnima tit'hi,* or time of full moon, in that month.

FIRST OPERATION.

To find the number of mean solar days from the creation to some part of the *purnima tit'hi* in *Cartic,* of the 4891st year of the *Cali Yug.*

Years expired of the *Calpa* to the end
    of the *Satya Yug,*   -   -   1970784000
Deduct the term of *Brahma's* employ-
    ment in the creation,   -   -   17064000
                                            _____

From the creation, when the planetary
    motions began, to the end of the
    Satya Yug,   -   -   -   1953720000
Add the *Treta Yug,*   -   -   1296000
        Dwapar Yug,   -   -   864000
        Present year of the *Cali Yug,*   4890
                                            _____

From the creation to the next approach-
    ing *Bengal year,*   -   -   1955884890

Or solar months, (× 12)   -   -   23470618680
Add seven months,   -   -   72
                                            _____
                                            23470618680

As the solar months in a *Yug*, 51840000, are to the intercalary *lunar* months in that cycle, 1593336, so are the solar months 23470618687, to their corresponding intercalary *lunar* months 721384677; which added together, give 24192003364 lunations. This number multiplied by thirty produces 725760100920 *tit'his*, or lunar days, from the creation to the new moon in *Cartic*; to which add fourteen *tit'his* for the same, to the *purnima tit'his* in that month 725760100934. Then, as the number of *tit'his* in a *Yug*, 1603000080, is to their difference exceeding the mean solar days in that cycle (called *cshaya tit'his*) 25082252, so are 725760100934 *tit'his*, to their excess in number over the solar days 11356017987, which subtracted, leaves 714404082947, as the number of mean solar days from the creation, or when the planetary motions began, to a point of time which will be midnight under the first meridian of *Lanca*, and near the time of full moon in *Cartic** . The first day after the creation being *Ravi-var*, or *Sunday*, divide the number of days by seven for the day of the week, the remainder after the division being two, marks the day *Soma-var*, or *Monday*.

SECOND OPERATION.

For the mean longitude of the sun, moon, and the ascending node. Say, as the number of mean solar days in a *Mahá Yug* is to the revolutions of any planet in that cycle, so are the days from the creation to even revolutions, which reject, and the fraction, if any, turned into sines, &c. is the mean longitude required.

---

* In the year of the *Cali Yug* 4891, corresponding with 1196 *Bengal* style, and with the month of *October* or *November* (hereafter to be determined) in the year of *Christ* 1789.

1st. Of the Sun.

$$\frac{71440408\,2947 \times 4320000}{1577917828} = \text{(19558489o)} \quad \begin{array}{l}\textit{Revolutions,} \quad \textit{Signs,} \quad ^\circ \quad ' \quad '' \quad ''' \\ 6 \ \ 22 \ \ 44 \ \ 2 \ \ 12\end{array}$$

2d. Of the Moon.

$$\frac{71440408\,2947 \times 57753336}{1577917828} = \text{(26147888255)} \quad 0 \ \ 21 \ \ 21 \ \ 58 \ \ 56$$

3d. Of the Moon's Apogee.

$$\frac{71440408\,2947 \times 488203}{1577917828} = \text{(221034460)} \quad 11 \ \ 5 \ \ 31 \ \ 13 \ \ 35$$

Correction of the *Bija* add.

$$\frac{71440408\,2947 \times 4}{1577917828} = (\ -- \ -- \ -- \ ) \quad \begin{array}{l}0 \ \ 37 \ \ 37 \ \ 52 \ \ 28 \\ \overline{11 \ \ 7 \ \ 9 \ \ 6 \ \ 3}\end{array}$$

4th. Of the Moon's ascending Node.

$$\frac{71440408\,2947 \times 232238}{1577917828} = \text{(105147017)} \quad + \ 27 \ \ 49 \ \ 48 \ \ --$$

Correction of the *Bija* add.

$$\frac{71440408\,2947 \times 4}{1577917828} = (\ -- \ -- \ -- \ ) \quad \begin{array}{l}0 \ \ 1 \ \ 37 \ \ 52 \ \ 28 \\ \overline{4 \ \ 29 \ \ 27 \ \ 40 \ \ 28}\end{array}$$

5th. Of the Sun's Apogee.

$$\frac{71440408\,2947 \times 387}{1577917828} \quad (\ -- \ .175 \ -- \ ) \ 2 \ 17 \ 17 \ 15 \ --$$

Vol. II.   'T

	Mean longitude for midnight under the meridian of Lanca.				Deduct for the longitude of Bhagalpur at * 80° 50' of equator east.		Mean longitude for midnight at Bhagalpur.			
	s	°	'	"	"'	'	"	s	°	'	"	"'
Of the Sun,	6	21	44	2	12	1	27	6	21	42	35	12
Moon,	—	21	21	58	56	19	34	—	21	2	25	—
Node,	4	29	37	40	28	—	4	4	29	37	36	—
Sun's Apogee,	2	17	17	15	—	inconsiderable		2	17	17	16	—
Moon's Apogee,	11	7	9	6	3	—	9	11	7	8	57	—

THIRD OPERATION.

For the equated longitude of the Sun and Moon, &c.

1st, Of the Sun.

The mean longitude of the sun is $6^s 21° 42' 35''$ $12'''$; of the apogee 2 17 17 15, the difference, or mean anomaly, $4^s 4° 25' 20''$; its complement to 6 signs or distance from the perigee $1^s 25° 34' 40''$, the equation for which is required. This may either be taken from the foregoing table, translated from *Macaranda*, or calculated in the manner explained as follows:

The sine of $1^s 25° 34' 40''$ is $2835' 31''$ and $\frac{2835' 11'' \times 10'}{3418'}$ $= 14' 30''$ to be subtracted from the *paridhi* degrees in *sama*; $14° - 14' 30'' = 13° 53' 30''$, the circumference of the epicycle in this point of anomaly; and $\frac{11° 41' 30'' \times 23' 5' 31'}{360°} = 108' 61''$ the sine of the angle of equation, considered as equal to its arc, or $1° 48' 6''$, to be deducted from the mean, for the true longitude;

---

* This longitude, assigned to *Bhagalpur*, is erroneous; but the error does not in the least affect the main object of the paper.

6' 21° 42 35″—1° 48' 6″= 6' 19° 54' 29″ for midnight agreeing with mean time; but as, in this point
of anomaly, the true or apparent midnight precedes
that estimated for mean time, for which the computation has been made, a proportionable quantity must
be deducted from the sun's place, which is thus
found : Say, as the minutes contained in the ecliptic
are to the sun's mean motion in one day 59' 8″, so is
the equation of his mean to his true place 180' 6″, to
the equation of time required, o' 18″ (= $\frac{59'8''×108'6''}{21600}$)
and 6' 19° 54' 29″—29″—18″ = 6' 19° 54' 11″ the
sun's true longitude for the apparent midnight.

For the sun's true motion. The co-sine of the sun's
distance from the perigee is 1941' 0″ 1‴, and
$\frac{1941'0''1''×1143 30}{360°}$ = 74' the co-sine of the epicycle, and
$\frac{59'8''×74}{341''}$ = 1' 16″ equation, to be added to the mean
for the true motion, 59' 8″ × 1' 16″ = 60' 24″ per day,
or 60″. 24‴ per *danda*.

2d. *Of the Moon.*

The moon's mean longitude for the mean midnight is 0' 21° 2' 25″, which exceeds her mean longitude for the true midnight, but $\frac{109×792 1 31}{21600}$ = 3' 57″,
her motion in the difference of time between the mean
and true midnight 0' 21° 2' 25″—3' 57″ = 0 20 58
28 mean longitude, for which the anomalistic equation is to be found. Place of the apogee 11' 7° 8' 45″
and the moon's distance from it 1' 13° 49' 33″. The
sine of the latter, 2379' 39″. By the rule before ex-
plained $\frac{2379'19''×15'}{343''}$ = 13' 51″, and $\frac{34°—11'51''×2379'19'}{360}$
= 210' the sine of the angle of equation equal to
its arc, or 3° 30″ to be subtracted, 0' 20' 58″ 28‴ —
3° 30 = 0° 17' 28' 28″ the moon's true place, agreeing with the true or apparent midnight.

T 2

For the moon's true motion. The co-sine of her distance from the apogee 2479. 13. Circumference of the epicycle 31° 46' 9", and $\frac{11° 46' 9'' \times 24 \cdot 9' 11''}{360°} =$ 218' 47" co-sine in the epicycle. The moon's mean motion from her apogee is 790' 35"—6' 41" = 783' 54", and $\frac{783' 54'' \times 118' 47''}{3038''} = 49' 53''$ the equation of her mean to her true motion, to be subtracted, 790. 35— 49 53 = 740. 42 the moon's true motion per day, or 740" 42''' per danda.

For the place of the moon's apogee reduced to the apparent midnight. The motion of the apogee is 6' 41" per day. $\frac{108' 6'' \times 6' 41''}{21600''} = 2''$, 11' 7° 8' 57"—2" =11' 7° 8' 55" its place.

For the same of the node. Its motion per day is 3' 11", and $\frac{108' 6'' \times 1' 11''}{21600''} = 1''$, and 4' 29° 27' 36"— 1" = 4' 29° 27' 35" its place.

The true longitude and motion, therefore, for the apparent time of midnight at *Bhagalpur*, 714404082947 solar days after the creation, or commencement of the planetary motions, will be

	Longitude.			Motion per day.	
	°	'	"	'	"
Of the Sun,	6	19 54	11	60 24	♄
Moon,	—	17 28	28	740 42	
Sun's Apogee,	2	17 17	15	inconsiderable	
Moon's Apogee,	11	7 8	55	6 41	
Moon's Node,	4	29 27	35	3 11	

FOURTH OPERATION.

Having the longitude and motion as above, to determine the *tit'hi* and time remaining unexpired to the instant of opposition, or full moon.

The moon's longitude subtracted from the sun's, leaves 5ʳ 27° 34′ 17″, or 10654′ 17″, which, divided by 720′, the minutes in a mean *tit'hi*, quotes fourteen even *tit'his* expired, and the fraction, or remainder 574′ 17″, is the portion expired of the 15th, or *purnima tit'hi*, which subtracted from 720′, leaves 145′ 43″ remaining unexpired of the same; which, divided by the moon's motion per *danda* from the sun, will give the time remaining unexpired from midnight to the instant of the full moon with as much precision as the *Hindu* astronomy requires. Deduct the sun's motion 60″ 24‴ per *danda* from the moon's 740′ 42‴, the remainder 680″ 8‴, is the moon's motion from the sun; by this divide the part remaining unexpired of the *purnima tit'hi* 145′ 43″.

$$\frac{145′ 43″ = 524580‴}{680″ 8‴ = 40818‴} = \begin{matrix} D. & P. \\ 12 & 51 \end{matrix}$$

therefore 12 *dundas*, 51 *palas* after midnight will be the end of the *purnima tit'hi*, or instant of opposition of the sun and moon.

FIFTH OPERATION.

Having the instant of opposition as above, to find the true longitude and motion of the sun and moon, the latitude of the latter, and the place of the node.

D. P.

Add the mean motion of each for 12 51 to the mean place, found before for the true midnight; and for the mean places so found, compute again the anomalistic equations. This being but a repetition of operation, the third is unnecessary to be detailed. The several particulars are as follows:

T 3

	Mean longitude for midnight.	Mean longitude at full moon.	Equation	True longitude at full moon.
	s ° ' "	s ° ' "	° ' "	s ° ' "
Of the Sun,	6 21 42 17	6 21 54 17	1 47 50	6 20 7 7
Moon,	— 20 58 28	— 23 47 47	3 40 20	— 20 7 27
Moon's Apogee,	11 7 8 55	11 7 10 21	—	—
Moon's Node,	4 29 27 35	4 29 28 16	—	—

	Mean motion.	Equation.	True motion at full moon.
Of the Sun,	59' 8"	x 1' 16"	60' 24"
Moon,	790 35	— 47 28	743 , 7

Hence it appears that, at the opposition, the moon will be near her descending node; for, $4' 29°$ $28' 16'' \times 6' = 10' 29° 28' 16''$, the place of the descending node *in antecedentia*, and $12'—10' 29° 28' 16'' = 1' 0° 31' 44''$ its longitude according to the order of the signs, and $1' 0° 31' 44''—20° 7' 27'' = 10° 24' 17''$ the moon's distance from her descending node, which, being within the limit of a lunar eclipse, shows that the moon will be then eclipsed. For her latitude at this time, say, as radius is to the inclination of her orbit to the ecliptic, $4° 30'$ or $270'$, so is the sine of her distance from the node $620' 57''$, to her latitude of $48' 45''$ ($= \frac{270' \times 6:0' 57''}{3435'}$).

SIXTH OPERATION.

From the elements now found, to compute the diameters of the moon and shadow, and the duration of the eclipse.

	Yojan.
The Sun's mean diameter is	6500
Moon's	480
Earth's	1600

Sun's mean motion,   - - -   59' 8"
Moon's,   - - - - - 790 35
Sun's true motion,   - - - 60 24
Moon's,   - - - - - 743 7
Moon's latitude,   - - - - 48 45

As the moon's mean motion is to her mean diameter, so is her true motion to her true diameter for the
time of opposition $\frac{741' 7'' \times 480}{790, 35} = 451$ 11 _Yojan_, which,
divided by fifteen, quotes $30' 5''$ of a great circle.

As the sun's mean motion is to his mean diameter,
so is his true motion to his diameter at the instant
of opposition $\frac{60' 24'' \times 6500}{59 8'} = 6639$ 14 _Yojun_.

As the moon's mean motion is to the earth's diameter, so is the moon's equated motion to the _Suchi_,
or a fourth number, which must be taken as the
earth's diameter, for the purpose of proportioning its
shadow to the moon's distance and apparent diameter
$\frac{1600 \times 743' 7'}{790 35} = 1503$ 56 _Yojun_, the _Suchi_.

Equated diameter of the sun,   - - 6639 14
Of the earth,   - - - - - - 1503 56
                              ——————
          Difference, 5039 14

As the sun's mean diameter is to the moon's diameter, so is the difference above 5039 14, to a fourth
number, which deducted from the _Suchi_, or equated
diameter of the earth, leaves the dimeter of the earth's
shadow at the moon, $\frac{480 \times 5039\ 14}{6500} = 372.$ 7, and

T 4

1503. 56—372. 7 = 1131. 49 *Yojan*, which divided by fifteen, quotes 75' 27" of a great circle for the same.

From the half sum of the diameters of the moon and shadow $\frac{75' 27'' \times 30' 5'}{2}$ = 52' 46", subtract the moon's latitude 48' 45", the remainder is the *Chch'anna*, or portion of the moon's diameter eclipsed, 4' 1" of a great circle, and by the nature of a right angled triangle, the square root of the difference of the squares of the moon's latitude, and the half sum of the diameters of the shadow and moon, will be the path of the moon's centre, from the beginning to the middle of the eclipse.

The diameter of the shadow is, 75 27
Of the moon, - - - - 30 5

Sum, - 105 32

Half sum, 52 46

The moon's latitude is, - 48 45

$\sqrt{52.46^2 \times 48.45^2}$ = 20' 11" which, divided by the moon's motion from the sun, quotes the half duration of the eclipse in *dandas* and *palas*, or *Hindu* mean solar hours, $\frac{20' 11'' - 1311''}{682' 43'} = \overset{D \quad P \quad V}{1 \ 46 \ 25}$; which doubled, is $\overset{D \quad P \quad V}{3 \ 32 \ 50}$, the whole duration of the eclipse; which will be partial, the moon's latitude being greater than the difference between the semidiameters of the moon's disk and the earth's shadow.

SEVENTH OPERATION.

To find the position of the equinoctial colures, and thence the declination of the sun, the length of day and night, and the time counted from sunrise, or hour of the civil day when the eclipse will happen.

1st. For the *ayanansa* or distance of the vernal equinox from the 1st of *Mesha.* $\frac{7144040823947 \times 600}{1577917848}$ = (271650) Period. 8s 4° 31′ 30″ 52‴ of which take the *bhuja* 8ˢ 4° 31′ 30″ 52‴ −6′ =2ˢ 4° 31′ 30″ 52″ which multiply by three, and divide by ten, $\frac{64° 31' 30'' 52 \times 3}{10}$ = 19° 21′ 27″ the *ayanansa*, which in the present age is added to the sun's longitude, to find his distance from the vernal equinox. The sun's equated longitude is 6s 19° 54′ 11″, and 6s 19° 54′ 11″ × 19° 21′ 27′ = 7s 9° 15′ 38″ his distance from the vernal equinox.

2d. For the declination, right ascension, and ascensional difference. The sun's place is 7s 9° 15′ 38″, and is 9° 15′ 38″ his distance from the autumnal equinox; the sine of which is 2174′ 41″, and as radius is to the sine of the greatest declination 24°, termed the *paramapacramajya* 1397′, so is 2174 41 to the sine of his declination 883′ 40″, the arc corresponding with which, in the canon of sines, is 14° 53′, ($\frac{1397 \times 2174' 41''}{3438}$ = 883′ 40″). The equinoctial shadow at *Bhagalpur* is 5, 30, and, as the *Gnomon* of twelve *angalas* is to the equinoctial shadow, so is the sine of the declination 883, 40, to the *cshitijya*, $\frac{5 \cdot 10 \times 883' 40''}{12}$ = 405′ 1″. And as the co-sine of the declination is to radius, so is the *cshitijya* to the sine of the *chara*, or ascensional difference, $\frac{405' 1 \times 3438}{3333 \cdot 36}$ = 419′ 4″ : its arc is 419′ 56″ the ascensional difference.

3d. For the length of the day and night.

The modern *Hindus* make their computations in mean solar time ; the *Surya Siddhanta* directs, that

they should be made in sydereal time. A sydereal day contains sixty *dandas*; each *danda*, sixty
viculas; and each *vicula* six respirations, in all 21600
respirations answering to the minutes of the equator.
A *nacshatra* day is exceeded in length by the *savan* or
solar day by reason of the sun's proper motion in the
ecliptic, the former measures time equably, but the
latter varies in its length from the inequality of the
sun's motion, and the obliquity of the ecliptic. The
sun's equated motion for the middle of the eclipse
was found 60′ 24″; and the oblique ascension for the
eighth sign from the vernal equinox, in which he will
be found at that time, is taken from the foregoing
table 343 *palas*, or 2058 respirations. As the number of minutes contained in one sine 1800, is to the
number of respirations, or the arc of the equator in
minutes answering to the oblique ascension of the
sine, the sun is in 2058, as above, so is the equated
motion 60′ 24″, to the excess in respirations of the
savan or solar day over the *nacshatra* or sydereal day
$\frac{2058' \times 60' \ 24'}{1800} = 69' \ 3''$; which added to 21600′ gives
the length of the solar day by civil account from
sunrise to sunrise, sydereal time 21669. 3 respirations.
From one-fourth of this deduct the ascensional difference, the sun being declined towards the south
pole, for the semidiurnal arc; and add it for the
seminocturnal arc : the former is 4997′ 19″, and the
latter 5837′ 11″; which may be reduced to *dandas* or
Hindu hours by a division of 360. Hence half the
day is 13 $\overset{D}{}$ 52 $\overset{P}{}$ 53 $\overset{V}{}$, and half the night 16 $\overset{D}{}$ 12 $\overset{P}{}$ 52 $\overset{V}{}$.
The whole day added to half the night shows the hour
counted from the preceding sunrise to midnight
43 $\overset{D}{}$ 59 $\overset{P}{}$ 38 $\overset{V}{}$, to which add the time at midnight unexpired of the *purnima tit'hi*, for the hour of the civil
day corresponding with the middle of the eclipse.'
The hour from midnight to the end of the *purnima-*

tit'hi is already found 12 ⁵¹ in mean solar time, and
to reduce it to sydereal time, say, as 21600′ is to
21600′ × 59′ 8″, so is 12 51, to sidereal hours 12 53,
equal to 2 51 solar hours.

From the preceding sunrise to midnight is, 43 59 —
At midnight will remain of the *purnima*
tit'hi, - - - } 12 53 —

Hour of the civil day at the middle of
the eclipse, - - } 56 52 —
Deduct the half duration, - - 1 46 25

Beginning of the eclipse, - - 55 5 35
Add the whole duration, - - 3 32 50

End of the eclipse, - - 58 38 25

And the day and night containing together 60 11
30, the eclipse should end 1 33 5 before sunrise, according to this calculation.

The first day after the creation, according to the
Hindus, was *ravi-var*, or *Sunday*: the number of days
for which the above calculation has been made, is
714404082947, which divided by seven, the number
of days in a week are 102057726135 weeks and two
days; the astronomical day therefore of *soma-var*,
or *Monday*, will end at midnight preceding the eclipse;
but the *soma-var* by civil computation will continue
to the next ensuing sunrise, and this *somavar*, by calculating the number of days elapsed from the instant
the sun entered the sign *Tula*, to his advance of 19° 54′
on that sign, will be found to fall on the 19th of the
month *Cartic*, answering to the third of November.

The time of the full moon and the duration of the eclipse, found by this computation, differ considerably from the Nautical Almanac. The *Siddhanta Rahasya* and *Grahalaghava*, comparatively modern treatises, are nearer the truth, yet far from correct. The *Hindus*, in determining these phenomena, are satisfied when within a few minutes of the true time.

A comparative statement of this eclipse as predicted in the Nautical Almanac, with computations of it made by different Hindu books. Those marked (*) are made for different meridians, the last I believe for Tirhut.

NAMES.	Equated longitude for midnight at *Bhagalpur*, supposed in 8° 50′ E. from *Lanca*, and 88° E. from *Greenwich*.		
	The Sun.	The Moon.	The Node.
Surya Siddhanta,	s o ′ ″ 6 19 54 11	s o ′ ″ — 17 28 28 1	— 31 44
Tables of Macaranda,	6 19 55 9	— 17 30 9 1	— 32 7
* Grahalaghava,			
Siddhanta Rahasya,	6 19 54 29	— 17 16 25 1	— 27 35

Add to each the *ayanansa* 19° 21′ 27″ for the longitude counted according to *European* astronomers from the Equinoctial colure.

NAMES.			
	s o ′ ″	s o ′ ″	9 o ′ ″
Surya Siddhanta,	7 9 15 38	1 6 49 55	1 19 53 11
Tables of Macaranda,	7 9 16 36	1 6 51 36	1 19 53 54
* Grahalaghava,			
Siddhanta Rahasya,	7 9 15 56	1 6 37 57	1 19 49 2
Nautical Almanac.	7 147 8	1 7 50 58	1 19 45 30

NAMES.	From midnight to the middle of the Eclipse.		Duration of the Eclipse.	
	Hindu time.	English time.	Hindu time.	Eng. time.
	D. V. P.	H. M. S.	D. P. V.	H. M. S.
Surya Siddhanta,	12 53 —	5 9 12	3 12 50	1 17 8
Tables of Macaranda,			4 50 —	1 46 20
* Grahalaghava,	*14 50 —	5 56 —	5 18 —	1 56 36
Siddhanta Rahasya,	13 53 —	5 33 —	4 58 —	1 49 16
* Grahana Mala, a Catalogue of Eclipses, }	16 6 —	6 26 24	5 26 —	2 10 24
Nautical Almanac.	16 — 37	0 24 15	5 22 23	2 0 —

XVI.

ANTIQUITY OF THE INDIAN ZODIAC.

BY THE PRESIDENT.

I ENGAGE to support an opinion (which the learned and industrious M. *Montucla* seems to treat with extreme contempt) that the *Indian* division of the Zodiac was not borrowed from the *Greeks* or *Arabs*, but, having been known in this country from time immemorial, and being the same in part with that used by other nations of the old *Hindu* race, was probably invented by the first progenitors of that race before their dispersion. " The *Indians*," he says, " have two " divisions of the Zodiac; one, like that of the " *Arabs*, relating to the moon, and consisting of " *twenty-seven* equal parts, by which they can tell " very nearly the hour of the night ; another relating " to the sun, and, like ours, containing twelve signs, " to which they have given as many names, corres- " ponding with those which we have borrowed from " the *Greeks*." All that is true; but he adds, " It " is highly probable that they received them at some " time or another by the intervention of the *Arabs* ; for " no man, surely, can persuade himself, that it is the " ancient division of the Zodiac formed, according " to some authors, by the forefathers of mankind, " and still preserved among the *Hindus*." Now I undertake to prove, that the *Indian* Zodiac was not borrowed mediately or directly from the *Arabs* or *Greeks*; and, since the solar division of it in *India* is the same in substance with that used in *Greece*, we may reasonably conclude, that both *Greeks* and *Hindus* received it from an older nation, who first gave names to the

luminaries of heaven, and from whom both *Greeks*
and *Hindus*, as their similarity in language and religion fully evinces, had a common descent.

The same writer afterwards intimates, that " the
" time when *Indian* astronomy received its most
" considerable improvement, from which it has now,
" as he imagines, wholly declined, was either the
" age when the *Arabs*, who established themselves
" in *Persia* and *Sogdiana*, had a great intercourse
" with the *Hindus*, or that, when the successors of
" *Chengiz* united both *Arabs* and *Hindus* under one
" vast dominion." It is not the object of this essay
to correct the historical errors in the passage last-
cited, nor to defend the astronomers of *India* from
the charge of gross ignorance in regard to the figure
of the earth and the distances of the heavenly bodies :
a charge, which *Montucla* very boldly makes on the
authority, I believe, of father *Souciet*. I will only remark, that, in our conversations with the *Pandits*, we
must never confound the system of the *Jyautishicas*,
or mathematical astronomers, with that of the *Paura-
nicas*, or poetical fabulists; for to such a confusion
alone must we impute the many mistakes of *Europeans* on the subject of *Indian* science. A venerable
mathematician of this province, named *Ramachandra*,
now in his eightieth year, visited me lately at *Crishnanagar* ; and part of his discourse was so applicable
to the inquiries, which I was then making, that, as
soon as he left me, I committed it to writing. " The
" *Pauranics*," he said, " will tell you, that our earth is
" a plane figure studded with eight mountains, and
" surrounded by seven seas of milk, nectar, and
" other fluids; that the part which we inhabit
" is one of seven islands, to which eleven smaller
" isles are subordinate; that a God, riding on a
huge *elephant*, guards each of the eight regions ; and

"that a mountain of gold rises and gleams in the
"centre; but we believe the earth to be sha,ed like
"a *Cadamba* fruit, or spheroidal, and admit only four
"oceans of salt water, all which we name from the four
"cardinal points, and in which are many great pen-
"insulas, with innumerable islands. They will tell you
"that a dragon's head swallows the moon, and thus
"causes an eclipse; but we know that the supposed
"head and tail of the dragon mean only the nodes, or
"points formed by intersections of the ecliptic and
"moon's orbit. In short, they have imagined a
"system which exists only in their fancy; but we
"consider nothing as true without such evidence as
"cannot be questioned." I could not perfectly understand the old Gymnosophist, when he told me
that the *Rasichacra*, or *Circle of Signs* (for so he called the Zodiac) was like a *Dhustura* flower; meaning
the *Datura*, to which the *Sanscrit* name has been
softened, and the flower of which is conical, or shaped
like a funnel. At first I thought that he alluded to a
projection of the hemisphere on the plane of the
colure, and to the angle formed by the ecliptic and
equator; but a younger astronomer, named *Vinayaca*,
who came forward to see me, assured me that they
meant only the circular mouth of the funnel, or the base
of the cone; and that it was usual among their ancient
writers to borrow from fruits and flowers their appellations of several plane and solid figures.

From the two *Brahmans*, whom I have just named,
I learned the following curious particulars; and you
may depend on my accuracy in repeating them, since
I wrote them in their presence, as well as corrected
what I had written, till they pronounced it perfect.
They divide a great circle, as we do, into three hundred and sixty degrees, called by them *arsas*, or *por-
sions*; of which they, like us, allot thirty to each of
the twelve signs, in this order:

VOL. II.   U

Mesha, the Ram,	*Tula*, the Balance.
Vrisha, the Bull.	8. *Vrishchica*, the Scorpion.
Mithana, the Pair.	*Dhanus*, the Bow.
🦀 *Carcata*, the Crab.	*Macara*, the Sea-Monster.
Sinha, the Lion.	*Cumbha*, the Ewer.
Canya, the Virgin.	12. *Mina*, the Fish.

The figures of the twelve asterisms, thus denominated
with respect to the sun, are specified by *Sripati*, author
of the *Retnamala*, in *Sanscrit* verses ; which I produce as my vouchers in the original, with a verbal
translation :

Meshadayo same tamasarupi,
Vinagadadhyam mit'hunam oriyugman,
Pradipasasye dadhati carabhyam
Navi st'hita variai canyacaiva.
Tula tulabhrit pretimanapanir
Dhanur dhanushman hayawat parangah
Mriganansh syan macaro'tha cumbhah
Scandhe nero rictaghatam dadhanah,
Anyanyapuchch'babbimac'ho hi minah
Matsyadwayam swast'halacharinomi.

" The *ram, bull, crab, lion,* and *scorpion,* have the fi-
" gures of those five animals respectively : the *pair*
" are a damsel playing on a *vina,* and a youth wielding
" a mace; the *virgin* stands on a boat in water, hold-
" ing in one hand a lamp, in the other an ear of
" rice-corn ; the *balance* is held by a weigher with a
" weight in one hand ; the *bow,* by an archer, whose .

" hinder parts are like those of a horse; the sea-
" monster has the face of an antelope; the ewer is a
" waterpot borne on the shoulder of a man, who
" empties it; the fish are two with their heads turned
" to each other's tail: and all these are supposed to
" be in such places as suit their several natures."

To each of the twenty-seven lunar stations, which
they call nucshatras, they allow thirteen ansas and
one-third, or thirteen degrees twenty minutes; and
their names appear in the order of the signs, but without any regard to the figures of them.

Aswini.	Magha.	Mula.
Bharani.	Purva p'halguni.	Purvashadha.
Critica.	Uttara p'halguni.	Uttarashadha.
Rohini.	Hasta.	Sravana.
Mrigasiras.	Chitra.	Dhanishta.
Ardra.	Swati.	Satabhisha.
Punarvasu.	Visac'ha.	Purva bhadrapada.
Pushya.	Anuradha.	Uttarabhadrapada.
9. Aslesha.	18. Jyeshi'ha.	27. Revati.

Between the twenty-first and twenty-second constellations, we find in the plate three stars, called Abhijit;
but they are the last quarter of the asterism immediately preceding, or the later Ashar, as the word is commonly pronounced. A complete revolution of the
moon, with respect to the stars, being made in twenty-seven days, odd hours, minutes, and seconds, and
perfect exactness being either not attained by the

U 2

Hindus, or not acquired by them, they fixed on the
number twenty-seven, and inserted *Abhijit* for some
astrological purpose in their nuptial ceremonies.
The drawing, from which the plate was engraved,
seems intended to represent the figures of the twenty-
seven constellations, together with *Abhijit,* as they
are described in three stanzas by the author of the
Retnamala :

1. Turagamuc'hasadricsham yonirupam cshurabham,
   Sacatasamam at'hainasyottamangena tulyam,
   Manigrihasara chacrabhani salopamam bham,
   Sayanasadrisamanyachchatra paryancarupam.

2. Hastacarayutam cha maucticasamam
         chanyat pravalopamam,
   Dhrishyam torana sannibham balinibham,
      satcundalabham param ;
   Crudhyatcesarivicramena sadrisam,
      · sayyasamanam param,
   Anyad dentivilasavat st'hitamatah
      sringatacavyacti bham.

3. Trivicramabham cha mridangarupam,
   Vrittam tatonyadyamalabhwayabham, ·
   Paryancarupam murajanucaram, _
   Ityevam aswadibhachacrarupam.   ' ' .'
                                                    . ?
   " A horse's head, *yoni* or *bhaga,* a razor, a wheel-
   " ed carriage, the head of an antelope, a gem, a
   " house, an arrow, a wheel, another house, a bed-
   " stead, another bedstead, a hand, a pearl, a piece
   " of coral, a festoon of leaves, an oblation to the
   " Gods, a rich ear-ring, the tail of a fierce lion, a
   " couch, the tooth of a wanton elephant, near which

" is the kernel òf the *sringataca* nut, the three foot-
" steps of *Vishnu*, a tabor, a circular jewel, a two-faced
" image, another couch, and a smaller sort of tabor ;
" such are the figures of *Aswini* and the rest in the
" circle of lunar constellations."

The *Hindu* draughtsman has very ill represented
most of the figures ; and he has transposed the two
Asharas as well as the two *Bhadrapads* ; but his figure
of *Abhijit*, which looks like our ace of hearts, has a
resemblance to the kernel of the *trapa* : a curious
water-plant described in a separate essay. In another
Sanscrit book the figures of the same constellations are
thus varied :

A horse's head.	A straight tail.	A couch.
Yoni, or *bhaga*.	Two stars S. to N.	A winnowing fan.
A flame.	Two, N. to S.	Another.
A waggon.	A hand.	An arrow.
A cat's paw.	A pearl.	A tabor.
One bright star.	Red saffron.	A circle of stars.
A bow.	A festoon.	A staff for burdens.
A child's pencil.	A snake.	The beam of a balance.

9. A dog's tail. 19. A boar's head. 27. A Fish.

From twelve of the asterisms just enumerated are
derived the names of the twelve *Indian* months, in the
usual form of patronymics ; for the *Pauranics*, who
reduce all nature to a system of emblematical mythology, suppose a celestial nymph to preside over
each of the constellations, and feign that the God
Soma, or. *Lunus*, having wedded twelve of them, became the father of twelve *Genii*, or months, who are
named after their several mothers ; but the *Jyautishi-*

U 3

ras assert, that, when their lunar year was arranged by former astronomers, the moon was at the full in each month on the very day when it entered the *nacshatra*, from which that month is denominated. The manner in which the derivatives are formed, will best appear by a comparison of the months with their several constellations:

Aswini.	Chaitra.
Cartica.	8. Vaisac'ha.
Margasirsha.	Jyaisht'ha.
4. Pausha.	Ashara.
Magha.	Sravana.
Phalguna.	12. Bhadra.

The third month is also called *Agrahayana* (whence the common word *Agran* is corrupted) from another name of *Mrigasiras*.

Nothing can be more ingenious than the memorial verses, in which the *Hindus* have a custom of linking together a number of ideas otherwise unconnected, and of chaining, as it were, the memory by a regular measure: thus by putting *teeth* for thirty-two, *Rudra* for eleven, *season* for six, *arrow* or *element* for five, *ocean*, *Veda*, or *age*, for four, *Rama*, *fire*, or *quality* for three, *eye*, or *Cumara* for two, and *earth* or *moon* for one, they have composed four lines, which express the number of stars in each of the twenty-seven asterisms:

Vahni tri ritwishu gunesdu critaguibbuta,
Banaswisetra sara bhucu yugabdhi ramah,
Rudrabdhiramagunavedasata dwiyugma,
Denta budhairabhjhitah cramaso bhatarah.

That is, "three, three, six; five, three, one;
" four, three, five; five, two, two; five, one, one;
" four, four, three; eleven, four, and three; three,.
" four, an hundred; two, two, thirty-two. Thus have.
" the stars of the lunar constellations, in the order
" as they appear, been numbered by the wise."

If the stanza was correctly repeated to me, the
two Atharas are considered as one asterism, and
Abhijit as three separate stars; but I suspect an error
in the third line, because *dwibana*, or *two and five*
would suit the metre as well as *bdhirama*; and because
there were only three *Vedas* in the early age, when, it
is probable, the stars were enumerated, and the technical verse composed.

Two lunar stations, or *mansions*, and a quarter are
co-extensive, we see, with one sign; and nine stations
correspond with four signs. By counting, therefore,
thirteen degrees and twenty minutes from the first star
in the head of the Ram, inclusively, we find the
whole extent of *Aswini*, and shall be able to ascertain
the other stars with sufficient accuracy; but first let
us exhibit a comparative table of both *Zodiacs*, denoting the mansions, as in the *Varanes* Almanac, by
the first letters or syllables of their names:

U 4

Months.	Solar Asterisms.	Mansions.
A'swin	Mesh	$A + bh + \frac{c}{4}$
Cartic	Vrish	$\frac{10}{4} + ro + \frac{M}{2}$
Agrahayan	Mit'hun	$\frac{M}{2} + a + \frac{2P}{4}$
Paush	Carcat 4.	$\frac{P}{4} + p + sl.\ 9.$
Magh	Sinh	$m + PU + \frac{U}{4}$
P'halgun	Canya	$\frac{3U}{4} + h + \frac{ch}{2}$
Chaitr	Tula	$\frac{ch}{2} + s + \frac{3v}{4}$
Vaisac'h	Vrischic. 8.	$\frac{v}{2} + a + j\ 18.$
Jaisht'h	Dhan	$mu + pu + \frac{s}{4}$
Ashar	Macar	$\frac{12}{4} + S + \frac{d}{2}$
Sravan	Cumbh	$\frac{d}{2} + s + \frac{m}{4}$
Bhadr	Min 12.	$\frac{M}{4} + u + r.\ 27.$

Hence we may readily know the stars in each mansion, as they follow in order:

Lunar Mansions.	Solar Asterisms.	Stars.
Aswini.	Ram	*Three* in and near the head.
Bharani.	———	*Three* in the tail.
Critica.	Bull	*Six* of the pleiads.
Rohini.	———	*Five* in the head and neck.
Mrigasiras.	Pair	{ *Three* in or near the feet, perhaps in the Galaxy.
Ardra.	———	*One* on the knee.

LUNAR MANSIONS.	SOLAR ASTERISMS.	STARS.
Punarvasu	—	*Four* in the heads, breast, and shoulder.
Pushya.	Crab	*Three* in the body and claws.
Aslesha.	Lion	*Five* in the face and mane.
Magha.	—	*Five* in the leg and haunch.
Purvap'halguni.	—	*Two* ; one in the tail.
Uttarap'halguni.	Virgin	*Two* on the arm and zone
Hasta.	—	*Five* near the hand.
Chitra.	—	*One* in the spike.
Swati.	Balance	*One* in the n. scale.
Visac'ha.	—	*Four* beyond it.
Anuradha.	Scorpion	*Four* in the body.
Jyesht'ha.	—	*Three* in the tail.
Mula.	Bow	*Eleven* to the point of the arrow.
Purvashara.	—	*Two* in the leg.
Uttarashara.	Sea-monster	*Two* in the horn.
Sravana.	—	*Three* in the tail.
Dhanisht'a.	—	*Four* in the arm.
Satabhisha.	Ewer	*Many* in the stream.
Purvabhadrapada.	—	*Two* in the first fish.
Uttarabhadrapada.	Fish	*Two* in the cord.
Revati.	—	*Thirty-two* in the second fish and cord.

Wherever the *Indian* drawing differs from the memorial verse in the *Retnamala*, I have preferred the authority of the writer to that of the painter, who has drawn some terrestrial things with so little similitude, that we must not implicitly rely on his representation of objects merely celestial. He seems particularly to have erred in the stars of *Dhanisht'a.*

For the assistance of those who may be inclined to re-examine the twenty-seven constellations with a chart before them, I subjoin a table of the degrees to which the *nacshatras* extend respectively from the first star in the asterism of *Aries*, which we now see near the beginning of the sign *Taurus*, as if it was placed in the ancient sphere.

N.	D.	M.	N.	D.	M.	N.	D.	M.
I.	13°.	20'.	X.	133°.	20'.	XIX.	253°.	20'.
II.	26°.	40'.	XI.	146°.	40'.	XX.	266°.	40'.
III.	40°.	0'.	XII.	160°.	0'.	XXI.	280°.	0'.
IV.	53°.	20'.	XIII.	173°.	20'.	XXII.	293°.	20'.
V.	66°.	40'.	XIV.	186°.	40'.	XXIII.	306°.	40'.
VI.	80°.	0'.	XV.	200°.	0'.	XXIV.	320°.	0'.
VII.	93°.	20'.	XVI.	213°.	20'.	XXV.	333°.	20'.
VIII.	106°.	40'.	XVII.	226°.	40'.	XXVI.	346°.	40'.
IX.	120°.	0'.	XVIII.	240°.	0'.	XXVII.	360°.	0'.

The asterisms of the *first* column are in the signs of *Taurus, Gemini, Cancer, Leo*; those of the *second*, in *Virgo, Libra, Scorpio, Sagittarius*; and those of the *third*, in *Capricornus, Aquarius, Pisces, Aries*. We cannot err much therefore, in any series of *three* constellations; for, by counting 13° 20' forwards and backwards, we find the spaces occupied by the two extremes, and the intermediate space belongs of course to the middlemost. It is not meant that the division of the *Hindu* Zodiac into such spaces is exact to a minute, or that *every* star of each asterism must necessarily be found in the space to which it belongs; but the computation will be accurate enough for our purpose, and no lunar mansion can be very remote from the path of the moon. How Father *Souciet* could dream that *Visac'ha* was in the Northern Crown, I can hardly comprehend; but it surpasses all comprehension that M. *Bailly* should copy his dream, and give reasons to support it; especially as four stars, arranged pretty much like those in the *Indian* figure, present themselves obviously near the Balance, or the Scorpion. I have not the boldness to exhibit the individual stars in each mansion, distinguished in *Bayer's* method, by *Greek* letters, because, though I have little doubt that the five stars of *Aslesha*, in the form of a wheel, are κ, γ, ζ, μ, ι, of the *Lion*, and those of *Mula* γ, ι, δ, ζ, φ, τ, σ, ν, ο, ξ, π, of the *Sagittary*: and though I think many of the others equally clear, yet, where the number of stars in a mansion is less than three, or even than four, it is not easy to fix on them with confidence; and I must wait, until some young *Hindu* astronomer, with a good memory and good eyes, can attend my leisure on serene nights at the proper seasons, to point out in the firmament itself the several stars of all the constellations for which he can find names in the *Sanscrit* language. The only stars, except those in the Zodiac, that have yet been distinctly named to me, are the *Septarshi*, *Dhruva*, *Arundhuti*, *Vishnupad*, *Matrimandel*; and, in the southern hemisphere, *Agastya*, or *Canopus*. The twenty-seven *Yoga* stars, indeed, have particular names, in the order of the *nacshatras*, to which they belong; and since we learn * that the *Hindus* have

---

* See p. 270.

determined *the latitude, longitude, and right ascension of each,* it might be useful to exhibit the list of them :: but at present I can only subjoin the names of twenty-seven *Yogas,* or divisions of the Ecliptic.

Vishcambha.	*Ganda.*	*Parigha.*
Priti.	*Vriddhi.*	*Siva.*
Ayushmat.	*Dhruva.*	*Siddha.*
Saubhagya	*Vyaghata.*	*Sadhya.*
Sobhana.	*Hershana.*	*Subha.*
Atiganda.	*Vajra.*	*Sucra.*
Sucarman.	*Asrij.*	*Brahman.*
Dhriti.	*Vyatipata.*	*Indra.*
Sula.	*Variyas.*	*Vaidhriti.*

Having shown in what manner the *Hindus* arrange the *Zodiacal* stars with respect to the sun and moon, let us proceed to our principal subject, *the antiquity of that double arrangement.* In the first place, the *Brahmans* were always too proud to borrow their science from the *Greeks, Arabs, Moguls,* or any nation of *Mlechch'has,* as they call those who are ignorant of the *Vedas,* and have not studied the language of the Gods. They have often repeated to me the fragment of an old verse, which they now use proverbially, *na nicho yavanatparah,* or *no base creature can be lower than a Yavan;* by which name they formerly meant an *Ionian* or *Greek,* and now mean a *Mogul,* or generally, a *Muselman.* When I mentioned to different *Pandits,* at several times, and in several places, the opinion of *Montucla,* they could not prevail on themselves to oppose it by serious argument; but some laughed heartily; others, with a sarcastic smile, said it was a *pleasant imagination;* and all seemed to think it a notion bordering on phrenzy. In fact, although the figures of the

I

twelve *Indian* signs bear a wonderful resemblance
to those of the *Grecian*, yet they are too much varied
for a mere copy, and the nature of the variation proves
them to be original; nor is the resemblance more extraordinary than that, which has often been observed,
between our *Gothic* days of the week and those of the
Hindus, which are dedicated to the same luminaries,
and (what is yet more singular) revolve in the same
order:—*Ravi*, the Sun; *Soma*, the Moon; *Mangala*,
Tuisco; *Budha*, Woden; *Vrihaspati*, Thor; *Sucra*,
Freya; *Sani*, Sater; yet no man ever imagined that
the *Indians* borrowed so remarkable an arrangement
from the *Goths* or *Germans*. On the planets I will
only observe, that *Sucra*, the regent of *Venus*, is, like
all the rest, a *male* deity, named also *Usanas*, and
believed to be a sage of infinite learning; but *Zohrah*,
the *Nahid* of the *Persians*, is a goddess like the *Freya*
of our *Saxon* progenitors. The drawing, therefore, of
the planets, which was brought into *Bengal* by Mr.
Johnson, relates to the *Persian* system, and represents
the genii supposed to preside over them, exactly as
they are described by the poet *Hatifi*: " He bedecked
" the firmament with stars, and ennobled this earth
" with the race of men; he gently turned the auspi-
" cious new moon of the festival, like a bright jewel,
" round the ancle of the sky; he placed the *Hindu*
" *Saturn* on the seat of that restive elephant, the re-
" volving sphere, and put the rainbow into his hand,
" as a hook to coerce the intoxicated beast; he made
" silken strings of sun-beams for the lute of *Venus*;
" and presented *Jupiter*, who saw the felicity of true
" religion, with a rosary of clustering pleiads. The
" bow of the sky became that of *Mars* when he was
" honoured with the command of the celestial host;
" for *God* conferred sovereignty on the Sun; and squa-
" drons of stars were his army."

The names and forms of the lunar constellations, especially of *Bharani* and *Abhijit*, indicate a simplicity of manners peculiar to an ancient people; and they differ entirely from those of the *Arabian* system, in which the very first asterism appears in the dual number, because it consists only of two stars. *Menzil*, or *the place of alighting*, properly signifies a *station* or *stage*, and thence is used for an ordinary day's *journey*; and that idea seems better applied than *mansion* to so incessant a traveller as the moon; the *menazilu'l kamar*, or *lunar stages*, of the *Arabs* have *twenty-eight* names, in the following order, the particle *al* being understood before every word:

Sharatan.	Nathrah.	Ghafr.	Dhabili.
Butain.	Tarf.	Zubaniyah.	Bulaa.
Thurayya.	Jabhah.	Iclil.	Saad.
Debaran.	Zubrah.	Kalb.	Akhbiya
Hakaah.	Sarfah.	Shaulah.	Mukdim.
Hanaah.	Awwa.	Naaim.	Mukhir.
7. Dhiraa.	14. Simac.	21. Beldah.	28. Risha.

Now, if we can trust the *Arabian* lexicographers, the number of stars in their several *menzils* rarely agrees with those of the *Indians*; and two such nations must naturally have observed, and might naturally have named, the principal stars near which the moon passes in the course of each day, without any communication on the subject. There is no evidence, indeed, of a communication between the *Hindus* and *Arabs* on any subject of literature or science; for, though we have reason to believe that a commercial intercourse subsisted in very early times between *Yemen* and the western coast of *India*, yet the *Brahmans*, who alone are permitted to read the six

Vedangas, one of which is the astronomical *Sastra*,
were not then commercial, and, most probably, neither could nor would have conversed with *Arabian*
merchants. The hostile irruption of the *Arabs* into
Hindustan, in the eighth century, and that of the *Moguls* under *Chengis*, in the thirteenth, were not likely
to change the astronomical system of the *Hindus*; but
the supposed consequences of *modern* revolutions are
out of the question ; for, if any historical records be
true, we know with as positive certainty, that *Amarsihn*
and *Calidas* composed their works before the birth of
Christ, as that *Menander* and *Terence* wrote before that
important epoch. Now the twelve *signs* and twenty-
seven *mansions* are mentioned, by the several names
before exhibited, in a *Sanscrit* vocabulary by the
first of those *Indian* authors; and the second of them
frequently alludes to *Rohini* and the rest by name in
his *Fatal Ring*, his *Children of the Sun*, and his *Birth
of Cumara*; from which poem I produce two lines, that
my evidence may not seem to be collected from mere
conversation :—

Maitre muhurte sasalanch'hanena,
Yogam gatasuttarap'halganishu,

" When the stars of *Uttarup'halgun* had joined in
" a fortunate hour the fawn-spotted moon."

This testimony being decisive against the conjecture
of M. *Montucla*, I need not urge the great antiquity
of *Menu's* Institutes, in which the twenty-seven asterisms are called the daughters of *Dacsha* and the con-
sorts of *Soma*, or the Moon ; nor rely on the testimony
of the *Brahmans*, who assure me with one voice, that
the names of the *Zodiacal* stars occur in the *Vedas* ;
three of which I firmly believe, from internal and
external evidence, to be more than *three thousand*

years old. Having therefore proved what I engaged to prove, I will close my essay with a general observation. The result of *Newton*'s researches into the history of the primitive sphere was, " that the practice of obser-" ving the stars began in *Egypt* in the days of *Ammon*, " and was propagated thence by conquest in the reign " of his son *Sisac*, into *Afric*, *Europe*, and *Asia*; " since which time *Atlas* formed the sphere of the *Ly-*" *bians*; *Chiron*, that of the *Greeks*; and the *Chal-*" *deans*, a sphere of their own." Now I hope, on some other occasions, to satisfy the public, as I have perfectly satisfied myself, that " the practice of ob-" serving the stars began, with the rudiments of civil " society, in the country of those whom we call *Chal-*" *deans*; from which it was propagated into *Egypt*, " *India*, *Greece*, *Italy*, and *Scandinavia*, before the " reign of *Sisac* or *Sacya*, who by conquest spread a " new system of religion and philosophy from the " *Nile* to the *Ganges* about a thousand years before " *Christ*; but that *Chiron* and *Atlas* were allegorical " or mythological personages, and ought to have no " place in the serious history of our species."

XVII.

ACCOUNT OF THE KINGDOM OF NEPAL,

BY FATHER GIUSEPPE,

Prefect of the Roman Mission.

COMMUNICATED BY JOHN SHORE, ESQ.

THE kingdom of *Nepal* is situated to the north-east of *Patna*, at the distance of ten or eleven days journey from that city. The common road to it lies through the kingdom of *Macwanpur*; but the missionaries and many other persons enter it on the *Bettia* quarter. Within the distance of four days journey from *Nepal* the road is good in the plains of *Hindustan*, but in the mountains it is bad, narrow, and dangerous. At the foot of the hills the country is called *Teriani*; and there the air is very unwholesome from the middle of *March* to the middle of *November*; and people in their passage catch a disorder, called in the language of that country *Aul*, which is a putrid fever, and of which the generality of people who are attacked with it die in a few days; but on the plains there is no apprehension of it. Although the road be very narrow and inconvenient for three or four days at the passes of the hills, where it is necessary to cross and recross the river more than fifty times, yet, on reaching the interior mountain before you descend, you have an agreable prospect of the extensive plain of *Nepal*, resembling an amphitheatre covered with populous towns and villages: the circumference of the plain is about 200 miles, a little irregular, and surrounded by hills on all sides, so that no person can enter or come out of it without passing the mountains.

X

308

There are three principal cities in the plain, each of which was the capital of an independent kingdom; the principal city of the three is situated to the northward of the plain, and is called *Cat'hmandu*: it contains about 18,000 houses; and this kingdom from south to north extends to the distance of twelve or thirteen days journey as far as the borders of *Tibet*, and is almost as extensive from east to west. The king of *Cat'hmandu* has always about fifty thousand soldiers in his service. The second city to the southwest of *Cat'hmandu* is called *Lelit Pattan*, where I resided about four years; it contains near 24,000 houses; the southern boundary of this kingdom is at the distance of four days journey, bordering on the kingdom of *Macwanpur*. The third principal city to the east of *Lelit Pattan* is called *B'hatgan*; it contains about 12,000 families, extends towards the east to the distance of five or six days journey, and borders upon another nation, also independent, called *Ciratas*, who profess no religion. Besides these three principal cities, there are many other large and less considerable towns or fortresses, one of which is *Timi*, and another *Cipoli*, each of which contains about 8,000 houses, and is very populous. All those towns, both great and small, are well built; the houses are constructed of brick, and are three or four stories high; their apartments are not lofty; they have doors and windows of wood, well worked and arranged with great regularity. The streets of all their towns are paved with brick or stone, with a regular declivity to carry off the water. In almost every street of the capital towns there are also good wells made of stone, from which the water passes through several stone-canals for the public benefit. In every town there are large square varandas, well built, for the accommodation of travellers and the public. These varandas are called *Pali*; and there are also many of them, as well as wells, in different parts of the country for public use. There are also, on the outside of the great towns, small square reservoirs of water, faced with brick, with a good road to walk upon, and a large flight of steps for the convenience of those who choose to bathe. A piece of water of this kind on the outside of the city of *Cat'hmandu*, was at least 200 feet long on each side of the square ; and every part of its work-manship had a good appearance.

The religion of *Nepal* is of two kinds : the more ancient is professed by many people who call them-selves *Boryesu :* they pluck out all the hair from their heads ; their dress is of coarse red woollen cloth, and they wear a cap of the same : they are considered as people of the religious order ; and their religion pro-hibits them from marrying, as it is with the *Lamas* of *Tibet*, from which country their religion was originally brought ; but in *Nepal* they do not observe this rule, except at their discretion. They have large monasteries, in which every one has a separate apartment, or place of abode; they observe also particular festivals, the principal of which is called *Yatra* in their language, and continues a month or longer, according to the pleasure of the king. The ceremony consists in drawing an idol, which at *Lelit Pattan* is called *Baghero* *, in a large and richly ornamented car, co-vered with gilt copper : round about the idol stand the king and the principal *Baryesus* ; and in this manner the vehicle is almost every day drawn through some one of the streets of the city by the inhabitants, who run about beating and playing upon every kind of instrument their country affords, which make an inconceiveable noise.

---

* I suppose a name of *Bhagwat* or *Crishna* ; but *Bharga* is *Mahadeva*, and *Bajri*, or *Vajri*, means the *Thunderer*.

The other religion, the more common of the two, is that of the *Brahmens*, and is the same as is followed in *Hindustan*, with the difference that in the latter country, the *Hindus* being mixed with the *Mohammedans*, their religion also abounds with many prejudices, and is not strictly observed; whereas in *Nepal*, where there are no *Musehmans* (except one *Cashmirian* merchant) the *Hindu* religion is practised in its greatest purity. Every day of the month they class under its proper name, when certain sacrifices are to be performed and certain prayers offered up in their temples. The places of worship are more in number in their towns than, I believe, are to be found in the most populous and most flourishing cities of *Christendom*; many of them are magnificent according to their ideas of architecture, and constructed at a very considerable expence; some of them have four or five square cupolas; and in some of the temples two or three of the extreme cupolas, as well as the doors and windows of them, are decorated with gilt copper.

In the city of *Lelit Pattan* the temple of *Baghero* was contiguous to my habitation, and was more valuable, on account of the gold, silver, and jewels it contained, than even the house of the king. Besides the large temples, there are also many small ones, which have stairs, by which a single person may ascend on the outside all around them; and some of those small temples have four sides, others six, with small stone or marble pillars, polished very smooth, with two or three pyramidal stories, and all their ornaments well gilt and neatly worked, according to their ideas of taste: and I think, that, if *Europeans* should ever go into *Nepal*, they might take some models from those little temples, especially from the two which are in the great court of *Lelit Pattan*, before the royal palace. On the outside of some of their temples there are also great square pillars of single stones, from twenty to

thirty feet high, upon which they place their idols, su‑
perbly gilt. The greatest number of their temples
have a good stone staircase in the middle of the
four squares, and at the end of each flight of stairs
there are lines cut out of stone on both sides. Round
about their temples there are also bells, which the peo‑
ple ring on particular occasions; and when they are
at prayers, many cupolas are also quite filled with
little bells, hanging by cords in the inside, about the
distance of a foot from each other, which make a
great noise on that quarter where the wind conveys
the sound. There are not only superb temples in
their great cities, but also within their castles.

To the eastward of *Cat'hmandu*, at the distance of
two or three miles, there is a place called *Tolu*, by
which there flows a small river, the water of which is
esteemed holy, according to their superstitious ideas;
and thither they carry people of high rank, when they
are thought to be at the point of death. At this place
there is a temple, which is not inferior to the best and
richest in any of the capital cities. They also have
it on tradition, that, at two or three places in *Nepal*,
valuable treasures are concealed under ground. One
of those places they believe is *Tolu*; but no one is
permitted to make use of them except the king, and
that only in cases of necessity. Those treasures, they
say, have been accumulated in this manner: When
any temple had become very rich from the offerings
of the people, it was destroyed, and deep vaults dug
under ground, one above another, in which the gold,
silver, gilt copper, jewels, and every thing of value
were deposited. When I was in *Nepal*, *Gainprejas*,
king of *Cat'hmandu*, being in the utmost distress for
money to pay his troops, in order to support himself
against *Prit'hwinarayan*, ordered search to be made
for the treasures of *Tolu*; and, having dug to a con‑
siderable depth under ground, they came to the first

X 3

vault; from which his people took to the value of a lac of rupees in gilt copper, with which *Gainprejas* paid his troops, exclusive of a number of small figures in gold, or gilt copper, which the people who had made the search had privately carried off; and this I know very well; because one evening as I was walking in the country alone, a poor man, whom I met on the road, made me an offer of a figure of an idol in gold, or copper gilt, which might be five or six sicca weight, and which he cautiously preserved under his arm; but I declined accepting it. The people of *Gainprejas* had not completely emptied the first vault, when the army of *Prit'hvinarayan* arrived at *Tolu*, possessed themselves of the place where the treasure was deposited, and closed the door of the vault, having first replaced all the copper there had been on the outside.

To the westward also of the great city of *Lelit Pattan*, at the distance of only three miles, is a castle called *Banga*, in which there is a magnificent temple. No one of the missionaries ever entered into this castle, because the people who have the care of it have such a scrupulous veneration for this temple, that no person is permitted to enter it with his shoes on; and the missionaries, unwilling to shew such respect to their false deities, never entered it. But when I was at *Nepal*, this castle being in the possession of the people of *Gore'ha*, the Commandant of the castle and of the two forts which border on the road, being a friend of the missionaries, gave me an invitation to his house, as he had occasion for a little physic for himself and some of his people. I then, under the protection of the Commandant, entered the castle several times, and the people durst not oblige me to take off my shoes. One day, when I was at the Commandant's house, he had occasion to go into the varanda, which is at the bottom of the great court

1

facing the temple, where all the chiefs dependent upon his orders were assembled, and where also was collected the wealth of the temple; and, wishing to speak to me before I went away, he called me into the varanda. From this incident I obtained a sight of the temple, and then passed by the great court which was in front: it is entirely marble almost blue, but interspersed with large flowers of bronze well disposed, to form the pavement of the great court-yard, the magnificence of which astonished me; and I do not believe there is another equal to it in *Europe*.

Besides the magnificence of the temples, which their cities and towns contain, there are many other rarities. At *Cat'hmandu*, on one side of the royal garden, there is a large fountain, in which is one of their idols, called *Narayan*. This idol is of blue stone, crowned and sleeping on a mattress of the same kind of stone; and the idol and mattress appear as floating upon the water. This stone machine is very large: I believe it to be eighteen or twenty feet long, and broad in pro-portion; but well worked, and in good repair.

In a wall of the royal palace of *Cat'hmandu*, which is built upon the court before the palace, there is a great stone of a single piece, which is about fifteen feet long, and four or five feet thick: on the top of this great stone there are four square holes at equal distances from each other. In the inside of the wall they pour water into the holes, and in the court-side, each hole having a closed canal, every person may draw water to drink. At the foot of the stone is a large ladder, by which people ascend to drink; but the curiosity of the stone consists in its being quite covered with characters of different languages cut upon it. Some lines contain the characters of the language of the country; others the characters of

X 4

Tibet, others *Persian*, others *Greek*, besides several
others of different nations; and in the middle there
is a line of *Roman* characters, which appears in this
form AVTOMNEW INTER LHIVERT; but
none of the inhabitants have any knowledge how they
came there, nor do they know whether or not any
European had ever been in *Nepal* before the missionaries, who arrived there only the beginning of the
present century. They are manifestly two *French*
names of seasons, with an *English* word between
them.

There is also to the northward of the city of *Cat'h-
mandu* a hill called *Simbi*, upon which are some tombs
of the *Lamas* of *Tibet*, and other people of high rank
of the same nation. The monuments are constructed
after various forms; two or three of them are pyramidal, very high and well ornamented; so that they
have a very good appearance, and may be seen at a
considerable distance. Round these monuments are
remarkable stones covered with characters, which
probably are the inscriptions of some of the inhabitants of *Tibet*, whose bones were interred there. The
natives of *Nepal* not only look upon the hill as sacred,
but imagine it is protected by their idols; and, from
this erroneous supposition, never thought of station-
ing troops there for the defence of it, although it be
a post of great importance, and only at a short mile's
distance from the city: but during the time of hostilities a party of *Prit'hwinarayan*'s troops being pur-
sued by those of *Gainprejus*, the former, to save themselves, fled to this hill, and, apprehending no danger from its guardian idols, they possessed themselves of it, and erected a fortification (in their own
style) to defend themselves. In digging the ditches
round the fort, which were adjoining to the tombs,
they found considerable pieces of gold, with a quantity of which metal the corpses of the grandees of *Tibet*

are always interred ; and when the war was ended, I myself went to see the monuments upon the hills.

I believe that the kingdom of *Nepal* is very ancient, because it has always preserved its peculiar language and independence ; but the cause of its ruin is the dissention which subsists among the three kings. After the death of their sovereign, the nobles of *Lelit Pattan* nominated for their king *Gainprejas*, a man possessed of the greatest influence in *Nepal*; altho' some years afterwards they removed him from his government, and conferred it upon the king of *Bhatgan* ; but he also a short time afterwards was deposed ; and, after having put to death another king who succeeded him, they made an offer of the government to *Prit'hwinarayàn*, who had already commenced war. *Prit'hwinarayan* deputed one of his brothers, by name *Delmerden Sah*, to govern the kingdom of *Lelit Pattan*, and he was in the actual government of it when I arrived at *Nepal*; but the nobles perceiving that *Prit'hwinarayan* still continued to interrupt the tranquillity of the kingdom, they disclaimed all subjection to him, and acknowledged for their sovereign *Delmerden Sah*, who continued the war against his brother *Prit'hwinarayan :* but some years afterwards they even deposed *Delmerden Sah*, and elected in his room a poor man of *Lelit Pattan*, who was of royal origin.

The king of *Bhatgan*, in order to wage war with the other kings of *Nepal*, had demanded assistance from *Prit'hwinarayan* ; but seeing that *Prit'hwinarayan* was possessing himself of the country, he was obliged to desist, and to take measures for the defence of his own possessions; so that the king of *Gorc'ha*, although he had been formerly a subject of *Gainprejas*, taking advantage of the dissentions which prevailed among the other kings of *Nepal*, attached to his party many mountain-chiefs, promising to keep them in possession, and also to augment their authority and importance; and if any of them were guilty of a breach of faith, he seized their country as he had done to the kings of *Murrcajis*, although his relations.

The king of *Gorc'ha* having already possessed himself of all the mountains which surround the plain of *Nepal*, began to descend into the flat country, imagining he should be able to carry on his operations with the same facility and success as had attended him on the hills; and, having drawn up his army before a town, containing about 8000 houses, situate upon a hill called *Cirtipur*, about a league's distance from *Cat'hmundu*, employed his utmost endeavours to get possession of it. The inhabitants of *Cirtipur* receiving no support from the king of *Lelit Pattan*, to whom they were subject, applied for assistance to *Guinprejas*, who immediatly marched with his whole army to their relief, gave battle to the army of the king of *Gorc'ha*, and obtained a complete victory. A brother of the king of *Gorc'ha* was killed on the field of battle; and the king himself, by the assistance of good bearers, narrowly escaped with his life, by fleeing into the mountains. After the action, the inhabitants of *Cirtipur* demanded *Guinprejas* for their king, and the nobles of the town went to confer with him on the business, but, being all assembled in the same apartment with the king, they were all surprised and seized by his people. After the seizure of those persons, *Guinprejas*, perhaps to revenge himself of these nobles for having refused their concurrence to his nomination as king, privately caused some of them to be put to death; another, by name *Danuvanta*, was led through the city in a woman's dress, along with several others, clothed in a ridiculous and whimsical manner, at the expence of the nobles of *Lelit Pattan*. They were then kept in close confinement for a long time. At last, after making certain promises, and interesting all the principal men of the country in their behalf, *Gainprejus* set them at liberty.

The king of *Gorc'ha*, despairing of his ability to get possession of the plain of *Nepal* by strength, hoped to effect his purpose by causing a famine, and with this design, stationed troops at all the passes of the mountains to prevent any intercourse with *Nepal*; and his orders were most rigorously obeyed, for every person who was found in the road, with only a little salt or cotton about him, was hung upon a tree; and he caused all the inhabitants of a neighbouring village to be put to death in a most cruel manner (even the women and children did not escape) for having supplied a little cotton to the inhabitants of *Nepal*; and, when I arrived in that country at the beginning of 1769, it was a most horrid spectacle to behold so many people hanging on the trees in the road. However the king of *Gorc'ha* being also disappointed in his expectations of gaining his end by this project, fomented dissentions among the nobles of the three kingdoms of *Nepal*, and attached to his party many of the principal ones, by holding forth to them liberal and enticing promises; for which purpose he had about 2000 *Brahmens* in his service. When he thought he had acquired a party sufficiently strong, he advanced a second time with his army to *Cirtipur*, and laid seige to it on the north-west quarter, that he might avoid exposing his army between the two cities of *Cat'hmandu* and *Lelit Patlan*. After a siege of several months, the king of *Gorc'ha* demanded the regency of the town of *Cirtipur*, when the commandant of the town, seconded by the approbation of the inhabitants, dispatched to him by an arrow a very impertinent and exasperating answer. The king of *Gorc'ha* was so much enraged at this mode of proceeding, that he gave im-

mediate orders to all his troops to storm the town on
every side : but the inhabitants bravely defended it, so
that all the efforts of his men availed him nothing ;
and, when he saw that his army had failed of gaining
the precipice, and that his brother, named *Suruparatna*,
had fallen wounded by an arrow, he was obliged to
raise the siege a second time, and o retreat with his army
from *Cirtipur*. The brother of the king was afterwards cured of his wound by our father *Michael Angelo*, who is at present in *Bettia*.

After the action, the king of *Gorc'ha* sent his army
against the king of *Lamji* (one of the twenty-four
kings who reign to the westward of *Nepal*) bordering
upon his own kingdom of *Gorc'ha*. After many desperate engagements, an accommodation took place with
the king of *Lamji*: and the king of *Gorc'ha* collecting all his forces, sent them for the third time to be-
siege *Cirtipur*; and the army on this expedition was
commanded by his brother *Suruparatna*. The inhabitants of *Cirtipur* defended themselves with their
usual bravery, and, after a siege of several months, the
three kings of *Nepal* assembled at *Cat'hmandu* to march
a body of troops to the relief of *Cirtipur*. One day in
the afternoon they attacked some of the *Tanas* of the
Gorc'hians, but did not succeed on forcing them, because the king of *Gorc'ha's* party had been reinforced
by many of the nobility, who, to ruin *Gainprejus*, were
willing to sacrifice their own lives. The inhabitants
of *Cirtipur* having already sustained six or seven
months siege, a noble of *Lelit Pattan*, called *Danuvanta*, fled to the *Gorc'ha* party, and treacherously introduced their army into the town. The inhabitants
might still have defended themselves, having many
other fortresses in the upper parts of the town to
retreat to ; but the people at *Gorc'ha* having published a general amnesty, the inhabitants, greatly
exhausted by the fatigues of a long siege, surrendered

themselves prisoners upon the faith of that promise. In the mean time the men of *Gorc'ha* 'seized all the gates and fortresses within the town; but two days afterwards *Prit'hwinarayan*, who was at *Navacuta* (a long day's journey distant) issued an order to *Surnparatna* his brother, to put to death all the principal inhabitants of the town, and to cut off the noses and lips of every one, even the infants, who were not found in the arms of their mothers; ordering at the same time all the noses and lips, which had been cut off, to be preserved, that he might ascertain how many souls there were, and to change the name of the town into *Naskatupur*, which signifies *the town of cut-noses*. The order was carried into execution with every mark of horror and cruelty, none escaping but those who could play on wind instruments; although father *Michael Angelo*, who, without knowing that such an inhuman scene was then exhibited, had gone to the house of *Surnparatna*, and interceded much in favour of the poor inhabitants. Many of them put an end to their lives in despair; others came in great bodies to us in search of medicines; and it was most shocking to see so many living people with their teeth and noses resembling the skulls of the deceased.

After the capture of *Cirtipur, Prit'hwinarayan* dispatched immediately his army to lay siege to the great city of *Lalit Pattan*. The *Gorc'hians* surrounded half the city to the westward with their *Tanas*; and, my house being situated near the gate of that quarter, I was obliged to retire to *Cat'hmandu*, to avoid being exposed to the fire of the besiegers. After many engagements between the inhabitants of the town of *Lalit Pattan* and the men of *Gorc'ha*, in which much blood was spilt on both sides, the former were disposed to surrender themselves, from the fear of having their noses cut off, like those at *Cirtipur*, and also their right hands: a barbarity the *Gorc'hians* had threatened them with, unless they would surrender within five days. One night all the *Gorc'hians* quitted the siege of *Lelit Pattan* to pursue the *English* army, which, under the command of Captain *Kinloch*, had already taken *Siduli*, an important fort at the foot of the *Nepal* hills, which border upon the kingdom of *Tirhut :* but Captain *Kinloch* not being able to penetrate the hills, either on the *Siduli* quarter or by the pass at *Hériapter*, in the kingdom of *Macwanpur*, the army of *Gorc'ha* returned to *Nepal* to direct their operations against the city of *Cat'hmandu*, where *Gainprejas* was, who had applied for succour to the *English*. During the siege of *Cat'hmandu* the *Brahmens* of *Gorc'ka* came almost every night into the city, to engage the chiefs of the people on the part of their king ; and the more effectually to impose upon poor *Gainprejas*, many of the principal *Brahmens* went to his house, and told him to persevere with confidence, that the chiefs of the *Gorc'ha* army were attached to his cause, and that even they themselves would deliver up their king *Prit'hwinarayan* to his hands. Having by these artifices procured an opportunity of detaching from his party all his principal subjects, tempting them with liberal promises according to their custom, one night the men of *Gorc'ha* entered the city without opposition, and the wretched *Gainprejas*, perceiving he was betrayed, had scarce time to escape with about three hundred of his best and most faithful *Hindustani* troops towards *Lelit Pattan*; which place however he reached the same night.

The king of *Gorc'ha* having made himself master of *Cat'hmandu* in the year 1768, persisted in the attempt of possessing himself also of the city of *Lelit Pattan*, promising all the nobles that he would suffer them to remain in the possession of their property, that he would even augment it ; and because the nobles of *Lelit Pattan* placed a reliance on the faith of his promises, he sent his domestic priest to make this protestation; that, if he

failed to acquit himself of his promise, he should draw
curses upon himself and his family even to the fifth
past and succeeding generation, so that the unhappy
Gainprejus and the king of *Lelit Pattan*, seeing that
the nobility were disposed to render themselves subject
to the king of *Gorg'ha*, withdrew themselves with
their people to the king of *B'hatgan*. When the city
of *Lelit Pattan* became subject to the king of *Gorc'ha*,
he continued for some time to treat the nobility with
great attention, and proposed to appoint a viceroy of
the city from among them. Two or three months
afterwards, having appointed the day for making his
formal entrance into the city of *Lelit Pattan*, he made
use of innumerable stratagems to get into his possession the persons of the nobility, and in the end succeeded. He had prevailed upon them to permit their
sons to remain at court as companions of his son ; he
had dispatched a noble of each house to *Navacut*, or
New Fort, pretending that the apprehensions he entertained of them had prevented his making a public
entrance into the city ; and the remaining nobles
were seized at the river without the town, where they
went to meet him agreeably to a prior engagement.
Afterwards he entered the city, made a visit to the
temple of *Baghero* adjoining to our habitation, and
passing in triumph thro' the city amidst immense numbers of soldiers who composed his train, entered the
royal palace which had been prepared for his reception ; in the mean time parties of his soldiers broke
open the houses of the nobility, seized all their effects,
and threw the inhabitants of the city into the utmost
consternation. After having caused all the nobles who
were in his power to be put to death, or rather their
bodies to be mangled in a horrid manner, he departed with a design of besieging *B'hatgan* ; and we obtained permission, through the interest of his son, to
retire with all the *Christians* into the possessions of the
English.

At the commencement of the year 1769, the king of *Gorc'ha* acquired possession of the city of *B'hatgan*, by the same expedients to which he owed his former successes; and on his entrance with his troops into the city, *Gainprejas*, seeing he had no resource left to save himself, ran courageously with his attendants towards the king of *Gorc'ha*, and, at a small distance from his palanquin, received a wound in his foot, which a few days afterwards occasioned his death. The king of *Lelit Pattan* was confined in irons till his death; and the king of *B'hatgan*, being very far advanced in years, obtained leave to go and die at *Benares*. A short time afterwards the mother of *Gainprejas* also procured the same indulgence, having from old age already lost her eye-sight; but before her departure they took from her a necklace of jewels (as she herself told me) when she arrived at *Patna* with the widow of her grandson: and I could not refrain from tears, when I beheld the misery and disgrace of this blind and unhappy queen.

The king of *Gorc'ha*, having thus in the space of four years effected the conquest of *Nepal*, made himself master also of the country of the *Ciratas* to the east of it, and of other kingdoms, as far as the borders of *Coch Bihar*. After his decease, his eldest son *Pratap Sinh* held the government of the whole country: but scarcely two years after, on *Pratap Sinh's* death, a younger brother, by name *Bahadar Sah*, who resided then at *Bettia* with his uncle *Delmerden Sah*, was invited to accept of the government: and the beginning of his government was marked with many massacres. The royal family is in the greatest confusion, because the queen lays claim to the government in the name of her son, whom she had by *Pratap Sinh*; and perhaps the oath violated by *Prit'hwinarayan* will in the progress of time have its effect. Such have been the successors of the kingdoms of *Nepal*, of which *Prit'hwinarayan* had thus acquired possession.

XVIII.

ON THE CURE OF PERSONS BITTEN BY SNAKES.

BY JOHN WILLIAMS, ESQ.

THE following statement of facts relative to the
cure of persons bitten by snakes, selected from a
number of cases which have come within my own
knowledge, require no prefatory introduction, as it
points out the means of obtaining the greatest self-
gratification the human mind is capable of experienc-
ing, That of the preservation of the life of a fellow-
creature, and snatching him from the jaws of death, by
a method which every person is capable of availing
himself of. Eau de Luce, I learn from many com-
munications which I have received from different parts
of the country, answers as well as the pure caustic
alkali spirit; and though, from its having some essential oils in its composition, it may not be so powerful, yet, as it must be given with water, it only requires
to encrease the dose in proportion; and, so long as
it retains its milky white colour, it is sufficiently efficacious.

From the effect of a ligature applied between the
part bitten and the heart, it is evident that the poison
diffuses itself over the body by the returning venous
blood; destroying the irritability, and rendering the
system paralytic. It is therefore probable that the volatile caustic alkali, in resisting the disease of the poison, does not act so much as a specific in destroying
its quality, as by counteracting the effect on the system, by stimulating the fibres, and preserving that irritability which it tends to destroy.

Vol. II.   Y

CASE I.

In the month of *August* 1780, a servant of mine
was bitten in the heel, as he supposed, by a snake; and
in a few minutes was in great agony, with convulsions
about the throat and jaws, and continual grinding of
the teeth. Having a wish to try the effects of volatile
alkali in such cases, I gave him about forty drops of
Eau de Luce in water, and applied some of it to the
part bitten. The dose was repeated every eight or ten
minutes, till a small phialful was expended: it was
near two hours before it could be said he was out of
danger. A numbness and pricking sensation was perceived extending itself up to the knee, where a ligature
was applied so tight, as to stop the returning venous
blood, which seemingly checked the progress of the
deleterious poison. The foot and leg, up to where
the ligature was made, were stiff and painful for several
days; and, which appeared very singular, were covered with a branny scale.

The above was the first case in which I tried the
effects of the volatile alkali, and, apprehending that
the essential oils in the composition of Eau de Luce,
though made of the strong caustic volatile spirit, would
considerably diminish its powers, I was induced, the
next opportunity that offered, to try the effects of pure
volatile caustic alkali spirit, and accordingly prepared some from quicklime and the sal ammoniac of
this country.

CASE II.

In *July* 1782, a woman of the *Brahmen* cast, who
lived in my neighbourhood at *Chunar*, was bitten by
a *Cobra de Capello* between the thumb and fore-finger
of her right hand. Prayers and superstitious incantations were practised by the *Brahmens* about her, till
she became speechless and convulsed, with locked

jaws,. and a profuse discharge of saliva running from her mouth. On being informed of the accident, I immediately sent a servant with a bottle of the volatile caustic alkali spirit, of which he poured about a teaspoonful, mixed with water, down her throat, and applied some of it to the part bitten. The dose was repeated a few minutes after, when she was evidently better, and in about half an hour was perfectly recovered.

This accident happened in a small hut, where I saw the snake, which was a middle-sized *Cobra de Capello*. The *Brahmens* would not allow it to be killed. In the above case, no other means whatever were used for the recovery of the patient than are here recited.

CASE. III.

A woman-servant in the family of a gentleman at *Benares*, was bitten in the foot by a *Cobra de Capello*. The gentleman immediately applied to me for some of the volatile caustic alkali, which I fortunately had by me. I gave her about sixty drops in water, and also applied some of it to the part bitten. In about seven or eight minutes after, she was quite recovered. In the above case, I was not witness to the deleterious effect of the poison on the patient; but saw the snake after it was killed.

CASE IV.

In *July* 1784, the wife of a servant of mine was bitten by a *Cobra de Capello* on the out-side of the little toe of her right foot. In a few minutes she became convulsed, particularly about the jaws and throat, with a continued gnashing of the teeth. She at first complained of a numbness extending from the

wound upwards; but no ligature was applied to the
limb.   About sixty drops of the volatile caustic spirit
were given to her in water, by forcing open her mouth,
which was strongly convulsed: in about seven minutes
the dose was repeated, when the convulsions left her:
and in three more she became sensible, and spoke to
those who attended her.   A few drops of the spirit
had also been applied to the wound.   The snake was
killed and brought to me, which proved to be a *Cobra de Capello.*

CASE V.

As it is generally believed that the venom of snakes
is more malignant during hot dry weather than at any
other season, the following case, which occurred in the
month of *July* 1788, when the weather was extremely
hot, no rain, excepting a slight shower, having fallen
for many months, may not be unworthy of notice :—

A servant belonging to an officer at *Juanpoor*, was
bitten by a snake on the leg, about two inches above
the outer ancle.   As the accident happened in the
evening, he could not see what species of snake it was.
He immediately tied a ligature above the part bitten ;
but was in a few minutes in such exquisite torture from
pain, which extended up his body and to his head,
that he soon became dizzy and senseless.   On being informed of the accident, I sent my servant with a phial
of the volatile caustic alkali, who found him, when
he arrived, quite torpid, with the saliva running out
of his mouth, and his jaws so fast locked, as to render it necessary to use an instrument to open them,
and administer the medicine.   About forty drops of
the volatile caustic spirit were given to him in water,
and applied to the wound; and the same dose repeated
a few minutes after.   In about half an hour he was per-

fectly recovered. On examining the part bitten, I could discover the marks of three fangs; two on one side, and one on the other; and, from the distance they were asunder, I should judge it a large snake. More than ten minutes did not appear to have elapsed from the time of his being bitten till the medicine was administered. The wounds healed immediately, and he was able to attend to his duty the next day. Though the species of snake was not ascertained, yet I judge, from the flow of saliva from the mouth, convulsive spasms of the jaws and throat, as well as from the marks of three fangs, that it must have been a *Cobra de Capello*; and, though I have met with five and six fangs of different sizes in snakes of that species, I never observed the marks of more than two having been applied in biting in any other case which came within my knowledge.

CASE VI.

In *September* 1786, a servant belonging to Captain S——, who was then at *Benares*, was bitten in the leg by a large *Cobra de Capello*. He saw the snake coming towards him, with his neck spread out in a very tremendous manner, and endeavoured to avoid him; but, before he could get out of his way, the snake seized him by the leg, and secured his hold for some time, as if he had not been able to extricate his teeth. Application was immediately made to his master for a remedy, who sent to consult me; but, before I arrived, had given him a quantity of sweet oil, which he drank. So soon as I saw him, I directed the usual dose of volatile caustic alkali to be given, which fortunately brought away the oil from his stomach, or it is probable that the stimulating effect of the volatile spirit would have been so much blunted by it, as to have become inefficacious: a second dose was immediately administered, and some time after, a third,

The man recovered in the course of a few hours. As oil is frequently administered as a remedy in the bite of snakes, I think it necessary to caution against the use of it with the volatile alkali, as it blunts the stimulating quality of the spirit, and renders it useless.

Of the numerous species of snakes which I have met with, not above six were provided with poisonous fangs; though I have examined many which have been considered by the natives as dangerous, without being able to discover any thing noxious in them.

The following is an instance of the deleterious effect of the bite of a snake, called by the natives *Krait*, a species of the *Boa*, which I have frequently met with in this part of the country :—

CASE VII.

On the 16th *September* 1788, a man was brought to me who had been bitten by a snake, with the marks of two fangs on two of his toes; he was said to have been bitten above an hour before I saw him: he was perfectly sensible, but complained of great pain in the parts bitten, with an unusual languor. I immediately gave him thirty drops of the volatile caustic alkali spirit in water, and applied some of it to the wounds. In a few minutes he became easier, and in about half an hour was carried away by his friends, with perfect confidence in his recovery, without having taken a second dose of the medicine, which indeed did not appear to have been necessary ; but, whether from the effect of the bite of the snake, or the motion of the dooly on which he was carried, I know not ; but he became sick at the stomach, threw up the medicine, and died in about a quarter of an hour after. The man said that the snake came up to him while he was sitting on the ground; and that he put him away with his hand once, but that he turned about and bit him, as described. The snake was brought to me, which I examined: it was about two feet and a half long, of a lightish brown colour on the back, a white belly, and annulated from end to end with 208 abdominal, and forty-six tail scuta. I have met with several of them from thirteen inches to near three feet in length : it had two poisonous fangs in the upper jaw, which lay naked, with their points without the upper lip. It does not spread its neck, like the *Cobra de Capello*, when enraged; but is very active and quick in its motion.

I have seen instances of persons bitten by snakes, who have been so long without assistance, that, when they have been brought to me, they have not been able to swallow, from convulsions of the throat and fauces, which is, I observe, a constant symptom of the bite of the *Cobra de Capello:* and indeed I have had many persons brought to me who had been dead some time; but never knew an instance of the volatile caustic alkali failing in its effect, where the patient has been able to swallow it.

XIX.

ON SOME ROMAN COINS FOUND AT NELORE.

TO THE PRESIDENT OF THE ASIATIC SOCIETY.

SIR,

I HAVE the honour to present you with an extract of a letter from Mr. *Alexander Davidson*, late Governor of *Madras*, giving an account of some *Roman Coins* and *Medals* lately found near *Nelore*, together with a drawing of them, copied from one transmitted by Mr. *Davidson*; which, I imagine, may be acceptable to the *Asiatic* Society.

I have the honour to be,

Sir,

Your most obedient humble servant,

S. DAVIS.

Calcutta, March 20, 1788.

Extract of a Letter from Alexander D.zidson, Esq.
Dated Madras, July 12, 1787.

A PEASANT near *Nelore*, about 100 miles north-
west of *Madras*, was ploughing on the side of a stony
craggy hill: his plough was obstructed by some
brick-work: he dug, and discovered the remains of
a small *Hindu* temple, under which a little pot was
found with *Roman* coins and medals of the second
century.

He sold them as old gold; and many no doubt
were melted, but the *Nawab Amirul Umura* recovered upwards of thirty of them. This happened
while I was governor; and I had the choice of two
out of the whole. I chose an *Adrian* and *Faustina*.

Some of the *Trajans* were in good preservation.
Many of the coins could not have been in circulation:
they were all of the purest gold, and many of them
as fresh and beautiful as if they had come from the
mint but yesterday. Some were much defaced and
perforated, and had probably been worn as ornaments on the arm, and others pending from the neck.

I send you drawings of my two coins, and have
no objection to your publishing an account of them
in the Transactions of the *Asiatic* Society. I received
my information respecting them from the young
Nawab; and if my name be necessary to authenticate
the facts I have related, you have my permission to
use it.

XX.

ON TWO HINDU FESTIVALS,

AND THE

INDIAN SPHINX.

BY THE LATE COLONEL PEARSE, MAY 12, 1785.

I BEG leave to point out to the Society, that the *Sunday* before last was the festival of *Bha-vani,* which is annually celebrated by the *Gopas,* and all other *Hindus* who keep horned cattle for use or profit. On this feast they visit gardens, erect a pole in the fields, and adorn it with pendants and garlands. The *Sunday* before last was our *first* of *May,* on which the same rites are performed by the same class of people in *England,* where it is well known to be a relique of ancient superstition in that country : it should seem, therefore, that the religion of the east and the old religion of *Britain* had a strong affinity. *Bhavani* has another festival ; but that is not kept by any one set of *Hindus* in particular, and this is appropriated to one class of people. This is con- stantly held on the *ninth* of *Baisac'h* ; which does not always fall on our *first* of *May,* as it did this year. Those members of the Society who are acquainted with the rules which regulate the festivals, may be able to give better information concerning this point. I only mean to point out the resemblance of the rites performed here and in *England,* but must leave abler hands to investigate the matter further, if it should be thought deserving of the trouble. I find that the festival which I have mentioned, is one of the most ancient among the *Hindus.*

II. During the *Huli*, when mirth and festivity reign among *Hindus* of every class, one subject of diversion is to send people on errands and expeditions, that are to end in disappointment, and raise a laugh at the expence of the person sent. The *Huli* is always in *March*, and the last day is the greatest holiday. All the *Hindus* who are on that day at *Jaggannai'h*, are entitled to certain distinctions, which they hold to be of such importance, that I found it expedient to stay there till the end of the festival; and I am of opinion, and so are the rest of the officers, that I saved above five hundred men by the delay. The origin, of the *Huli* seems lost in antiquity; and I have not been able to pick up the smallest account of it.

If the rites of *May-day* show any affinity between the religion of *England* in times past and that of the *Hindus* in these times, may not the custom of making *April-fools*, on the first of that month, indicate some traces of the *Huli?* I have never yet heard any account of the origin of the *English* custom ; but it is unquestionably very ancient, and is still kept up even in great towns, though less in them than in the country. With us it is chiefly confined to the lower classes of people ; but in *India* high and low join in it ; and the late *Shujaul Daulah*, I am told, was very fond of making *Huli*-fools, though he was a *Muselman* of the highest rank. They carry it here so far, as to send letters making appointments, in the names of persons who, it is known, must be absent from their house at the time fixed on ; and the laugh is always in proportion to the trouble given.

III. At *Jagannat'h* I found the *Sphinx* of the *Egyptians*, and present the Society with a drawing of it. *Murari Pandit*, who was deputy *Faujdar* of *Balasor*, attended my detachment on the part of the *Mahrattas*

He is now the principal *Faujdar*, and is much of the
gentleman : a man of learning, and very intelligent.
From him I learned that the *Sphinx*, here called *Singh*,
is to appear at the end of the world, and, as soon as
he is born, will prey on an elephant. He is, therefore,
figured seizing an elephant in his claws ; and the elephant is made small, to show that the *Singh*, even a
moment after his birth, will be very large in proportion to it.

When I told *Murari* that the *Egyptians* worshipped
the bull, and chose the God by a black mark on his
tongue, and that they adored birds and trees, he immediately exclaimed, " their religion then was the same
" with ours ; for we also chuse our *sacred bulls* by the
" *same marks*; we reverence the *hansa*, the *garura*, and
" other birds; we respect the *pippal* and the *vata*
" among trees, and the *tulast* among shrubs ; but as
" for onions (which I had mentioned) they are eaten
" by low men, and are fitter to be eaten than wor-
" shipped."

REMARK BY THE PRESIDENT.

Without presuming to question the authority of
Murari Pandit, I can only say, that several *Brahmans*
now in *Bengal*, have seen the figure at *Jagannat'h*,
where one of the gates is called *Sinhadwar* ; and they
assure me, that they always considered it as a mere representation of a *Lion* seizing a young elephant ; nor
do they know, they say, any sense for the word *Sinha*
but a *Lion*, such as Mr. *Hastings* kept near his garden. The *Huli*, called *Holaca* in the *Vedas*, and
Phalgutsava in common *Sanscrit* books, is the festival of the vernal season, or *Nauruz* of the *Persians*.

XXI.

A SHORT DESCRIPTION OF CARNICOBAR,
BY MR. G. HAMILTON.

COMMUNICATED BY MR. ZOFFANY.

THE island, of which I propose to give a succinct account, is the northernmost of that cluster in the *Bay* of *Bengal*, which goes by the name of the *Nicobars*. It is low, of a round figure, about forty miles in circumference, and appears at a distance as if entirely covered with trees: however, there are several well cleared and delightful spots upon it. The soil is a black kind of clay, and marshy. It produces in great abundance, and with little care, most of the tropical fruits, such as pine-apples, plantains, papayas, cocoa-nuts, and areca-nuts; also excellent yams, and a root called *cachu*. The only four-footed animals upon the island are hogs, dogs, large rats, and an animal of the lizard kind, but large, called by the natives *tolonqui*; these frequently carry off fowls and chickens. The only kind of poultry are hens, and those not in great plenty. There are abundance of snakes, of many different kinds; and the inhabitants frequently die of their bites. The timber upon the island is of many sorts, in great plenty, and some of it remarkably large, affording excellent materials for building or repairing ships.

The natives are low in stature, but very well made, and surprizingly active and strong; they are copper-coloured, and their features have a cast of the *Malay*; quite the reverse of elegant. The women, in particular, are extremely ugly. The men cut their hair short, and the women have their heads shaved quite bare, and wear no covering but a short petticoat, made of a sort of rush or dry grass, which reaches half way down the thigh. This grass is not interwoven, but hangs round the person something like the thatching of a house. Such of them as have received presents

of cloth-petticoats from the ships, commonly tie them
round immediately under the arms.   The men wear
nothing but a narrow strip of cloth about the middle,
in which they wrap up their privities so tight, that
there hardly is any appearance of them.   The ears of
both sexes are pierced when young, and by squeez-
ing into the holes large plugs of wood, or hanging
heavy weights of shells, they contrive to render them
wide, and disagreeable to look at.   They are naturally disposed to be good humoured and gay, and are
very fond of sitting at table with *Europeans*, where
they eat every thing that is set before them; and they
eat most enormously.   They do not care much for
wine, but will drink bumpers of arrack as long as they
can see.   A great part of their time is spent in feast-
ing and dancing.   When a feast is held at any village, every one that chuses goes uninvited, for they
are utter strangers to ceremony.   At those feasts they
eat immense quantities of pork, which is their favourite food.   Their hogs are remarkably fat, being fed
upon the cocoa-nut kernel and sea-water: indeed all
their domestic animals, fowls, dogs, &c. are fed upon
the same.   They have likewise plenty of small sea-fish,
which they strike very dexterously with lances, wading
into the sea about knee deep.   They are sure of killing a very small fish at ten or twelve yards distance.
They eat the pork almost raw, giving it only a hasty
grill over a quick fire.   They roast a fowl, by running a piece of wood through it, by way of spit, and
holding it over a brisk fire, until the feathers are
burnt off, when it is ready for eating, in their taste.
They never drink water; only cocoa-nut milk, and
a liquor called *sourn*, which oozes from the cocoa-nut
tree after cutting off the young sprouts or flowers.
This they suffer to ferment before it is used, and
then it is intoxicating, to which quality they add
much by their method of drinking it, by sucking
it slowly through a small straw.   After eating, the

young men and women, who are fancifully drest with
leaves, go to dancing, and the old people surround them
smoking *tobacco* and drinking *smra.* The dancers,
while performing, sing some of their tunes, which are
far from wanting harmony, and to which they keep
exact time. Of musical instruments they have only
one kind, and that the simplest. It is a hollow bamboo about 2¼ feet long and three inches in diameter ;
along the outside of which there is stretched from end
to end a single string made of the threads of a split
cane; and the place under the string is hollowed a
little, to prevent it from touching. This instrument
is played upon in the same manner as a guitar. It is
capable of producing but few notes ; the performer
however makes it speak harmoniously, and generally
accompanies it with the voice.

What they know of physic is small and simple. I
had once occasion to see an operation in surgery performed on the toe of a young girl, who had been stung
by a scorpion or centipee. The wound was attended
with a considerable swelling, and the little patient
seemed in great pain. One of the natives produced
the under jaw of a small fish, which was long, and
planted with two rows of teeth as sharp as needles :
taking this in one hand, and a small stick by way of
hammer in the other, he struck the teeth three or four
times into the swelling, and made it bleed freely : the
toe was then bound up with certain leaves, and next
day the child was running about perfectly well.

Their houses are generally built upon the beach in
villages of fifteen or twenty houses each ; and each
house contains a family of twenty persons and upwards.
These habitations are raised upon wooden pillars, about
ten feet from the ground ; they are round and, having no windows, look like bee-hives, covered with

thatch. The entry is through a trap-door below, where the family mount by a ladder, which is drawn up at night. This manner of building is intended to secure the houses from being infested with snakes and rats; and for that purpose the pillars are bound round with a smooth kind of leaf, which prevents animals from being able to mount; besides which, each pillar has a broad round flat piece of wood near the top of it, the projecting of which effectually prevents the further progress of such vermin as may have passed the leaf. The flooring is made with thin strips of bamboos, laid at such distances from one another as to leave free admission for light and air; and the inside is neatly finished and decorated with fishing lances, nets, &c.

The art of making cloth of any kind is quite unknown to the inhabitants of this island; what they have is got from the ships that come to trade in cocoa-nuts. In exchange for their nuts (which are reckoned the finest in this part of *India*) they will accept of but few articles; what they chiefly wish for is cloth of different colours, hatchets and hanger-blades, which they use in cutting down the nuts. Tobacco and arrack they are very fond of; but expect these in presents. They have no money of their own, nor will they allow any value to the coin of other countries, further than as they happen to fancy them for ornaments; the young women sometimes hanging strings of dollars about their necks. However, they are good judges of gold and silver; and it is no easy matter to impose baser metals upon them as such.

They purchase a much larger quantity of cloth than is consumed upon their own island. This is intended for the *Choury* market. *Choury* is a small island to the southward of theirs, to which a large fleet of their boats sails every year about the month of *November*, to exchange cloth for canoes; for they

cannot make these themselves. This voyage they
perform by the help of the sun and stars, for they
know nothing of the compass.

In their disposition there are two remarkable qualities. One is their entire neglect of compliment and
ceremony, and the other, their aversion to dishonesty.
A *Carnicobarian* travelling to a distant village upon
business or amusement, passes through many towns
in his way without perhaps speaking to any one. If
he is hungry or tired, he goes up into the nearest house,
and helps himself to what he wants, and sits till he
is rested, without taking the smallest notice of any of
the family, unless he has business or news to communicate. Theft or robbery is so very rare amongst
them, that a man going out of his house, never
takes away his ladder, or shuts his door, but leaves
it open for any body to enter that pleases, without
the least apprehension of having any thing stolen from
him.

Their intercourse with strangers is so frequent, that
they have acquired in general the barbarous language
of the *Portuguese*, so common over *India*; their own
tongue has a sound quite different from most others,
their words being pronounced with a kind of stop,
or catch in the throat, at every syllable. The few following words will serve to shew those who are acquainted with other *Indian* languages, whether there
is any similitude between them.

A man,	*Kegonia*	To eat,	*Gnia.*
A woman,	*Kecunna.*	To drink,	*Okk.*
A child,	*Chu.*	Yams,	*T'owls.*
To laugh,	*Ayeluur.*	To weep,	*Poing.*
A canoe,	*App.*	A pine-apple,	*Frung.*

Z 2

A house,	*Albamun.*	To sleep,	*Loom loom.*
A fowl,	*Hayam.*	A dog,	*Tamam.*
A hog,	*Hown.*	Fire,	*Tamia.*
Fish,	*Ka.*	Rain,	*Koomra.*

They have no notion of a God; but they believe firmly in the Devil, and worship him from fear. In every village there is a high pole erected with long strings of ground-rattans hanging from it, which, it is said, has the virtue to keep him at a distance. When they see any signs of an approaching storm, they imagine that the Devil intends them a visit; upon which many superstitious ceremonies are performed. The people of every village march round their own boundaries, and fix up at different distances small sticks split at the top, into which split they put a piece of cocoa-nut, a wisp of tobacco, and the leaf of a certain plant. Whether this is meant as a peace-offering to the Devil, or a scarecrow to frighten him away, does not appear.

When a man dies, all his live stock, cloth, hatchets, fishing-lances, and in short every moveable thing he possessed is buried with him; and his death is mourned by the whole village. In one view, this is an excellent custom, seeing it prevents all disputes about the property of the deceased amongst his relations. His wife must conform to custom, by having a joint cut off from one of her fingers; and, if she refuses this, she must submit to have a deep notch cut in one of the pillars of her house.

I was once present at the funeral of an old woman. When we went into the house, which had belonged to the deceased, we found it full of her female relations; some of them were employed in wrapping up the corpse in leaves and cloth, and others tearing to pieces all the cloth which had belonged to her. In another house hard by, the men of the village, with a great many others from the neighbouring towns, were sitting drinking *soura* and smoking tobacco. In the mean time two stout young fellows were busy digging a grave in the sand near the house. When the woman had done with the corpse, they set up a most hideous howl, upon which the people began to assemble round the grave, and four men went up into the house to bring down the body; in doing this they were much interrupted by a young man, son to the deceased, who endeavoured with all his might to prevent them, but finding it in vain, he clung round the body, and was carried to the grave along with it : there, after a violent struggle, he was turned away, and conducted back to the house. The corpse now put into the grave, and the lashings which bound the legs and arms cut, all the live stock which had been the property of the deceased, consisting of about half a dozen hogs and as many fowls, was killed, and flung in above it. A man then approached with a bunch of leaves stuck upon the end of a pole, which he swept two or three times gently along the corpse, and then the grave was filled up. During the ceremony, the women continued to make the most horrible vocal concert imaginable : the men said nothing. A few days afterwards, a kind of monument was erected over the grave, with a pole upon it, to which long strips of cloth of different colours were hung.

Polygamy is not known among them ; and their punishment of adultery is not less severe than effectual. They cut, from the man's offending member, a piece of the foreskin proportioned to the frequent commission or enormity of the crime.

There seems to subsist among them a perfect equality. A few persons, from their age, have a little

more respect paid to them; but there is no appearance
of authority one over another. Their society seems
bound rather by mutual obligations continually conferred and received: the simplest and best of all
ties.

The inhabitants of the *Andamans* are said to be
Cannibals. The people of *Carnicobar* have a tradition
among them, that several conoes came from *Andaman*
many years ago, and that the crews were all armed,
and committed great depredations, and killed several
of the *Nicobarians*. It appears at first remarkable,
that there should be such a wide difference between
the manners of the inhabitants of islands so near to
one another; the *Andamans* being savage *Cannibals*,
and the others, the most harmless inoffensive people
possible. But it is accounted for by the following
historical anecdote, which, I have been assured, is
matter of fact. Shortly after the *Portuguese* had discovered the passage to *India* round the *Cape of Good
Hope*, one of their ships, on board of which were a
number of *Mozambique* negroes, was lost on the *Andaman* islands, which were till then uninhabited. The
blacks remained on the island and settled there: the
Europeans made a small shallop, in which they sailed to
Pegu. On the other hand, the *Nicobar* islands were
peopled from the opposite main and the coast of *Pegu*;
in proof of which, the *Nicobar* and *Pegu* languages are
said, by those acquainted with the latter, to have
much resemblance.

XXII.

THE DESIGN OF A TREATISE ON THE PLANTS OF INDIA.

BY THE PRESIDENT.

THE greatest, if not the only, obstacle to the progress of knowledge in these provinces, except in those branches of it which belong immediately to our several professions, is our want of leisure for general researches; and, as *Archimedes*, who was happily master of his time, had not *space* enough to move the greatest weight with the smallest force, thus we, who have ample space for our inquiries, really want *time* for the pursuit of them. " Give me a place to " stand on, said the great mathematician, and I will " move the whole earth :" *Give us time*, we may say, *for our investigations, and we will transfer to* Europe *all the sciences, arts, and literature of* Asia. " Not to have despaired," however, was thought a degree of merit in the *Roman* General, even though he was defeated; and, having some hope that others may occasionally find more leisure than it will ever, at least in this country, be my lot to enjoy, I take the liberty to propose a work, from which very curious information, and possibly very solid advantage, may be derived.

Some hundreds of plants, which are yet imperfectly known to *European* botanists, and with the virtues of which they are wholly unacquainted, grow wild on the plains and in the forests of *India*. The *Amarcosh*, an excellent vocabulary of the *Sanscrit* language, contains in one chapter the names of about three hundred medicinal vegetables; the *Medini* may com-

Z 4

346 THE DESIGN OF A TREATISE

prize many more; and the *Dravyabidana*, or *Dictionary of Natural Productions*, includes, I believe, a far greater number; the properties of which are distinctly related in medical tracts of approved authority. Now the first step, in compiling a treatise on the plants of *India*, should be to write their true names in *Roman* letters, according to the most accurate orthography, and in *Sanscrit* preferably to any vulgar dialect; because a learned language is fixed in books, while popular idioms are in constant fluctuation, and will not perhaps, be understood a century hence by the inhabitants of these *Indian* territories, whom future botanists may consult on the common appellations of trees and flowers. The childish denominations of plants from the persons who first described them, ought wholly to be rejected; for *Champaca* and *Hinna* seem to me not only more elegant, but far properer, designations of an *Indian* and an *Arabian* plant, than *Michelia* and *Lawsonia*; nor can I see without pain, that the great *Swedish* botanist considered it as *the supreme and only reward of labour* in this part of natural history, to preserve a name by hanging it on a blossom, and that he declared this mode of promoting and adorning botany, worthy of being *continued with holy reverence*, though so high an honour, he says, *ought to be conferred with chaste reserve, and not prostituted for the purpose of conciliating the good-will, or eternizing the memory, of any but his chosen followers; no; not even of saints.* His list of *an hundred and fifty* such names, clearly shows that his excellent works are the true basis of his just celebrity, which would have been feebly supported by the stalk of the *Linnea*. From what proper name the *Plantain* is called *Musa*, I do not know; but it seems to be the *Dutch* pronunciation of the *Arabic* word for that vegetable, and ought not, therefore, to have appeared in his list; though, in my opinion, it is the only rational name in the muster-roll. As to the system of *Linnaeus*, it is the system of Nature, subordinate indeed to the beautiful arrangement of *natural*

orders, of which he hath given a rough sketch, and
which may hereafter, perhaps, be completed : but the
distribution of vegetables into *classes*, according to the
number, length, and position of the stamens and pistils, and of those *classes* into *kinds* and *species*, according to certain marks of discrimination, will
ever be found the clearest and most convenient of methods, and should therefore be studiously observed
in the work which I now suggest; but I must be
forgiven, if I propose to reject the *Linnæan* appellations of the twenty-four *classes*, because, although
they appear to be *Greek* (and, if they really were so,
that alone might be thought a sufficient objection) yet
in truth they are not *Greek*, nor even formed by analogy to the language of *Grecians*; for *Polygamos*, *Mo-
naudros*, and the rest of that form, are both masculine
and feminine; *Polyandra*, in the abstract, never occurs, and *Polyandrion* means a public cemetery;
diæcia and *hiæcus* are not found in books of authority;
nor, if they were, would they be derived from *dis*, but
from *dia*, which would include the *triæcia*; let me add
that the *twelfth* and *thirteenth* classes are ill distinguished by their appellations, independently of other
exceptions to them, since the real distinction between
them consists not so much in the *number* of their stamens, as in the *place* where they are inserted; and
that the *fourteenth* and *fifteenth* are not more accurately discriminated by two words formed in defiance
of grammatical analogy, since there are but *two* powers, or two *diversities of length* in each of those classes.
Calycopolyandros might, perhaps, not inaccurately denote a flower of the *twelfth* class; but such a compound would still savour of barbarism or pedantry;
and the best way to amend such a system of words is
to efface it, and supply its place by a more simple
nomenclator, which may easily be found. Numerals
may be used for the *eleven* first classes, the former of
two numbers being always appropiated to the *stamens*,
and the latter to the *pistils*. Short phrases, as *on th*

calyx or *calice, in the receptacle, two long, four long from one base, from two or many bases, with anthers connected, on the pistils, in two flowers, in two distinct plants, mixed, concealed,* or the like, will answer every purpose of discrimination ; but I do not offer this as a perfect substitute for the words, which I condemn. The allegory of *sexes* and *nuptials,* even if it were complete, ought, I think, to be discarded, as unbecoming the gravity of men, who, while they search for truth, can have no business to inflame their imaginations ; and, while they profess to give descriptions, have nothing to do with metaphors. Few passages in *Aloisia,* the most impudent book ever composed by man, are more wantonly indecent than the hundred-forty-sixth number of the *Botanical Philosophy,* and the broad comment of its grave author, who *dares,* like *Octavius* in his epigram, *to speak with* Roman *simplicity;* nor can the *Linnæan* description of the *Arum,* and many other plants, be read in *English* without exciting ideas which the occasion does not require. Hence it is that no well-born and well educated woman can be advised to amuse herself with botany as it is now explained, though a more elegant and delightful study, or one more likely to assist and embellish other female accomplishments, could not possibly be recommended.

When the *Sanscrit* names of the *Indian* plants have been correctly written in a large paper-book, one page being appropriated to each, the fresh plants themselves, procured in their respective seasons, must be concisely, but accurately, *classed* and *described;* after which their several *uses* in medicine, diet, or manufactures, may be collected with the assistance of *Hindu* physicians, from the medical books in *Sanscrit,* and their accounts either disapproved or established by repeated experiments, as fast as they can be made with exactness.

By way of example, I annex the descriptions of five *Indian* plants ; but am unable, at this season, to re-examine them, and wholly despair of leisure to exhibit others, of which I have collected the names, and most of which I have seen in blossom.

I. MUCHUCUNDA.

Twenty, from One Base.

Cal. Five-parted, thick ; leafleats oblong.
Cor. Five petals, oblong.
Stam. From twelve to fifteen, rather long, fertile ; five shorter, sterile. In some flowers, the *unprolific* stamens longer.
Pist. *Style* cylindric.
Peric. A capsule, with five cells, many-seeded.
Seeds. Roundish, compressed; winged.
Leaves. Of many different shapes.
Uses. The quality refrigerant.

One flower, steeped a whole night in a glass of water, forms a cooling mucilage, of use in virulent gonorrhœas. The *Muchucunda*, called also *Pichuça*, is exquisitely fragrant : its calyx is covered with an odoriferous dust ; and the dried flowers in fine powder, taken as snuff, are said, in a *Sanscrit* book, almost instantaneously to remove a nervous head-ach.

Note. This plant differs a little from the *Pentapetes* of *Linnæus*.

II. BILVA, or MALURA.

Many on the Receptacle, and One.

Cal. Four or five cleft beneath.

Cor. Four or five petals; mostly reflex.

Stam. Forty to forty-eight filaments; anthers mostly erect.

Pist. *Germ,* roundish; *Style* smooth, short; *Stigma* clubbed.

Peric. A spheroidal berry, very large; many-seeded.

Seeds. Toward the surface ovate, in a pellucid mucus.

Leaves. Ternate; common petiole long; leaflets subovate; obtusely notched with short petioles; some almost lanced.

Stem. Armed with sharp thorns.

Uses. The fruit nutritious, warm, cathartic; in taste delicious, in fragrance exquisite: its aperient and detersive quality, and its efficacy in removing habitual costiveness, having been proved by constant experience. The mucus of the seed is, for some purposes, a very good cement.

Note. This fruit is called *Srip'hala,* because it sprang, say the *Indian* poets, from the milk of *Sri,* the Goddess of Abundance, who bestowed it on mankind at the request of *Iswara,* whence he alone wears a chaplet of *Bilva* flowers: to him only the *Hindus* offer them; and, when they see any of them fallen on the ground, they take them up with reverence, and carry them to his temple. From the first blossom of this plant, that I could inspect, I had imagined that it belonged to the same class with the *Durio,* because the filaments appeared to be distributed in five sets; but in all that I have since examined, they are perfectly distinct.

III. SRINGATACA.

Four and One.

Cal. Four cleft, with a long peduncle above.

Cor. Four petals.

Stem. Anthers kidney-shaped.

Pist. *Germ* roundish; *Style* long, as the filaments; *Stigma* clubbed.

Seed. A *Nut* with four opposite angles (two of them sharp thorns) formed by the *Calyx.*

Leaves. Those which float on, the water are rhomboidal; the two upper sides unequally notched, the two lower, right lines. Their petioles buoyed up by spindle-shaped spongy substances, not bladders.

Root. Knotty, like coral.

Uses. The fresh kernel, in sweetness and delicacy, equals that of the filbert. A mucus, secreted by minute glands, covers the wet leaves, which are considered as cooling.

Note. It seems to be the floating *Trapa* of *Linnæus.*

IV. PUTICARAJA.
Ten and One.

Cal. Five-cleft.

Cor. Five equal petals.

Peric. A thorny legumen ; two seeds.

Leaves. Oval, pinnated.

Stem. Armed.

Uses. The seeds are very bitter, and, perhaps, tonic ; since one of them, bruised and given in two doses, will, as the *Hindus* assert, cure an intermittent fever.

V. MADHUCA. *(See Vol. 1. page 300.)*
Many, *not* on the Receptacle, and One.

Cal. *Perianth* four or five-leaved.

Cor. One-petaled. *Tube* inflated, fleshy. *Border* nine, or ten, parted.

Stam. *Anthers* from twelve to twenty-eight, erect, acute, subvillous.

Pist. *Germ* roundish ; *Style* long, awl-shaped.

Peric. A *Drupe*, with two or three *Nuts?*

Leaves. Oval, somewhat pointed.

Uses. The *tubes* esculent, nutritious; yielding, by distillation, an inebriating spirit, which, if the sale of it were duly restrained by law, might be applied to good purposes. A useful oil is expressed from the seed.

Note. It resembles the *Bassia* of *Koenig.*

Such would be the method of the work which I recommend ; but even the specimen which I exhibit, might, in skilful hands, have been more accurate. Engravings of the plants may be annexed ; but I have more than once experienced, that the best anatomical and botanical prints give a very inadequate, and sometimes a very false notion of the objects which they were intended to represent. As we learn a new language by reading approved compositions in it with the aid of a Grammar and Dictionary, so we can only study with effect the natural history of vegetables by analysing the plants themselves with the *Philosophia Botanica*, which is the *Grammar*, and the *Genera et Species Plantarum*, which may be considered as the *Dictionary* of that beautiful language, in which Nature would teach us what plants we must avoid as noxious, and what we must cultivate as salutary ; for that the qualities of plants are *in some degree* connected with the *natural orders* and *classes* of them, a number of instances would abundantly prove.

XXIII.

ON THE DISSECTION OF THE PANGOLIN,

In a Letter to General Carnac
from Adam Burt, Esq.

COMMUNICATED BY THE GENERAL.

' S I R,

IN compliance with your desire, I most willingly
do myself the honour to present to you my observations and reflections on the dissection of one of those
animals, of which we have a print, with a very short
account, in the *First Volume* of the *Transactions of
the Asiatic Society*. The animal, from which that
likeness has been taken, was sent by Mr. *Leslie*, from
Chitra, to the President Sir *William Jones*. It is distinguished in the *Transactions* by a name, which I do
not at present remember; but probably the animal
is of the same genus with the *Manis*, as described in
the former edition of the *Encyclopædia Britannica*, or,
perhaps, not different from the *Pangolin* of *Buffon*.

The representation of this animal in the *Memoirs
of the Asiatic Society*, makes it unnecessary for me to
enter into any general description of its external figure
and appearance. There are on each foot five claws, of
which the outer and inner are small when compared
with the other three. There are no distinct toes; but
each nail is moveable by a joint at its root. This
creature is extremely inoffensive : it has *no teeth*; and
its feet are unable to grasp. Hence it would appear
that Nature, having furnished it with a coat of mail
for its protection, has, with some regard to justice, denied it the powers of acting with hostility against

its fellow-creatures. The nails are well adapted
for digging in the ground ; and the animal is so dexterous in eluding its enemies, by concealing itself in
holes and among rocks, that it is extremely difficult
to procure one.

The upper jaw is covered with a cross cartilaginous
ridge, which though apparently not at all suited to any
purposes of mastication, may, by increasing the surface of the palate, extend the sense of taste. The œso-
phagus admitted my fore-finger with ease. The tongue
at the bottom of the mouth is nearly about the size
of the little finger, from whence it tapers to a point.
The animal at pleasure protrudes this member a great
way from the mouth. The tongue arises from the
ensiform cartilage, and the contiguous muscles of the
belly, and passes in form of a round distinct muscle
from over the stomach, through the thorax, immediately under the sternum ; and interior to the wind-
pipe in the throat. When dissected out, the tongue
could be easily elongated so as to reach more than the
length of the animal, exclusive of its tail. There is
a cluster of salivary glands seated around the tongue,
as it enters the mouth. These will necessarily be
compressed by the action of the tongue, so as occasionally to supply a plentiful flow of their secretion.

The stomach is *cartilaginous*, and analogous to that
of the gallinaceous tribe of birds. It was filled with
small stones and gravel, which in this part of the
country, are almost universally calcareous. The inner surface of the stomach was rough to the feel, and
formed into folds, the interstices of which were
filled with a frothy secretion. The guts were filled
with a sandy pulp, in which, however, were interspersed
a few distinct small stones. No vestiges of any animal or vegetable food could be traced in the whole
primæ viæ. The gall-bladder was distended with a

fluid, resembling in colour and consistence the dregs of beer.

The subject was a female: its dugs were two, seated on the breast. The uterus and organs of generation were evidently those of a viviparous animal.

Forcibly struck with the phenomena which this quadruped exhibited, my imagination at once overleaped the boundaries by which science endeavours to circumscribe the productions and the ways of Nature; and believing with *Buffon, que tout ce qui peut etre est,* I did not hesitate to conjecture that this animal might possibly derive its nourishment from mineral substances. This idea I accordingly hazarded in an address to Colonel *Kyd.* The spirit of inquiry, natural to that gentleman, could be ill satisfied by ideas thrown out apparently at random; and he soon called on me to explain my opinion, and its foundation.

Though we have perhaps no clear idea of the manner in which vegetables extract their nourishment from earth, yet the fact being so, it may not be unreasonable to suppose that some animal may derive nutriment by a process somewhat similar. It appears to me, that facts produced by *Spallanzani* directly invalidate the experiments, from which he has drawn the inference, that fowls swallow stones merely from stupidity; and that such substances are altogether unnecessary to those animals. He reared fowls, without permitting them ever to swallow sand or stones; but he also established the fact, that carnivorous animals may become frugivorous; and herbivorous animals may come to live on flesh. A wood-pidgeon he brought to thrive on putrid meat. The experiment on fowls, then, only corroborates the proof, that we have it in our power by habits to alter the natural constitution of animals. Again the eminent investigator of truth found, that fowls died when fed

on stones alone; but surely that fact is far short of
proving that such substances are not agreeable to the
original purposes of nature in the digestive process of
these animals. When other substances shall have
been detected in the stomach of this animal, my inference, from what I have seen, must necessarily fall
to the ground. But if, like other animals with mus-
cular and cartilaginous stomachs, this singular quadruped consumes grain, it must be surprising that no
vestige of such food was found present in the whole
alimentary canal, since in that thinly inhabited country, the wild animals are free to feed without intrusion
from man. Nor can it be inferred from the structure
of the stomach, that this animal lives on ants or on
insects. Animals devoured as food, though of considerable size and solidity, with a proportionably small
extent of surface to be acted on by the gastric juice
and the action of the stomach, are readily dissolved
and digested by animals possessing not a cartilaginous, but a membranaceous stomach; as for instance,
a frog in that of a snake.

In the stomach many minerals are soluble, and the
most active things which we can swallow. Calcareous
substances are readily acted on. Dr. *Priestly* has
asked, " May not phlogistic matter be the most es-
" sential part of the food and support of both vege-
" table and animal bodies?" I confess, that
Dr. *Priestly's* finding cause to propose the question,
inclines me to suppose that the affirmative to it may
be true. Earth seems to be the basis of all animal
matter. The growth of the bones must be attended
with a constant supply; and in the human species
there is a copious discharge of calcareous matter
thrown out by the kidneys and salivary glands.
May not the quadruped in question derive phlogiston
from earth? salt, from mineral substances? And, as
it is not deprived of the power of drinking water,

what else is necessary to the subsistence of his corporeal machine?

Considering the scaly covering of this animal, we may conceive that it may be at least necessary for its existence, on that account, to imbibe a greater proportion of earth than is necessary to other animals. It may deserve consideration, that birds are covered with feathers, which in their constituent principles approach to the nature of horn and bone. Of these animals the gallinaceous tribe swallow stones; and the carnivorous take in the feathers and bones of their prey: the latter article is known to be soluble in the membranaceous stomachs; and hence is a copious supply of the earthy principles. In truth, I do not know that any thing is soluble in the stomach of animals, which may not be thence absorbed into their circulating system; and nothing can be so absorbed without affecting the whole constitution.

What I have here stated is all that I could advance to the Colonel; but my opinion has been since not a little confirmed, by observing the report of experiments by M. *Hruquatelli* of *Pavia*, on the authority of M. *Crell*, by which we learn, that some birds have so great a dissolvent power in the gastric juice, as to dissolve in their stomachs flints, rock-crystal, calcareous stones, and shells.

I beg only farther to observe, that some things in *Buffon*'s description of the Pangolin, not apparently quite applicable to this animal, might have been owing to his description being only from the view of a dried preparation, in which the organs of generation would be obliterated, and the dugs shrivelled away so as to be imperceptible; else that elegant philosopher could not have asserted that, " *tous les animaux qua-* " *drupedes, qui sont couverts d'ecailles, sont ovipares.*"

A a 2

Excuse my prolixity, which is only in me the necessary attendant of my superficial knowledge of things. In ingenuousness, however, I hope that I am not inferior to any man : and I am proud to subscribe myself,

Sir,

Your most obedient and humble servant,

ADAM BURT.

Gya, September 14, 1789.

A Letter from Doctor Anderson to Sir William Jones.

DEAR SIR,

THE male *Lac* insect having hitherto escaped the observation of naturalists, I send the enclosed description, made by Mr. *William Roxburgh*, surgeon on this establishment, and botanist to the Honourable Company, in hopes you will give it a place in the publication of your Society, as Mr. *Roxburgh's* discovery will bring Lac a genus into the class Hemiptera of *Linnæus*.

I am, with esteem,

Dear Sir,

Your very obedient servant,

JAMES ANDERSON.

Fort St. George, January 2, 1790.

A a 3

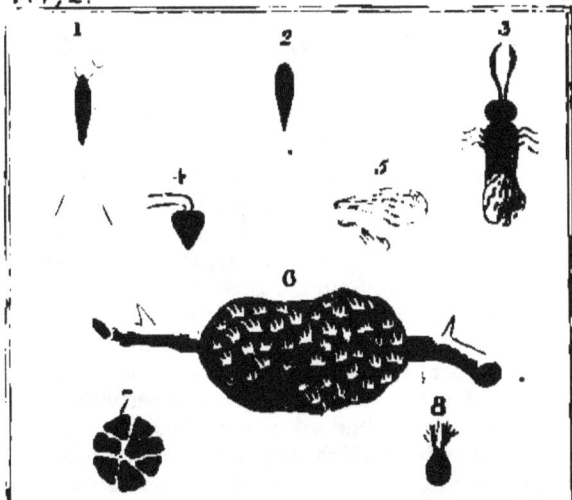

P. 333.

P. 343.

XXIV.

ON THE LACSHA, OR LAC INSECT.

BY MR. WILLIAM ROXBURGH.

SOME pieces of very fresh-looking lac adhering to small branches of *mimosa cinerea*, were brought me from the mountains on the 20th of last month. I kept them carefully, and to-day, the 4th of *December*, fourteen days from the time they came from the hills, myriads of exceedingly minute animals were observed creeping about the lac and branches it adhered to, and more still issuing from small holes over the surface of the cells: other small and perforated excrescences were observed with a glass amongst the perforations, from which the minute insects issued, regularly two to each hole, and crowned with some very fine white hairs. When the hairs were rubbed off, two white spots appeared. The animals, when single, ran about pretty briskly; but in general they were so numerous as to be crowded over one another. The body is oblong, tapering most towards the tail, below plain, above convex, with a double, or flat margin: laterally on the back part of the thorax are two small tubercles, which may be the eyes: the body behind the thorax is crossed with twelve rings; legs six; feelers (antennæ) half the length of the body, jointed, hairy, each ending in two hairs as long as the antennæ; rump, a white point between two terminal hairs, which are as long as the body of the animal; the mouth I could not see. On opening the cells, the substance that they were formed of cannot be better described, with respect to appearance, than by saying it is like the transparent amber that beads are made of: the external covering of the cells may be about half a line thick, is remarkably strong and able to resist injuries; the partitions are much thinner; the cells are in general

A a 4

irregular squares, pentagons, and hexagons, about an eighth of an inch in diameter, and ⅓ deep; they have no communication with each other: all these I opened during the time the animals were issuing, contained in one-half a small bag filled with a thick red jelly-like liquor, replete with what I take to be eggs; these bags, or utriculi, adhere to the bottom of the cells, and have each two necks, which pass through perforations in the external coat of the cells, forming the fore-mentioned excrescences, and ending in some very fine hairs. The other half of the cells have a distinct opening, and contain a white substance, like some few filaments of cotton rolled together, and numbers of the insects themselves ready to make their exit. Several of the same insects I observed to have drawn up their legs, and to lie flat; they did not move on being touched, nor did they show any signs of life with the greatest irritation.

December 5. The same minute hexapedes continue. issuing from their cells in numbers; they are more lively, of a deepened red colour, and fewer of the motionless sort. To-day I saw the mouth; it is a flattened point, about the middle of the breast, which the little animal projects on being compressed.

December 6. The male insects I have found to-day. A few of them are constantly running among the females most actively: as yet they are scarce more, I imagine, than one to 5000 females, but twice their size. The head is obtuse; eyes black, very large; antennæ clavated, feathered, about ⅓ the length of the body; below the middle an articulation, such as those in the legs; colour between the eyes a beautiful shining green; neck very short; body oval, brown; abdomen oblong, the length of body and head; legs six; wings membranaceous, four, longer than the body, fixed to the sides of the thorax, narrow at their insertions, growing broader for two-thirds of their length, then rounded; the anterior pair is twice the size of the posterior; a strong fibre runs along their anterior margins; they lie flat, like the wings of a common fly, when it walks or rests; no hairs from the rump; it springs most actively to a considerable distance on being touched; mouth in the under part of the head; maxillæ transverse. To-day the female insects continue issuing in great numbers, and move about as on the 4th.

December 7. The small red insects still more numerous, and move about as before: winged insects, still very few, continue active. There have been fresh leaves and bits of the branches of both *mimosa cinerea* and *corinda* put into the wide mouthed bottle with them: they walk over them indifferently, without showing any preference, nor inclination to work nor copulate. I opened a cell whence I thought the winged flies had come, and found several, eight or ten, more in it, struggling to shake off their incumbrances: they were in one of those utriculi mentioned on the 4th, which ends in two mouths, shut up with fine white hairs, but one of them was open for the exit of the flies; the other would no doubt have opened in due time: this utriculus I found now perfectly dry, and divided into cells by exceeding thin partitions. I imagine, before any of the flies made their escape, it might have contained about twenty. In these minute cells with the living flies, or whence they had made their escape, were small dry dark coloured compressed grains, which may be the dried excrements of the flies.

Note by the President.

THE *Hindus* have six names for *Lac*; but they generally call it *Lacsha*, from the *multitude* of small insects, who, as they believe, discharge it from their stomachs, and at length destroy the tree on which they form their colonies. A fine *Pippala* near *Crishnanagar*, is now almost wholly destroyed by them.

XXV.

THE SEVENTH

ANNIVERSARY DISCOURSE,

DELIVERED 25 FEBRUARY, 1790.

BY THE PRESIDENT.

Gentlemen,

ALTHOUGH we are at this moment considerably nearer to the frontier of *China* than to the farthest limit of the *British* dominions in *Hindustan*, yet the first step that we should take in the philosophical journey, which I propose for your entertainment at the present meeting, will carry us to the utmost verge of the habitable globe known to the best geographers of *Old Greece* and *Egypt*; beyond the boundary of whose knowledge we shall discern from the heights of the northern mountains an empire nearly equal in surface to a square of fifteen degrees; an empire, of which I do not mean to assign the precise limits, but which we may consider, for the purpose of this dissertation, as embraced on two sides by *Tartary* and *India*, while the ocean separates its other sides from various *Asiatic* isles of great importance in the commercial system of *Europe*. Annexed to that immense tract of land is the peninsula of *Corea*, which a vast oval bason divides from *Nifon*, or *Japan*, a celebrated and imperial island, bearing in arts and in arms, in advantage of situation, but not in felicity of government, a pre-eminence among eastern kingdoms analogous to that of *Britain* among the nations of the west. So many climates are included in so prodigious an area, that while the principal emporium of *China* lies nearly under the tropic, its metropolis enjoys the temperature of *Sa-*

markand : such too is the diversity of soil in its fifteen
provinces, that, while some of them are exquisitely
fertile, richly cultivated, and extremely populous,
others are barren and rocky, dry and unfruitful, with
plains as wild or mountains as rugged as any in *Scythia,*
and those either wholly deserted, or peopled by savage
hordes, who, if they be not still independent, have
been very lately subdued by the perfidy, rather than
the valour, of a monarch, who has perpetuated his
own breach of faith in a *Chinese* poem, of which I
have seen a translation.

The word *China,* concerning which I shall offer
some new remarks, is well known to the people whom
we call the *Chinese ;* but they never apply it (I speak
of the learned among them) to themselves or to their
country. Themselves, according to Father *Visdelou,*
they describe as the *people of Han,* or of some other
illustrious family, by the memory of whose actions
they flatter their national pride ; and their country
they call *Chum-cue,* or the *Central Kingdom,* representing it in their symbolical characters by a parallelogram
exactly bisected. At other times they distinguish it
by the words *Tien-hia,* or *What is under Heaven ;*
meaning *all that is valuable on earth.* Since they
never name themselves with moderation, they would
have no right to complain, if they knew that *European* authors have ever spoken of them in the extremes
of applause or of censure. By some they have been
extolled as the oldest and the wisest, as the most learned
and most ingenious of nations ; whilst others have
derided their pretensions to antiquity, condemned their
government as abominable, and arraigned their manners
as inhuman, without allowing them an element of science, or a single art for which they have not been indebted to some more ancient and more civilized race of
men. The truth perhaps lies, where we usually find it,

between the extremes; but it is not my design to ac-
cuse or to defend the *Chinese*, to depress or to aggrandize them : I shall confine myself to the discussion of
a question connected with my former discourses, and
far less easy to be solved than any hitherto started :
" Whence came the singular people, who long had
" governed *China*, before they were conquered by the
" *Tartars?*" On this problem (the solution of which
has no concern, indeed, with our political or commercial interests, but a very material connection, if I
mistake not, with interests of a higher nature) four
opinions have been advanced, and all rather peremp-
torily asserted than supported by argument and evidence. By a few writers it has been urged, that the
Chinese are an original race, who have dwelt for
ages, if not from eternity, in the land which they
now possess; by others, and chiefly by the missionaries, it is insisted that they sprang from the same stock
with the *Hebrews* and *Arabs*; a third assertion is
that of the *Arabs* themselves and of M. *Pauw*,
who hold it indubitable, that they were originally
Tartars descending in wild clans from the steeps
of *Imaus*; and a fourth, at least as dogmatically
pronounced as any of the preceding, is that of
the *Brahmens*, who decide, without allowing any ap-
peal from their decision, that the *Chinas* (for so they
are named in *Sanscrit*) were *Hindus* of the *Cshatriya*,
or military class, who, abandoning the privileges of
their tribe, rambled in different bodies to the north-
east of *Bengal*; and, forgetting by degrees the rites
and religion of their ancestors, established separate
principalities, which were afterwards united in the plains
and valleys, which are now possessed by them. If any
one of the three last opinions be just, the first of them
must necessarily be relinquished; but of those three,
the first cannot possibly be sustained, because it rests
on no firmer support than a foolish remark, whether
true or false, that *Sem* in *Chinese* means *life* and *pro-
creation*; and because a tea-plant is not more different

from a palm than a *Chinese* from **&** *Arab*. They are men, indeed, as the tea and the palm are vegetables; but human sagacity could not, I believe, discover any other trace of resemblance between them. One of the *Arabs*, indeed (an account of whose voyage to *India* and *China* has been translated by *Renaudot*) thought the *Chinese* not handsomer (according to his ideas of beauty) than the *Hindus*; but even more like his own countrymen in features, habiliments, carriage, manners, and ceremonies: and this may be true, without proving an actual resemblance between the *Chinese* and *Arabs*, except in dress and complexion. The next opinion is more connected with that of the *Brahmens* than M. *Pauw*, probably, imagined; for, though he tells us expressly that by *Scythians* he meant the *Turks*, or *Tartars*, yet the Dragon on the standard, and some other peculiarities, from which he would infer a clear affinity between the old *Tartars* and the *Chinese*, belonged indubitably to those *Scythians* who are known to have been *Goths*; and the *Goths* had manifestly a common lineage with the *Hindus*, if his own argument, in the preface to his *Researches on the. Similarity of Language* be, as all men agree that it is, irrefragable. That the *Chinese* were anciently of a *Tartarian* stock, is a proposition which I cannot otherwise disprove for the present, than by insisting on the total dissimilarity of the two races in manners and arts, particularly in the fine arts of imagination, which the *Tartars*, by their own account, never cultivated; but, if we show strong grounds for believing that the first *Chinese* were actually of an *Indian* race, it will follow that M. *Pauw* and the *Arabs* are mistaken. It is to the discussion of this new and, in my opinion, very interesting point, that I shall confine the remainder of my discourse.

In the *Sanscrit Institutes* of civil and religious duties, revealed, as the *Hindus* believe, by *Menu*, the son of *Brahma*, we find the following curious passage:

" Many families · of the military class having gra-
" dually abandoned the ordinances of the *Veda*, and
" the company of *Brahmens*, lived in a state of degra-
" dation; as the people of *Pundraca* and *Odra*, those
" of *Dravira* and *Camboja*, the *Yavanas* and *Sacas*,
" the *Paradas* and *Pahlrvas*, the *Chinas*, and some
" other nations." A full comment on his text would
here be superfluous; but, since the testimony of the
Indian author, who, though certainly not a divine personage, was as certainly a very ancient lawyer, mora-
list, and historian, is direct and positive, disinterested
and unsuspected, it would, I think, decide the question before us, if we could be sure that the word *China*
signified a *Chinese*, as all the *Pandits*, whom I have separately consulted, assert with one voice. They assure
me, that the *Chinas* of *Menu* settled in a fine country
to the north-east of *Gaur*, and to the east of *Camarup*
and *Nepal*; that they have long been, and still are,
famed as ingenious artificers; and that they had themselves seen old *Chinese* idols, which bore a manifest
relation to the primitive religion of *India* before *Buddha*'s appearance in it. A well-informed *Pandit* showed
me a *Sanscrit* book in *Cashmirian* letters, which, he
said, was revealed by *Siva* himself, and entitled *Sac-
tisangama*: he read to me a whole chapter of it on the
heterodox opinions of the *Chinas*, who were divided,
says the author, into near two hundred clans. I then
laid before him a map of *Asia*; and, when I pointed
to *Cashmir*, his own country, he instantly placed his
finger on the north-western provinces of *China*, where
the *Chinas*, he said, first established themselves; but
he added, that *Mahachina*, which was also mentioned
in his book, extended to the eastern and southern
oceans. I believe, nevertheless, that the *Chinese* empire, as we now call it, was not formed when the laws of
Menu were collected; and for this belief, so repugnant
to the general opinion, I am bound to offer my reasons.
If the outline of history and chronology for the last
two thousand years be correctly traced (and we must

be hardy sceptics to doubt it) the poems of *Calidas*
were composed before the beginning of our era. Now
it is clear, from internal and external evidence, that
the *Ramayan* and *Mahabharat* were considerably older
than the productions of that poet; and it appears from
the style and metre of the *Dherma Sastra*, revealed by
Menu, that it was reduced to writing long before the
age of *Valmic* or *Vyasa*, the second of whom names
it with applause. We shall not, therefore, be thought
extravagant if we place the compiler of those laws between a thousand and fifteen hundred years before
Christ; especially as *Buddha*, whose age is pretty well
ascertained, is not mentioned in them; but, in the
twelfth century before our era, the *Chinese* empire
was at least in its cradle. This fact it is necessary to
prove; and my first witness is *Confucius* himself. I
know to what keen satire I shall expose myself by citing that philosopher, after the bitter sarcasms of M.
Pauw against him and against the translators of his
mutilated, but valuable works; yet I quote without
scruple the book entitled *Lun Yu*, of which I possess
the original with a verbal translation, and which I
know to be sufficiently authentic for my present purpose. In the second part of it *Con fu-tsu* declares, that
" Altho' he, like other men, could relate, as mere lessons
" of morality, the histories of the first and second im-
" perial houses, yet, *for want of evidence*, he could
" give no certain account of them." Now, if the *Chinese* themselves do not even pretend that any historical monument existed in the age of *Confucius*, preceding the rise of their third dynasty, about eleven
hundred years before the *Christian* epoch, we may
justly conclude that the reign of *Vivam* was in the
infancy of their empire, which hardly grew to maturity
till some ages after that prince; and it has been asserted
by very learned *Europeans*, that even of the third
dynasty, which he has the fame of having raised, no
unsuspected memorial can now be produced. It was
not till the eighth century before the birth of our

Saviour, that a small kingdom was erected in the province of *Shen-si*, the capital of which stood nearly in the *thirty-fifth* degree of northern latitude, and about *five* degrees to the west of *Si-gan:* both the country and its metropolis were called *Chin*; and the dominion of its princes was gradually extended to the east and west. A king of *Chin*, who makes a figure in the *Shahnamah* among the allies of *Afrasiyab*, was, I presume, a sovereign of the country just mentioned; and the river of *Chin*, which the poet frequently names as the limit of his eastern geography, seems to have been the *Yellow River*, which the *Chinese* introduce at the beginning of their fabulous annals. I should be tempted to expatiate on so curious a subject, but the present occasion allows nothing superfluous, and permits me only to add, that *Mangukhan* died in the middle of the thirteenth century, before the city of *Chin*, which was afterwards taken by *Kublai*, and that the poets of *Iran* perpetually allude to the districts around it which they celebrate, with *Chegil* and *Khoten*, for a number of musk animals roving on their hills. The territory of *Chin*, so called by the old *Hindus*, by the *Persians*, and by the *Chinese* (while the *Greeks* and *Arabs* were obliged by their defective articulation to miscall it *Sin)* gave its name to a race of emperors, whose tyranny made their memory so unpopular, that the modern inhabitants of *China* hold the word in abhorrence, and speak of themselves as the people of a milder and more virtuous dynasty; but it is highly probable that the whole nation descended from the *Chinas* of *Menu*, and, mixing with the *Tartars* (by whom the plains of *Honan* and the more southern provinces were thinly inhabited) formed by degrees the race of men whom we now see in possession of the noblest empire in *Asia*.

In support of an opinion, which I offer as the result of long and anxious inquiries, I should regularly

proceed to examine the language and letters, religion
and philosophy of the present *Chinese*, and subjoin
some remarks on their ancient monuments, on their
sciences, and on their arts, both liberal and mechanical; but their spoken *language* not having been preserved by the usual symbols of articulate sounds, must have
been for many ages in a continual flux; their *letters*,
if we may so call them, are merely the symbols of ideas;
their popular *religion* was imported from *India* in an
age comparatively modern; and their *philosophy* seems
yet in so rude a state as hardly to deserve the appellation; they have no *ancient monuments*, from which
their origin can be traced even by plausible conjecture;
their *sciences* are wholly exotic; and their *mechanical
arts* have nothing in them characteristic of a particular family; nothing which any set of men, in a country so highly favoured by nature, might not have
discovered and improved. They have indeed both
national music and national poetry, and both of them
beautifully pathetic; but of painting, sculpture, or architecture, as arts of imagination, they seem (like other
Asiatics) to have no idea. Instead, therefore, of en-
larging separately on each of those heads, I shall
briefly inquire, how far the literature and religious
practices of *China* confirm or oppose the proposition
which I have advanced.

The declared and fixed opinion of M. *De Guignes*, on
the subject before us, is nearly connected with that of
the *Bráhmans:* he maintains, that the *Chinese* were
emigrants from *Egypt*; and the *Egyptians*, or *Ethiopians* (for they were clearly the same people) had indubitably a common origin with the old natives of *India*,
as the affinity of their languages and of their institutions, both religious and political, fully evince; but
that *China* was peopled a few centuries before our era by
a colony from the banks of the *Nile*, tho' neither *Persians* nor *Arabs*, *Tartars* nor *Hindus*, ever heard of such
an emigration, is a paradox, which the bare authority

even of so learned a man cannot support; and, since reason grounded on facts can alone decide such a question, we have a right to demand clearer evidence and stronger arguments than any that he has yet adduced. The hieroglyphics of *Egypt* bear, indeed, a strong resemblance to the mythological sculptures and paintings of *India*, but seem wholly dissimilar to the symbolical system of the *Chinese*, which might easily have been invented (as they assert) by an individual, and might very naturally have been contrived by the first *Chinas*, or outcast *Hindus*, who either never knew, or had forgotten, the alphabetical characters of their wiser ancestors. As to the table and bust of *Isis*, they seem to be given up as modern forgeries; but, if they were indisputably genuine, they would be nothing to the purpose; for the letters on the bust appear to have been designed as alphabetical; and the fabricator of them (if they really were fabricated in *Europe*) was uncommonly happy, since two or three of them are exactly the same with those on a metal pillar yet standing in the north of *India*. In *Egypt*, if we can rely on the testimony of the *Greeks*, who studied no language but their own, there were two sets of alphabetical characters; the one *popular*, like the various letters used in our *Indian* provinces; and the other *sacerdotal*, like the *Devanagari*, especially that form of it which we see in the *Veda*; besides which they had two sorts of *sacred sculpture*; the one simple, like the figures of *Buddha* and the three *Ramas*; and the other allegorical, like the images of *Ganesa*, or *Divine Wisdom*, and *Isani*, or *Nature*, with all their emblematical accompaniments; but the *real character* of the *Chinese* appears wholly distinct from any *Egyptian* writing, either mysterious or popular: and, as to the fancy of M *de Guignes*, that the complicated symbols of *China* were at first no more than *Phenician* monograms, let us hope that he has abandoned so wild a conceit, which he started probably with no other view than to display his ingenuity and learning.

We have ocular proof that the few radical characters of the *Chinese* were originally (like our astronomical and chymical symbols) the pictures or outlines
of visible objects, or figurative signs for simple ideas,
which they have multiplied by the most ingenious
combinations and the liveliest metaphors ; but, as the
system is peculiar, I believe, to themselves and the
Japanese, it would be idly ostentatious to enlarge on
it at present ; and, for the reasons already intimated,
it neither corroborates nor weakens the opinion which
I endeavour to support. The same may as truly be
said of their *spoken* language ; for, independently of
its constant fluctuation during a series of ages, it has
the peculiarity of excluding four or five sounds which
other nations articulate, and is clipped into monosyl-
lables, even when the ideas expressed by them, and
the written symbols for those ideas, are very complex. This has arisen, I suppose, from the singular
habits of the people ; for, though their common
tongue be so *musically* accented as to form a kind of re-
citative, yet it wants those *grammatical* accents, without which all human tongues would appear monosyl-
labic. Thus *Amita*, with an accent on the first syllable,
means, in the *Sanscrit* language, *immeasurable*; and
the natives of *Bengal* pronounce it *Omito*; but when
the religion of *Buddha*, the son of *Maya*, was carried
hence into *China*, the people of that country, unable
to pronounce the name of their new God, called him
Foe, the son of *Mo-ye*, and divided his epithet *Amita*
into three syllables *O-mi-to*, annexing to them certain
ideas of their own, and expressing them in writing
by three distinct symbols. We may judge from this
instance, whether a comparison of their spoken tongue
with the dialects of other nations can lead to any certain conclusion as to their origin ; yet the instance
which I have given, supplies me with an argument
from analogy, which I produce as conjectural only, but
which appears more and more plausible the oftener I

I

consider it. The *Buddha* of the *Hindus* is unquestionably the *Foe* of *China*; but the great progenitor of
the *Chinese* is also named by them *Fo-hi*, where the
second monosyllable signifies, it seems, a *victim*. Now
the ancestor of that military tribe, whom the *Hindus*
call the *Chandravansa*, or *Children of the Moon*, was,
according to their *Puranas* or legends, *Buddha*, or the
genius of the planet *Mercury*, from whom, in the
fifth degree, descended a prince named *Druhya*; whom
his father *Yayati* sent in exile to the east of *Hindustan*, with this imprecation, " May thy progeny be
" ignorant of the *Veda*." The name of the banished
prince could not be pronounced by the modern *Chinese*;
and, though I dare not conjecture that the last syllable of it has been changed into *Yao*, I may nevertheless observe that *Yao* was the *fifth* in descent from
Fo hi, or at least the fifth mortal in the first imperial
dynasty; that all *Chinese* history before him is considered by the *Chinese* themselves as poetical or fabulous;
that his father *Ti-co*, like the *Indian* king *Yayati*, was
the first prince who married several women; and that
Fo-hi, the head of their race, appeared, say the *Chinese*, in a province of the west, and held his court in
the territory of *Chin*, where the rovers, mentioned by
the *Indian* legislator, are supposed to have settled.
Another circumstance in the parallel is very remarkable : — According to Father *De Premare*, in his tract
on *Chinese* Mythology, the mother of *Fo-hi* was the
Daughter of Heaven, surnamed *Flower-loving*; and
as the nymph was walking alone on the bank of a *river*
with a similar name, she found herself on a sudden
encircled by a *rainbow*; soon after which she became
pregnant, and at the end of twelve years was delivered
of a son radiant as herself, who, among other titles,
had that of *Sui*, or *Star of the Year*. Now, in the
mythological system of the *Hindus*, the nymph *Rohini*,
who presides over the fourth lunar mansion, was the
favourite mistress of *Soma*, or the Moon, among

whose numerous epithets we find *Cumudanayaca*, or *Delighting in a* species of *water-flower* that blossoms at night; and their offspring was *Budha*, regent of a planet, and called also, from the names of his parents *Rauhineya*, or *Saumya*. It is true that the learned missionary explains the word *Sui* by *Jupiter*; but an exact resemblance between two such fables could not have been expected; and it is sufficient for my purpose that they seem to have a family-likeness. The God *Budha*, say the *Indians*, married *Ila*, whose father was preserved in a miraculous ark from an universal deluge. Now, although I cannot insist with confidence, that the *rainbow* in the *Chinese* fable alludes to the *Mosaic* narrative of the flood, nor build any solid argument on the divine personage *Nu-va*, of whose character, and even of whose sex, the historians of *China* speak very doubtfully, I may, nevertheless, assure you, after full inquiry and consideration, that the *Chinese*, like the *Hindus*, believe this earth to have been wholly covered with water, which, in works of undisputed authenticity, they describe as *flowing abundantly*, *then subsiding, and separating the higher from the lower age of mankind*; that the *division of time*, from which their poetical history begins, just preceded the appearance of *Fo-hi* on the mountains of *Chin*; but that the great *inundation* in the reign of *Yao* was either confined to the lowlands of his kingdom, if the whole account of it be not a fable, or, if it contain any allusion to the flood of *Noah*, has been ignorantly misplaced by the *Chinese* annalists.

The importation of a new religion into *China* in the first century of our era, must lead us to suppose that the former system, whatever it was, had been found inadequate to the purpose of restraining the great body of the people from those offences against conscience and virtue, which the civil power could not reach; and it is hardly possible that, without such restrictions, any government could long have subsisted with felicity; for no government can long subsist without equal justice, and justice cannot be administered without the sanctions of religion. Of the religious opinions entertained by *Confucius* and his followers, we may glean a general notion from the fragments of their works translated by *Couplet*. They professed a firm belief in the Supreme God, and gave a demonstration of his being and of his providence from the exquisite beauty and perfection of the celestial bodies, and the wonderful order of nature in the whole fabric of the visible world. From this belief they deduced a system of ethics, which the philosopher sums up in a few words at the close of the *Lun-yu*: " He," says *Confucius*, " who will be fully " persuaded that the Lord of Heaven governs the " universe, who shall in all things chuse moderation, " who shall perfectly know his own species, and so act " among them that his life and manners may con- " form to his knowledge of God and man, may be " truly said to discharge all the duties of a sage, and " to be far exalted above the common herd of the " human race." But such a religion and such morality could never have been general; and we find that the people of *China* had an ancient system of ceremonies and superstitions, which the government and the philosophers appear to have encouraged, and which has an apparent affinity with some parts of the oldest *Indian* worship. They believed in the agency of genii, or tutelary spirits, presiding over the stars and the clouds, over lakes and rivers, mountains, valleys, and woods, over certain regions and towns, over all the elements (of which, like the *Hindus*, they reckoned *five)* and particularly over *fire*, the most brilliant of them. To those deities they offered victims on high places : and the following passage from the *Shi-cin*, or *Book of Odes*, is very much in the style of the *Brahmans* :— " Even they, who perform a sacrifice with due reve- " rence, cannot perfectly assure themselves that the di- " vine spirits accept their oblations; and far less can " they, who adore the Gods with languor and oscitancy,

" clearly perceive their sacred illapses." These are imperfect traces indeed, but they are traces of an affinity
between the religion of *Menu* and that of the *Chinas*,
whom he names among the apostates from it. M. *Le
Gentil* observed, he says, a strong resemblance between
the funeral rites of the *Chinese* and the *Sraddha* of the
Hindus; and M. *Bailly*, after a learned investigation,
concludes, that " Even the puerile and absurd stories
" of the *Chinese* fabulists, contain a remnant of an-
" cient *Indian* history, with a faint sketch of the first
" *Hindu* ages." As the *Bauddhas*, indeed, were
Hindus, it may naturally be imagined that they carried into *China* many ceremonies practised in their own
country; but the *Bauddhas* positively forbade the im-
molation of cattle; yet we know that various animals,
even bulls and men, were anciently sacrificed by the
Chinese; besides which we discover many singular
marks of relation between them and the old *Hindus*:
as in the remarkable period of *four hundred and thirty-
two thousand*, and the cycle of *sixty* years; in the
predilection for the mystical number *nine*; in many
similar fasts and great festivals, especially at the solstices and equinoxes; in the just-mentioned obsequies
consisting of rice and fruits offered to the manes of
their ancestors; in the dread of dying childless, lest
such offerings should be intermitted; and, perhaps, in
their common abhorrence of *red* objects, which the
Indians carried so far, that *Menu* himself, where he allows a *Brahmen* to trade, if he cannot otherwise support life, absolutely forbids "his trafficking in any sort
" of *red* cloths, whether linen or woollen, or made
" of woven bark." All the circumstances, which have
been mentioned under the two heads of *Literature* and
Religion, seem collectively to prove (as far as such a
question admits proof) that the *Chinese* and *Hindus*
were originally the same people; but having been separated near four thousand years, have retained few
strong features of their ancient consanguinity, especially as the *Hindus* have preserved their old language and

ritual, while the *Chinese* very soon lost both ; and the *Hindus* have constantly intermarried among themselves, while the *Chinese*, by a mixture of *Tartarian* blood from the time of their first establishment, have at length formed a race distinct in appearance both from *Indians* and *Tartars*.

A similar diversity has arisen, I believe, from similar causes, between the people of *China* and *Japan*; on the second of which nations we have now, or soon shall have, as correct and as ample instruction as can possibly be obtained without a perfect acquaintance with the *Chinese* characters. *Kæmpfer* has taken from M. *Titsingh* the honour of being the first ; and he from *Kæmpfer* that of being the only *European* who, by a long residence in *Japan*, and a familiar intercourse with the principal natives of it, has been able to collect authentic materials for the natural and civil history of a country *secluded* (as the *Romans* used to say of our own island) *from the rest of the world.* The works of those illustrious travellers will confirm and embellish each other ; and when M. *Titsingh* shall have acquired a knowledge of *Chinese*, to which a part of his leisure in *Java* will be devoted, his precious collection of books in that language, on the laws and revolutions, the natural productions, the arts, manufactures, and sciences of *Japan*, will be in his hands an inexhaustible mine of new and important information. Both he and his predecessor assert with confidence, and, I doubt not, with truth, that the *Japanese* would resent, as an insult on their dignity, the bare suggestion of their descent from the *Chinese*, whom they surpass in several of the mechanical arts, and, what is of greater consequence, in military spirit; but they do not, I understand, mean to deny that they are a branch of the same ancient stem with the people of *China* ; and, were that fact ever so warmly contested by them, it might be proved by an invinci-

ble argument, if the preceding part of this discourse,
on the origin of the *Chinese*, be thought to contain
just reasoning.   In the first place, it seems incon-
ceivable that the *Japanese*, who never appear to have
been conquerors or conquered, should have adopted
the whole system of *Chinese* literature with all its in-
conveniences and intricacies, if an immemorial con-
nexion had not subsisted between the two nations, or,
in other words, if the bold and ingenious race who
peopled *Japan* in the middle of the thirteenth century before *Christ*, and, about six hundred years
afterwards established their monarchy, had not carried with them the letters and learning which they
and the *Chinese* had possessed in common; but my
principal argument is, that the *Hindu* or *Egyptian*
idolatry has prevailed in *Japan* from the earliest ages;
and among the idols worshipped, according to
Kæmpfer, in that country before the innovations of
Sacya or *Buddha*, whom the *Japanese* also called *Ami-
da*, we find many of those which we see every day
in the temples of *Bengal*; particularly *the goddess
with many arms*, representing the powers of nature; in
Egypt named *Isis*, and here *Isani* or *Isi*; whose image,
as it is exhibited by the *German* traveller, all the
Brahmans to whom I showed it, immediately recog-
nized with a mixture of pleasure and enthusiasm. —
It is very true that the *Chinese* differ widely from
the natives of *Japan* in their vernacular dialects, in
external manners, and perhaps in the strength of their
mental faculties; but as wide a difference is observa-
ble among all the nations of the *Gothic* family; and
we might account even for a greater dissimilarity, by
considering the number of ages during which the several swarms have been separated from the great *Indian* hive, to which they primarily belonged. The
modern *Japanese* gave *Kæmpfer* the idea of polished
Tartars; and it is reasonable to believe, that the people of *Japan*, who were originally *Hindus* of the mar-

tial class, and advanced farther eastward than the *Chi-nus*, have, like them, insensibly changed their fea-tures and characters by intermarriages with various *Tartarian* tribes, whom they found loosely scattered over their isles, or who afterwards fixed their abode in them.

Having now shown in five discourses, that the *Arabs* and *Tartars* were orignally distinct races, while the *Hindus*, *Chinese*, and *Japanese* proceeded from another ancient stem, and that all the three stems may be traced to *Iran*, as to a common centre, from which it is highly probable that they diverged in various direc-tions about four thousand years ago, I may seem to have accomplished my design of investigating the ori-gin of the *Asiatic* nations ; but the questions which I undertook to discuss, are not yet ripe for a strict analy-tical argument ; and it will first be necessary to exa-mine with scrupulous attention all the detached or insulated races of men, who either inhabit the borders of *India*, *Arabia*, *Tartary*, *Persia*, and *China*, or are interspersed in the mountainous and uncultivated parts of those extensive regions. To this examination I shall, at our next annual meeting, allot an entire dis-course; and if, after all our inquiries, no more than *three* primitive races can be found, it will be a subse-quent consideration whether those three stocks had one common root ; and, if they had, by what means that root was preserved amid the violent shocks which our whole globe appears evidently to have sustained.

XXVI.

THE TRANSLATION OF AN INSCRIPTION
IN THE MAGA LANGUAGE,
Engraved on a Silver Plate, found in a Cave near Islamabad.

COMMUNICATED BY JOHN SHORE, ESQ.

ON the 14th of *Magha* 904, *Chandi Lâh Raja**, by the advice of *Bowangari Rauli*, who was the director of his studies and devotions, and in conformity to the sentiments of twenty-eight other *Raulis*, formed the design of establishing a place of religious worship; for which purpose a cave was dug, and paved with bricks, three cubits in depth, and three cubits also in diameter; in which were deposited one hundred and twenty brazen images of small dimensions, denominated *Tahmudas*; also, twenty brazen images larger than the former, denominated *Langula*; there was likewise a large image of stone call *Langudagari*, with a vessel of brass, in which were deposited two of the bones of *T'hacur*. On a silver plate were inscribed the *Hauca*, or the mandates of the deity; with that also styled *Taumah Chucksowna Tahma*, to the study of which twenty-eight *Raulis* devote their time and attention; who, having celebrated the present work of devotion with festivals and rejoicings, erected over the cave a place of religious worship for the *Magas*, in honour of the deity.

God sent into the world *Buddha Avatar* to instruct and direct the steps of angels and of men; of whose birth and origin the following is a relation:—When *Buddha Avatar* descended from the region of souls, in

---

* Perhaps *Sandilyab.*

the month of *Mugh*, and entered the body of *Muha-maya*, the wife of *Sootah Dannah, Raja* of *Cailas*, her womb suddenly assumed the appearance of clear transparent crystal, in which *Buddha* appeared, beautiful as a flower, kneeling and reclining on his hands. After ten months and ten days of her pregnancy had elapsed, *Mahamaya* solicited permission from her husband, the *Raja*, to visit her father : in conformity to which the roads were directed to be repaired and made clear for her journey ; fruit-trees were planted, water-vessels placed on the road-side, and great illuminations prepared for the occasion. *Mahamaya* then commenced her journey, and arrived at a garden adjoining to the road, where inclination led her to walk and gather flowers. At this time, being suddenly attacked with the pains of child-birth, she laid hold on the trees for support, which declined their boughs at the instant, for the purpose of concealing her person, while she was delivered of the child ; at which juncture *Brahma* himself attended with a golden vessel in his hand, on which he laid the child, and delivered it to *Indra*, by whom it was committed to the charge of a female attendant ; upon which the child, alighting from her arms, walked seven paces, whence it was taken up by *Mahamaya* and carried to her house, and, on the ensuing morning, news were circulated of a child being born in the *Raja*'s family. At this time *Tupaswi Muni*, who, residing in the woods, devoted his time to the worship of the deity, learned by inspiration that *Buddha* was come to life in the *Raja*'s palace : he flew through the air to the *Raja*'s residence, where, sitting on a throne, he said, " I have repaired " hither for the purpose of visiting the child." *Buddha* was accordingly brought into his presence. The *Muni* observed two feet fixed on his head, and, divining something both of good and bad import, began to weep and laugh alternately. The *Raja* then questioned him with regard to his present impulse, to whom he answered, " I must not reside in the same place

" with *Buddha* when he shall arrive at the rank of
" *Avatar*; this is the cause of my present affliction;
" but I am even now affected with gladness by his
" presence, as I am hereby absolved from all my
" transgressions." The *Muni* then departed; and,
after five days had elapsed, he assembled four *Pandits*
for the purpose of calculating the destiny of the child;
three of whom divined, that, as he had marks on his
hands resembling a wheel, he would at length become
a *Raja Chacraverti*: another divined, that he would
arrive at the dignity of *Avatar*.

The boy was now named *Surya*, and had attained
the age of sixteen years; at which period it happened
that the *Raja Chuhidan* had a daughter named *Vasu-
tara*, whom he had engaged not to give in marriage
to any one, till such time as a suitor should be found
who could brace a certain bow in his possession,
which hitherto many *Rajas* had attempted to accomplish without effect. *Surya* now succeeded in the
attempt, and accordingly obtained the *Raja*'s daughter in marriage, with whom he repaired to his own
place of residence.

One day as certain mysteries were revealed to him,
he formed the design of relinquishing his dominion;
at which time a son was born in his house, whose
name was *Raghu*. *Surya* then left his palace with
only one attendant and a horse, and, having crossed
the river *Ganga*, arrived at *Balucali*, where, having
directed his servant to leave him and carry away his
horse, he laid aside his armour.

When the world was created, there appeared five
flowers, which *Brahma* deposited in a place of safety;
three of them were afterwards delivered to the three
Thcurs, and one was presented to *Surya*, who

discovered, that it contained some pieces of wearing-apparel, in which he clothed himself, and adopted the manners and life of a mendicant. A traveller one day passed by him with eight bundles of grass on his shoulders, and addressed him, saying, " A " long period of time has elapsed since I have seen " the *T'hacur*; but now since I have the happiness " to meet him, I beg to present him an offering, con- " sisting of these bundles of grass." *Sacya* accord- ingly accepted of the grass, and reposed on it. At that time there suddenly appeared a golden temple, containing a chair of wrought gold ; and the height of the temple was thirty cubits, upon which *Brahma* alighted, and held a canopy over the head of *Sacya :* at the same time *Indra* descended, with a large fan in his hand, and *Naga*, the *Raja* of serpents, with shoes in his hand, together with the four tutelar deities of the four corners of the universe ; who all attended to do him service and reverence. At this time likewise the chief of *Asurs* with his forces arrived, riding on an elephant, to give battle to *Sacya* ; upon which *Brahma*, *Indra*, and the other deities deserted him and vanished. *Sacya*, observing that he was left alone, invoked the assistance of the earth ; who, at- tending at his summons, brought an inundation over all the ground, whereby the *Asur* and his forces were vanquished, and compelled to retire.

At this time five holy scriptures descended from above, and *Sacya* was dignified with the title of *Bud- dha Avatar*. The scriptures confer powers of know- ledge and retrospection, the ability of accomplishing the impulses of the heart, and of carrying into effect the words of the mouth. *Sacya* resided here, without breaking his fast, twenty-one days, and then returned to his own country, where he presides over *Rajas*, governing them with care and equity.

Whoever reads the *Caric*, his body, apparel, and the place of his devotions must be purified; he shall be thereby delivered from the evil machinations of demons and of his enemies; and the ways of redemption shall be open to him. *Buddha Avatar* instructed a certain *Rauli*, by name *Anguli Mula*, in the writings of the *Caric*, saying, "whoever shall read and study them, his soul shall not undergo a transmigration:" and the scriptures were thence called *Anguli Mala*. There were likewise five other books of the *Caric*, denominated *Vachanam*, which if any one peruse, he shall therefore be exempted from poverty and the machinations of his enemies; he shall also be exalted to dignity and honours, and the length of his days shall be protracted. The study of the *Caric* heals afflictions and pains of the body; and whoever shall have faith therein, Heaven and bliss shall be the reward of his piety.

XXVII.

A SUPPLEMENT TO THE ESSAY
ON INDIAN CHRONOLOGY.

BY THE PRESIDENT.

OUR ingenious associate Mr. *Samuel Davis* (whom I name with respect and applause, and who will soon, I trust, convince M. *Bailly* that it is very possible for an *European* to translate and explain the *Surya Siddhanta*) favoured me lately with a copy, taken by his *Pandit*, of the original passage, mentioned in his paper on the Astronomical Computations of the *Hindus* concerning the places of the colures in the time of *Varaha*, compared with their position in the age of a certain *Muni*, or ancient *Indian* philosopher; and the passage appears to afford evidence of two actual observations, which will ascertain the chronology of the *Hindus*, if not by rigorous demonstration, at least by a near approach to it.

The copy of the *Varahisanhita*, from which the three pages received by me had been transcribed, is unhappily so incorrect (if the transcript itself was not hastily made) that every line of it must be disfigured by some gross error; and my *Pandit*, who examined the passage carefully at his own house, gave it up as inexplicable; so that, if I had not studied the system of *Sanscrit* prosody, I should have laid it aside in despair: but though it was written as prose, without any sort of distinction or punctuation, yet, when I read it aloud, my ear caught, in some sentences, the cadence of verse, and of a particular metre, called *Arya*, which is regulated (not by the *number* of syllables, like other *Indian* measures, but) by the proportion of

C c 2

times, or *syllabic moments,* in the four divisions of
which every stanza consists. By numbering those moments and fixing their proportion, I was enabled to re-
store the text of *Varaha,* with the perfect assent of the
learned *Brahmen* who attends me ; and, with his assistance, I also corrected the comment, written by
Bhattotpala, who, it seems, was a son of the author,
together with three curious passages, which are cited
in it. Another *Pandit* afterwards brought me a copy
of the whole original work, which confirmed my conjectural emendations, except in two immaterial syllables, and except that the first of the six couplets in
the text is quoted in the commentary from a different
work, entitled *Panchasiddhantica,* five of them were
composed by *Varaha* himself; and the third chapter
of his treatise begins with them.

Before I produce the original verses, it may be useful to give you an idea of the *Arya* measure ; which
will appear more distinctly in *Latin* than in any modern language of *Europe:*

Tigridas, apros, thoas, tyrannos, pessima monstra, venemur:
Die hinnulus, die lepus male quid egerint graminivori.

The couplet might be so arranged as to begin and end
with the cadence of an hexameter and pentameter, six
moments being interposed in the middle of the long,
and seven in that of the short hemistich :

Thoas, apros, tigridas nos *venemur,* pejoresque tyrannos :
Die tibi cerva, lepus *tibi die male quid* egerit herbivorus.

Since the *Arya* measure, however, may be almost infinitely varied, the couplet would have a form completely *Roman,* if the proportion of *syllabic instants,*

in the long and short verses, were *twenty-four* to
twenty, instead of *thirty* to *twenty seven:*

Venor apros tigridasque, et, pessima monstra, tyrannos :
Cerva mali quid agunt herbivorusque lepus?

I now exhibit the five stanzas of *Varaha* in *European* characters, with an etching of the two first,
which are the most important, in the original *Dewa-
nagari:*

Asleshardhaddacshinamuttaramayananraverdhanishthadyan
Nunan cadachidasidyenoctan purva sastreshu.
Sampratamayananan savituh carcatacadyan inrigaditascbanyat:
Uctabhave vicritih pratyacshapericshanair vyactih.
Durast'hacbihnavedyadudaye'stamaye'piva sahasramoh,
Ch'hayapravesanirgamachihnairva mandale mahati.
Aprapya macaramago vinivritto hanti saparan yamyan,
Carcatacamasanprapno vinivrittaschottaran saindrin.
Uttaramayanamatitya vyavrittah cshemasasya vriddhicarah,
Pracritist'haschapycvan vicritigatir bhayacriduahnansuh.

Of the five couplets thus exhibited, the following
translation is most scrupulously literal :

" Certainly the southern solstice was once in the
" middle of *Asleshu ;* the northern in the first *degree* of
" *Dhanisht'ha,* by what *is* recorded in former *Sastras.*
" At present, one solstice is in the first *degree* of *Car-
" cata,* and the other in the first of *Macara.* That
" which *is* recorded not appearing, a change *must*

" have happened; and the proof arises from ocular
" demonstrations; that is, by observing the remote
" object and its marks at the rising or setting of the
" sun, or by the marks in a large graduated circle,
" of the shadow's ingress and egress. The sun, by
" turning back without having reached Macara, de-
" stroys the south and the west; by turning back
" without having reached Carcata, the north and
" east. By returning when he has just passed the
" winter solstitial point, he makes wealth secure and
" grain abundant, since he moves thus according to
" nature; but the sun, by moving unnaturally, ex-
" cites terror."

Now the Hindu astronomers agree, that the 1st of
January 1790, was in the year 4891 of the Caliyuga,
or their fourth period; at the beginning of which, they
say, the equinoctial points were at the first degrees of
Mesha and Tula; but they are also of opinion, that
the vernal equinox oscillates from the third of Mina to
the twenty-seventh of Mesha, and back again in 7200
years, which they divide into four padas, and consequently that it moves in the two intermediate padas
from the first to the twenty-seventh of Mesha and back
again in 3600 years; the colure cutting their ecliptic
in the first of Mesha, which coincides with the first
of Aswin, at the beginning of every such oscilla-
tory period. Varaha, surnamed Mihira, or the Sun,
from his knowledge of astronomy, and usually distinguished by the title of Acharya, or teacher of the
Veda, lived, confessedly, when the Caliyuga was far
advanced; and, since by actual observation he found
the solstitial points in the first degrees of Carcata and
Macara, the equinoctial points were at the same time
in the first of Mesha and Tula; he lived, therefore, in
the year 3600 of the fourth Indian period, or 1291
years before the 1st of January 1790, that is, about the
year 499 of our era. This date corresponds with the

avanansa, or prec_ssion, calculated by the rule of the *Surya Siddhanta*; for 19° 21′ 54″ would be the precession of the equinox in 1291 years, according to the *Hindu* computation of 54″ annually, which gives us the original of the *Indian* Zodiac nearly; but, by *Newton*'s demonstrations, which agree as well with the phenomena as the varying density of our earth will admit, the equinox recedes about 50″ every year, and has receded 17° 55′ 50″ since the time of *Varaha*; which gives us more nearly in our own sphere the first degree of *Mesha* in that of the *Hindus*. By the observation recorded in older *Sastras*, the equinox had gone back 23° 20′; or about 1680 years had intervened between the age of the *Muni* and that of the modern astronomer: the former observation, therefore, must have been made about 2971 years before the 1st of *January* 1790; that is, 1181 before *Christ*.

We come now to the commentary, which contains information of the greatest importance. By former *Sastras* are meant, says *Bhattotpala*, the books of *Parasara* and of other *Munis*; and he then cites from the *Parasari Sanhita* the following passage, which is in modulated prose, and in a style much resembling that of the *Vedas*:

Sravishtadyat paushnardhantan charah sisiro; vasantah paushnardhat rohinyantan; saumyadyadasleshardhantan grishmah; pravri dasleshardhat hastantan; chitradyat jyesht'hardhantan sarat; hemanto jyesht'hardhat vaishnavantan.

" The season of *Sisira* is from the first of *Dha-*
" *nishi'ha* to the middle of *Revati*; that of *Vasanta*
" from the middle of *Revati* to the end of *Rohini*;
" that of *Grishma* from the beginning of *Mrigasiras*
" to the middle of *Aslesha*; that of *Versha* from
" the middle of *Aslesha* to the end of *Hasta*; that

" of *Sarad* from the first of *Chitra* to the middle of
" *Jyesht'ha*; that of *Hemanta* from the middle of
" *Jyesht'ha* to the end of *Sravana*."

This account of the six *Indian* seasons, each of
which is co-extensive with two signs, or four lunar
stations and a half, places the solstitial points, as *Varaha* has asserted, in the first degree of *Dhanisht'ha*,
and the middle, or 6° 40′, of *Aslesha*, while the
equinoctial points were in the *tenth* degree of *Bharani*
and 3° 20′ of *Visac'ha*; but, in the time of *Varaha*,
the solstitial colure passed through the tenth degree
of *Punarvasu* and 3° 20′ of *Uttarashara*, while the
equinoctial colure cut the *Hindu* ecliptic in the first of
Aswini and 6° 40′ of *Chitra*, or the *Yoga* and only
star of that mansion, which, by the way, is indubitably the *Spike* of the Virgin, from the known
longitude of which all other points in the *Indian*
Zodiac may be computed. It cannot escape notice,
that *Parasara* does not use in this passage the phrase
at present, which occurs in the text of *Varaha*; so
that the places of the colures might have been ascertained *before* his time, and a considerable change
might have happened in their true position without
any change in the phrases by which the seasons were
distinguished, as our popular language in astronomy
remains unaltered, though the Zodiacal asterisms are
now removed a whole sign from the places where they
have left their names. It is manifest, nevertheless,
that *Parasara* must have written *within twelve centuries* before the beginning of our era; and that single
fact, as we shall presently show, leads to very momen-
tous consequences in regard to the system of *Indian*
history and literature.

On the comparison which might easily be made
between the colures of *Parasar* and those ascribed by

Endœus to *Chiron*, the supposed assistant and instructor of the *Argonauts*, I shall say very little; because the whole *Argonautic* story (which neither was, according to *Herodotus*, nor, indeed, could have been originally *Grecian*) appears, even when stripped of its poetical and fabulous ornaments, extremely disputable; and whether it was founded on a league of the *Helladian* princes and states for the purpose of checking, on a favourable opportunity, the overgrown power of *Egypt*, or with a view to secure the commerce of the *Euxine* and appropriate the wealth of *Colchis*; or, as I am disposed to believe, on an emigration from *Africa* and *Asia* of that adventurous race, who had first been established in *Chaldea*; whatever, in short, gave rise to the fable, which the old poets have so richly embellished, and the old historians have so inconsiderately adopted, it seems to me very clear, even on the principles of *Newton*, and on the same authorities to which he refers, that the voyage of the *Argonauts* must have preceded the year in which his calculations led him to place it. *Battus* built *Cyrene*, says our great philosopher, on the scite of *Irasa*, the city of *Antæus*, in the year 633 before *Christ*; yet he soon afterwards calls *Euripylus*, with whom the *Argonauts* had a conference, king of *Cyrene*; and in both passages he cites *Pindar*, whom I acknowledge to have been the most learned, as well as the sublimest of poets. Now, if I understand *Pindar* (which I will not assert, and I neither possess nor remember at present the *Scholia*, which I formerly perused) the fourth *Pythian* Ode begins with a short panegyric on *Arcesilas* of *Cyrene*; " where" says the bard, " the priestess, who sat near the golden " eagles of *Jove*, prophesied of old, when *Apollo* was " not absent from his mansion, that *Battus*, the cole- " nizer of fruitful *Lybia*, having just left the sacred " isle *(Thera)* should build a city excelling in cars, " on the splendid breast of earth, and, *with the se-* " *venteenth generation*, should refer to himself the " *Therean* prediction of *Medea* which that princess of " the *Colchians*, that impetuous daughter of *Æetes*,

" breathed from her immortal mouth, and thus deli-
" vered to the half-divine mariners of the warrior
" *Jason*." From this introduction to the noblest and
most animated of the *Argonautic* poems, it appears
that *fifteen complete generations* had intervened between
the voyage of *Jason* and the emigration of *Battus*;
so that, considering *three* generations as equal to *an
hundred*, or an *hundred and twenty* years, which *Newton* admits to be the *Grecian* mode of computing
them, we must also place that voyage a: least *five* or *six
hundred years* before the time fixed by *Newton* himself, according to his own computation, for the building of *Cyrene*; that is, *eleven* or *twelve hundred and
thirty-three* years before *Christ*: an age very near on
a medium to that of *Parasara*. If the poet means afterwards to say, as I understand him, that *Arcesilas*,
his contemporary, was the *eighth* in descent from *Battus*, we shall nearly draw the same conclusion, without
having recourse to the unnatural reckoning of *thirty-
three* or *forty* years to a generation; for *Pindar* was
forty years old when the *Persians*, having crossed the
Hellespont, were nobly resisted at *Thermopylæ*, and
gloriously defeated at *Salamis*. He was born, therefore, about the sixty-fifth *Olympiad*, or five hundred
and twenty years before our era; so that, by allowing
more naturally *six* or *seven hundred* years to *twenty-
three* generations, we may at a medium place the
voyage of *Jason* about one thousand one hundred and
seventy years before our Saviour, or about *forty-five*
years before the beginning of the *Newtonian* chronology.

The description of the old colures by *Eudoxus*, if
we implicitly rely on his testimony and on that of *Hip-
parchus*, who was, indisputably, a great astronomer
for the age in which he lived, affords, I allow, sufficient evidence of some rude observation about 937
years before the *Christian* epoch; and, if the cardinal points had receded from those colures 36° 29′

10" at the beginning of the year 1690, and 37° 52′
30" on the first of *January* in the present year, they
must have gone back 3° 23′ 20" between the observation implied by *Parasara* and that recorded by *En-
doxus*; or, in other words, 244 years must have
elapsed between the two observations. But this dis-
quisition having little relation to our principal subject,
I proceed to the last couplets of our *Indian* astronomer
Varaha Mihira, which, although merely astrological,
and consequently absurd, will give occasion to remarks
of no small importance. They imply, that when the
solstices are not in the first degrees of *Carcata* and
Macara, the motion of the sun is contrary to nature;
and being caused, as the commentator intimates, by
some *utpata*, or preternatural agency, must necessarily
be productive of misfortune; and this vain idea
seems to indicate a very superficial knowledge even of
the system which *Varaha* undertook to explain; but
he might have adopted it solely as a religious tenet,
on the authority of *Garga*, a priest of eminent sanctity, who expresses the same wild notion in the following couplet:

Yada nivertate'praptah sravishtamuttarayane,
Asleshan dacshine'praptastadavidyanmahadbhayan.

" When *the sun* returns, not having reached *Dha-*
" *nisht'ha* in the northern solstice, *or* not having
" reached *Aslesha* in the southern, then let *a man*
" feel great apprehension of danger."

Parasara himself entertained a similar opinion,
that any irregularity in the solstices would indicate
approaching calamity: *Yadaprapto vaishnavantum,*
says he, *udanmarge prepadyate daeshine asleskam va
mahabhayaya*; that is, " When, having reached the
" end of *Sravana*, in the northern path, or half of
" *Aslesha* in the southern, he still advances, *it is* a
" cause of great fear." This notion, possibly, had

its rise before the regular precession of the cardinal points had been observed; but we may also remark, that some of the lunar mansions were considered as inauspicious, and others as fortunate; thus *Menu*, the first *Indian* lawgiver, ordains, that certain rites shall be performed under the influence of a happy *Narshatra*; and, where he forbids any female name to be taken from a constellation, the most learned commentator gives *Ardra* and *Revoti* as examples of ill-omened names, appearing by design to skip over others that must first have occurred to him. Whether *Dhanisht'ha* and *Aslesha* were inauspicious or prosperous, I have not learned; but, whatever might be the ground of *Varaha's* astrological rule, we may collect from his astronomy, which was grounded on observation, that the solstice had receded *at least* 25° 20' between his time and that of *Parasara*; for, though it refers its position to the *signs*, instead of the *lunar mansions*, yet all the *Pandits* with whom I have conversed on the subject, unanimously assert, that the first degrees of *Mesha* and *Aswini* are coincident. Since the two ancient sages name only the lunar asterisms, it is probable, that the solar division of the Zodiac into twelve signs was not generally used in their days; and we know from the comment on the *Surya Siddhanta*, that the lunar month, by which all religious ceremonies are still regulated, was in use before the solar. When M. *Bailly* asks "Why the " *Hindus* established the beginning of the precession, " according to their ideas of it, in the year of *Christ* " 499?" to which his calculations also had led him, we answer, Because in that year the vernal equinox was found by observation in the origin of their ecliptic; and since they were of opinion that it must have had the same position in the first year of the *Caliyuga*, they were induced by their erroneous theory to fix the beginning of their fourth period 3600 years before the time of *Varaha*, and to account for *Parasara's* observation, by supposing an *utpata*, or *prodigy*.

To what purpose, it may be asked, have we ascertained the age of *Munis?* Who was *Parasara?* Who was *Garga?* With whom were they contemporary, or with whose age may theirs be compared? What light will these inquiries throw on the history of *India* or of mankind? I am happy in being able to answer those questions with confidence and precision.

All the *Brahmens* agree, that only one *Parasara* is named in their sacred records; that he composed the astronomical book before cited, and a law-tract, which is now in my possession; that he was the grandson of *Vasisht'ha,* another astronomer and legislator, whose works are still extant, and who was the preceptor of *Rama,* king of *Ayodhya;* that he was the father of *Vyasa,* by whom the *Vedas* were arranged in the form which they now bear, and whom *Crishna* himself names with exalted praise in the *Gita;* so that, by the admission of the *Pandits* themselves, we find only three generations between two of the *Ramas,* whom they consider as incarnate *portions* of the divinity; and *Parasara* might have lived till the beginning of the *Caliyuga,* which the mistaken doctrine of an oscillation in the cardinal points has compelled the *Hindus* to place 1920 years too early. This error, added to their fanciful arrangement of the four ages, has been the source of many absurdities; for they insist that *Vulmic,* whom they cannot but allow to have been contemporary with *Ramachandra,* lived in the age of *Vyasa,* who consulted him on the composition of the *Mahabharat,* and who was personally known to *Balarama,* the brother of *Crishna.* When a very learned *Brahmen* had repeated to me an agreeable story of a conversation between *Valmic* and *Vyasa,* I expressed my surprize at an interview between two bards, whose ages were separated by a period of 864,000 years; but he soon reconciled himself to so monstrous an anachronism, by observing that the longevity of the

Munis was preternatural, and that no limit could be
set to Divine power. By the same recourse to miracles or to prophesy, he would have answered another
objection equally fatal to his chronological system. It
is agreed by all, that the lawyer *Yagyawalcya* was an
attendant on the court of *Janaca*, whose-daughter
Sita was the constant but unfortunate wife of the
great *Rama*, the hero of *Valmic*'s poem; but that
lawyer himself, at the very opening of his work, which
now lies before me, names both *Parasara* and *Vyasa*
among twenty authors, whose tracts form the body of
original *Indian* law. By the way, since *Vasisht'ha* is
more than once named in the *Manavisanhita*, we may
be certain that the laws ascribed to *Menu*, in whatever age they might have been first promulgated,
could not have received the form in which we now
see them, above *three thousand* years ago. The age
and functions of *Garga* lead to consequences yet
more interesting : he was confessedly the *purohita*, or
officiating priest, of *Crishna* himself, who, when
only a herdsman's boy at *Mat'hara*, revealed his divine
character to *Garga*, by running to him with more than
mortal benignity on his countenance, when the priest
had invoked *Narayan*. His daughter was eminent
for her piety and her learning, and the *Brahmens*
admit, without considering the consequence of
their admission, that she is thus addressed in the
Veda itself : *Yata urdhwan no va samopi, Gargi, esha
adityo dyanurdhanan tapati, dya va bhumin tapati,
bhumya subhran tapati, locan tapati, antaran tapaty-
anantaran tapati* ; or, " That Sun, O daughter of
" *Garga*, than which nothing is higher, to which no-
" thing is equal, enlightens the summit of the sky ;
" with the sky enlightens the earth ; with the earth
" enlightens the lower worlds ; enlightens the higher
" worlds, enlightens other worlds ; it enlightens the
" breast, enlightens all besides the breast." — From
these facts, which the *Brahmans* cannot deny, and from

these concessions, which they unanimously make, we may reasonably infer that, if *Vyasa* was not the composer of the *Vedas*, he added at least something of his own to the scattered fragments of a more ancient work, or perhaps to the loose traditions which he had collected; but whatever be the comparative antiquity of the *Hindu* scriptures, we may safely conclude that the *Mosaic* and *Indian* chronologies are perfectly consistent; that *Menu*, son of *Brahma* was the *Adima*, or *first* created mortal, and consequently our *Adam*; that *Menu*, child of the Sun, was preserved with *seven* others in a *bahitra*, or capacious ark, from an universal deluge, and must therefore be our *Noah*; that *Hiranyacasipu*, the giant *with a golden axe*, and *Vali*, or *Bali*, were impious and arrogant monarchs, and most probably our *Nimrod* and *Belus*; that the three *Ramas*, two of whom were invincible warriors, and the third not only valiant in war but the patron of agriculture and *wine*, which derives an epithet from his name, were different representations of the *Grecian Bacchus*, and either the *Rama* of scripture, or his colony personified, or the Sun first adored by his idolatrous family; that a considerable emigration from *Chaldea* into *Greece*, *Italy*, and *India*, happened about *twelve* centuries before the birth of our Saviour; that *Sacya*, or *Sisak*, about two hundred years after *Vyasa*, either in person or by a colony from *Egypt*, imported into this country the mild heresy of the ancient *Bauddhas*; and that the dawn of true *Indian* history appears only three or four centuries before the *Christian* era, the preceding ages being clouded by allegory or fable.

As a specimen of that fabling and allegorizing spirit which has ever induced the *Brahmens* to disguise their whole system of history, philosophy, and religion, I produce a passage from the *Bhagavat*, which, however strange and ridiculous, is very curious in itself, and closely connected with the subject of this essay.

It is taken from the fifth *Scandha*, or section, which is written in modulated prose. "There are some," says the *Indian* author, "who, for the purpose of me-
" ditating intensely on the holy son of *Vasudeva*, ima-
" gining on celestial sphere to represent the figure of
" that aquatic animal which we call *Sisumara* : its head
" being turned downwards, and its body bent in a
" circle, they conceive *Dhruva*, or the pole-star, to
" be fixed on the point of its tail ; on the middle
" part of the tail they see four stars, *Prejapati, Agni,*
" *Indra, Dherma,* and on its base two others, *Dhatri*
" and *Vidhatri :* on its rump are the *Septarshis,* or
" seven stars of the *Sacata,* or *Wain* ; on its back
" the path of the Sun, called *Ajavit'hi,* or the *Series*
" *of Kids* ; on its belly the *Ganga* of the sky : *Punar-*
" *vasu* and *Pushya* gleam respectively on its right and
" left haunches ; *Ardra* and *Aslesha* on its right and left
" feet, *or fins* ; *Abhijit* and *Uttarashad'ha* in its right
" and left nostrils ; *Sravana* and *Purvashad'ha* in its
" right and left eyes ; *Dhanisht'ha* and *Mula* on its
" right and left ears.   Eight constellations, belonging
" to the summer solstice, *Magha, Purvap'halguni,*
" *Uttarap'halguni, Hasta, Chitra, Swati, Visac'ha,*
" *Anuradha,* may be conceived in the ribs of its left
" side ; and as many asterisms, connected with the win-
" ter solstice, *Mrigasiras, Rohini, Crittica, Bharani, As-*
" *wini, Revati, Uttarabhadrapada, Purvabhadrapada,*
" may be imagined on the ribs of its right side in an
" inverse order.   Let *Satabhisha* and *Jyeshi'ha* be placed
" on its right and left shoulders.   In its upper jaw is
" *Agastya,* in its lower *Yama* ; in its mouth the pla-
" net *Mangala* ; in its part of generation, *Sanais-*
" *chara* ; on its hump, *Vrihaspati* ; in its breast, the
" Sun ; in its heart, *Narayan* ; in its front, the Moon ;
" in its navel, *Usanas* ; on its two nipples, the two *As-*
" *wins* ; in its ascending and descending breaths,
" *Budha* ; on its throat, *Rahu* ; in all its limbs, *Cetus,*
" or comets ; and in its hair, or bristles, the whole

" multitude of stars." It is necessary to remark, that, although the *sisumara* be generally described as the *sea-hog* or *porpoise*, which we frequently have seen playing in the *Ganges*, yet *susmar*, which seems derived from the *Sanscrit*, means in *Persian* a large *lizard*. The passage just exhibited may nevertheless relate to an animal of the cetaceous order, and possibly to the dolphin of the antients. Before I leave the sphere of the *Hindus*, I cannot help mentioning a singular fact :—In the *Sanscrit* language *Ricsha* means a *constellation* and a *bear*, so that *Maharcsha* may denote either a *great bear* or a *great asterism*. Etymologists may, perhaps, derive the *Megas arctos* of the *Greeks* from an *Indian* compound ill understood ; but I will only observe, with the wild *American*, that a bear *with a very long tail* could never have occurred to the imagination of any one who had seen the animal. I may be permitted to add, on the subject of the *Indian* Zodiac, that, if I have erred in a former essay, where the longitude of the lunar mansions is computed from the first star in our constellation of the Ram, I have been led into an error by the very learned and ingenious M. *Bailly*, who relied, I presume, on the authority of M. *Le Gentil*. The origin of the *Hindu* Zodiac, according to the *Surya Siddhanta*, must be nearly ♈ 19° 21' 54", in our sphere, and the longitude of *Chitra*, or the Spike, must of course be 199° 21' 54" from the vernal equinox ; but since it is difficult by that computation to arrange the twenty-seven mansions and their several stars, as they are delineated and enumerated in the *Retnamala*, I must for the present suppose with M. *Bailly*, that the Zodiac of the *Hindus* had two origins, one constant and the other variable ; and a farther inquiry into the subject must be reserved for a season of retirement and leisure.

Vol. 2.

P. 405.

JATAMANSI.

or Indian Spikenard.

P. 391.

अन्स्रोबाईमैद्मिराग्नायसिग्नद्रेहोर्मि्यांते
दलेठमैद्गिदानगिख्नालैंभूर्स्रागहेहु
भोद्मैद्गौत्रिकिहिह्रेलुँहद्यालेगुभोदिन्स्रान्प्रव
उस्रांगोगौदेहिस्रालैं अरप्सास्रौस्ट्रेरास्रा

XXVIII.

ON THE SPIKENARD OF THE ANTIENTS.

BY THE PRESIDENT.

IT is painful to meet perpetually with words that
convey no distinct ideas; and a natural desire of
avoiding that pain excites us often to make inquiries,
the result of which can have no other use than to give
us clear conceptions. Ignorance is to the mind what
extreme darkness is to the nerves: both cause an
uneasy sensation; and we naturally love knowledge
as we love light, even when we have no design of ap-
plying either to a purpose essentially useful. This is
intended as an apology for the pains which have
been taken to procure a determinate answer to a
question of no apparent utility, but which ought to
be readily answered in *India*: " What is *Indian* Spikenard?" All agree that it is an odoriferous plant, the
best sort of which, according to *Ptolemy*, grew about
Rangamritica or *Rangamati*, and on the borders of
the country now called *Butan*. It is mentioned by
Dioscorides, whose work I have not in my possession;
but his description of it must be very imperfect, since
neither *Linnæus* nor any of his disciples pretend to
class it with certainty; and, in the latest botanical
work that we have received from *Europe*, it is marked as *unknown*. I had no doubt, before I was personally acquainted with *Koenig*, that he had ascertained it: but he assured me that he knew not what
the *Greek* writers meant by the nard of *India*; he
had found, indeed, and described a sixth species of
the nardus, which is called *Indian* in the Supplement

to *Linnæus*; but the *nardus* is a grass which, though it bear a *spike*, no man ever supposed to be the *true* Spikenard, which the great botanical philosopher himself was inclined to think a species of *Andropogon*, and places in his *Materia Medica*, but with an expression of doubt, among his polygamous plants. Since the death of *Koenig* I have consulted every botanist and physician with whom I was acquainted, on the subject before us; but all have confessed without reserve, though not without some regret, that they were ignorant what was meant by the *Indian* Spikenard.

In order to procure information from the learned natives, it was necessary to know the *name* of the plant in some *Asiatic* language. The very word *nard* occurs in the *Song of Solomon*; but the name and the thing were both exotic: the *Hebrew* lexicographers imagine both to be *Indian*; but the word is, in truth *Persian*, and occurs in the following distich of an old poet:

An chu bikbeft, in chu nardeft, an chu shakest, in chu bar,
An chu bikhi payidarest, in chu nardi payidar.

It is not easy to determine in this couplet, whether *nard* means the *stem*, or, as *Anju* explains it, the *pith*; but it is manifestly a part of a vegetable, and neither the *root*, the *fruit*, nor the *branch*, which are all separately named. The *Arabs* have borrowed the word *nard* but in the sense, as we learn from the *Kamis*, of a *compound medicinal unguent*. Whatever it signified in old *Persian*, the *Arabic* word *sumbul*, which, like *sumbalah*, means an *ear* or *spike*, has long been substituted for it; and there can be no doubt that, by the *sumbul* of *India* the *Muselmans* understand the same plant with the *nard* of *Ptolemy* and the *Nardostachys*, or *Spikenard*, of *Galen*; who, by the way, was deceived by the dry specimens which he had seen, and mistook them for *roots*.

A singular description of the *sumbul* by *Abu'lfazl*, who frequently mentions it as an ingredient in *Indian* perfumes, had for some time almost convinced me that the true *Spikenard* was the *Cetaca*, or *Pandanus* of our botanists: his words are, *Sumbul panj berg dared, ceh dirazii an dah angoshtestu pahnai, seh*, or, " The *sumbul* has five leaves, ten fingers long, and " three broad." Now I well knew that the minister of *Achar* was not a botanist, and might easily have mistaken a thyrsus for a single flower : I had seen no blossom, or assemblage of blossoms, of such dimensions, except the male *Cetaca*; and, though the *Persian* writer describes the female as a different plant, by the vulgar name *Cyora*, yet such a mistake might naturally have been expected in such a work : but what most confirmed my opinion, was the exquisite fragrance of the *Cetaca*-flower, which to my sense far surpassed the richest perfumes of *Europe* or *Asia*. Scarce a doubt remained, when I met with a description of the *Cetaca* by *Forskohl*, whose words are so perfectly applicable to the general idea which we are apt to form of *Spikenard*, that I give you a literal translation of them :—" The *Pandanus* is an incomparable " plant, and cultivated for its odour, which it breathes " so richly, that one or two *Spikes*, in a situation ra- " ther humid, would be sufficient to diffuse an odo- " riferous air for a long time through a spacious " apartment; so that the natives in general are not " solicitous about the living plants, but *purchase the* " *spikes at a great price.*" I learned also, that a fragrant essential oil was extracted from the flowers; and I procured from *Banares* a large phial of it, which was adulterated with sandal ; but the very adulteration convinced me, that the genuine essence must be valuable, from the great number of thyrsi that must be

D d 3

required in preparing a small quantity of it. Thus
had I nearly persuaded myself, that the true nard was
to be found on the banks of the *Ganges*, where the
Hindu women roll up its flowers in their long black
hair after bathing in the holy river; and I imagined,
that the *precious alabaster-box* mentioned in the scripture, and the *small onyx*, in exchange for which the
poet offers to entertain his friend with *a cask of old
wine*, contained an essence of the same kind, though
differing in its degree of purity with the nard which
I had procured; but an *Arab* of *Mecca*, who saw in
my study some flowers of the *Cetaca*, informed me
that the plant was extremely common in *Arabia*,
where it was named *Cudhi*; and several *Muhomedans*
of rank and learning have since assured me, that
the true name of the *Indian Sumbul* was not *Cetaca*,
but *Jatamansi*. This was important information: finding, therefore, that the *Pandanus* was not peculiar to
Hindustan, and considering that the *Sumbul* of *Abulfazl* differed from it in the precise number of leaves
on the thyrsus, in the colour, and in the season of
flowering, though the length and breadth corresponded very nearly, I abandoned my first opinion, and began to inquire eagerly for the *Jatamansi*, which grew,
I was told, in the garden of a learned and ingenious
friend, and fortunately was then in blossom. A fresh
plant was very soon brought to me. It appeared on
inspection to be a most elegant *Cyperus* with a polished three-sided culm, an umbella with three or four
ensiform leaflets minutely serrated, naked proliferous
peduncles, crowded spikes, expanded daggers; and
its branchy root had a pungent taste with a faint aromatic odour; but no part of it bore the least resemblance to the drug known in *Europe* by the appellation of *Spikenard*; and a *Muselman* physician from
Dehli assured me positively, that the plant was not
Jatamansi, but *Sud*, as it is named in *Arabic*, which
the author of the *Tohfatu'l Mumenin* particularly dis-
tinguishes from the *Indian Sumbul*. He produced on

the next day an extract from the Dictionary of Natural History, to which he had referred; and I present you with a translation of all that is material in it.

" 1. *Sud* has a roundish olive-shaped root, exter-
" nally black, but white internally, and so fragrant as
" to have obtained in *Persia* the name of *Subterranean
" Musk*: its leaf has some resemblance to that of a
" leek, but is longer and narrower, strong, somewhat
" rough at the edges, and tapering to a point. 2. *Sum-
" bul* means a *spike* or *ear*, and was called *nard* by
" the *Greeks*. There are three sorts of *Sumbul* or
" *Nardin*; but, when the word stands alone, it means
" the *Sumbul* of *India*, which is an herb *without flower
" or fruit* (he speaks of the drug only) like the tail
" of an ermine, or of a small weasel, but not quite so
" thick, and about the length of a finger. It is dark-
" ish, inclining to yellow, and very fragrant; it is
" brought from *Hindustan*; and its medicinal virtue
" lasts three years." It was easy to procure the dry
Jatamansi, which corresponded perfectly with the description of the *Sumbul*; and, though a native *Muselman* afterwards gave me a *Persian* paper, written by
himself, in which he represents the *Sumbul* of *India*,
the *Sweet Sumbul*, and the *Jatamansi* as three different
plants, yet the authority of the *Tohfatu'l Mumenin* is
decisive that the *Sweet Sumbul* is only another denomination of nard; and the physician who produced
that authority, brought, as a specimen of *Sumbul*,
the very same drug which my *Pandit*, who is also a
physician, brought as a specimen of the *Jatamanti*.
A *Brahmen* of eminent learning gave me a parcel of
the same sort, and told me that it was used in their
sacrifices; that, when fresh, it was exquisitely sweet,
and added much to the scent of rich essences, in which
it was a principal ingredient; that the merchants
brought it from the mountainous country to the
north-east of *Bengal*; that it was the entire plant,

not a part of it, and received its *Sanscrit* names
from its resemblance to *locks of hair*; as it is called
Spikenard, I suppose, from its resemblance to a spike
when it is dried, and not from the configuration of its
flowers, which the *Greeks*, probably, never examined.
The *Persian* author describes the whole plant as resembling the tail of an ermine; and the *Jatamansi*,
which is manifestly the *Spikenard* of our druggists,
has precisely that form, consisting of withered stalks
and ribs of leaves, cohering in a bundle of yellowish
brown capillary fibres, and constituting a spike about
the size of a small finger. We may, on the whole,
be assured, that the *nardus* of *Ptolemy*, the *Indian
Sumbul* of the *Persians* and *Arabs*, the *Jatamansi* of
the *Hindus*, and the *Spikenard* of our shops, are one
and the same plant; but to what class and genus it
belongs in the *Linnean* system, can only be ascertained
by an inspection of the fresh blossoms. Dr. *Patrick
Russel*, who always communicates with obliging facility his extensive and accurate knowledge, informed
me by letter, that " Spikenard is carried over the de-
" sert" (from *India*, I presume) " to *Aleppo*, where
" it is used in substance, mixed with other perfumes,
" and worn in small bags, or in the form of essence,
" and kept in little boxes or phials, like *atar* of roses."
He is persuaded, and so am I, that the *Indian* nard
of the antients and that of our shops, is one and the
same vegetable.

Though diligent researches have been made at my
request on the borders of *Bengal* and *Behar*, yet the
Jatamansi has not been found growing in any part of
the *British* territories. Mr. *Saunders*, who met with
it in *Butan*, where, as he was informed, it is very
common, and whence it is brought in a dry state
to *Rangpur*, has no hesitation in pronouncing it a
species of the *Baccharis*; and, since it is not possible that he could mistake the *natural order* and

essential character of the plant, which he examined, I had no doubt that the *Jatamansi* was composit and corymbiferous with stamens connected by the anthers, and with female prolific florets, intermixed with hermaphrodites. The word *Spike* was not used by the antients with botanical precision, and the *Stachys* itself is verticillated with only two species out of fifteen, that could justify its generic appellation. I therefore concluded that *the true Spikenard* was a *Baccharis*, and that, while the philosopher had been searching for it to no purpose,

———————————— the dull swain
Trod on it daily with his clouted shoon;

for the *Baccharis*, it seems, as well as the *Conyza*, is called by our gardeners, *Ploughman's Spikenard*. I suspected, nevertheless, that the plant which Mr. *Saunders* described was not *Jatamansi*; because I knew that the people of *Butan* had no such name for it, but distinguished it by very different names in different parts of their hilly country: I knew also that the *Butias*, who set a greater value on the drug than it seems, as a perfume, to merit, were extremely reserved in giving information concerning it, and might be tempted, by the narrow spirit of monopoly, to mislead an inquirer for the fresh plant. The friendly zeal of Mr. *Purling* will probably procure it in a state of vegetation; for, when he had the kindness, at my desire, to make inquiries for it among the *Butan* merchants, they assured him, that the living plants could not be obtained without an order from their sovereign the *Devaraja*, to whom he immediately dispatched a messenger with an earnest request, that eight or ten of the growing plants might be sent to him at *Rangpur*. Should the *Devaraja* comply with that request, and should the vegetable flourish in the plain of *Bengal*, we shall have ocular proof of its class, order, genus, and species; and if it prove the same with the

Jatamansi of *Nepal*, which I now must introduce to your acquaintance, the question with which I began this essay will be satisfactorily answered.

Having traced the *Indian* Spikenard, by the name of *Jatamansi*, to the mountains of *Nepal*, I requested my friend Mr. *Law*, who then resided at *Gaya*, to procure some of the recent plants by the means of the *Nepalese* pilgrims; who, being orthodox *Hindus*, and possessing many rare books in the *Sanscrit* language, were more likely than the *Butias* to know the true *Jatamansi*, by which name they generally distinguish it. Many young plants were accordingly sent to *Gaya*, with a *Persian* letter specifically naming them, and apparently written by a man of rank and literature; so that no suspicion of deception or of error can be justly entertained. By a mistake of the gardener they were *all* planted at *Gaya*, where they have blossomed, and at first seemed to flourish. I must therefore, describe the *Jatamansi* from the report of Mr. *Burt*, who favoured me with a drawing of it, and in whose accuracy we may perfectly confide; but, before I produce the description, I must endeavour to remove a prejudice, in regard to the *natural order* of the Spikenard, which they, who are addicted to swear by every word of their master *Linnæus*, will hardly abandon, and which I, who love truth better than him, have abandoned with some reluctance. *Nard* has been generally supposed to be a *grass*; and the word *stachys* or *spike*, which agrees with the habit of that natural order, gave rise, perhaps, to the supposition. There is a plant in *Java*, which most travellers and some physicians call *spikenard*; and the Governor of *Chinsura*, who is kindly endeavouring to procure it thence in a state fit for examination, writes me word, that a " *Dutch* author pronounces it a *grass like the Cypirus*, " but insists that what we call the *spike* is the fibrous " part above the root, as long as a man's little finger,

" of a brownish hue inclining to red or yellow, rather
" fragrant, and with a pungent, but aromatic scent."
This is too slovenly a description to have been written
by a botanist; yet I believe the latter part of it to be
tolerably correct, and should imagine that the plant
was the same with our *Jatamansi*, if it were not commonly asserted that the *Javan* spikenard was used as
a condiment; and if a well informed man, who had
seen it in the island, had not assured me that it was a
sort of *Pimento*, and consequently a species of *Myrtle*,
and of the order now called *Hesperian*. The resemblance before mentioned between the *Indian sumbul*
and the *Arabian Sud*, or *Cyperus*, had led me to suspect that the true nard was a *grass*, or a *reed*; and, as
this country abounds in *odoriferous grasses*, I began to
collect them from all quarters. Colonel *Kyd* oblig-
ingly sent me two plants with sweet-smelling roots;
and, as they were known to the *Pandits*, I soon found
their names in a *Sanscrit* dictionary: one of them is
called *gandhasat'hi*, and used by the *Hindus* to scent
the red powder of *Supan*, or *Bukkam*-wood, which they
scatter in the festival of the vernal season; the other
has many names, and, among them, *naguramastac*
and *gonarda*; the second of which means *rustling in
the water*; for all the *Pandits* insist that *nard* is never used as a noun in *Sanscrit*, and signifies, as the root
of a verb, *to sound*, or *to rustle*. Soon after, Mr. *Burrow* brought me, from the banks of the *Ganges* near
Heridwar, a very fragrant grass, which in some places
covers whole acres, and diffuses, when crushed, so
strong an odour, that a person, he says, might easily
have smelt it, as *Alexander* is reported to have smelt
the nard of *Gedrosia* from the back of an elephant:
its blossoms were not preserved, and it cannot, therefore, be described. From Mr. *Blane* of *Lucnow*, I
received a fresh plant, which has not flowered at *Calcutta*; but I rely implicitly on his authority, and have
no doubt that it is a species of *Andropogon*: it has

rather a rank aromatic odour, and, from the virtue
ascribed to it of curing intermittent fevers, is known
by the *Sanscrit* name of *jwarancusa*, which literally
means a *fever-hook*, and alludes to the *iron-hook* with
which the elephants are managed. Lastly, Dr. *Anderson* of *Madras*, who delights in useful pursuits and
in assisting the pursuits of others, favoured me with a
complete specimen of the *Andropogon Nardus*, one
of the most common grasses on the coast, and
flourishing most luxuriantly on the mountains, never
eaten by cattle, but extremely grateful to bees, and
containing an essential oil, which, he understands,
is extracted from it in many parts of *Hindustan*, and
used as an *atar*, or *perfume*. He adds a very curious
philological remark, that, in the *Tamul* dictionary,
most words beginning with *nar* have some relation to
fragrance; as *narukeradu* to yield an odour; *narium
pillu*, lemon-grass; *nartei*, citron; *narta manum*, the
wild orange-tree; *narum panei*, the *Indian Jasmin*; *narum alleri*, a strong smelling flower; and *nartu*, which
is put for *nard* in the *Tamul* version of our Scriptures;
so that not only the *nard* of the *Hebrews* and *Greeks*,
but even the *copia narium* of *Horace*, may be derived
from an *Indian* root. To this I can only say, that I
have not met with any such root in *Sanscrit*, the oldest
polished language of *India*; and that in *Persian*, which
has a manifest affinity with it, *nar* means a *pomegra-
nate*, and *nargil* (a word originally *Sanscrit*) a *cocoa-
nut*; neither of which has any remarkable fragrance.

Such is the evidence in support of the opinion given
by the great *Swedish* naturalist, that the true nard was
a gramineous plant, and a species of *Andropogon*;
but since no grass, that I have yet seen, bears any resemblance to the *Jatamansi*, which I conceive to be the
nardus of the antients, I beg leave to express my dis-
sent, with some confidence as a philologer, though with
humble diffidence as a student in botany. I am not,
indeed, of opinion that the *nardum* of the *Romans*

was merely the essential oil of the plant from which
it was denominated, but am strongly inclined to believe
that it was a *generic* word, meaning what we now call
atar, and either the *atar* of roses from *Cashmir* and
Persia, that of *Cetaca*, or *Pandanus*, from the western coast of *India*, or that of *Aguru*, or aloe-wood,
from *Asam* or *Cochinchina*, the process of obtaining
which is described by *Abulfazl*, or the mixed perfume, called *abir*, of which the principal ingredients
were yellow sandal, violets, orange-flowers, wood of
aloes, rose-water, musk, and true Spikenard: all those
essences and compositions were costly; and, most of
them being sold by the *Indians* to the *Persians* and
Arabs, from whom, in the time of *Octavius*, they
were received by the *Syrians* and *Romans*, they must
have been extremely dear at *Jerusalem* and at *Rome*.
There might also have been a pure *nardine oil*, as
Athenæus calls it; but *nardum* probably meant (and
Koenig was of the same opinion) an *Indian* essence *in
general*, taking its name from that ingredient which
had, or was commonly thought to have, the most exquisite scent. But I have been drawn by a pleasing
subject to a greater length than I expected, and proceed to the promised description of the *true nard* or
Jatamansi, which, by the way, has other names in the
Amarcosh, the smoothest of which are *jatila* and *lomasa*,
both derived from words meaning *hair*. Mr. *Hurt*, after
a modest apology for his imperfect acquaintance with
the language of botanists, has favoured me with an
account of the plant, on the correctness of which I
have a perfect reliance, and from which I collect the
following *natural characters* :

AGGREGATE.

Cal. Scarce any. *Margin* hardly discernible.
Cor. One petal. *Tube* somewhat gibbous. *Bor-
der* five cleft.
Stam. Three *anthers*.
Pist. *Germ* beneath. One *style* erect.

Seed solitary, crowned with a pappus.
Root fibrous.
Leaves hearted, fourfold ; *radical* leaves petioled.

It appears, therefore, to be the *Protean* plant, *Vale-
rian*, a sister of the Mountain and *Celtic* Nard, and
of a species which I should describe in the *Linnæan*
style, *Valeriana Jatamansi floribus triandris, foliis cor-
datis quaternis, radiculibus petiolatis.* The radical
leaves, rising from the ground and enfolding the
young stem, are plucked up with a part of the root,
and, being dried in the sun, or by an artificial heat,
are sold as a drug, which from its appearance has been
called *spikenard*; though, as the *Persian* writer observes, it might be compared more properly to the
tail of an ermine. When nothing remains but the dry
fibres of the leaves, which retain their original form,
they have some resemblance to a *lock of hair*, from
which the *Sanscrit* name, it seems, is derived. Two
mercantile agents from *Butan* on the part of the *Devaraja* were examined, at my request, by Mr. *Har-
rington*, and informed him that the drug, which the
Bengalese called *Jatamansi*, "grew erect above the
"surface of the ground, resembling in colour an ear
"of green wheat; that, when recent, it had a faint
"odour, which was greatly increased by the simple
"process of drying it; that it abounded on the hills,
"and even on the plains, of *Butan*, where it was
"collected and prepared for medicinal purposes."
What its virtues are, experience alone can ascertain ;
but, as far as botanical analogy can justify a conjecture, we may suppose them to be antispasmodic; and,
in our provinces, especially in *Behar*, the plant will
probably flourish; so that we may always procure it
in a state fit for experiment. On the description of
the *Indian* Spikenard, compared with the drawing, I
must observe, that, though all the leaves, as delineated, may not appear of the same shape, yet all of

them are not fully expanded. Mr. *Burt* assures me
that the four radical leaves are *hearted and petioled*;
and it is most probable, that the cauline and floral
leaves would have a similar form in their state of perfect expansion; but, unfortunately, the plants at *Gaya*
are now shrivelled; and they who seek farther information, must wait with patience until new stems and
leaves shall spring from the roots, or other plants shall
be brought from *Nepal* and *Butan.* On the proposed
inquiry into the virtues of this celebrated plant, I must
be permitted to say, that, although many botanists
may have wasted their time in enumerating the qualities of vegetables, without having ascertained them by
repeated and satisfactory experiments, and although
mere botany goes no farther than technical arrangement
and description, yet it seems indubitable that the great
end and aim of a botanical philosopher is to discover
and prove the several uses of the vegetable system;
and, while he admits with *Hippocrates* the *fallaciousness
of experience,* to rely on experiment alone as the basis
of his knowledge.

APPENDIX.

A

METEOROLOGICAL DIARY,

KEPT AT CALCUTTA,

By *HENRY TRAIL, Esq.*

From 1st February 1784, to 31st Decem. 1785.

REMARKS.

IN the following Diary of the Weather, begun the
1st of February 1784, every change in the air was
marked down with the greatest precision three times
every day, and always nearly at the same hours, viz.
at sun-rising at three, or half past three o'clock in the
afternoon, and at eleven o'clock at night.

While the wind continued southerly, the Thermometer was placed in a Verandah open to the Esplanade,
where there was at all times a free circulation of air;
and when the wind became northerly, the instrument
was removed to the opposite side of the house, and
equally exposed, as in the preceding part of the year.

The Barometer continued always in the same
place.

The Hygrometer made use of, was a bit of fine
sponge, suspended in a scale (on the end of a steel-
yard) first prepared for more easily imbibing the
moisture, by dipping it in a solution of Salt of Tartar, afterwards drying it well, and bringing it to an
equilibrium by a weight in the opposite scale, at a
time when the atmosphere appeared to have the
least degree of moisture.

A semicircular scale at the top, divided from o to
90° on each side, with the needle of the yard, pointed
out the quantity of moisture gained or lost daily;
but in the following Diary the degrees of moisture
have seldom been taken down.

E e 2

Every fall of rain was likewise taken, and the quantity in cubic inches daily noted down.

The winds were also observed, and the figures 0, 1, 2, 3, 4, denote the force thereof.

Here it may be remarked, that at sun-rising, there is seldom or ever any wind ; but no sooner is the air a little rarefied by its rays, than a little breeze begins, and this generally increases till about noon, when again it begins to lose its force, and dies away, from the same cause.

In order to ascertain the influence of the Moon upon the weather, the mean temperature, as well as the weight of the atmosphere of each quarter, is accurately marked down by taking in the three days preceding, and the three days after the change with the intermediate day. From these, the density is discovered, by the following rule given by Dr. *Bradely*, viz.

A, altitude of barometer; B, altitude of thermometer; D, density.

$$\frac{A}{B \times 350} = D - \text{or density.}$$

N. B. In this, the mean morning density is only taken. However, the mean density for the whole may be found by the same rule.

January 1, 1785. From an examination of one year's observations on the influence of the Moon on the mercury in the Barometer, it does not appear that there is any certain rule to be laid down regarding it. However, it may be affirmed that the direc-

tion of the winds has more effect upon it, as we never
fail to see the mercury highest when the wind blows
from the NW; in a lesser degree from the N, and
lowest of all when it proceeds from the SE quarter.

A General State of the Weather for February 1785.

	M.	N.	E
Greatest altitude of the Thermometer,	73°	86	78
Least ditto,	66	70	68
Mean ditto,	72	78	71

74 11-3d Mean temperature.

Clear, - - - 3 days.
Cloudy, - - - 26 do.
N° of days on which it rained, 8 do.
Quantity of rain, - 4·3 Inch

This month the wind very variable, and the atmosphere for the most part cloudy, and sometimes several days succeeding without any sun; the air also damp and cold. Frequently thunder, and on the 8th there was a fall of hail in the afternoon, accompanied with thunder.

The mornings generally foggy.

Calcutta, February 1784.

D	Thermometer M	N	E	Mean morning declivity of each quarter of the Moon.		Wind Points	Force	Appearance of the air.	REMARKS.
1	68	75	72			W	0	Cloudy,	Sunday.
2	68	78	72			N	0	ditto,	Heavy, with a great appearance of rain.
3	67	74	69			NE	0	ditto,	ditto.
4	68	77	68			S	0	ditto,	ditto.
5	71	79	71			SW	1	ditto,	ditto.
6	72	80	74	Full Moon 70 3–7ths	1	NW	1	ditto,	A thick fog all day.
7	71	82	75			S	1	Clear,	
8	70	80	74				1	Cloudy,	Some hail in the afternoon, with thunder.
9	74	80	75				2	ditto,	
10	75	80	74				1	ditto,	A great appearance of rain, very dark.
11	72	77	73		.2	NW	1	ditto,	ditto, a few drops of rain.
12	73	79	76	L. Q. 71 6 7ths	.1	S	3	ditto,	ditto.
13	73	80	74		.1	NW	2	ditto,	ditto.
14	74	81	75		0.5		1	ditto,	Much thunder this morning, with a heavy shower.
15	75	78	74			S	0	ditto,	
16	72	81	74				1	Clear,	A few drops of rain.
17	70	76	71			var.	0	Hazy,	
18	69	79	70			S	1	ditto,	Very gloomy, and a great appearance of rain, very close, no sun all day.
19	69	77	69			W	2	ditto,	
20	70	77	70	New Moon 70 3–7ths	0.5	N	3	Cloudy,	ditto.
21	73	75	73		.4	W	0	Hazy,	
22	70	83	70				0	ditto,	ditto.
23	72	84	72				0	Cloudy,	Clear at intervals.
24	71	76	77		.1	NW	1	ditto,	ditto.
25	76	76	68	F. Q. 67 1–7ths		W	0	ditto,	Very thick.
26	68	68	67			NW	0	ditto,	Thunder, very moist and wet.
27	67	74	67				1	Clear.	Very chilly.
28	67	76	60						
	72	79	73		4.2	var.	2	Cloudy,	Mean state of the atmosphere.

A General State of the Weather for March.

Greatest altitude of Thermometer,
Least ditto, - -
Mean ditto, - -

M	N.	E.
84	89	85
66	75	71
75	84	79

} 79 1-3d Mean temperature.

Clear,   16 days
Cloudy,   15 do.
Rain,   3 do.
Quantity of do. 1.8 inch.

The wind almost continually southerly, and strong blasts towards the end of the month ; the weather throughout clear and serene, and heavy dews at night ; which indeed must always be the case when they are preceded by a clear warm sun.

In blowing weather dews are seldom seen, the moisture as it falls being dispelled by the wind.

The heat of the earth this month about mid-day, about 120°.

Calcutta, March 1784.

Days	Thermometer			Mean morning heat at each quarter of the Moon	Inch. of rain	Wind		Appearance of the air	REMARKS.
	M.	N.	E.			Points.	Force.		
1	66	80	71			SW	1	Clear,	Monday.
2	67	80	71			W	1	ditto,	Moist.
3	70	81	76			9	4	ditto,	Thunder, but no rain.
4	71	85	76		1	W	0	Cloudy,	Thunder, early this morning.
5	71	84	74			SE	1	Hazy,	
6	73	81	74					Cloudy,	
7	72	78	74	Full Moon 7h 57m				ditto,	Great appearance of rain.
8	69	75	71			S.	1	Clear,	The weather very fine and dry.
9	70	80	74					ditto,	ditto.
10	70	81	75			var.	0	ditto,	ditto
11	70	82	75				1	ditto,	ditto
12	69	81	75				1	ditto,	ditto.
13	70	83	77	L. Q. 7h 6m		9	3	ditto,	
14	75	86	83				0	ditto,	The morning foggy.
15	76	86	82				0	Cloudy,	Very close and sultry.
16	72	86	81				0	Clear,	ditto.
17	74	83	81			var.	0	ditto,	ditto.
18	78	87	83		0.3		8	Hazy,	ditto.
19	80	80	83				3	Clear,	The wind high.
20	80	86	82	New Moon 7h 3.7m		W	3	Cloudy,	ditto, thunder.
21	77	85	83			S	2	ditto,	ditto,
22	80	86	84				0	Clear,	
23	80	83	82				2	Cloudy,	Moist.
24	80	81	83				1	ditto,	ditto.
25	81	85	85	P. Q. 8h 2.7m	0.5			ditto,	Very thick.
26	83	84	84			var.	4	ditto,	A great appearance of rain.
27	84	86	80			S	3	ditto,	The wind boisterous.
28	77	84	81				3	ditto,	ditto.
29	75	81	83				1	ditto,	ditto.
30	72	86	81				1	Clear,	
31	76	84	81					ditto,	
mean	75	84	79		1.3		5	Clear.	Mean state of the atmosphere.

A General State of the Weather for April.

	M.	N.	E.	
Greatest altitude of the Thermometer,	86	97	87	
Least ditto,	71	87	79	} 86 1-3d Mean temperature.
Mean ditto,	83	91	83	

Clear,	14 days
Cloudy,	16 do.
Rain,	6 do.
Quantity of do.	3-1 inch.

The prevailing wind this month, as well as the former, south; the mean heat of the earth at mid-day, 126°. Blowing and heavy weather in general, and frequent thunder-storms about the end, although many of the nights were close and sultry.

The thunder-storms that generally prevail at this time of the year, always happen in the afternoon or evening, and come from the NW, and are attended with loud peals and heavy falls of rain. Before these storms begin, the clouds become very dark and low; and the winds being thus confined between the clouds and earth, must of course, be greatly augmented.

Calcutta, April 1784.

Day.	M.	N.	E.	Mean morning heat at each quarter of the Moon.		Wind Point.	Force.	Appearance of the air.	REMARKS.
1	79	89	85			S	1	Clear,	Thursday.
2	81	97	91				0	ditto,	
3	83	91	85				4	Cloudy,	Disagreeable blowing weather.
4	83	89	89				3	ditto,	ditto.
5	83	87	84				4	ditto,	ditto.
6	83	85	85				3	Cloudy,	ditto.
7	83	91	86	Full M. 81 6-7ths			2	Hazy,	ditto.
8	83	91	86				4	Clear,	
9	84	97	87				2	ditto,	
10	84	94	87				1	ditto,	The night very close.
11	86	97	95				0	ditto,	ditto.
12	86	95	93	L. Q. 84 3-7ths			0	ditto,	
13	86	91	84			SE	0	ditto,	Hard blowing weather with much dust.
14	87	91	86			8	8	Cloudy,	ditto.
16	85	90	80				3	ditto,	A heavy thunder-storm in the evening.
17	84	88	84		0.4	SW	3	ditto,	
18	80	87	79		1.5	NW	3	ditto,	High wind.
19	74	89	85	New M. 81 3-7ths	0.5	9	4	ditto,	Very close.
20	83	91	86				2	Clear,	Strong wind.
21	85	95	91				9	ditto,	ditto.
22	85	91	87				3	Hazy,	
23	83	92	91				3	Clear,	Close and sultry.
24	83	91	86		0.4		9	ditto,	
25	83	90	84	P. Q. 83 1-7ths	0.2		1	Cloudy,	With rain and thunder.
26	84	88	85				4	ditto,	ditto, from NW.
27	80	88	86		0.1		4	ditto,	ditto. ditto.
28	83	90	88				1	ditto,	ditto.
29	85	88	85				0	ditto,	
30	84	89	85				4	ditto,	High wind.
mean	83	91	85		3.1	S	4	Cloudy,	Mean state of the atmosphere.

A General State of the Weather for May.

	M.	N.	E.	
Greatest altitude of the Thermometer,	85		88	
Least ditto,	75	82	74	} 84 21-31st Mean temperature
Mean ditto,	81	84	84	

Clear, 7 days.
Cloudy, 84 do.
Rain, 14 do.
Quantity of do. 9-6 inches.

The wind southerly, with a few pretty violent storms from the NW, at the beginning of the month, while the latter part was close, gloomy, and warm ; but in general, the whole month was exceedingly cloudy, and scarcely a single day of bright sun-shine.

The rains began on the 22d, and from that day to the end, the nights were very close and sultry, and the air very damp.

Calcutta, May 1784.

Days	Thermometer		Mean morning heat of each quarter of the Moon.	d. M.	Wind		Appearance of the air.	REMARKS.
	M	N	E		Point.	Force		
1	81	86	81		4.	S	3	Cloudy,	Saturday, a violent storm.
2	77	88	74		1.		3	ditto,	Very heavy do. No sun.
3	77	83	79		0.6		4	ditto,	ditto.
4	78	87	84				1	Hazy,	And close.
5	81	89	84	Full Moon 79 6-7ths	0.5		1	ditto,	No sun all day.
6	83	90	87				3	ditto,	A thunder storm in the evening.
7	84	90	83				3	ditto,	High wind at times.
8	83	90	86				1	Clear,	ditto.
9	83	90	87				3	Hazy,	
10	84	84	87		0.4		3	Cloudy,	Very thick and dark.
11	77	90	78	Last Quarter 79 6-7ths	0	SE	3	ditto,	A thunder-storm in the evening.
12	75	84	84		4.	E	3	ditto,	No wind.
13	77	83	80			S	8	ditto,	
14	75	85	83			var.	0	Clear,	
15	80	86	84		0.1	8	0	ditto,	Thunder in the evening.
16	83	90	83				0	ditto,	The weather very close and still.
17	78	91	86				0	ditto,	ditto.
18	81	91	87	New Moon 83 6-7ths			1	ditto,	ditto.
19	84	90	87		0.6		3	Cloudy,	At intervals.
20	85	93	83		0.4		0	Clear,	Very still.
21	85	91	85				3	Cloudy,	Thunder in the evening.
22	84	91	83		0.1	SE	4	ditto,	ditto.
23	84	90	89		0.1	NW	4	ditto,	ditto.
24	82	89	85	F. Q. 83 6-7ths		NW	1	ditto,	ditto.
25	83	92	84		0.4	NW	8	ditto,	ditto.
26	84	86	84				4	ditto,	ditto.
27	81	82	81				4	ditto,	ditto.
28	80	86	83		0.4		3	ditto,	A great appearance of rain.
29	81	89	84				3	ditto,	The night very sultry.
30	51	89	51				3	ditto,	ditto.
31	42	60	46		0.2	S	2	ditto,	Thunder. &c.
	80	88	84		9.6	8	3	Cloudy,	Mean state of the atmosphere.

A General State of the Weather for June.

	Mt.	N.	E.
Greatest altitude of the Thermometer, . . .	84	90	86
Least do.	7	40	78
Mean do.	81	85	85

85 Mean temperature.

Clear, 3 days,
Cloudy, 19 do.
Rain, 14
Quantity of do. 17·4 inches.

The wind, this month, inclining sometimes to the E. of S. The atmosphere exceedingly moist and wet, and much rain from the 10th to 17th, the sky mostly clouded throughout, and very little variation in the temperature of the air.

Calcutta, June 1794.

Days	M.	N.	E.	Mean height of each quarter of the Moon.	Rain.	Wind Points	Wind Force	Appearance of the air.	REMARKS.
1	86	82	82		0.7	S	1	Cloudy,	Tuesday, thunder
2	80	86	84		1.2		1	ditto,	
3	81	84	85	Fall M. 68 3-7th		var.	1	ditto,	A gentle shower. Close.
4	82	85	85		0.8		3	ditto,	
5	81	87	85				0	ditto,	
6	82	82	84		0.5	NE	0	ditto,	Several showers.
7	82	72	82		1.8		1	ditto,	
8	81	84	82				0	ditto,	No sun all day.
9	80	84	83	L Q 80 1-7th		S	0	ditto,	Incessant rain all day. Ditto.
10	81	83	81		1.1		2	ditto,	
11	79	86	80		1.6		1	ditto,	
12	78	78	78		4.6		1	ditto,	
13	77	80	80		0.1	W,	3	ditto,	Thunder in the evening
14	81	85	86		0.4	var.	1	Hazy,	No sun all day.
15	81	85	81		0.1	3	1	Cloudy,	Ditto.
16	80	82	79	New M. 81 1-7th	1.3		0	ditto,	Ditto.
17	81	83	85		0.8		1	Hazy,	Ditto.
18	81	89	85				1	ditto,	Sun very faint.
19	81	86	86			SE	1	ditto,	Very thick, and no sun.
20	80	83	85			SE	1	ditto,	The night very close.
21	84	90	95				1	ditto,	Ditto.
22	84	89	89	F. Q 82		var.	0	ditto,	Ditto.
23	81	90	84			SE	0	4 ito,	D tto.
24	83	89	84			3	0	Cloudy,	Ditto.
25	84	87	81				0	Cloudy,	Ditto.
26	91	97	87			var.	1	Hazy,	Thunder.
27	81	81	81		2.2	3		ditto,	High wind.
28	9.	98	81					Clear,	
29						SASE	4	Cloudy,	Mean state of the atmosphere
30					17.4				

A General State of the Weather for July.

	M.	N.	E.	
Greatest altitude of the Thermometer,	84	90	85	
Least ditto,	77	77	78	} 83 Mean temperature.
Mean ditto,	81	85	83	

Clear,   1 day
Cloudy,   30 ditto
Rain,   30 ditto
Quantity of ditto, 15 inches.

The prevailing wind SE, and the atmosphere, as the former month, exceedingly thick and humid, and very little sun-shine. The mean temperature exactly the same as last month, and very little variation between the heat at mid-day and that of the morning and evening.

During the rains the wind is often variable, but commonly it comes round to the eastward, when there falls much rain.

Calcutta, July 1784.

Day	Thermometer E.	M.	N.	Mean morning heat of each quarter of the Moon.	Rain	Winds Points	Force	Appearance of the air.	Remarks.
1	84	87	83	THURSDAY.		S	2	Clear,	The wind strong in the morning, but the night very still and clear.
2	84	88	83				2	Cloudy,	
3	81	85	83			SE	4	ditto,	
4	80	86	84	Full Moon 88.	0.4		3	ditto,	
5	84	89	84				2	Hazy,	
6	84	89	84				0	Cloudy,	
7	85	85	84		0.1		6	ditto,	The night very bright.
8	86	86	91		0.1	var.	2	ditto,	ditto, thunder.
9	82	83	82	L.Q. 80 3-7ths	1.1		2	ditto,	ditto.
10	84	86	83		0.9		2	ditto,	ditto.
11	83	86	81		0.3		3	ditto,	Much lightning in the evening.
12	84	86	83		0.2		2	ditto,	
13	83	84	81		2.6		2	ditto,	Several small showers.
14	82	83	82			SE	2	ditto,	
15	82	91	82				3	ditto,	Rained all day.
16	82	83	78		0.9		0	ditto,	
17	82	83	77	New M. 79 5-7ths	0.1	S	2	ditto,	Small rain, very dark.
18	82	85	79		0.8	SE	2	ditto,	On the 9th there had been no rain at Chunar, many persons sick, but chiefly among the natives.
19	80	85	80				3	ditto,	
20	80	83	77				2	ditto,	
21	81	84	72		0.1	F.	0	ditto,	Much thunder and lightning.
22	80	85	72		0.3	SE	2	ditto,	
23	80	85	80	F.Q. 79 6-7ths	1.7		1	ditto,	
24	79	83	80			SW	2	ditto,	Thunder.
25	80	83	81		0.1	S	2	ditto,	
26	81	86	81		0.1	SW	3	ditto,	
27	81	86	83		0.2		2	ditto,	High winds.
28	81	86	84				2	ditto,	Thunder.
29	81	83	83		1.9		3	ditto,	Rain all the day.
30	79	82	73		3.6		2	ditto,	
31	78	79	79					ditto,	
mean	82	85	81		15.	SASE	2	Cloudy	Mean state of the atmosphere.

A General State of the Weather for August.

		M.	N.	L.	
Thermometer,	Greatest altitude,	83°	89°	84°	} 81° 2-3ds Mean tempera-ture.
	Least do.	77	80	80	
	Mean do.	81	85	82	
Barometer,	Greatest do.	29.75	29.75	29.76	} Mean state of the atmosphere—29.57.
	Least do.	29.57	29.56	29.61	
	Mean do.	29.67	29.66	29.70	
	Greatest variation,	.18	.19	.15	
	Mean d-rainy,	.693	.698	.598	} .686 density.
Hygrometer,	Greatest moisture,	50°	45°	45°	
	Ditto drought,	3 15	10	10	
	Mean drought and moist,	d 21 8m	1d 18m	2d 15m	

Clear,   5 days.
Cloudy,   16 do.
Rain,   13 do.
Quantity do. 16.4 inches.

The air still very moist and very little sun-shine, although the nights in general were very bright and fine: frequently thunder, and on the 22d, an exceeding loud peal early in the morning. The quantity of rain that fell this month was very considerable, and every thing inhibiting the moisture to the highest degree.

The Barometer is almost invariably higher at night than in the morning, and lowest always at mid-day. The air being much loaded with moisture the whole of this month, the variation of the mercury was very insensible. The same causes kept the Thermometer nearly stationary also.

Calcutta, August 1784.

Days	Thermometer			Mean density of each quarter of the Moon	Barometer			Hygrometer						Rain	Wind and Force				Hour
	M.	N.	E.		M.	N.	E.	M. d.	N. d.	N. m.	d.	fi.			Point	W.	N.	E.	
1	77	83	80	F.M. SUNDAY	29.64	29.64	29.73	10	15		10		1.1	S	0	1	0	Cloudy.
2	80	86	81		.69	.69	.73	15	13	20	5		0.4		0	1	0	ditto.
3	80	86	83		.70	.63	.70	15	10	20				SE	1	1	0	ditto.
4	82	84	83		.66	.64	.66	15	15	19	0		0.4	E	0	1	0	Clear.
5	81	86	83		.61	.61	.71	11	19	10			0.1	SE	0	1	0	Cloudy.
6	81	86	84		.70	.70	.74	30	30	10			0.1		1	1	0	ditto.
7	82	86	84		.75	.75	.75	21	40	30	0		0.3	S	0	1	0	ditto.
8	81	85	83		.74	.74	.74	30	35	30					0	1	0	ditto.
9	81	87	83		.70	.70	.73	11	35	30		30	0.4		1	0	0	Clear.
10	82	87	83	L.Q.	.71	.71	.75	13	40	40		40	0.7		0	0	0	ditto.
11	83	85	83	687	.72	.72	.72	45	45			8	0.8	SE	0	0	0	Cloudy.
12	81	86	81		.70	.70	.74	45	45	10			0.7		1	0	0	ditto.
13	81	87	82		.74	.74	.77	10	10	35		15	1.9	S	0	0	0	ditto.
14	81	85	81		.74	.72	.74	10	10	35		11	1.8	SE	0	0	0	ditto.
15	81	81	81		.70	.60	.61	15	15	40		30	0.8		1	0	0	ditto.
16	79	83	80		.60	.56	.64	45	43	30	0	40	0.5		0	0	0	ditto.
17	81	83	80		.69	.69	.64	45	45	45		30			0	1	0	ditto.
18	77	80	81	N.M.	.74	.74	.74	40	40	35	0	45	.19	SW	1	1	1	ditto.
19	77	78	80	689	.71	.75	.72	50	45	15	0	10	.03		0	0	1	Clear.
20	78	84	81		.71	.64	.69	45	50	10		5			0	0	0	Hazy.
21	79	86	83		.65	.61	.67	10	10	0	0			S	0	0	0	Cloudy.
22	82	85	83		.67	.64	.66	30	30	0	0	5	0.1	SE	0	1	1	ditto.
23	82	85	84	F.Q.	.64	.61	.64	15	15	0			0.1	E	0	1	1	ditto.
24	82	85	82	689	.64	.64	.63	10	10		10	6	0.7	SE	0	0	1	ditto.
25	81	85	84		.60	.56	.61	8	8			8	0.2		1	1	1	ditto.
26	80	84	81		.59	.59	.65	10	10	5		10	0.6		1	1	3	ditto.
27	80	84	83	F.M.	.19	.19	.65	10	10	5		10		SW	4	3	3	ditto.
28	80	81	83	688	.44	.64	.58	33	33	15			1.0	SW	4	3	3	ditto.
29	81	85	83		.62	.65	.69	20	20	10					4	2	1	ditto.
30	81	85	82		.66	.60	.74	45	45	5						1	1	ditto.

A General State of the Weather for September.

		M.	N.	E.	
Thermometer,	Greatest altitude,	8.?	90°	85°	} 8·¼ mean temperature.
	Least do.	76	77	74	
	Mean do.	80	85	81¾	
Barometer,	Greatest do. in.	29·45	27·95	29·97	} Mean state of the atmosphere —29.81.
	Least do.	20·12	29·58	30·75	
	Mean do.	29·81	29·90	29·83	
	Greatest variation,	0·33	0·21	0·22	
	Mean density,	·693	·645	·692	} ·690 density.
Pygrometer,	Greatest moisture,	60¾	65°	65°	
	Prime drought,	10	40	15	
	Mean density and moisture,	5d 14m	10d 14m	5d 15m	

Clear,　　　10 Days.
Cloudy,　　20 do.
Rain,　　　12 do.
Quantity do.　11·3 inches.

The wind generally S and SE, much lightning in the evenings, but not attended either with rain or thunder. The air still damp and cloudy, although the Barometer stood considerably higher than the preceding month.

It is worthy of observation, that upon the rains going off, the water falls in larger drops than at any other period of the season, and probably this may be occasioned from the height it has to fall: and in proof of this, the opposite stations of the Barometer need only be consulted, where it appears that the weight of the atmosphere was greatly increased about the last period of the rains.

Calcutta, September 1784.

Days	Thermometer.			Mean density at each quarter of the Moon.	Barometer.			Hygrometer.							Rain	Wind and Force.			
	M.	N.	E.		M.	N.	E.	M.		N.		E.				Point.	M.	N.	N.
1	81	86	83	WEDNESDAY.	29.71	29.72	29.79	40		5		10			2.0	S.	0		Cloudy.
2	81	89	84		.79	.81	.84	15		20		5				SE.	0		Clear.
3	83	83	83		.84	.81	.84	35		20		15				SW.	0		Cloudy.
4	83	87	83		.82	.78	.76	30		20		30					0		Hazy.
5	81	83	83		.74	.77	.75	20		20		40					0		ditto.
6	82	89	83		.75	.82	.78	15		0		20					0		Cloudy.
7	81	89	83		.77	.81	.81	15				10		10		S	0		Cl.a.
8	82	82	84		.80	.81	.85	15		10		0				S	0		ditto.
9	83	89	83		.79	.72	.78	5	10	0		15	5			SW			ditto.
10	83	90	85		.76	.71	.78	5		20		30	20			SE			ditto.
11	84	90	85		.72	.73	.82					40	25			NE			ditto.
12	84	87	84		.81	.80	.79	0		0		20	20						Cloudy &c
13	81	84	83		.77	.75	.78	15	10	5		10	10			N			Heavy
14	82	81	83		.77	.80	.80	15	10	10		0	0		0.7	NE			ditto.
15	77	81	81		.78	.80	.78	20		38		0			0.3	SE			ditto.
16	79	80	80		.93	.79	.78	18		30					1.5				ditto.
17	79	81	79		.79	.77	.84	35		55					0.9				ditto.
18	77	77	78		.84	.79	.87	30		55					1.2				ditto.
19	76	80	79		.86	.89	.91	60				15			1.1				d.to.
20	78	80	78		.91	.87	.95	65				45			0.3				ditto.
21	78	80	78		.95	.90	.97	60	45	45					1.1	SE			ditto.
22	78	80	80		.94	.88	.98	45	35	35					0.7	E			ditto.
23	78	83	80		.91	.84	.82	40	30	30						SE			ditto.
24	79	84	80		.91	.84	.86	35		5		0				S			ditto.
25	78	85	86		.87	.86	.86	20		0		0			1.6	SE			Clear.
26	78	83	79		.80	.54	.80		10							ver.			Cloudy.
27	80	81	82		.80	.72	.81	5	20	5		0				S			Clean.
28	79	82	84		.84	.81	.80	10	35	0						SE			ditto.
29	80	86	84		.89	.87		10	15										ditto.
30	81	69	81				.41												Cloudy.

A General State of the Weather for October.

		M.	N.	E.	
Thermometer,	Greatest altitude,	8½	90	85	} 61¾ Mean temperature.
	Least do.	74	77	76	
	Mean do.	79	66¼	81½	
Barometer,	Greatest do. in.	30.04	30.00	30.02	} Mean state of the atmosphere.—29.91
	Least do.	29.74	29.77	29.78	
	Mean do.	29.91	29.91	29.91	
	Greatest variation,	0.30	0.11	0.26	
Hygrometer,	Mean density,	.697	686	.693	} .693 density.
	Greatest moisture,	41	85	30	
	Ditto drought,	30	50	41	
	Mean moist and drought	3d 7m 3pd 10s 2d 3m			

Clear,   19 days
Cloudy,   12 do.
Rain,   3 days.
Quantity of do. 2-8 inches.

The air very clear and elastic, and heavy dews at night. The Barometer very high, and the wind W and NW.

About the middle of the month the mornings became a little foggy, which indicates the approach, or beginning, of the cold season: the atmosphere thin and dry, and cleared of its vapours; of course the mercury rose in the Barometer.

As the difference between the day and the night heat begins now to be greater than in any of the eight preceding months, the fogs we have at this season of the year are by that means formed.

Calcutta, October 1784.

Day	Thermometer M.	N.	E.	Mean density at each quarter of the Moon	Barometer M.	N.	E.	Hygrometer						Rain	Wind and Force Point	M.	N.	E.	
1	83	84	94	Friday.	29.91	29.93	29.93	3		10	39		10	0.6	SE	0	3	1	Cloudy
2	81	89	83		94	90	87			15	15		0	0.2	S	0	3	1	ditto
3	82	88	80		90	83	87			15	15				SE	0	1	1	ditto
4	80	84	83		83	78	86	5		40	45				9	0	3	0	ditto
5	81	88	84		76	78	78	5		80	45				NE	0	1	1	Clear
6	81	90	83		76	77	75	9		40	45				var.	0	1	0	ditto
7	82	97	82	L. Q. 698	74	77	77	0		40	35					0	1	0	Cloudy
8	82	88	81		77	37	83			44	35				W	0	1	0	Clear
9	80	82	83		81	87	86			44	30				W	1	1	0	ditto
10	79	89	86		88	87	66	10		41	15			0.1		0	1	0	ditto
11	83	90	89	New Moon 696	30.03	90	30	10		15	13		30			0	1	0	ditto
12	92	96	95		29.98	94	29.97	15		23	15		15			0	1	0	ditto
13	80	89	94		99	91	94	15		30	20				SW	0	1	0	ditto
14	80	85	95		91	89	91	18		40	18				SW	0	1	0	ditto
15	80	87	93		91	93	93	0		35	30				W	0	1	0	ditto
16	80	83	88		94	P.	94	0		35	30				NW	0	1	0	ditto
17	78	87	91		94	23.97	96	0		40	25					0	1	0	ditto
18	80	87	91		30.01	98	30.01	0		43	30					0	1	0	ditto
19	80	82	83		04	98	29.98	10		41	30					0	1	0	ditto
20	77	83	81		29.95	96	97	10		58	45		30		N	0	2	0	ditto
21	78	88	61		10.	99	98	30		50	46		15		N	0	2	0	ditto
22	78	87	74	F. Q. 702	29.95	94	93	10		0	40		5			3	3	0	Cloudy
23	75	80	76		96	89	93		40	3	10			ses	NW	3	1	0	ditto
24	75	77	79		91	88	91		35	15	40					1	1	0	ditto
25	74	84	80		93	90	93		20	30	40					1	1	0	ditto
26	76	93	86		93	89	94		0	30	35					1	1	0	ditto
27	76	66	90		94	94	96		0	44	30					1	1	0	Clear
28	76	88	91		94	94	99			35	40					0	1	0	ditto
29	77	83	78	Full Moon 705	99	30.	99	10		40	40					0	1	1	ditto
30	75	85	86		95	29.95	30	10		45	40					0	1	0	ditto
31	75	81	80		30.	30.	30.66	70								0	1	0	ditto
m.	79	86	83		30.63	30.03	30.66							0.8	WNW	0.6	1	0.6	Clear.

A General State of the Weather for November.

		M.	N.	E.	
Thermometer,	Greatest altitude,	78°	84	90	⎫ 78 Mean temperature.
	Least do.	66	75	71	
	Mean do.	71½	80½	75½	⎭
Barometer,	Greatest do. in.	30.12	30.05	30.28	⎫ 30.00 mean standard at-
	Least do.	29.60	29.88	29.92	mosphere.
	Mean do.	30.00	29.99	30.02	⎭
	Greatest variation,	00.48	00.17	00.36	
Hygrometer,	Mean density,	.78½	.696	.706	⎫ 70½ density.
	Greatest moisture,	40	15	15	
	Ditto drought,	44	51	52	⎭
	Mean moist and drought,	42	33	33½	sum 284

Clear,   23 days.
Cloudy,   7 do.
Rain,   1 do.
Quantity of do. 0·9 inches.

The NW winds prevailed this month; but nothing remarkable in the change of the atmosphere, although there were several appearances of rain in the course of it. The air more elastic than any of the former months, also more serene and dry. The foggy mornings still keep off.

In clear dry weather there is always a very sensible change on the Barometer two or three hours after sun-rising; it being often near one-tenth of an inch higher about nine o'clock than at six, or sun-rise. May not this be owing to the load of vapour condensed and kept near the surface of the earth from the coldness of the night, which, as it is gradually rarefied by the heat of the sun, must increase the weight and spring of the atmosphere, and produce this variation? From hence, the Barometer is always higher in the evening before these watery particles fall than in the morning when the air is replete.

Calcutta, November 1784.

Days	Thermometer M.	N.	E.	Mean density at each quarter of the Moon.	Barometer M.	N.	E.	Inst-meter M. d.	N. m.	d.	Rain.	Wind and Force Point.	W.	N.	E.	
1	74	85	80	Monday.	30.01	29.99	30.03			35		NW	0	1	0	Clear.
2	77	84	80		.05	.96	.05			40			0	1	0	Cloudy.
3	77	86	82		.00	.98	.66			30			0	1	0	Clear.
4	76	85	80		.00	30.00	.03			35			0	1	0	Cloudy.
5	74	85	79	L.Q.	.00	29.97	.01			35			0	1	0	Clear.
6	76	74	80	705	.00	30.00	.01			38			1	1	0	ditto.
7	76	86	78		.01	.01	.01			45			0	1	1	ditto.
8	73	81	78		.04	.02	.02			40			1	1	0	ditto.
9	73	83	78		.08	.02	.06			45		N	0	1	0	ditto.
10	72	81	76		.10	.08	.08			50		NE	1	1	3	Cloudy.
11	74	79	76	N.M.	.11	.04	.05			45		N	0	1	0	ditto.
12	74	79	77	707	.06	.04	.07		15	35			0	1	0	Clear.
13	75	71	75		.04	.95	.02						1	1	0	ditto.
14	77	77	73		29.63	29.93	.No	40	15	15 15	0.9		1	1	0	ditto.
15	73	70	73		30.05	.95	29.94	40		18		NE	1	1	0	ditto.
16	73	80	71		.05	30.05	30.00	10		15		N	1	1	0	ditto.
17	67	78	74		.04	.01	.06	20		15		NE	0	1	0	ditto.
18	65	73	75	P.Q.	.03	.01	.04	20		35		NW	1	1	0	ditto.
19	69	73	75	718	.04	29.99	.05	0		40		N	0	1	0	Hazy.
20	69	79	74		.03	30.02	.01			35		NW	0	1	0	Clear.
21	64	79	73		.12	29.97	29.97			30			0	1	0	Cloudy.
22	65	73	73		29.98	.91	.91	5	5	15		N	0	1	0	Clear.
23	70	78	71		.97	.98	.93	15		35			0	1	0	ditto.
24	68	78	71	F.M.	.96	.93	30.02	40		35			0	1	0	Cloudy.
25	67	79	73	717	.03	30.03	.01		5	15		N	0	1	0	Clear.
26	67	79	67		.00	.06	.04			20		NW	0	1	0	ditto.
27	69	80	75		.00	.00	.01			30			0	1	0	ditto.
28	67	80	73		.01	29.99	.04			30			0	1	0	ditto.
29	67	80	77		.01	30.01	.18			15			0	1	1	ditto.
30												NW				Clear.
mean	71	80	75					8		18	0.9	NW				

A General State of the Weather for December 1784.

		M.	N.	E.	
Thermometer,	Greatest altitude,	6½	72	71	68 a–yds
	Least do.	58	68	65	Mean beat.
	Mean do.	63⅜	74	65⅜	
Barometer,	Greatest do.	30.17	30.17	30.14	30°.08
	Least do.	30.02	30.02	30.00	Mean state of the at-
	Mean do.	30.09	30.09	30.07	mosphere.
	Greatest variation,	00.15	00.15	00.14	
	Mean density,	.717	.709	.711	.717 M. D.
Hygrometer,	Mean moist and drought,	14 d.	48 d.	18 d.	

Clear,   16 days.
Cloudy,   5 do.
Rain,   1 do.
Quantity of do. 0.03 inch.

The winds were constantly NW, except a few days, when it was inclined a little to the E, which always brings on cloudy thick weather. The whole month remarkably dry, and the atmosphere of such a density as greatly to exceed any of the former. At this season of the year there is generally a thick disagreeable fog in the mornings and evenings : however, this month, on the contrary, has been very clear and serene, and but seldom thick fogs at either of these times.

Days	Thermometer			Mean density of each quarter of the Moon	Barometer			Hygrometer				Rain	Wind and Force				Weather
	M.	N.	E.		M.	N.	E.	N.j	N.m	g.d	g.m		Point	M.	N.	E.	

Moon quarters: L. Q. 72¹ — N. M. 728 — F. Q. 725 — F. M. 73²

A General State of the Weather for January 1785.

		M.	S.	L.	
Thermometer,	Greatest altitude,	70	78	74	} M. h.
	Least do.	57	69	63	66
	Mean do.	61	73	66 a-gds	
Barometer,	Greatest do.	30.17	30.14	30.17	} Mean state of the atmosphere 30.0².
	Least do.	29.98	29.97	30.03	
	Mean do.	30.08	30.12	30.09	
	Greatest variation,	00.19	00.17	00.14	
	Mean density,	.732	.718	.733	} 732 M. D.
Hygrometer,	Moisture and drought.	30 d.	30 d.	40 d.	
	Clear, 29 days.				
	Cloudy, 2 do.				

The atmosphere very dry and elastic.

The winds variable; but from the middle of the month were almost constantly from the SW and S, and often pretty strong.

The mercury in the Barometer stood very high till about the end of the month, when a very sensible change took place, both with regard to the warmth and serenity of the weather. Frequent heavy dews about the same time.

The mornings always very foggy.

The medium heat of the sun at mid-day (the instrument being exposed five minutes) was 90°.

Calcutta, January 1785.

Days	Thermometer			Mean density of each quarter of the Moon.	Barometer			Hygrometer			Rain	Wind and Force				
	M.	N.	E.		M.	N.	E.	M.	N.	E.		Point.	M.	N.	R.	
1	60	69	64		30.09	30.09	30.09	30	50	45		WN	0	1	0	Clear.
2	57	69	64		.09	.09	.11	40	50	41		NW	0	1	0	ditto.
3	59	71	65		.11	.06	.07	35	45	40			0	1	0	ditto.
4	63	69	66		.04	.08	.08	30	50	41		WNW	0	2	0	ditto.
5	63	70	66		.07	.03	.11	35	50	46			0	2	0	ditto.
6	63	70	67		.11	.13	.17	36	50	50		W	1	2	0	ditto.
7	59	72	65	Last Quarter 732.	.14	.13	.10	35	60	50		NW	1	1	0	ditto.
8	59	71	67		.10	.09	.09	35	60	45		N	0	1	0	ditto.
9	58	70	65		.17	.10	.14	40	66	50		NW	0	1	0	ditto.
10	55	71	65		.17	.11	.13	35	60	45			1	1	0	ditto.
11	55	72	66	N. M. 736.	.12	.11	.11	37	51	45		N	0	1	0	ditto.
12	60	77	67		.14	.14	.14	35	46	50		NW	1	2	0	ditto.
13	58	77	65		.15	.15	.17	40	50	50			0	1	0	ditto.
14	57	70	65		.17	.15	.10	45	55	55		N	0	1	0	ditto.
15	60	69	65		.08	.05	.06	40	60	55		NW	1	2	0	ditto.
16	53	70	65	F. Q. 730.	.15	.05	.07	45	55	50			0	1	0	ditto.
17	58	72	67		.03	.00	.08	45	40	55		SW	0	2	0	ditto.
18	59	74	65		.04	.04	.03	40	55	50		W	0	2	0	ditto.
19	52	72	67		.44	.03	.07	42	60	55		SW	0	2	0	ditto.
20	52	70	66	F. M. 728.	.08	.08	.03	40	55	50		W	0	1	0	ditto.
21	59	70	68		.07	.01	.03	30	45	45			0	1	0	ditto.
22	62	72	69		29.98	29.97	.03		40	40		SW	0	3	0	ditto.
23	61	74	70		30.01	30.01	.44	10	55	30	10	S	0	1	0	ditto.
24	67	75	73		.07	.02	.05	40	60	30	10	SW	2	2	1	Cloudy.
25	66	76	73		.00	.01	.03		0	50	10	S	0	1	1	ditto.
31	70	79	74													Clear.
mean	61	72	66½		30.08	30.00	30.00									

A General State of the Weather for February 1785.

	M.	N.	E.	
Thermometer, Greatest altitude,	74	86	76	} 75 Mean temperature.
Least do.	63	75½	69	
Mean do.	71	79½	74	
Barometer, Greatest do.	30.14	30.17	30.15	} 30.01 Mean state of
Least do.	29.59	29.69	29.96	the atmosphere.
Mean do.	30.03	30.01	31.04	
Greatest variation,	0.55	2.18	0.19	
Mean density,	.713	.698	.765	} .706
Hygrometer, Moisture and drought.	0	31 d.	21 d.	

Clear,   17 days,
Cloudy,   11 do.
Rain,   4 ditto.
Quantity do.   2·9 inches.

Thunder five times. Mean heat of the sun at mid-day, the Thermometer being exposed five minutes 56°.

The beginning of this month the air was very moist, which is generally the case when the wind comes from the S and SE.

On the contrary, the NW winds which prevailed, renders it very dry and elastic, and has always a very great effect in raising the mercury in the barometer. During the whole of this month the mornings were extremely thick and foggy: on the 1st, 8th, and 12th, moderate storms from the NW.

Calcutta, February 1784.

Day	Thermometer			Mean density of each quarter of the Moon.	Barometer.			Hygrometer.								Rain.	Wind and Force.				Weather
	M.	N.	E.		M.	N.	E.	M.		N.		L.						Point.	M.	N.	E.	
1	71	77	74		30.00	29.92	29.95	90		0		40					0.5	S	1	4	1	Cloudy.
2	73	76	71		29.99	.89	.96	40		15		20						SE	0	1	0	ditto.
3	69	77	77		.96	.96	.11	30		5		30		30					0	1	0	Clear.
4	72	83	74		30.08	30.07	.04	4				25		15				s	0	1	0	Cloudy.
5	72	79	73		.08	.04	.04	4				20							1	1	1	Clear.
6	71	80	76		29.98	29.99	.04	50		15									1	1	1	Cloudy.
7	71	80	75		.98	30.04	.03	45		30		0						SE	1	1	0	Clear.
8	68	78	74		30.03	.04	.03	30		35		5					d.	E	1	1	0	ditto.
9	72	78	75		.97	29.99	.08	15				5						W	1	0	0	Cloudy.
10	72	80	72		29.97	.99	30.08	10										N	0	0	0	Clear.
11	73	85	69		.98	30.03	.12			40		30							3	3	3	ditto.
12	73	89	74		30.03	.03	.08	30		60		55					1.3	NW	0	1	0	ditto.
13	69	81	74		.05	.01	.06	35		45		40							0	1	0	Clear.
14	70	81	73		.04	.06	.08	30		50		30						SW	1	1	0	Cloudy.
15	70	75	73		.06	.06	.05	35		45		45							0	1	0	Cloudy.
16	67	80	71		.01	.01	.03	40		55		50					0.7	NW	1	0	0	ditto.
17	70	71	72		.06	.06	.05	35		35		55						SW	0	0	0	ditto.
18	67	75	73		.03	.03	.03	40		60									0	3	0	Clear.
19	69	79	73		.04	.04	.03	35		30		15						NW	1	1	0	ditto.
20	64	77	76		29.98	29.97	29.97			15		20						W	0	1	1	ditto.
21	70	81	76		.99	.96	30.00	15		10		15							0	1	1	ditto.
22	74	84	75		30.00	.98	29.98	10				45							0	0	1	ditto.
23	71	88	75		29.98	.96	.97	20		10		55						NW	0	0	1	Cloudy.
24	72	86	75		.96	.96	30.00			20		55						NW	0	0	0	Clear.
25	72	81	74		30.03	30.03	.10			60		55							0	0	0	ditto.
26	73	83	76		.03	.03	.10			65		57							0	0	0	ditto.
27	70	61	71		.14	.17	.11												0	0	0	ditto.
mean	71	79½	74		30.01	30.01	30.04										3.9					

A General State of the Weather for March 1785.

		M.	N.	E.	
Thermometer,	Greatest altitude,	80°	90°	83°	} 79°
	Least ditto,	61	80	73	
	Mean do.	71	85	78	
Barometer,	Greatest do.	30.11	30.12	30.11	
	Least do.	29.85	29.84	29.86	} 29.95
	Mean do.	29.95	29.92	29.97	
	Greatest variation,	.27	.16	.27	
	Mean density,	.073	.845	.700	} .698
	Moisture and drought,	0.0	36 d.	11 d.	

Clear,   10 days.
Cloudy,   11 do.
Rain,   3 do.
Quantity do. 0-5 inches

Thunder five times. Mean heat of the sun 100°.

There were two or three thunder-storms this month; but gentle, and attended with little rain. Several mornings about the beginning were very foggy and damp, and continued so; but in a lesser degree nearly throughout the month. Heavy dews from the 15th.

The barometer continued low, which may proceed from the high winds that prevailed, as well as from the extreme rarefaction of the atmosphere at this season of the year. We had often the appearance of rain (as must always be the case) while the wind comes from the south quarter, and bringing with it so much vapour.

Calcutta, March 1785.

Days	Thermometer M.	N.	E.	Mean density at each quarter of the M.	Barometer M.	N.	E.	Hygrometer M.	d.	N.	d.	E.	℞ Rain	Wind Points	M.	N.	E.	
1	68	84	73		30.14	30.10	30.11	55		60		60		NW	1	2	0	Clear
2	68	84	73		.10	.07	.08	50		60		55			0	1	0	ditto
3	69	80	74		.05	.04	.04	50		55		50			0	1	0	ditto
4	72	81	75		.04	.02	.04	15		35		35		SW	2	4	2	ditto
5	73	87	75		.05	.03	.00	10		55		35			1	3	1	ditto
6	73	81	76		.03	29.98	.04			55		44			0	4	1	ditto
7	73	85	77	L. Q. .713	29.97	.99	.07	40		45		40		SE	0	4	1	Cloudy
8	73	87	77		30.01	30.02	.07	45		55		45	0.1		0	3	0	Clear
9	74	84	77		.06	.02	.05	15		50		40			0	3	1	Cloudy
10	74	85	76		.15	.04	.01	10		40		40		S	0	2	1	Clear
11	74	85	77		.01	29.98	19.93		5	30	10	30	0.3	SE	1	2	1	Cloudy
12	75	84	75	N. M. .709	19.98	.90	.89		5	15	10	15	(some hail)	SW	0	3	1	Clear
13	73	84	74		.90	.84	.93	35	0	40	25	40		SE	3	3	4	Cloudy
14	77	83	74		.93	.85	.93			20	35	15			4	3	3	ditto
15	77	86	77		.87	.87	.97	10		15	20	30	10	S	1	4	1	ditto
16	78	86	80		.96	.89	.93			21	25	21		SW	0	1	1	Clear
17	78	90	80	F. Q. .702	.91	.86	.88		10	50	35	50	10	SE	3	2	3	ditto
18	79	86	81		.85	.87	.87		10	40	30	40	10	SW	0	3	4	Cloudy
19	79	85	81		.84	.85	.89		10	30	20	30		SE	1	3	1	ditto
20	77	85	81		.87	.84	.89			10	30	10		S	0	3	0	ditto
21	78	87	81		.85	.87	.89			80	30	80	10		0	2	0	Clear
22	79	84	80		.87	.84	.93			10	20	10			1	2	2	ditto
23	79	88	81	F. M. .696	.85	.85	.86			80	30	30			1	1	1	ditto
24	79	88	81		.89	.91	.91			30	30	30			0	2	0	Cloudy
25	79	84	85		.87	.93	.91			15	35	15	5		2	2	2	Clear
26	60	84	84		.85	.87	.91			20	25	20	5		2	2	2	ditto
27	79	86	84		.90	.87	.95			80	30	80	10		0	0	0	Cloudy
31	79				.90	.95	.98	5		60		40			0	1	0	Clear
Sum	75	85	78		29.95	29.91	29.97	5					80	0.5		5	3	1	

A General State of the Weather for April 1785.

		M.	N.	E.	
Thermometer,	Greatest altitude.	83	91	85	
	Least do.	69	73	74	} 84
	Mean do.	79	86½	82	
Barometer,	Greatest do.	29.97	29.92	29.97	
	Least do.	29.70	29.68	29.74	} 69.83
	Mean do.	29.83	29.91	29.86	
	Greatest variation,	.87	.14	.13	
Hygrometer,	Mean density,	.695	.684	.691	Apl } 490
	Moisture and drought,	20 m.	20 d.	4 d	
	Clear,	17 days.			
	Cloudy,	13 do.			
	Rain,	6 do.			
	Quantity do.	8 inches.			

The quantity of rain that fell on the sixteenth and seventeenth was very considerable; and the variation that appeared on the mercury before and after the thunder-storms was very great, sometimes 00'.30 in the space of a few minutes.

Thunder six times. Mean heat of the sun 108° to 110°.

The temperature of the air throughout this month was less warm and sultry than it is generally found at this time of the year; as also, the storms that came from the NW were fewer in number. The air rather moist, and little or no variation in the winds, they being always directly S and SE.

Calcutta, April 1785.

Day	Thermometer			Mean density at each quarter of the Moon	Barometer			Hygrometer						Rain	Wind and Force				Weather
	M.	N.	E.		M.	N.	E.	M. d	M. m	N. d	N. m	H. d	H. m		Point	W.	N.	E.	
1	79	84	80		29.90	29.86	29.90	10							S	0	1	4	Clear.
2	75	85	80		.89	.89	.85	15			50					0	1	1	ditto.
3	77	90	84		.81	.77	.81				50					1	3	3	ditto.
4	77	92	83		.85	.80	.84				30					1	3	5	ditto.
5	79	93	83		.85	.80	.83				80					0	3	1	ditto.
6	79	90	81		.81	.81	.84				80		10			0	4	3	ditto.
7	78	88	80		.86	.85	.84				15					0	4	3	ditto.
8	78	87	84		.88	.83	.84	15			10					6	4	1	Cloudy.
9	80	87	84		.84	.81	.85	30	10					2.2	NW	1	7	4	Clear.
10	80	88	85		.81	.81	.86	30		40				3.8		1	4	4	Cloudy.
11	81	87	85		.78	.77	.85	50		80				3.5	NE	1	7	0	ditto.
12	81	85	85		.81	.82	.87	30		40					S	1	6	0	ditto.
13	81	83	83		.81	.80	.89	30		50						2	4	0	ditto.
14	83	84	83		.87	.86	.87	12		30				0.9		2	3	4	ditto.
15	81	85	83		.90	.91	.97	20								1	4	8	Clear.
16	78	84	83		.97	.92	.96	45				10			SE	1	3	0	Clear.
17	79	81	81		.96	.92	.81					80	80			2	0	1	Cloudy.
18	77	83	80		.81	.79	.94						80			0	1	1	Clear.
19	77	84	80		.81	.84	.90					10	10			0	1	0	Cloudy.
20	78	85	80		.85	.79	.93						10			1	1	1	Clear.
21	75	84	80		.85	.82	.90								W	1	3	1	Clear.
22	74	81	80		.83	.80	.87					10	10			1	1	0	Clear.
23	79	85	83		.83	.81	.80									1	4	1	Clear.
24	78	88	83		.77	.73	.78					10	10			2	3	1	ditto.
25	81	89	85		.76	.75	.77					20	10			4	4	4	Cloudy.
26	82	89	85		.71	.68	.73					10	10			4	4	4	ditto.
27	81	90	81		.71	.75	.74					15	16			1	3	3	ditto.
28	78	88	81		.70	.79	.84					15	15			1	4	3	ditto.
29	64	84	81		.76	.79	.83									0	3	1	ditto.
30	82	82	81		.82	.81	.84									0	3	1	Cloudy.
means	79	87	82		29.83	29.81	29.86												

A General State of the Weather for May 1785.

	M.	N.	E.	
Thermometer, Greatest altitude,	87	94	90	} 86
Least do.	79	67	80	
Mean do.	83	89¾	83	
Barometer, Greatest do.	29.96	89.92	30.03	
Least do.	29.60	29.53	29.63	} 29.77
Mean do.	29.77	29.74	29.62	
Greatest variation,	.36	.39	.30	
Hygrometer, Mean moisture,	1 m	30 d	20 d	
Mean density.	.625	.576	.685	} .682
Clear,	16 days.			
Cloudy,	15 days.			
Rain,	10 times.			
Quantity	6 inches.			

Thunder fourteen times. Mean heat of the sun 110° to 111°.

The air this month has been drier than that of the preceding; but the winds being more from the SE quarter, is the reason of the mercury being so low: much close and sultry weather about the middle. The variation on the Barometer much greater than usual.

Calcutta, May 1785.

Days.	Thermometer. M.	N.	E.	Mean density of each quarter of the Moon.	Barometer. M.	N.	E.	Hygrometer. M. d.	m.	N. d.	m.	E. d.	m.	Rain.	Wind and Force. Point.	M.	N.	E.	
1	82	92	86		29.82	29.80	29.81		40	10			10		S	1	0	1	Clear.
2	83	91	85		.77	.74	.75		35	20			10			0	2	2	ditto.
3	83	98	87	L.Q. .686	.75	.68	.75		30	20		20				1	1	2	ditto.
4	87	91	86		.76	.73	.81	15		40		10				6	3	1	ditto.
5	85	89	86		.78	.83	.87	0		30		20				1	4	4	Cloudy.
6	83	90	83		.96	.86	30.03	15		10		20		0.5		2	3	2	Clear.
7	81	87	93		.73	.73	29.94	10		35		30			E	1	1	1	Cloudy.
8	82	90	97	N.M. .690	.95	.98	.97		30	30		20			S	0	2	0	Clear.
9	83	[illegible]	85		.94	.89	.95		10	50		25				0	2	1	ditto.
10	85	89	95		.92	.85	.87	10		45		20		0.3	SE	0	4	0	ditto.
11	84	90	83		.80	.79	.83	10		50		30				0	2	2	ditto.
12	83	90	83		.80	.77	.85			50		15		0.1		0	2	2	ditto.
13	84	87	95		.80	.78	.83		10	45		15				3	3	0	ditto.
14	94	91	95		.83	.77	.82	25		50		30				0	1	0	Cloudy.
15	84	92	86		.84	.77	.80		10	60		55				0	1	0	Clear.
16	86	93	84	F.Q. .688	.81	.76	.86	40		60		35			SW	0	0	0	ditto.
17	82	[illegible]	95		.83	.81	.90	20		56		30				0	1	0	Cloudy.
18	80	[illegible]	84		.77	.86	.93		10	40		20		1.4	S	0	1	0	ditto.
19	81	[illegible]	86		.89	.81	.83	10		50		40			SW	1	0	0	Clear.
20	83	89	86		.80	.72	.79	10		50		40			S	0	0	0	Cloudy.
21	84	91	83		.75	.67	.79	10		55		40				0	1	1	Clear.
22	82	90	87		.74	.65	.75	30		40		40				0	1	0	Cloudy.
23	83	91	89	F.M. .685	.69	.55	.66	10		40		35			SE	0	1	0	Clear.
24	87	91	[illegible]		.63	.51	.66	20		20		20		0.2	S	0	0	4	Cloudy.
25	84	[illegible]	[illegible]		.60	.57	.61		10	60		10		0.3		1	0	0	ditto.
26	70	[illegible]	83		.65	.63	.70		10	50		20			SE	1	0	0	ditto.
27	[illegible]	90	80		.65	.63	.76		20	40			10	0.5		0	3	1	ditto.
28	[illegible]	88	85		.70	.70	.78		20	40			10			0	1	3	Clear.
29	81	88	82		.73	.70	.75	10		40		10		0.4	S	1	3	1	Cloudy.
30	84	90	85		.74	.66	.78		20	0				0.1		3	3	2	Clear.
31	[illegible]	87	85		.61	.68	.78		40		20		40	1.2	SW	2	1	1	Cloudy.
mean	83	89	83		29.77	29.74	29.80	8	9	40	1	23	3	6.0		4	2	2	Clear.

A General State of the Weather for June 1785.

		M.	N.	E.	
Thermometer,	Greatest altitude,	84	90	81	} 82
	Least do.	79	80	79	
	Mean do.	81½	84½	81	
Barometer,	Greatest do.	29.70	29.68	29.72	} 29.58
	Least do.	29.44	29.47	29.47	
	Mean do.	29.55	29.56	29.61	
	Greatest variation,	.26	.28	.25	
	Mean density,	.687	.681	.665	.684
Hygrometer,	Mean moisture,	30 m	30 m	40 m	

Clear, 4 days.
Cloudy, 16 do.
Rain, 14 times.
Thunder, 16 do.
Quantity rain, 14.4 inches.

Mean heat of the Sun 106°.

The quantity of rain this month has been uncommonly great: and scarce a day has passed without some falling; the weather of course disagreeable and unhealthy.

The mercury in the Barometer very low, which seldom fails to be the case while the winds come from the SE and E quarters.

Calcutta, June 1785.

Days	Thermometer.			Mean density at each quarter of the Moon.	Barometer.			Hygrometer.						Rain.	Winds.				Clear.
	M.	N.	E.		M.	N.	E.	M. d.	m.	N. d.	m.	E. d.	m.		Point.	M.	N.	E.	

A General State of the Weather for July 1785.

		M.	N.	E.	
Thermometer,	Greatest altitude,	8.4°	89	87	} 84
	Least do.	70	80	80	
	Mean do.	61	82	71	
Barometer,	Greatest do.	29.73	29.67	29.73	
	Least do.	29.44	29.45	29.47	} 29.59
	Mean do.	29.59	29.56	29.8	
	Greatest variation,	.49	.22	.26	
	Mean density,	.636	.681	.646	.684
Hygrometer,	Mean moisture,	50 m	35 m	45 m	

Clear,   4 days.
Cloudy,   27 do.
Rain,   14 times.
Quantity do. 11.6 inches.
Thunder,   11 times.

Mean heat of exposed air 100°.

The weather this, as the preceding month, very relaxing and disagreeable, although the quantity of rain only about one half. The low state of the mercury is undoubtedly affected by the easterly winds, as is no less the animal spirits.

Calcutta, July 1785.

Days	Thermometer			Mean density of each quarter of the Moon.	Barometer			Hygrometer			Rain.	Wind and Force				Clouds.
	M.	N.	E.		M.	N.	E.	M. d	N. m	E. d		points	M.	N.	E.	
1	81	86	85		29.47	29.46	29.52	40	30	40	0.1	SE	0	0	0	Cloudy.
2	80	86	83		.51	.51	.50	42	30	40	0.3	NE	1	1	0	ditto
3	79	83	81		.58	.53	.17	60	30	50	0.6		1	0	0	ditto
4	80	84	81		.56	.54	.39	60	58	60	0.3	S	0	1	0	ditto
5	81	80	83		.58	.54	.47	60	60	60	1.8	S	0	0	3	ditto
6	80	80	81		.54	.45	.57	60	60	60	0.1	SE	1	1	1	fine
7	80	82	82		.44	.47	.43	60	60	60	0.4	SE	1	1	1	ditto
8	80	79	81		.55	.37	.66	60	60	60		S	1	0	1	ditto
9	81	82	83		.60	.59	.18	60	60	60	8		1	0	1	ditto
10	80	83	82		.66	.65	.70	50	40	40	1.3	SE	1	0	1	ditto
11	81	83	83		.68	.57	.34	50	30	40	1.7		1	1	1	ditto
12	83	82	82		.66	.44	.61	50	40	50	0.1	SW	2	1	1	ditto
13	82	83	83		.55	.51	.68	50	40	50		SW	0	1	0	ditto
14	83	81	82		.51	.51	.44	50	40	40	0.3	S	1	0	3	date.
15	82	83	83		.61	.37	.57	50	40	40	0.3	SW	1	1	1	ditto.
16	82	85	84		.67	.49	.30	50	30	40	0.5	S	2	1	0	ditto.
17	80	83	81		.61	.50	.37	50	40	40	0.6	SE	1	1	4	Clear.
18	80	84	81		.58	.54	.80	50	30	40		SW	2	0	0	Cloudy.
19	80	84	83		.47	.55	.63	50	40	50	0.1		1	1	1	ditto.
20	80	82	82		.57	.62	.66	50	40	40	0.1	S	1	1	0	ditto.
21	81	82	82		.60	.64	.74	55	44	50		SE	1	0	1	ditto.
22	80	84	83		.66	.67	.71	55	42	60	R		1	0	0	ditto.
23	80	84	84		.73	.67	.73	55	30	10		s	0	0	0	Clear
24	84	85	85		.71	.69	.71	30	20	10	0.1	SE	0	0	0	ditto.
25	84	87	84		.72	.63	.67	30	10	20		S	1	1	1	Cloudy.
26	84	87	86		.70	.67	.64	30	0		0.3		0	0	0	date.
27	84	86	85		.67	.60	.66	30	0	20		NE	1	1	0	Clear.
28	84	89	87		.64	.58	.61	40	10	10	0.1		1	1	1	Cloudy.
29	84	87	85		.60	.56		40	20	20	0.3		0	1	0	ditto.
30	82	86	84		.57	.46		50	30	20	0.1		0	0	0	Cloudy.
31											0.1		0	0	0	ditto.
mean					29.59	29.56	29.61	50	33	45	12.0		4	1	6	Cloudy.

Mean density of each quarter of the Moon:
N. M. 66.4
F. Q. 68.6
F. M. 67.8
Last Quarter 73.1.

A General State of the Weather for August 1785.

		M.	k.	t.	
Thermometer,	Greatest altitude,	84	89	86	
	Least do.	79	80	80	
	Mean do.	81 1/4	84 1/2	61 1/2	82 2-3ds.
Barometer,	Greatest do.	29.78	29.78	29.78	
	Least do.	29.50	29.49	29.57	
	Mean do.	29.61	29.59	29.64	29.62
	Greatest variation,	1.2	.41	.121	
	Mean density,	.687	.681	.696	.695.
Hygrometer,	Moisture,	50 m	30 m	40 m	

Clear,   9 days
Cloudy,   19 do
Thunder,   15 times
Rain   no do.
Quantity of do. 9.3 inches.

The heat of the sun at mid-day 100°.

Much cloudy weather, but seldom any very heavy falls of rain, and the quantity altogether but moderate. The river very full; and accounts of heavy rains up the country.

The Barometer remarkably low the whole month: a proof of there being still much water in the clouds.

Calcutta, August 1785.

Days	Thermometer M.	N.	E.	Mean density of each quarter of the Moon	Barometer M.	N.	E.	Hygrometer M. d.	N. m. d.	E. m. d.	Rain	Wind and Force Point.	M.	N.	E.	Weather
1	80	84	84		29.53	29.50	29.58	50	40	40	0.3	SE	0	—	—	Cloudy, h. air.
2	81	86	89		.56	.53	.85	50	30	30			0	—	0	Cloudy
3	83	84	88		.59	.58	.63	50	30	30	0.1		0	—	0	ditto
4	82	87	85		.59	.58	.60	40	40	40	1.3		0	—	0	ditto
5	81	85	81		.56	.56	.61	40	40	40	0.9		1	—	0	ditto
6	80	84	81		.54	.56	.65	60	40	50	0.2		1	—	0	ditto
7	81	84	83		.61	.63	.74	50	40	50	1.4		0	—	1	ditto
8	80	84	81		.74	.74	.76	60	48	50	0.7		0	—	0	ditto
9	80	80	80	N. M. 685	.74	.68	.70	60	50	50			3	—	1	ditto
10	79	84	85		.74	.74	.61	60	30	50			0	—	1	Clear.
11	83	87	85		.60	.61	.64	50	40	40			2	—	1	Cloudy
12	81	85	83		.63	.59	.62	50	30	40	0.3	NE	0	0	1	ditto
13	81	87	82		.56	.50	.57	50	40	40	0.4	SE	0	0	—	ditto
14	81	86	84		.53	.49	.57	50	40	40	0.1		3	0	1	ditto
15	82	87	83		.53	.53	.81	50	20	20	1.3		0	0	0	ditto
16	82	84	83		.50	.54	.44	40	40	40			2	1	1	ditto
17	81	84	85		.61	.53	.63	40	30	30			0	0	—	ditto
18	83	84	87	F. M. 687	.60	.60	.61	50	30	30			0	0	—	d. Mn.
19	84	89	86		.58	.55	.66	40	20	20			0	0	0	ditto
20	80	89	85		.81	.60	.67	20	0	0	0.2		3	—	—	Clear.
21	84	83	85		.61	.37	.64	20	10	20	0.1	NE	4	1	1	Cloudy
22	83	87	91		.61	.60	.66	40	30	30	0.3		1	—	1	d ito.
23	81	84	81		.68	.62	.72	40	30	30			—	—	—	ditto.
24	83	85	84	L. Q. 690	.70	.70	.71	40	35	40	0.2	SE	0	0	0	ditto.
25	82	84	81		.78	.72	.75	40	30	30	0.1		0	0	0	ditto.
26	81	85	83		.74	.67	.72	40	20	20	0.2		0	0	0	ditto.
27	81	84	83		.72	.67	.73	40	20	20			0	0	0	ditto.
28	81	84	83		.67	.61	.69	70	30	30	1.4		1	—	0	ditto.
mean	81	85	83		29.52	29.59	29.64	50	30	40	9.3	SE	14	7	9	Cloudy.

General State of the Weather for September 1785.

		M.	N.	E.	
Thermometer,	Greatest altitude,	84°	83°	85	} 82 2-3ds.
	Least do.	80	61	80	
	Mean do.	82	82	82½	
Barometer,	Greatest do.	29.81	29.92	29.87	} 29.72.
	Least do.	29.7	29.68	29.66	
	Mean do.	29.	.21	29.75	
	Greatest variation,	.1		.11	
Hygrometer,	Moisture,	45 m	40 m	45 m	} .686.
	Density,	.681	.688	.678	.688

Clear,	8 days.
Cloudy,	11 do.
Thunder,	13 times.
Rain,	16 do.
Quantity do.	11.7 inches.

Mean heat of the sun at mid-day 110°.

The Barometer higher than the former month: about the middle and end, great quantities of rain. By account from Berhampore, the quantity of rain there must have been very considerable, and many parts above, the whole country being under water, and the river swelling prodigiously. This month very unhealthy and many people dying.

Calcutta, September 1785.

Days	Thermometer M.	Thermometer N.	Mean density at each quarter of the Moon	Barometer M.	Barometer N.	Barometer r.	Hygrometer M. d.	Hygrometer N. d.	Hygrometer N. m.	Hygrometer E. d.	Hygrometer E. m.	Rain	Wind Point	Wind M.	Wind N.	Wind E.	Weather
1	80	84		29.65	29.64	29.74	40		10		30		NE	2	3	2	Cloudy.
2	80	81		.70	.69	.77	30		20		30			1	1	1	ditto.
3	80	83		.73	.74	.71	50		20		20			1	1	0	Clear.
4	81	83		.77	.73	.80	40		10		20			0	1	0	ditto.
5	81	88	N. M. 692	.78	.76	.84	30	10						0	0	0	ditto.
6	81	89		.80	.74	.80	10	20						1	0	0	ditto.
7	84	89		.77	.73	.77	20	20						0	1	0	ditto.
8	82	89		.80	.73	.80	30	10						1	1	0	Cloudy.
9	84	87		.80	.76	.85	10	10				0.4		0	0	0	ditto.
10	81	84		.81	.82	.87	10		10		10			0	0	0	ditto.
11	81	84		.81	.77	.80	40		20		20	.5		1	1	0	ditto.
12	82	86		.97	.48	.73	40		20		20	.3	E	0	1	0	Clear.
13	81	84		.64	.43	.70	40		10		10	.6		0	0	0	Cloudy.
14	82	91	F. Q. 656	.66	.61	.69	40		30		20			1	0	0	Cloudy.
15	83	85		.84	.60	.63	40		30		30	.4	NE	2	1	1	ditto.
16	81	86		.66	.64	.73	50		40		30	.3		2	1	0	ditto.
17	81	88		.67	.64	.73	53		40		30	.1	E	1	1	0	Cloudy.
18	82	88	F. M. 688	.64	.61	.66	55		40		47	.4	NE	2	1	0	ditto.
19	80	86		.62	.59	.70	55		40		50	.5	SE	2	1	2	ditto.
20	80	82		.63	.60	.78	50		40		50	.1		2	1	1	ditto.
21	80	81		.72	.71	.80	50		30		10		E	3	3	3	ditto.
22	80	82		.78	.77	.74	42		40		10			2	2	2	ditto.
23	80	87		.73	.86	.72	10		10		20	1.3		1	0	0	Clear.
24	81	86	L. Q. 696	.66	.64	.71	10		0		10	1.7	SE	0	0	0	Cloudy.
25	80	82		.66	.61	.68	20		20		10	.6		1	1	1	ditto.
26	80	82		.66	.60	.67	30		20		20			2	2	2	ditto.
27	80	83		.61	.60	.71	50		50		50	3.5		2	2	3	ditto.
28	80	84		.66	.65	.72	50		10		20	.1		0	1	2	ditto.
29	80	85		.70	.71	.78							SE				ditto.
mean	81	85	81½	29.71	29.68	29.73	45	2	30	1	65	11.7	SE				

A General State of the Weather for October 1785.

		M.	N.	E.	
Thermometer,	Greatest altitude,	84	89	95	} .81
	Least do.	77	82	77	
	Mean do.	81	85½	81	
Barometer,	Greatest do.	29.78	19.96	29.03	} 29.92
	Least do.	21.63	29.81	27.35	
	Mean do.	29.90	29.87	29.92	
	Greatest variations,	.15	.15	.13	} .691
Hygrometer,	Mean density,	.694	.694	7 d.	

Clear,   21 days.
Cloudy,   10 do.
Thunder,   4 times.
Rain,   7 do.
Quantity,   1.4 inch.

The mean heat of the sun at mid-day 110°.

The wind began to set in from the NW about the 12th and 13th.

Calcutta, October 1785.

Days.	Thermometer. M	N.	E.	Mean density of each quarter of the Moon.	Barometer. M.	N.	E.	Hygrometer. M. d.	M. m.	N. d.	N. m.	E. d.	E. m.	Rain.	Wind and Force. Point.	M.	N.	E.	
1	83	85	84		29.84	29.80	29.85		30	20		10			NE	0	0	0	Clear.
2	82	89	83		.83	.82	.85		10	40		30				0	0	0	ditto.
3	83	87	85		.83	.81	.86	10		30		10				0	0	0	ditto.
4	82	87	84	N. M. 691	.84	.85	.90	20		40		10				0	0	1	ditto.
5	82	87	84		.88	.86	.93		0	30		0				0	0	0	ditto.
6	84	88	85		.95	.88	.92		10	10		0				0	0	0	ditto.
7	83	87	85		.90	.82	.90		0	10		0				0	0	1	ditto.
8	82	85	81		.89	.82	.90		0	10		0	10	0.3		1	1	1	Cloudy.
9	81	82	80		.88	.85	.91		10	0			10	0.6		1	2	2	ditto.
10	78	84	81		.91	.88	.96		10	30						1	1	1	ditto.
11	81	85	83	F. Q. 665.	.96	.90	.94		10	20		20		0.1		0	1	0	Clear.
12	83	87	82		.94	.90	.96		0	30		10			NW	0	1	1	ditto.
13	82	87	85		.93	.90	.96		0	40		20				0	1	0	ditto.
14	85	88	85		.95	.89	.93	10		40		10				0	1	1	ditto.
15	84	88	84		.93	.91	.98		0	40		10				0	1	0	ditto.
16	83	85	83		.98	.93	.96		0	10		0				0	1	1	ditto.
17	91	87	84	F.M. 693.	.97	.92	.93		10	40		20				1	1	0	ditto.
18	84	89	85		.93	.89	.93		0	30		20				1	1	0	ditto.
19	92	83	83		.92	.98	.94		0	30		20				0	1	2	ditto.
20	82	85	83		.90	.84	.98	20		50		30				1	1	1	ditto.
21	81	96	83		.90	.88	.91	20		50		50				0	1	0	ditto.
22	79	87	82		.92	.84	.89	10		50		20				0	1	2	ditto.
23	79	86	82		.91	.87	.93	10		50		30				0	2	0	ditto.
24	80	85	83		.92	.90	.93	20		40		20				2	0	0	ditto.
25	79	86	84	L. Q. 698.	.94	.90	.94		0	30		20	10			0	1	0	ditto.
26	78	83	79		.90	.88	.90		0	20			20	02	SW	0	2	2	Cloudy.
27	79	82	80		.86	.82	.86		30		10		20	R	NE	0	2	1	ditto.
28	78	82	79		.87	.84	.88		30		0		20			0	2	1	ditto.
29	77	82	79		.85	.82	.92		30		20		10			0	2	2	ditto.
30	78	82	79		.90	.96	.92		30		10		10	0.3	NW	0	1	0	ditto.
31	87	82	80		.92	.90	.95		20				10	0.1	NE	0	0	0	ditto.
mean	82	85½	82½		29.90	29.87	29.96	3	8	25	3	12	3	1.4	NW	½	1	½	Clear.

A General State of the Weather for November 1785.

	M.	N.	E.	
Thermometer, Greatest altitude,	Kc	85	82	} 75.
Least do.	67	74	71	
Mean do.	77	79d	71	
Barometer, Greatest do.	30.10	30.08	30.18	} 69.p.M.
Least do.	29.90	29.82	29.60	
Mean ditto.	29.99	29.98	30.80	
Greatest variation,	.80	.16	.78	} .703.
Hygrometer, Mean density,	.15d	.85d	.2dd	
	.709	.700	.706	

Clear, 16 days.
Cloudy, 4 do.
Rain, 4 times.
Quantity of do. 0-5 inches.

Mean heat of the sun at mid-day 100.

Calcutta, November 1785.

Days	Thermometer			Mean morning density at each Quarter.	Barometer			Hygrometer							Rain	Wind and Force				
	M.	N.	E.		M.	N.	E.	M.	N.	N. m.	d.	E. m.		Point	M.	V.	E.	
1	79	85	81		29.93	29.90	29.96	20	10			10		NW	0	2	0	Clear.
2	80	85	81		.95	.91	30.00	22	16			10		NE	0	2	0	ditto.
3	79	85	80	N. M.	.93	.97	29.96	20	20			10		NE	1	2	1	ditto.
4	77	81	79	.696	.94	.87	.91	20							1	1	1	ditto.
5	77	82	79		.88	.85	.80	10					30		1	1	0	ditto.
6	78	81	80		.91	.90	.97	20	30					R	0	1	1	Cloudy
7	77	80	75		.93	.91	.91	30	10						0	1	3	ditto.
8	71	77	77	F. Q.	.90	.94	.97	10			30				0	1	0	Clear.
9	71	80	77	704	.91	.44	0.03	30				30		R	0	1	0	ditto.
10	71	77	76		30.14	30.20	.10	10			10	10			0	1	0	ditto.
11	74	77	75		.48	.44	.77	15			10				0	1	0	ditto.
12	71	77	76		.08	.07	.11	10	10		40		0.4		0	1	0	ditto.
13	73	77	76	F. M.	.00	29.96	29.91	40	30		30				0	1	0	ditto.
14	74	79	76	710	29.90	.91	.95	40	0		40				0	1	0	ditto.
15	71	77	76		.96	.96	30.00	40	40		40				0	1	0	ditto.
16	71	77	73		30.02	30.04	.06	30	50		40				0	1	0	ditto.
17	71	77	73		.10	.04	.07	30	10		50				2	1	0	ditto.
18	69	77	74		.07	.04	.11	30	30		40				0	1	0	ditto.
19	71	77	73		.06	.02	.10	10	40		40				0	1	0	ditto.
20	71	77	74	L. Q.	.05	.02	.04	10	10		20			d	2	1	1	Cloudy
21	69	77	74	712	.01	29.91	29.97	20	30		40				0	1	2	Clear.
22	71	77	74		29.99	.94	.94	30	30		40				0	1	0	ditto.
23	71	73	73		.94	.90	.96	10	10		40				0	1	1	ditto.
24	70	73	72		.93	.78	.91	20	20		40				0	1	1	ditto.
25	70	77	72		.95	.00	30.06	40	50		50				0	1	1	ditto.
26	70	77	72		.00	30.01	.06	40	50		50				1	1	1	ditto.
27	68	73	71		.03	.00	.04	40	40		90				1	1	1	ditto.
28	67	74	71		.05	29.97	.00	40	50		60				1	1	1	ditto.
29	67	74	72		.52	.44	.00	40	50		50				0	1	0	ditto.
Mean	73	78¼	75		29.99	29.98	30.05									1 1½		4	Clear.

A General State of the Weather for December 1785.

		M.	N.	V.
Thermometer,	Greatest altitude,	70	76	73
	Least do.	6	71	66 } 69
	Mean do.	63½	73½	69
Barometer,	Greatest do.	30.09	30.06	30.10
	Least do.	29.97	29.90	29.99 } 30.01
	Mean do.	30.02	29.98	30.03
	Greatest variation,	.12	.16	.11
Hygrometer,	Mean density,	30 d	50 d	40 d } .716
		.716	.709	.719

Clear, 31 days.

The weather throughout the month remarkably clear and pleasant, and much milder than it is usually at this season of the year.

Mean heat of the sun at mid-day about 96°.

Calcutta, December 1785.

Days.	Thermometer. M.	Thermometer. N	Thermometer. E.	Mean density of each quarter of the Moon.	Barometer. M.	Barometer. N.	Barometer. E.	Hygrometer. M. d.	Hygrometer. M. m.	Hygrometer. N. d.	Hygrometer. N. m.	Hygrometer. E. d.	Hygrometer. E. m.	Rain.	Wind and Force. Points.	Wind and Force. M.	Wind and Force. N.	Wind and Force. E.	
1	68	76	78		30.00	29.97	29.99	30		50		40		NW	WW	1	1	0	Clear.
2	70	75	72	N. M. 714.	29.99	.95	30.00	30		50		40				0	1	0	ditto.
3	70	75	72		30.03	.98	.02	30		50		40				0	2	0	ditto.
4	69	75	72		.04	.98	.03	30		50		40				0	0	0	ditto.
5	68	75	71		.01	.96	.00	30		50		40				1	1	1	ditto.
6	67	75	71		29.98	.95	29.99	25		45		45				0	1	0	ditto.
7	67	74	71		.99	.96	.79	25		45		35				1	1	1	ditto.
8	67	74	69		.94	.99	30.04	30		45		35				0	1	1	ditto.
9	67	74	69	F. Q. 720	30.06	.99	.05	30		40		35				0	1	1	ditto.
10	67	74	69		.05	.97	.04	35		45		40				0	1	0	ditto.
11	67	75	70		.05	.94	.10	30		50		40				1	1	0	ditto.
12	68	75	70		.08	.99	.08	30		55		40				0	1	1	ditto.
13	66	75	70		.09	30.05	.04	30		55		40				0	2	1	ditto.
14	64	74	69		.06	.04	.09	30		55		45				0	1	0	ditto.
15	61	71	66	F. M. 728	.07	.03	.09	30		60		45				1	1	1	ditto.
16	63	71	67		.08	.02	.05	30		55		40				1	1	0	ditto.
17	63	72	67		.04	02	.04	25		35		40				0	1	1	ditto.
18	66	73	67		.03	00	.02	25		35		40				0	1	1	ditto.
19	64	73	68		.00	00	.01	25		40		30				1	1	0	ditto.
20	63	73	69		29.97	29.97	.05	50		40		40				1	1	1	ditto.
21	65	73	69		30.01	.98	.02	30		50		45				0	1	1	ditto.
22	65	74	69		.00	.98	.03	35		40		30				0	1	0	ditto.
23	66	73	69	Last Quarter 731.	.05	.97	.03	35		40		30				0	1	0	ditto.
24	67	74	68		03	.91	.06	35		45		35				0	1	1	ditto.
25	65	73	67		.01	.90	.02	30		45		40				0	1	1	ditto.
26	64	73	67		.00	.98	00	30		50		40				1	1	0	ditto.
27	63	72	63		29.99	.95	.00	30		55		45				0	1	1	ditto.
28	64	73	68		.98	.97	01	30		55		50				1	1	1	ditto.
29	64	73	67		.99	.97	.04	30		55		45				0	1	0	ditto.
30	64	73	68	N. M. 728.	30.06	30.04	07	30		50		40				0	1	1	ditto.
31	61	74	6-		07	.06	.09	30		50		40				0	1	0	ditto.
Mean	65½	73½	69		30.08	29.98	30.03	30		50		40				½	1	½	

From the foregoing *Diary* of the Weather, it may
be remarked in regard to the variation of the Barometer, that during the cold season, from November to
March, the mercury is at its greatest height; and at the
lowest during the rainy months of May, June, July,
August, and September. The variation of the Thermometer, or the difference between the temperature
of mid-day and that of the morning and evening is
very trifling, seldom exceeding 3 or 4° during the
rains, whereas, during the cold season, the difference
is 8 or 10°.

II.

A Synopsis of the different Cases that may happen in deducing the Longitude of one Place from another, by Means of Arnold's Chronometers, and of finding the Rates when the Difference of Longitude is given.

BY MR. REUBEN BURROW.

IT was formerly the custom to give rules for calculation, without any investigation of their principles; but the contrary method has so much taken place of late, that those who are not acquainted with the theory of a subject are seldom in a capacity of calculating at all; and those who are acquainted with it, must either lose time by recurring thereto continually, or run the hazard of often making mistakes. Indeed, the use of practical rules is so obvious, that *Newton* has often given them when he has omitted their demonstrations; and the want of them has been noted by *Bacon* among the deficiencies of learning. The Hindoos were so particularly attentive in that respect, that they usually gave two rules for the same operation; one couched in the shortest terms possible, and often in verse, for the ease of the memory; and the other more at length, as an explanation. It therefore is much to be wished that authors would revert to the ancient custom so far, as to pay some attention to the reduction of their knowledge to practice; that people may not be under the necessity of investigating rules at the time they want to use them.

The following is one rule, out of a great number, that I drew up for my own use, in determining the situations of places in India ; and I insert it on account of its utility and easiness of application.

Let $E=$ Error of the Watch from mean time at the first place ;

    $e=$ Error from mean time at the second place ;

    $T=$ Time by the Watch at the second place, when the error was e ;

    $D=$ Difference of Longitude between the places ;

    $N=$ Interval of mean time between the observations at the two places (found by taking the interval by the Watch, and correcting it according to the estimated rate, &c.)

    $r=$ Rate of the Watch, or what it gains or loses in a day of mean time. Then,

If the Watch be too

If the Watch be too		In the mean time at the first place when the Watch was T at the second, or when the mean time at the second place was	Then, if the second place be from the first to the		Is the rate of the Watch, and		Is the difference of Longitude
Fast for mean time at both places, and the Watch be	Gaining, then	T—E—nr	T—e	E	(D—E+e):n	E—e+nr
	Losing,	T—E+nr	T—e	W	(e—E—D):n	—E—nr
				E	(E—D):n	E—e—nr
				W	(D+E—e):n	e—E+nr
Slow for mean time at both places, and the Watch be	Gaining,	T+E—nr	T+e	E	(D+E—e):n	e—E+nr
	Losing,	T+E—nr	T+e	W	(E—D—e):n	E—e+nr
				E	(e—E—D):n	E—e—nr
				W	(D—E+e):n	E—e+nr
Slow for mean time at first place and fast at second place, and the Watch be	Gaining, then	T+E+nr	T—e	E	(D+E+e):n	nr—e—E
	Losing,	T+E+nr	T—e	W	(E—D+e):n	E+e—nr
					Impossible	E+e—nr
					(D—E—e):n	
Fast for mean time at first place and slow for mean time at second place, and the Watch be	Gaining, then	T—E—nr	T+e	E	(D—E—):n	E+e+nr
	Losing,	T—E+nr	T+e		Impossible	E+c—nr
				E	(E—D+e):n	nr—E—e
				W	(D+E+e):n	

III.

MEMORANDUMS

CONCERNING AN OLD BUILDING

In the Hadjipore District, near the Gunduc River, &c.

BY MR. REUBEN BURROW.

THE pyramids of *Egypt*, as well as those lately discovered in *Ireland* (and probably too the *Tower* of *Babel*) seem to have been intended for nothing more than images of *Mahadeo*.

Two of the *Sakkara* pyramids described by *Norden*, are, like many of the small ones, usually built of mud in the villages of *Bengal*. One of the pyramids of *Dushour*, drawn by *Pocock*, is nearly similar to that I am going to mention, except in the acuteness of the angle. Most of the *Pagodas* of the *Carnatic* are either complete or truncated pyramids; and an old stone-building without any cavity, which I saw in *Yumbeah*, near the *Catabeda* river, on the *Arracan* coast, differed so little from a pyramid, that I did not suspect it was meant for the image of *Seeva*, till I was told it by the natives.

The largest building of the kind which I have yet seen in *India*, is about two days journey up the *Gunduc* river, near a place called *Kessereah*: it goes by the name of *Bheem Sain's Dewry*; but seems evidently intended for the well-known image of *Mahadeo*; having originally been a cylinder placed upon the frustum of a cone, for the purpose of being seen at a distance. It is at present very much decayed; and it is not easy to tell whether the upper part of the cylinder has been globular or conical; a considerable quantity of the outside is fallen down, but it still may be seen a good distance up and down the river.

The day I went from the river to view it was so uncommonly hot, that the walk and a fever together obliged me to trust to the measurements of a servant. For want of a better instrument, he took the circumference of the cylindrical part, in length of a spear, and from that as a scale, and a sketch of the building taken at a distance, I deduced the following dimensions. What dependence there may be on his measures, I cannot determine; but probably they are not very erroneous.

Diameter of the cylindrical part, - - 64 feet
Height of the cylinder, - - - 65
Height of the conic frustum on which the
    cylinder is placed, . - - - 93
Diameter of the cone at the base, - 363

Both the cone and the cylinder were of bricks; those of the last were of different sizes, many of them two spans long and one broad; others were of the common size, but thinner; and they were well burnt, though bedded in mortar little better than mud: There did not appear any signs of the cylinder's being hollow: the conical part was overgrown with jungle; but I broke through it in several places, and found it everywhere brick.

I do not recollect whether it be visible from the site of the ancient city where the famous pillar of *Singeah* stands, or not; but have a faint idea that it

ia. What the intention of these extraordinary columns
may have been originally, is perhaps not so easy to
tell: at first sight it would seem that they were for
holding inscriptions, because those of *Bettiah, Dehli,*
and *Illahabad,* have inscriptions (though in a character that has not been yet decyphered); but the
pillar of *Singeah* seems to have none whatever, for
some *Bramins* told me they attended at the time it was
dug to the foundation, near twenty feet under ground,
by a gentleman of *Patna,* who had hopes to have
found some treasures; and that there were not the
least vestige of any inscription upon it. Probably
those pillars, *Cleopatra's Needle,* and the *Devil's Bolts,*
at *Boroughbridge,* may all have the same religious
origin.

Perhaps the connection of time and place may apo-
logize for the diversity of the subject, in mentioning,
that while I sat under the shade of a large tree near
the pyramid, on account of the sultry heat, some of
the people of the adjacent village came and played
there with *cowries* on a diagram, that was formed
by placing five points in a circular order, and joining
every pair of alternate points by a line, which formed
a kind of pentagon; this brought to my recollection
a circumstance told me by a gentleman in *England,*—
That an old piece of silver plate had been dug out of
the earth with such a figure upon it; the use of it was
totally unknown, as well as the age; and I was desired to find what geometrical properties the figure
possessed. One, I remember, was, that if any number
of points whatever were placed in a circular order, and
each two alternate points joined, then the sum of all
the salient angles of the figure would be equal to two
right angles when the number of points was odd;
but equal to four right angles when the number was
even. *Euclid's* properties of the angles of the triangle
and trapezium, are particular cases of these; but I had

no suspicion of the real intention of the figure till I
saw the use here made of it. It seems, however, an argument in favour of the identity of the *Druids* and
Bramins, as well as another well-known diagram,
usually called the *Walls of Troy*, which was used
originally in the *Hindoo* astrology. These figures, however, appear to have flowed from a much higher source,
and to have relation to what *Leibnitz* had a distant
idea of in his Analysis of Situation, *Euclid* in his Po-
risms, and *Girard* perhaps in his Restitution of them.
In fact, as the modern Algebraists have the advantage
of transferring a great part of their labour from the
head to the hands, so there is reason to believe that
the *Hindoos* had mechanical methods of reasoning geome-
trically, much more extensive than the elementary
methods made use of at present; and that even their
games were deduced from and intended perhaps to
be examples of them : but this deserves to be treated
more at length elsewhere.

   The same apology may perhaps excuse my mentioning here, that the idea of the *Nile's* deriving its
floods from the melted snows, as well as the *Ganges*,
appears to be rather imaginary: they seem to be caused
principally by the rains; for the high hills beyond the
Herdwar apparently retain the snow all the year, and
therefore the quantity melted could never produce
the enormous swell of the *Ganges*; not to mention
that the effect of a thaw seems different from what
would arise from the mere difference of heat, and
therefore might partly take place in winter and the dry
season.   That the rains are sufficient for the purpose,
without recurring to the hypothesis of melted snows,
appears from the following fact :—A little before I
observed the aforesaid pyramid, I had been a considerable distance up the *Gunduc*; the river was low
for the time of the year, and the hills that skirt the
borders of *Nepaul* were clear, and apparently not above

fifteen cose distant: soon after, a heavy shower fell upon them for some hours, and the river was in a short time filled to the very banks, and continued so for many days; and large trees were torn up by the roots, and came driving down with such force by the torrent, that my boat was often endangered. Now, on these hills there was actually no snow whatever; and as the rise was obviously caused by the rains, it may reasonably be concluded that the same effect has the same cause in other places.

IV.

OBSERVATIONS ON SOME OF THE ECLIPSES OF JUPITER'S SATELLITES.

BY MR. REUBEN BURROW.

The following in the Ganges and Burrampooter Rivers.

Apparent time 1787. d h ′ ″	Sat.	Weather.	Im. or Em.	Place of Observation.
Sept. 23 11 41 9	2	Moderate,	Imm.	Bankipore Granary.
24 15 41 22	3	Ditto,	Imm.	Ditto.
Oct. 11 12 45 14	1	Ditto,	Imm.	Colgong ; Cleveland's Bungalo.
23 10 26 20	3	Ditto,	Emer.	Mouth of Jellingy.
25 11 47 39	2	Ditto,	Imm.	Shore of Ganges South of Pulna
25 16 42 40	1	Ditto,	Imm.	Ditto.
27 11 13 59	1	Ditto,	Imm.	Casundab, Nullah.
30 14 35 18	3	Ditto,	Emer.	Dacca ; Nabob's boate.
Nov. 19 8 56 32	2	Ditto,	Imm.	Tralcopee, Burrampooter.
26 11 33 45	2	Ditto,	Imm.	Bakkamar Chorr.
26 13 13 57	1	Ditto,	Imm.	Ditto.
28 7 42 52	1	Ditto,	Imm.	Carycorta.
Dec. 3 14 20 54	2	Hazy,	Imm.	Goalpauah.
3 15 8 1	1	Moderate,	Imm.	Ditto.
5 7 51 59	3	Ditto,	Imm.	Ditto.
5 9 35 26	1	Ditto,	Imm.	Ditto.
10 16 45 14	2	Very hazy,	Imm.	Bedjapoor.
10 16 57 58	1	Moderate,	Imm.	Ditto.
12 11 26 9:	1	Hazy,	Imm.	Tingarchof.
12 11 48 40	3	Ditto,	Imm.	Ditto.
19 15 20 59	1	Ditto,	Emer.	Luchipore.

The following on the Arracan Coast.

Apparent time 1788. d h ′ ″	Sat.	Weather.	Im. or Em.	Place of Observation.
Feb. 5 10 18 12;	1	Moderate,	Emer.	Cheduba, Flag-staff Point.
12 14 13 54	1	A little hazy,	Emer.	Ditto, Maykawoody Fort.
21 8 39 19	1	Moderate,	Emer.	Yambrah Ty Fort.
23 10 17 53	2	Ditto,	Emer.	Ditto, Mysorema.
28 10 35 13	2	Ditto,	Emer.	Cheduba ; Cedar Point.

The following were observed at Colonel Watson's Docks at Kidderpore, near the Mouth of the Nullah.

Apparent time 1788. d h ′ ″	Sat.	Weather.	Im.or Em.	Place of Observation.
March, 13 8 36 36	1	Moderate	Emer.	
19 7 34 3	2	ditto,	Emer.	
21 10 34 41	1	ditto,	Emer.	
31 7 1 24	3	ditto,	Emer.	

The following in the Ganges and Rohilcund, &c.

Apparent time 1788. d h ′ ″	Sat.	Weather.	Im.or Em.	Place of Observation.
Oct.	8 14 35 30	3′	Moderate,	Emers.	Bankipore.
	19 14 3 4	1	Ditto,	Imm.	Benares Observatory
Nov.	7 15 42 36	2	ditto,	Imm.	Chunar Camp
	28 17 44 23	1	Heavy,	Imm.	Illahabad Fort.
	14 12 17 19	1	Ditto,	Imm.	Currahcoua.
	20 10 43 28	3	Moderate.	Imm.	In the Ganges 3m below Nedjiff
	20 14 9 50:1	3	Ditto,	Emer.	Ghat.
	21 11 55 31	1	ditto,	Imm.	Janjemow.
	27 14 44 19	5	ditto,	Imm.	Cawopore; Magazine Gaut.
	28 15 49 21	1	ditto,	Imm.	Ditto.
	30 10 17 2	1	ditto,	Emm.	Dain.
Dec.	3 15 1 23	2	ditto,	Imm.	Jongapore Gaut.
	7 12 6 3	1	ditto,	Imm.	East of Champate° 2′ 29″.
	14 17 54 67	7	ditto,	Imm.	Futtyghur M.; mine.
	21 9 20 53	2	ditto,	Imm.	Ditto, Pr. Cook's Gaut.
	21 15 44 51	1	ditto,	Imm.	Ditto.
	21 10 12 34	1	ditto,	Imm.	Ditto.
	28 17 33 23:1	1	Heavy,	Imm.	Cotterub.
	30 12 2 43	1	Moderate,	Imm.	Ferozepore.
	1789.				
Jan.	4 14 26 28	1	Ditto,	Emm.	Nabobgunge.
	6 13 53 41	1	ditto,	Imm.	Pillibeet; End Gain.
	8 8 20 26	1	ditto,	Imm.	Shabgur.
	9 14 10 39	3	ditto,	Imm.	Howerkah.
	21 14 15 50	1	ditto,	Emer.	Shyrah.
	24 8 44 7	1	ditto,	Imer.	Takon udwar.
	26 14 15 36	2	ditto,	Emer.	Sidjibarad.
	29 16 7 14	1	Heavy,	Emer.	Ditto.
Feb.	14 13 22 29	3	Moderate,	Emer.	Antrouab.
	14 14 23 40	1	Ditto,	Emer.	Ditto.
	16 8 43 8	2	ditto,	Emer.	Hussenpore.
	16 8 51 53	1	Heavy,	Emer.	Ditto.
	17 6 53 11:1	4	Ditto,	Imm.	Seetrah.
	17 11 6 44:2	4	rain,	Emer.	Ditto.
	21 10 40 1	1	ditto,	Emer.	Chardowry.
March	1 11 45 13	1	Moderate,	Emer.	Futtyghur, Pr. Cook's Gaut.
	2 14 11 13	2	Ditto,	Emer.	Ditto.

APPENDIX.   485

Apparent time 1749 d h ' "	Sat.	Weather.	Im.or Em	Place of Observations.
March 11 9 11 11:	1	Moderate.	Emers.	Mobariekpore Gaut.
18 11 23 56	1	Ditto.	Emer.	Chunar Fort.
20 9 4 43	2	Ditto.	Emer.	Benares Observatory.
27 7 59 16	1	Ditto.	Emer	Bankypore Granary.
27 11 53 1	2	Ditto.	Emer.	Ditto.
29 10 31 10	3	Ditto.	Imm.	Ditto.
Apr. 3 9 56 45:	1	Ditto.	Emer.	Patna ; Chehelsuttoun.
10 11 59 48:	1	Verhazy.	Emer.	Mongeer, Rocky Point.
19 8 30 56	2	Hazy.	Emer.	Rajmahal.
26 10 31 22	1	Moderate.	Emer.	Fenially Dundutuma.

The following were observed at Russahpugly, near Calcutta.

Apparent time 1789 d h ' "	Sat.	Weather.	Im.or Em.	Place of Observation.
May 11 8 45 50	1	Moderate.	Emer.	
Dec. 19 11 59 15	1	Hazy.	Imm.	
19 14 5 33	3	Ditto.	Imm.	
21 11 23 4	2	Moderate.	Imm.	
26 13 49 36	1	Ditto.	Imm.	
1790.				
Jan. 2 15 39 32	1	Ditto.	Imm.	
18 13 44 51	1	Mist & wind	Imm.	
23 1 49 48	2	Ditto.	Imm.	
24 9 42 57	3	Hazy.	Imm.	
27 10 6 19	1	Moderate.	Imm.	
31 11 35 15	3	Very hazy.	Imm.	
Feb. 1 17 32 45	1	Hazy.	Imm.	
3 11 1 30	1	Moderate.	Imm.	
17 10 36 18	2	Ditto.	Emer.	
10 12 33 56	1	Ditto.	Emer.	
26 14 28 36	1	Hazy.	Emer.	
28 8 57 11	1	Moderate.	Emer.	
March 1 9 0 52	3	Ditto.	Emer.	
5 16 24 13	1	Hazy.	Emer.	
16 7 18 14	1	Moderate.	Emer.	
21 9 14 25	1	Ditto.	Emer.	
26 7 36 11	4	Ditto.	Imm.	

The two following were at Jowgatta, near Krishnagur.

Apparent time 1790 d h ' "	Sat.	Weather.	Im.or Em.	Place of Observation.
Apr. 22 10 27 30	2	Moderate.	Emer.	
28 11 33 10	1	Ditto.	Emer.	

VOL. II.   I i

Those to the 31st of March 1788, were observed with a glass made by *Watkins*, that magnified about 110 times; those from thence to the 12th of May 1790, were observed with one of *Ramsden*'s telescopes of the sort lately made for the navy; and the remainder with a glass made by *Dolland*, that magnifies about eighty times.

I shall conclude these observations with a remark that highly concerns both the buyers and makers of telescopes; namely, that the parts which compose the object glass of an Achromatic, are generally put together in such a manner that they cannot be taken asunder; and the brass part that they are bedded in, shoots a number of chymical ramifications between the glasses, that in the course of a year renders a telescope of little or no service. This defect the maker may easily remove by making the compound object glass capable of being taken to pieces, or the parts in some other substance not liable to this defect.

V.

A PROOF THAT THE HINDOOS HAD THE
BINOMIAL THEOREM.

BY MR. REUBEN BURROW.

THE *Islands* in the Bay of *Bengal* are, many of them, covered with shells and marine productions to a great height, and there are beds of large smooth pebbles near the *Herdwar*, some hundreds of feet above the present level of the *Ganges*; the sea has therefore gradually been retiring, and consequently the position of the Equator was formerly farther north than it is at present in this part of the earth : and if a few similar observations were made in other countries, it is evident that the ancient situation of the pole upon the surface of the earth might be determined sufficiently near for explaining many difficulties and paradoxes in geographical antiquities. For this purpose also it would be adviseable to have permanent meridian lines drawn in high northern latitudes, to be compared in succeeding ages, and also to have marks cut upon rocks in the sea, to shew the proper level of the water.

In the aforesaid position of the Equator, the sands of *Tartary* were inhabitable and the Siberian climates temperate ; the deserts of the *Lesser Bukharia* were then part of the seat of the *Paradise of Moses*; and the four sacred rivers of *Eden* went through *India, China, Siberia*, and into the *Caspian Sea*, respectively. This appears from a *Bramin* map of the world in the

Sanscrit language, which I met with about two years
ago in the higher parts of *India,* together with a valuable treatise of geography upon the system of *Boodh*;
both of which I communicated, with my idea on the .
subject, to Mr. *Wilford,* of the *Bengal* Engineers; and
from him the world may expect shortly to be favoured
with the first true representation of Scriptural and
Hindoo Geography.

From the aforesaid country the *Hindoo* religion probably spread over the whole earth : there are signs of
it in every northern country, and in almost every system of worship. In *England* it is obvious; Stonehenge
is evidently one of the temples of *Boodh*; and the
arithmetic, the astronomy, astrology, the holidays,
games, names of the stars, and figures of the constellations, the ancient monuments, laws, and even the
languages of the different nations, have the strongest
marks of the same original. The worship of the sun
and fire, human and animal sacrifices, &c. have apparently once been universal : the religious ceremonies
of the papists seem in many parts to be a mere servile
copy of those of the *Goseigns* and *Fakeers*; the christian ascetics were very little different from their filthy
original the *Byraggys,* &c; even the hell of the
northern nations is not at all like the hell of the scripture, except in some few particulars; but it is so
striking a likeness of the hell of the *Hindoos,* that I
should not at all be surprised if the story of the sol-
dier that saw it in *Saint Patrick*'s purgatory, described
in *Matthew Paris*'s history, should hereafter turn out
to be merely a translation from the *Sanscrit,* with the
names changed. The different tenets of *Popery* and
Deism have a great similarity to the two doctrines of
Brahma and *Boodh*; and as the *Bramins* were the authors of the Ptolemaic system, so the *Boodhists* appear
to have been the inventors of the ancient *Philolaic,* or
Copernican, as well as of the doctrine of attraction ; and

probably too the established religion of the *Greeks* and the *Eleusinian* mysteries may only be varieties of the two different sects. That the *Druids* of *Britain* were *Bramins* is beyond the least shadow of a doubt; but that they were all murdered and their sciences lost, is out of the bounds of probability; it is much more likely that they turned Schoolmasters, Freemasons, and Fortune-tellers, and in this way part of their sciences might easily descend to posterity, as we find they have done. An old paper, said to have been found by *Locke*, bears a considerable degree of internal evidence both of its own antiquity and of this idea; and on this hypothesis it will be easy to account for many difficult matters that perhaps cannot so clearly be done on any other, and particulary of the great similarity between the *Hindoo* sciences and ours: a comparison between our oldest scientific writers and those of the *Hindoos* will set the matter beyond dispute; and fortunately the works of *Bede* carry us twelve hundred years back, which is near enough to the times of the *Druids* to give hopes of finding there some of their remains. I should have made the comparison myself, but *Bede* is not an author to be met with in this country; however, I compared an astrolabe in the *Nagry* character (brought by Dr. *Mackinnon* from *Jynagur*) with *Chaucer's* description, and found them to agree most minutely: even the center-pin which *Chaucer* calls " the horses" has a horse's head upon it in the instrument; therefore if *Chaucer's* description should happen to be a translation from *Bede*, it will be a strong argument in favour of the hypothesis, for we then could have nothing from the *Arabians*. What *Bungey* and *Swisset* may contain, will also deserve inquiry; and that the comparison may be the readier made, where the books are procurable, I mean very shortly to publish translations of the *Leelavotty* and *Beej Geneta*, or the arithmetic and algebra of the *Hindoos*.

It is much to be feared, however, that many of the best treatises of the *Hindoos* are lost, and that many of those that remain are imperfect. By the help of a *Pundit* I translated part of the *Beej Ganeta* near six years ago, when no *European* but myself, I believe, even suspected that the *Hindoos* had any Algebra; but finding that my copy was imperfect, I deferred completing the translation, in hopes of procuring the remainder. I have since found a small part more, and have seen many copies; but from the plan of the work (which in my opinion is the best way of judging) they still seem to be all imperfect, though the copier generally takes care to put at the end of them that they are complete. I have the same opinion of the *Leelavatty*, and for the same reason: indeed, it is obvious that there must have been treatises existing where algebra was carried much farther; because many of their rules in astronomy are approximations deduced from infinite series, or at least have every appearance of it; such, for instance, as finding the sine from the arc, and the contrary; and finding the angles of a right angled triangle from the hypothenuse and sides, independent of tables of sines; and several others of a similar nature, much more complicated. I have been informed by one of their *Pundits*, that, some time ago, there were other treatises of Algebra besides that just mentioned, and much more difficult, though he had not seen them; and therefore as it is possible they may still be existing, and yet be in danger of perishing very soon, it is much to be wished that people would collect as many of the books of science as possible (their poetry is in no danger) and particularly those of the doctrine of *Boodh*, which perhaps may be met with towards *Thibet*. That many of their best books are depraved and lost is evident, because there is not now a single book of geometrical elements to be met with; and yet that they had elements not long ago, and apparently more extensive than those of *Euclid*, is obvious from some of their works of no great antiquity ; the same remarks are applicable to their cosmographical remains, in some of which there are indications of an astronomy superior to that of the *Sourya Siddhant*, and such popular treatises.

Till we can therefore find some of their more superior works, it must be rather from the form and construction of their astronomical tables and rules, and the properties implied in their accidental solutions of questions, &c. that we can judge what they formerly knew, than otherwise. That they were acquainted with a differential method similar to *Newton's*, I shall give many reasons for believing, in a treatise on the principles of the *Hindoo* astronomy, which I began more than three years ago, but was prevented from finishing, by a troublesome and laborious employment that for two years gave me no leisure whatever ; and which (though the small time I had to spare since has been employed in writing a comment on the works of *Newton*, and explaining them to a very ingenious native who is translating them into *Arabic)* I hope ere long to have an opportunity of completing. At present I shall only give an extract of a paper explaining the construction of some tables, which first led me to the idea of their having a differential method : it is part of one, out of a number of papers that were written in the latter part of the year 1783 and the beginning of 1784, and of which several copies were taken by different people, and some of them sent to *England*. This particular extract was to investigate the rules at pages 253, 254, and 255 of Mons. *Gentil's* Voyage, of which the author says, " Je n'ai pu savoir sur quels " principes cette table est fondée," &c. and is as follows :

" Now, by proceeding in the manner explained in " the aforesaid paper, to calculate the right ascension

" and ascensional difference for *Tircalour*, and af-
" terwards taking the differences algebraically, and re-
" ducing them to puls of a *Gurry*, as in the follow-
" ing table, the principles of the method will be
" evident.

s	Obl. Ascens. R.A.	Obl. Ascens. Asc. Diff.	First diff. of Obl. Ascension.	Do., reduced to Puls of a Gurry.	Do. farther reduced.
0	0	0—0 0			
1	27 54	—2 19	27 54—2 19	279—23	256
2	57 49	—4 13	29 55—1 54	299—19	280
3	90 0	—4 59	32 11—0 46	322— 8	314
4	122 11	—4 13	32 11+0 46	322+ 8	330
5	152 6	—2 19	29 55+1 54	299+19	318
6	180 0	+0 0	27 54+2 19	279+23	302
7	200 54	+2 19	27 54+2 19	279+23	302
8	237 49	+4 13	29 57+1 54	299+19	318
9	270 0	+4 59	32 11+0 46	322+ 8	330
10	302 11	+4 13	32 11—0 46	322— 8	314
11	332 6	+2 19	29 55—1 54	299—19	280
12	360 0	+0 0	27 54—2 19	279—23	256

" The fifth and sixth columns sufficiently. explain
" the tables in page 253 and 254 of M. *Gentil*; but
" there remains a part more difficult, namely, why in
" calculating the *Bauja*," or the doubles of the first
differences of the ascensional difference " $\frac{10}{10}$ of the
" length of the shadow is taken for the first ; $\frac{4}{4}$ of
" the first term for the second, and $\frac{1}{2}$ of the first
" term for the third." " The primary reason of
" taking differences here, seems to be that the
" chords may be nearly equal to the arcs, and

" that, by adding of the differences, the arcs them-
" selves may be found nearly ; the reason will appear
" from the following investigation. Let N be the equa-
" torial shadow of the *Bramins* in *Bingles*, then 720 the
" length of the *Gnomon*, or twelve *Ongles*, will be to N
" the shadow, as radius to the tangent of the latitude ;
" and radius to the tangent of the latitude as the tangent
" of the declination to the sine of the ascensional dif-
" ference ; consequently 720 is to N as the tangent of
" declination to the sine of the ascensional difference.
" Now if the declinations for one, two, and three sines
" be substituted in the last proportion, we get the sines
" of the three ascensional differences in terms of N
" and known quantities ; and, if these values be sub-
" stituted in the Newtonian form for finding the arc
" from the sine, we get the arcs in parts of the radius ;
" and if each of these be multiplied by 3600 and
" divided by 6,28318, the values comes out in puls
" of a *Gurry* if N be in *Bingles*, but in parts of a
" *Gurry* if N be in *Ongles* ; and by taking the doubles,
" we get the values nearly as follows :

Values.	*Difference.*	
0,00000 N		
0,33056 N	0,33056 N = 1·3 N nearly,	⎫ the values
0,59928 N	0,26872 N = 4·5 of 1·3 N nearly,	⎬ used by the
0,70060 N	0,10932 N = 1·3 N nearly,	⎭ *Bramins.*

" Now, because the values in the first column are
" doubles of the ascensional differences for one, two,
" and three sines, their halves are the ascensional dif-
" ferences in parts of a *Gurry*, supposing N to be
" in *Ongles*; and if each of these halves be mul-
" tiplied by sixty, the products, namely, 9,9168 N,
" 17,9784 N, and 21,2580 N will be the same in
" puls of a *Gurry* ; and if to get each of these nearly
" in round numbers, the whole be multiplied by three,
" and afterwards divided by three, the three products

" will be 29,75 N, 53,94 N, and 63,77 N, which are
" nearly equal to thirty N ; fifty-four N, and sixty-
" four N respectively; and hence the foundation of the
" *Bramin* rule is evident, which directs to multiply
" the equatorial shadow by thirty, fifty-four, and
" sixty-four respectively ; and to divide the products
" by three for the *Chorardo* in puls : and these parts
" answer to one, two, and three signs of longitude
" from the true equinox; and therefore the *Ayanangsh*,
" or *Bramin* precession of the equinox, must be add-
" ed to find the intermediate *Chorardo* by propor-
" tion."

Though the agreement of this investigation with
the *Bramin* results, is no proof that the *Hindus* had
either the differential method, or Algebra, it gave me
at the time a strong suspicion of both; and yet, for
want of knowing the name that Algebra went by in
Sanscrit, I was near two years before I found a treatise
on it, and even then I should not have known what to
enquire for, if it had not come into my mind to ask
how they investigated their rules. Of the differential
method, I have yet met with no regular treatise, but
have no doubt whatever that there were such, for the
reasons I before hinted at ; and I hope others will be
more fortunate in their enquiries after it than myself.

With respect to the *Binomial Theorem*, the application of it to fractional indices will perhaps remain for
ever the exclusive property of *Newton*; but the following question and its solution evidently shew that
the *Hindoos* understood it in whole numbers to the
full as well as *Briggs*, and much better than
Pascal. Dr. *Hutton*, in a valuable edition of *Sher-
win's* tables, has lately done justice to *Briggs*; but
Mr. *Whitchell*, who some years before pointed out
Briggs as the undoubted inventor of the differential

method, said he had found some indications of the
Binomial Theorem in much older authors. The method however by which that great man investigated
the powers independent of each other, is exactly the
same as that in the following translation from the
Sanscrit.

" A *Raja*'s palace had eight doors; now these doors.
" may either be opened by one at a time, or by two
" at a time, or by three at a time, and so on through
" the whole, till at last all are opened together. It is
" required to tell the numbers of times that this can
" be done?

" Set down the number of the doors, and proceed
" in order, gradually decreasing by one to unity,
" and then in a contrary order, as follows:

$$8\ 7\ 6\ 5\ 4\ 3\ 2\ 1$$
$$1\ 2\ 3\ 4\ 5\ 6\ 7\ 8$$

" Divide the first number eight by the unit beneath
" it, and the quotient eight shews the number of
" times that the doors can be opened by one at a
" time. Multiply this last eight by the next term seven,
" and divide the product by the two beneath it, and
" the result twenty-eight is the number of times that
" two different doors may be opened; multiply the
" last found twenty-eight by the next figure six, and
" divide the product by the three beneath it, and the
" quotient fifty-six shews the number of times that
" three different doors may be opened. Again, this
" fifty-six multiplied by the next five, and divided by
" the four beneath it, is seventy, the number of
" times that four different doors may be opened. In
" the same manner fifty-six is the number of fives that
" can be opened: twenty-eight the number of times
" that six can be opened: eight the number of times

" that seven can be opened ; and lastly, one is the
" number of times the whole may be opened together;
" and the sum of all the different times is 255."

The demonstration is evident to mathematicians ;
for as the second term's coefficient in a general equation shews the sum of the roots, therefore, in the
n power of $1 + 1$ where every root is unity, the coefficient shews the different *ones* that can be taken in
n things : also, because the third term's coefficient is
the sum of the products of all the different twos.
of the roots, therefore when each root is unity the
products of each two roots will be unity, and therefore the number of units, or the coefficient itself, shews
the number of different *twos* that can be taken in n
things. Again, because the fourth term is the sum of
the products of the different threes that can be taken
among the roots, therefore, when each root is unity,
the product of each three will be unity, and therefore
every unit in the fourth will shew a product of three
different roots, and consequently the coefficient itself
shews all the different *threes* that can be taken in n
things ; and so for the rest. I should not have added
this, but that I do not know well where to refer to it.

P. S. There is an observation, perhaps worth remarking, with respect to the change of the *poles*; namely, that the small rock-oysters are generally all dead
within about a foot above high water-mark ; now possibly naturalists may be able to tell the age of such shells
nearly by their appearance ; and if so, a pretty good
estimate may be formed of the rate of alteration of the
level of the sea in such places where they are ; for I made
some astronomical observations on a rock in the sea near
an island about seven miles to the south of the island
of *Cheduba*, on the *Aracan* coast, whose top was eighteen feet above high water-mark, and the whole rock
covered with those shells fast grown to it, but all of

them dead, except those which were a foot above the high water-mark of that day, which was February 2, 1789. The shells were evidently altered a little in proportion to their height above the water, but by no means so much as to induce one to believe that the rock had been many years out of it. All the adjacent islands and the coast shewed similar appearances, and therefore it was evidently no partial elevation by subterranean fires, or any thing of that sort; this is also apparent from the island of *Cheduba* itself, in which there is a regular succession of sea-beaches and shells more and more decayed to a great height. By a kind of vague estimation from the trees and the coasts and shells, &c. (on which however there is not the least dependence) I supposed that the sea might be subsiding at the rate of about three inches in a year.

ADDITIONS.

Page 154. Note. The *gunja*, I find, is the *Abrus* of our botanists; and I venture to describe it from the wild plant compared with a beautiful drawing of the flower magnified, with which I was favoured by Dr. *Anderson.*

CLASS XVII. *Order* IV.,

Cal. Perianth funnel-shaped, indented above.
Cor. Cymbiform; *Awning* roundish, pointed, nerved.
   Wings lanced, shorter than the awning.
   Keel rather longer than the wings.

Stam. Filaments nine, some shorter; united in two sets at the top of a divided, bent, awl-shaped body.

Pist. Germ inserted in the calyx. *Style* very minute at the bottom of the divided body. *Stigma*, to the naked eye, obtuse; in the microscope, feathered.

Per. A legume. *Seeds*, spheroidal; black or white, or scarlet with black tips.

·Leaves pinnated; some with, some without, an odd leaflet.

Page 361. See the Plate Fig. 1. The female insect in its *larva* state. 2. The egg, which produces the male. 3. The male insect. 4. The head with jointed antennæ. 5. The wings on one side. The preceding figures are much magnified, but in just proportion. 6. A piece of *Lac*, of its natural size. 7. The inside of the external coat of the cells. 8. One of the utriculi. The two last figures are a little magnified.

CONTENTS

OF THE

SECOND VOLUME.

*** There was not room in this volume for the Dissertations on the Music of the *Hindus* and the Laws of *Siam*; but they will appear in the Third volume, for which ample materials have been collected.

www.ingramcontent.com/pod-product-compliance
Lightning Source LLC
Chambersburg PA
CBHW020448270326
41926CB00008B/524